NYC Subway

- Express, local and terminal stops
- Express stop
- Local stop
- Transfer stations (2 lines or more)

MANHATTAN

BROOKLYN

Hudson River

East River

Upper Bay

215 St
207 St
190 St
181 St
175 St
168 St/Washington
163 St
157 St
155 St
145 St
137St/City College
135 St
125 St
116 St/Columbia University
110 St
103 St
96 St
86 St
79 St
72 St
66 St/Lincoln
59 St/Columbus
50 St
42 St/Time Sq.
34 St
28 St
23 St
18 St
14 St

207 St
Dyckman
191 St
181 St

148 St/Lenox
145 St
135 St
125 St
116 St
110 St
103 St
96 St
86 St
81 St
72 St
7 Av
57 St
5 Av
49 St
47 St
42 St
33 St
28 St
23 St
6 Av
W.4 St/Wash
Christopher/Sheridan
Houston
Canal
Franklin
Chambers
Cortlandt
Rector
South Ferry
Bowling Green
Wall
Broad
Whitehall/S.Ferry

Dyckman
207 St
191 St
181 St

145 St
135 St
125 St
116 St
110 St
103 St
96 St
86 St
77 St
68 St/Hunter Coll
Lexington Av
5 Av/59 St
Lexington Av
5 Av
Lexington/3 Av-51 St
42 St/Grand Central
Penn Station
34 St
49 St
7 Av
50 St

Fordham
183 St
Burnside
176 St
Mt.Eden
170 St
167 St
161 St/Yankee Stadium
155 St
149 St/Grand Concourse
145 St
138 St/Grand Concourse
125 St

Fordham
162-183 Sts
Tremont
174-175 Sts
170 St
167 St

149 St/Grand Concourse
3 Av
3 Av/138 St
Brook
Cypress

Freeman
Simpson
Intervale
Prospect
Jackson

Morrison/Sound View
Elder
Whitlock
Hunts Point
Longwood
E.149 St
E.143 St

3 Av/138 St

Ditmars Blvd
Astoria
30 Av
Broadway
36 Av
39 Av
21 St/Queensbridge
Queensboro
Queens Plaza
23 St/Ely
45 Rd
21 St
Court Sq
Hunters Point
Vernon/Jackson
Roosevelt Island

Greenpoint
Nassau
Bedford

Lexington Av
14 St/Union Sq
Astor
Bwy/Lafayette
Prince
Spring
Canal
Park Place
City Hall
Bwy/Nassau
Fulton
Wall
3 Av
1 Av
Bleeker
2 Av
Bowery
Canal
Grand
Brooklyn Bridge
Delancy/Essex
E.Broadway
York
High/Bklyn
Jay/Borough
Clark
Court/Borough Hall
Hoyt/Schermer
Bergen
Carroll

NEW YORK CITY

François Rémillard

ULYSSES
TRAVEL PUBLICATIONS
Travel better... enjoy more

Editorial *Series Director:* Claude Morneau; *Project Supervisor:* Pascale Couture;

Research and Composition *Author:* François Rémillard; Karl Lemay, François Brodeur, Alain Legault;

Production *Design:* Patrick Farei (Atoll Direction); *Proofreading:* Tara Salman, Stephanie Heidenreich; *Translation:* Tracy Kendrick, Sarah Kresh, Danielle Gauthier, *Cartography:* André Duchesne, Patrick Thivièrge (Assistant), Marc Rigole, Isabelle Lalonde; *Layout:* Christian Roy, Stéphane G. Marceau.

Illustrations *Cover Photo: East Side Skyline* Patti McConville (Image Bank); *Interior Photos:* Tibor Bognár, New York Convention & Visitors Bureau; *Chapter Headings:* Jennifer McMorran; *Drawings:* Lorette Pierson, Marie-Annick Viatour.

Thanks to Stéphanie Jukes-Amer, David Birn, April Black, Marcella Carberry, Felicity Campbell, Donald Lineberg, Jennifer McGuire, Pierre Miville-Deschênes, Paul Van Wijk, Susan Murray, Diana Wells, Muriel Wiltord, Nell Barrett and Ann Godfrey (New York Convention and Visitors Bureau), and finally to SODEC and the Department of Canadian Heritage for their financial Support.

DISTRIBUTORS

AUSTRALIA: Little Hills Press, 11/37-43 Alexander St., Crows Nest NSW 2065, ☎ (612) 437-6995, Fax: (612) 438-5762

BELGIUM AND LUXEMBOURG: Vander, Vrijwilligerlaan 321, B-1150 Brussel, ☎ (02) 762 98 04, Fax: (02) 762 06 62

CANADA: Ulysses Books & Maps, 4176 Saint-Denis, Montréal, Québec, H2W 2M5, ☎ (514) 843-9882, ext.2232, 800-748-9171, Fax: 514-843-9448, www.ulysses.ca

GERMANY AND AUSTRIA: Brettschneider, Fernreisebedarf, Feldfirchner Strasse 2, D-85551 Heimstetten, München, ☎ 89-99 02 03 30, Fax: 89-99 02 03 31

GREAT BRITAIN AND IRELAND: World Leisure Marketing, Unit 11, Newmarket Court, Newmartket Drive, Derby DE24 8NW, ☎ 1 332 57 37 37, Fax: 1 332 57 33 99

ITALY: Centro Cartografico del Riccio, Via di Soffiano 164/A, 50143 Firenze, ☎ (055) 71 33 33, Fax: (055) 71 63 50

NETHERLANDS: Nilsson & Lamm, Pampuslaan 212-214, 1380 AD Weesp (NL), ☎ 0294-494949, Fax: 0294-494455, E-mail: nilam@euronet.nl

PORTUGAL: Dinapress, Lg. Dr. Antonio de Sousa de Macedo, 2, Lisboa 1200, ☎ (1) 395 52 70, Fax: (1) 395 03 90

SCANDINAVIA: Scanvik, Esplanaden 8B, 1263 Copenhagen K, DK, ☎ (45) 33.12.77.66, Fax: (45) 33.91.28.82

SPAIN: Altaïr, Balmes 69, E-08007 Barcelona, ☎ 454 29 66, Fax: 451 25 59, altair@globalcom.es

SWITZERLAND: OLF, P.O. Box 1061, CH-1701 Fribourg, ☎ (026) 467.51.11, Fax: (026) 467.54.66

U.S.A.: The Globe Pequot Press, 6 Business Park Road, P.O. Box 833, Old Saybrook, CT 06475, ☎ 1-800-243-0495, Fax: 800-820-2329, sales@globe-pequot.com

Other countries, contact Ulysses Books & Maps (Montréal), Fax: (514) 843-9448

"We must never believe
that our diversity is a weakness"

– Bill Clinton

TABLE OF CONTENTS

LIST OF MAPS

CANADIAN CATALOGUING

Rémillard, François
  New York City
  (Ulysses Travel Guide) - Translation of: New York - includes
  index
  ISBN 2-89464-088-9
  1. New York (N.Y.) - Guidebooks. I. Title. II. Series
  F128.18.R4513 1998   917.47'10443   C97-941456-3

SYMBOLS

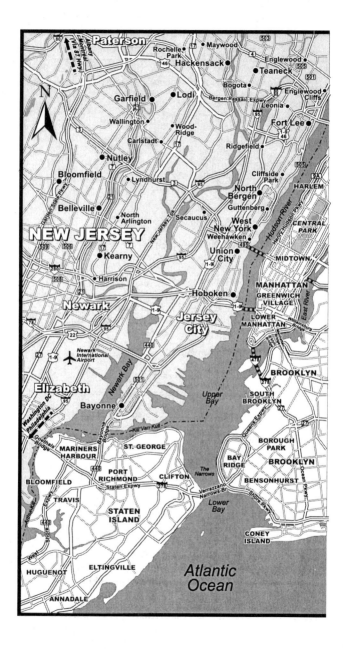

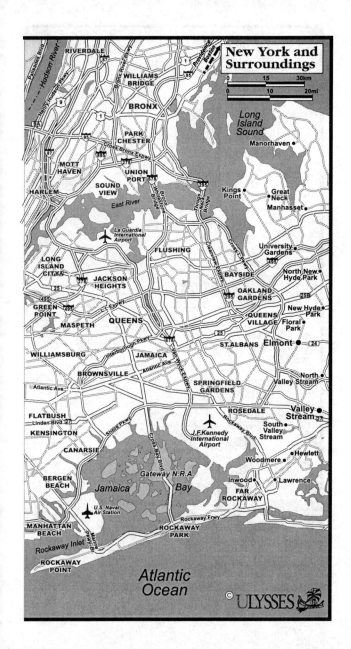

Hudson Bay

C A N A D A

New York

New York City

U N I T E D
S T A T E S

Atlantic Ocean

Pacific Ocean

MEXICO

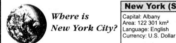

*Where is
New York City?*

New York (State)	New York (City)
Capital: Albany Area: 122 301 km² Language: English Currency: U.S. Dollar	Population (City): 7 700 000 inhab. Population (Metropolitan area): 16 000 000 inhab.

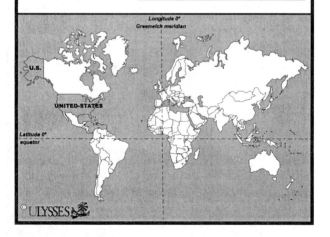

Longitude 0°
Greenwich meridian

U.S.

UNITED-STATES

Latitude 0°
equator

© ULYSSES

PORTRAIT

In 1621, what was to become Manhattan was visited by Dutch trappers. They settled here and named their trading post New Amsterdam. The island was already populated as it had been since the dawn of time by Native Americans, specifically Algonquins. A relationship budded between the two peoples, but the colony was not profitable, despite the considerable efforts of Peter Stuyvesant, and passed into the hands of the English in 1664. New Amsterdam was no longer – and New York was born! And what the city underwent to become the megalopolis it is today!

This age-old ancestry is visible on the streets of the southern part of Manhattan Island, where curving sidewalks lead through the maze work of America from another century. It is hard to believe that forests once stretched as far as the eye could see where now some of the most beautiful buildings in the world stand, forests alive with the call of wild animals that colonists tried with mixed success to tame. Hints of the rustic nature of that bygone land are no longer to be found in neighbourhoods like Greenwich Village or in the flashy window displays of stylish Fifth Avenue shops. Who would have known that one day the greatest artists would live here long enough to create their masterpieces, that the greatest athletes would be cheered by crowds of fans, and that Wall Street, the city's core, would be emblazoned in the eyes of millions of businessmen striving for wealth and luxury.

New York's unique appeal, which is not to be seen on such a great scale anywhere else in the world, is its cosmopolitan blend of people from all over the world: African Americans, Puerto Ricans, Irish, Chinese, Italians, and many more. Just witnessing the multicultural ensemble that is the Big Apple – that indescribable feeling you get when going from Chinatown to Little Italy or another neighbourhood – is worth the trip in itself. Stroll streets with the most varied architecture in all of the United States; watch an impromptu streetcorner performance along with a frenzy of people united for one brief moment, bonded only by the memory of a guitar virtuoso or the enchanting voice of a singer; hop into the Village Vanguard or the Five Spot to hear the newest giants of jazz and blues. You'll never feel alone anywhere in this city, no matter how dingy or upscale the place: over 18 million people live in the metropolitan area and 7.4 million New Yorkers are squeezed into the five boroughs of the behemoth.

Just like the millions of souls spread over the four corners of New York, visitors don't have to look far for entertainment: they can rush headlong to Broadway to see famous productions or new talents; they can stare enthralled at screenings of the latest Woody Allen movie; they can ride on the ferry to Staten Island to see the queen of the Atlantic, the Statue of Liberty; and from the port, they can just hear the cheers of Yankee fans celebrating yet another victory for the home team.

A full experience of New York involves drinking in its unique atmosphere, being drawn along by the flow of its streets and avenues, and being swept up in the folly of a city built on the dreams of millions.

GEOGRAPHY

New York City is situated at a latitude of 40 degrees, 43 minutes north and a longitude of 74 degrees west. For the sake of comparison, Madrid, Naples, Istanbul and Beijing are all at the same latitude.

New York's location at the mouth of the Hudson River makes the city a natural entrance way to the entire region south of the Great Lakes and for the United States as a whole. The favourable terrain on which New York and its port were built was created by the slow work of glaciers that buried the entire region under several hundred metres of ice about 15,000 years ago. The main islands of the city were formed by the movement of the glaciers, which dug the beds of the Hudson and East Rivers.

The nearest large American cities are Boston to the north, and Philadelphia, Baltimore and Washington to the south.

What Is New York?

Everyone knows what New York is. Or, rather, everyone thinks he or she knows what New York is. The name New York actually designates many different entities.

First of all New York is a large state (128,401 square kilometres, or 51,360 miles) in the United Sates of America, the capital of which is Albany. The State of New York is in the shape of a triangle: its northern border divides it from Canada, from Lake Erie to Lake Champlain; its southern border separates it east-west from New Jersey and Pennsylvania; to the east, from north to south, New York State adjoins Vermont, Massachusetts and Connecticut. Only the southeastern tip of the state has a seaside, where the Hudson empties into the Atlantic Ocean. Three large islands at the mouth of the Hudson extend the territory of the state: Manhattan, Staten Island and Long Island. A large protected bay between these islands called Upper Bay forms an exceptional natural harbour. Manhattan especially benefits from this port, because the island is sort of at the heart of the bay, bathed to the west by the Hudson River and to the east by the East River.

New York State is divided into electoral districts called counties, one of which, unsurprisingly, is also called New York and covers the territory of Manhattan Island. Bronx County is on the mainland just north of Manhattan. The territory of Staten Island constitutes the geographical basis of Richmond County. Long Island is divided into many counties: Kings

County (Brooklyn) is on the southwestern part of the island and the northwestern section of the island makes up Queens County.

Together, the territories of New York County, Bronx County, Richmond County, Kings County and Queens County have an area of 787 square kilometres (314.8 miles). This is what the State of New York officially recognizes as City of New York. Each of the five counties is called a borough within the city jurisdiction and has its own mayor. Although Bronx and Queens were kept as the names of their corresponding boroughs, Manhattan, Staten Island and Brooklyn were adopted as the designations of the three others.

Finally, for many, many visitors, and for New Yorkers themselves, New York is a reality that extends beyond the five boroughs. Manhattan's skyline remains the most important landmark, but the urban network of this megalopolis extends far beyond it. All of the neighbouring cities are part of it, whether north of the Bronx, on Long Island, or even in New Jersey. This conurbation, with a population of 16 million, is the largest in the world.

Manhattan

From Inwood Hill Park in the north to Battery Park in the south, the island of Manhattan is barely over 20 kilometres (12.4 miles) long. The widest section of the island is a narrow four kilometres – not much space for 1,488,000 people. In this confined area, New York manages to show off its tendency toward excess. Skyscrapers, Central Park, Wall Street, Harlem and Broadway are just a few of the sights that haunt the imaginations of visitors.

The island is cut off from the rest of the city by the Hudson to the west, the Harlem River to the north, and the East River to the east. The entire southern portion of the island is ringed by docks. At the southern tip, ferries run to New Jersey, Staten Island and Governor's Island. Other shuttles serve Ellis Island and Liberty Island, the latter being the home of a certain very tall lady who has lit up the world for a very long time. Many bridges and tunnels permit pedestrians, drivers, trains and subways to reach the other boroughs and New Jersey from the island, and although none of these is more famous than the Brooklyn Bridge, which offers one of the "classic" views of New York. The George Washington Bridge, with its one-kilometre span across the Hudson to New Jersey, is just as spectacular.

One of Manhattan's overriding characteristics is its grid layout, which makes it much easier to get around. With the notable exception of the southern part of the island, the majority of streets are numbered. When they run north-south they are called avenues; these are about 30 metres (98.4 feet) wide and are numbered from the eastern shore of the island to the western bank. East-west thoroughfares are called streets; these are about 20 metres wide (65.6 feet), and are numbered from south to north. Streets are also divided between east and west at Fifth Avenue. This sort of grid is also in evidence, although not so uniformly, in other parts of the city, especially in Brooklyn.

The Other Boroughs

The other parts of New York City are by no means uninteresting, but that doesn't prevent them from living somewhat in Manhattan's shadow.

Staten Island lies just southwest of Manhattan. It is larger than the latter, and is separated from New Jersey only by a secondary waterway that is spanned by many bridges. With only 379,000 residents, it is still relatively sparsely populated. Upper Bay creates quite a distance between Staten Island and Manhattan. This bay, and Lower Bay, its southern extension, separate Staten Island from Brooklyn. The point of Staten Island is linked to Brooklyn by a unique bridge that represents the symbolic finish line for ships coming in from the Atlantic: Verrazano Bridge is the longest suspension bridge in the world with a centre span that is almost 1,300 metres (4,264 feet) long!

The trip across Brooklyn from north to south or from east to west is barely over 15 kilometres (9.3 miles). The most populous borough in New York with 2,301,000 residents, Brooklyn occupies the western end of Long Island and, along with Staten Island, it encloses Upper Bay. It is therefore no surprise that the Brooklyn shore facing the bay and Manhattan is lined with docks. Coney Island with its beaches on the Atlantic is just south of Brooklyn.

Queens numbers 1,952,000 residents and boasts the most cosmopolitan electoral district in the United States. It is also the largest of the boroughs – almost the size of Manhattan, the Bronx and Staten Island combined. The East River separates Queens from Manhattan and the Bronx. Queens is bordered by Brooklyn to the southwest, and the suburbs that make up the rest of Long Island, including Long Beach, are its eastern neighbours. A long bay, the Long Island Sound, separates Queens from the mainland. Flushing Meadows is in Queens, just next to Shea Stadium, but most visitors come to Queens because it is home to New York's two international airports, La Guardia and John F. Kennedy Airport.

Finally, the Bronx is about a dozen kilometres across at its widest point between the Hudson and the East River and about the same length from north to south. As the only part of the city on the mainland, this borough automatically serves as an access way between Manhattan, Long Island, New Jersey and the northern suburbs of New York. The Bronx numbers 1,204,000 residents and is also home to Yankee Stadium, the city's botanical garden and zoo. This borough has acquired an undesirable reputation in terms of safety, which undoubtedly explains why tourists do not explore it in great numbers.

HISTORY

The First Explorers

In 1524, 10 years before Jacques Cartier made his famous voyage to Canada, Giovanni da Verrazano explored the North American coast in service of Francis I, King of France. He spotted the site of New York, but did not explore further than the Narrows, because he still had several kilometres of coast land to survey before returning to France for the winter. Verrazano disembarked briefly on Staten Island, met some of the Algonquians who lived around New York Bay, noted the potential of the site and named the area "Angoulême" in honour of the king's father, the count of Angoulême. Over the course of the following winter, the Spanish navigated the waterways that surround Manhattan, but discovering neither gold nor silver and discouraged by the cold and the ice, they left the area without further ado.

Almost 100 years passed before Europeans disturbed the peace of local Native Americans again. In 1609, the Englishman Henry Hudson explored the region in the service of the Dutch East Indies Company and left his name on the great river that runs along the western shore of Manhattan. Even though he failed in his mission of finding a route to the Orient, the logs of his voyage attracted the attention of a group of merchants in Amsterdam. In 1621, these businessmen founded the Dutch West Indies Company, to which Holland granted a trading monopoly in America. The company wanted to establish a fur trading post at the mouth of the Hudson. It was also entrusted with the responsibility of populating the colony. However, the Dutch colony in North America, New Holland, never grew to the expected size, because the company had other more lucrative projects in South America.

New Amsterdam

In 1624, a first group of colonists settled on present-day Governor's Island, in New York Bay. They named the island the "Island of Nuts" because of the hazel trees that grew there at the time. They then moved to Manhattan Island, which was more hospitable and more importantly larger. Recruiting colonists from the Dutch population proved quite difficult, and the persecuted residents of border zones like Flanders were more attracted to the adventure than others, so most of these pioneers were French-speaking Protestant Walloons. From its very beginnings, therefore, New York acquired a characteristic that would mark it all through its history: a safe-haven for oppressed peoples of the world who desire to improve their lot.

Among the persecuted groups that were welcomed to New York as early as the 17th century were numerous Jews, who strengthened the commercial activity of the city. (The Shearith Israel Congregation of New York is the oldest still-active Jewish congregation in North America.) It is estimated that

18 languages were spoken in the streets of the little agglomeration in the 17th century, illustrating its precociously cosmopolitan nature, and French was prominent among these.

Once it was established on the southern tip of Manhattan, the colony was renamed New Amsterdam. In an incident that has since become legendary, the colonial governor, Peter Minuit, bought the entire island from the Algonquins for a meagre shipload of trinkets evaluated by some historians at a value of 24 dollars on May 6, 1626. A fort was built of earth south of what is now Bowling Green, and about 30 brick houses with typical Flemish-style stepped gables were put up alongside the East river. A canal was even dug at the site of Broad Street. Apart from the narrow streets in the financial district, no physical traces remain of this first settlement, except for some plans, maps and a few furniture pieces. However, many of the names that the Dutch used have survived: Brooklyn, Staten Island, Harlem and the Bronx are just a few examples. The other boroughs of New York are almost as old as Manhattan. Brooklyn, which was originally one of the large agricultural estates that the Dutch called *bouwerie*, was founded in 1646, while the village of Harlem was born in 1658.

The most famous governor of New Amsterdam was also the last. Peter Stuyvesant, a controversial and intransigent figure, ruled the colony with an iron fist. Despite his determination to make the region into an exclusively Dutch territory, his orders were flouted on several occasions. In 1653, the first municipal government, modelled on those of the homeland with its burgomasters and its *schepens*, saw the light of day on the island. The war of 1652 between Great Britain and Holland forced authorities to construct a fortified wall to protect the northern border of New Amsterdam.

The British had never accepted the Dutch presence on the Atlantic coast, which they had always considered their realm from northern Florida to Nova Scotia. Even more offensive to them was the fact that the Dutch colony drove a wedge between the British colonies, isolating New England to the north from Maryland and Virginia to the south. On the other hand, as the years passed, British-born farmers established themselves closer and closer to the tiny Dutch colony of 1,400 residents. Moreover, the little settlement was constantly threatened by Native American tribes that were allied with the

English, as well as by friendly tribes that had turned hostile after squabbles with Dutch colonists and governors.

One fine day in 1664, the King of England Charles II decided without warning to offer the territory of the Dutch colony as a gift to his brother James, Duke of York, snapping his fingers at the Dutch presence and at past treaties. The latter sent an armed flotilla led by Colonel Richard Nicolls to unwrap the present. Unable to withstand the siege, the inhabitants of New Amsterdam surrendered September 8, 1664, before even a single shot was fired. The Dutch West Indies Company, in poor financial shape, could not afford any attempts to recapture the colony, which was handed over to England by the Treaty of Breda (1667). The town was immediately renamed New York.

The English Colony

The Dutch, Swedish, Jewish and Walloon inhabitants that populated the colony back then were guaranteed that they could keep their possessions and above all that they would be free to continue doing business. No one felt threatened by the new masters of the area. On the contrary, the English were more able to ensure the security and prosperity of the colonists than the Dutch administrators. The resident's enterprising spirit quickly spread to newly arriving British settlers, despite a little bit of friction between both groups and the narrow views of the Duke of York himself. Very early on there were marriages between members of the Dutch and British elites. In the spirit of partnership, the English extended the territory of New York to the whole of Manhattan Island.

In 1673, the Dutch briefly recaptured the city, which they renamed New Orange in honour of their sovereign, William of Orange. The following year, New York was returned to the English by treaty. In 1679, the construction of the first major docks gave a serious boost to commerce, particularly to the fur trade and grain exports (corn and wheat flour). A beaver and a stalk of wheat are depicted on the city flag, illustrating the importance of this economic activity in the history of New York. The port quickly became a target of pirates who scoured the seas pillaging the shipments of enemy countries. All of this was seen as perfectly legal by British authorities. William Kidd was the most famous of these pirates, not only because of the considerable fortune he amassed, but also because he was a pastor's son.

The revocation of the Edict of Nantes in 1685, brought New York hundreds of French Huguenots, who would greatly contribute to the prosperity of the city. Louis XIV had forbidden them from settling in New France, which he wanted to maintain exclusively Catholic. The Huguenots founded New Rochelle, today a simple suburb northeast of the Bronx. At the end of the 17th century, the fortified wall of New York was demolished to be replaced by a thoroughfare, Wall Street, and the Dutch canal was filled in. Slowly, the city grew northward. All the same, during all of the next century, New York remained a relatively modest town compared to Boston and Philadelphia, then the largest cities in North America. In 1760, New York numbered 16,000 inhabitants (Quebec City, the capital of New France, had a population of 8,000 at the time).

At the end of the Seven Years' War, New France was ceded to the British, putting an end to the French threat that loomed over New York – an invasion from Montreal in the north had been a constant fear. In the wake of these events, the British quickly realized the advantages of the port of New York and constructed a shipyard and many loading docks, developments that saw New York supplant Boston in the area of trade a few decades later. Finally, the Jewish community was growing, and many Jews who had arrived with the British Army during the war established themselves as arms and military equipment dealers.

The American Revolution

The American colonies greatly benefitted from the outcome of the Seven Years' War. The conflict was very costly to the city, however, which had to empty its royal coffers to pay its suppliers. The Crown enacted various measures to make the colonies bear the brunt of these debts. In 1764, it prohibited New Yorkers from printing their own paper money in order to better control the local economy. The next year, London enacted the Stamp Act, a law that imposed a tax on a whole range of products and services in the British colonies – glasses of beer served in taverns, newspaper advertisements, marriage licenses, etc. – through the mandatory purchase of stamps. The American colonists were not accustomed to taxes and duties and revolted against these measures so strongly that the London Parliament was forced to acquiesce. However, in 1767, Parliament revisited the issue with the Townshend Acts, which imposed duties on a series of products including tea, the "sacred" beverage of Anglo-Saxons.

The New York elite of the era cursed these imposed taxes but was fearful of the independence movement that arose in resistance to them. Seated firmly on the fence, New Yorkers ultimately played only a secondary role in the creation of the United States. In 1773, word came that the American Revolution was underway in Boston, ignited by the famous Boston Tea Party (Bostonians disguised as Native Americans threw a British shipment of tea overboard). Fearing that the revolution would have an ill effect on the city's economic growth and that the British Army stationed in the port might definitively crush the city, 15,000 New Yorkers fled to the countryside. When American independence was proclaimed in Philadelphia in 1776, the colony of New York abstained, remaining for some time further in the British fold. As a result, the city was attacked by both sides who battled fiercely for it. August 22, 1776, George Washington lost the Battle of Long Island (18,000 men against 32,000 Englishmen on almost 500 ships). To top it all off, a fire broke out on September 21, destroying one third of the city.

New York was the nerve centre of the British administration in America and was the principal centre for detaining American prisoners of war. Loyalists, subjects that remained faithful to the Crown, converged here, occupying houses abandoned by New Yorkers who had temporarily fled the city. When their cause was defeated at the Battle of Yorktown in 1781, they in their turn began to desert the city. The Treaty of Versailles, signed June 28, 1783, consecrated the independence of the United States. General panic broke out in the streets of New York and in many cities in the state. The number of Loyalists who fled the region over the course of the summer is estimated at 100,000. Many of them headed for Canada, the only remaining bit of British North America, where they settled in the regions of the Eastern Townships, the Outaouais and in what would become Upper Canada (Ontario). The resulting turmoil was beneficial to black slaves, among others, who were finally able to acquire the status of free people. November 25, 1783, George Washington entered the ruined city while the last of the British troops boarded ships back to England.

The Port City

Few American cities suffered as much in the War of Independence as did New York. Luckily, the geographic assets of the city allowed it to rebound quickly. In addition, the city was chosen as the capital of the United States in 1785. On April 30, 1789, George Washington took the Oath of Office on the balcony of Federal Hall and was sworn in as the first President of the United States. The capital was tansferred to Philadelphia only a few months later, however, before being permanently moved to a brand new city named for Washington and built expressly to house the American government. The decision to create a new city for the capital, although it disappointed New Yorkers, aimed to preserve the cohesion of the nascent nation, especially in the choice of a strategic site on the Potomac River, on the borderline between the southern and northern colonies. Then, in 1797, the political influence of rural constituents led to the relocation of the state government from New York to Albany, a city in the middle of the countryside near the geographic centre of the state.

Despite all this, New York experienced lightning-pace growth, surpassing Boston and Philadelphia to become the largest city in the United States in 1820 with a population of more than 100,000. Simultaneously, its port became the first ranked in the country. The renowned New York Stock Exchange was born in 1817 and quickly became the most important stock market on the continent. The city was already welcoming hundreds of immigrants annually, among them many aristocrats who fled France and the Reign of Terror that arose following the French Revolution of 1789.

The construction of the Erie Canal (1817-1825), spanning a distance of over 580 kilometres (232 miles) into the continental interior, gave New York a firm hold over its east coast rivals. The canal made it unnecessary to pass through Montreal to reach the Great Lakes and the Mississippi Valley. Instead, boats could navigate up the Hudson to Albany, then take the canal to Buffalo, and from there cover all of the American Midwest. The Lachine Canal in Montreal, inaugurated the same year, simply was not up to the task. Everything was now in place to make New York the gateway to the North American continent from Europe. Merchandise and immigrants flooded into the port in larger and larger numbers year after year, and continued to do so until the middle of the 20th century.

From this point on, the histories of New York and of the global economy became intimately linked. Not only were products shipped through the port, but an export manufacturing sector developed in the city that soon made New York the foremost industrial centre in the United States, a title it held until the First World War. New York became the most important trade centre for domestic products and services by the beginning of the 19th century, one hundred years before the United States emerged from the World Wars as the preeminent global power and New York became the most important business centre on the planet. The flow of goods and money soon gravitated around New York as it had in the past around London and Paris.

The quasi-permanent conflicts all over Europe, religious persecution in Russia, and misery and hunger in Ireland brought immigrants who dreamed of a better world, swelling New York's population from 100,000 in 1820 to close to one million in 1870. The face of the city changed completely in just 50 years. It ceased to be a small trading city centred around its port, and had become a great cosmopolitan metropolis with which the rest of the world would have to reckon.

Beginning in 1830, New York reconstructed itself every 15 or 20 years – buildings were not even given the time to age. This renewal was completed after a fire destroyed the entire old section of the city in 1825, obliterating the last vestiges of its Dutch past. New York was already being described in superlatives. The Astor was the largest hotel in the world in 1836, with 300 rooms, the restaurant Taylor's served 3,000 meals a day, and the largest luxury stores in the Western World sprouted up on Broadway.

However, the occasionally ostentatious wealth of some New Yorkers was an affront to the masses living in the decrepit neighbourhoods of the Lower East Side. As early as 1849, bloody riots at Astor Place highlighted the tensions between the rich and the poor. Two rival actors appearing in the same play on the same night served as the trigger of this unfortunate event that led to the deaths of about 30 people. The tragedy was a principal cause of the desertion of the commercial nexus of Broadway by the better-off, who were drawn to the budding neighbourhoods of Midtown and the Upper East Side – still considered the poshest in the city – that began to develop after it was decided in 1857 to build a large park north of 59th Street (Central Park). When construction of St. Patrick's Cathedral began, in the same period, Fifth Avenue was still just a plain country road – 20 years later it would be the most prestigious thoroughfare in the United States.

The Astor Place riots were a mere prelude to the Draft Act Riots of 1863. As the United States slipped into the Civil War, the number of Union volunteers, which included many New Yorkers, proved insufficient to the task. President Lincoln imposed conscription. The law was gravely unjust, however, since the better off could buy their way out of service for 300 dollars and avoid battle altogether. The poor had no choice. For four days, rioters, mainly penniless Irish people, sacked the city, burning down public buildings and business that supported conscription. These events, the bloodiest in the city's history, resulted in over 2,000 deaths.

New York's Golden Age

With the advent of peace, New York entered a golden age unprecedented in human history. Many of the famous personalities and traditions that would win the city its worldwide acclaim emerged during this rosy period that began in 1865, the year that marked the end of the Civil War, and lasted until the Great Crash on Wall Street in 1929. The Astor, Vanderbilt, Carnegie, Steinway, Cunard, Rockefeller, Morgan and Tiffany families had all been in business for a long time, but they all had their greatest successes in this period, which was also the era in which they ascended to the apex of American high society and infiltrated the best salons in Europe.

PORTRAIT

Caroline Astor reigned over all of these beautiful people, parsimoniously selecting those who would be admitted to the inner circle. By enacting a rigorous code of etiquette, she contributed to the training and refinement, among other aspects, of an upper class that until then had been somewhat vulgar and flashy. It was a time of memorable equipages, balls and ceremonies. The famous Easter Parade, an Easter Sunday procession down Fifth Avenue of couples decked out in their most beautiful hats and most fashionable outfits, was born in this context of abundance and prosperity.

Most of the city's structural layout and major cultural institutions also made their appearance during this era. The Metropolitan Museum of Art was founded in 1870. A few years later, it moved to Central Park, which was inaugurated in 1878 after 20 years of work. The Metropolitan Opera opened in 1883, and in the years that followed it, was the setting of triumphant performances by Enrico Caruso, Arturo Toscanini and Vaslav Nijinsky. The opening night concert at Carnegie Hall in May 1891 was conducted by Tchaikovsky himself. The ribbon cutting that most solidified New York's identity, however, was the inauguration of the Statue of Liberty, a gift from France to the United States, in 1886.

New Yorkers of the era had still bigger ambitions. At the turn of the century, the city developed its profile of skyscrapers, which has become the symbol of the American metropolis and which was soon copied all over the world. In fact, between 1890 and 1914, the city's appearance changed radically. The race to build the tallest skyscraper, the ultimate symbol of prestige, started with the construction of the 16 stories of the World Building (1890) and saw its pre-war apotheosis at the inauguration of the Woolworth Building, a flamboyant, 60-floor neo-Gothic tower, in 1913. At first these skyscrapers were concentrated in Lower Manhattan, but after 1920 they sprouted up like mushrooms in Midtown. The process of construction, demolition and reconstruction accelerated and reached an unprecedented scale. For example, in 1897 the Waldorf-Astoria was erected at the corner of Fifth Avenue and 34th Street; it had no fewer than 1,000 rooms on 17 floors, which made it the largest and most luxurious hotel on the planet. Then, just 30 years later, this mammoth was razed to make way for the 102 stories of the Empire State Building!

The importers and shipowners of South Street, who had controlled the city's economy until then, were ousted by the financiers of Wall Street and the railway, oil and steel magnates who would make New York the hub of the global economy. It is estimated that 70 percent of the headquarters of large American companies were based in New York in 1900, in the restricted area of Lower Manhattan. The proximity of head offices to each other allowed for deals to be made more quickly and new projects to be begun more easily.

While Manhattan was developing in an anarchic frenzy, the other urban areas on the shores of New York Bay also experienced phenomenal growth. Brooklyn was already the third largest American city in 1880; three years later it was connected to Manhattan by the Brooklyn Bridge. In 1898, Brooklyn, the Bronx, Queens and Staten Island merged with New York, which until then had been limited to Manhattan Island, to form the largest city in the world with over three million residents in 1900. To link these five boroughs, the construction of a sprawling underground subway system was begun in 1904. Above ground trains and ferries completed the network, shuttling their cargo of bustling workers every morning, and two large train stations in Midtown, Pennsylvania Station and Grand Central Terminal, were added to this infrastructure.

Between 1880 and 1914, New York experienced a massive wave of immigration. With the introduction of transatlantic liners, the trip from Europe to the United States could be made in under a week, making the dream of America more real than ever. Immigrants crowded into the holds of these giant ships, ascending to their decks when they arrived in the Port of New York to behold the Statue of Liberty. Immigrants were so numerous that authorities built an entire complex on Ellis Island to serve as a welcoming and processing centre for new arrivals. Among them were hundreds of thousands of Italians, as well as Russian and Polish Jews fleeing the pogroms unleashed by the assassination of Tzar Alexander II in 1881. Jews would make up more than a quarter of the city's population beginning in 1910.

The First World War (1914-1918) was a boon to New York's economy. Blacks from the southern states, attracted by the general prosperity, moved to Harlem starting in 1916. This neighbourhood was in full swing with new jazz clubs and other nightclubs opening like wildfire. New York in the 1920s was gigantic party that people thought would never end. The only dark spot on the horizon was Prohibition. This federal law of 1920 prohibited the consumption of alcohol in the United States. To circumvent the law, a mafia-controlled network of clandestine bars called "speakeasies" sprouted up, to which the very corrupt local authorities turned a blind eye. This period lasted until 1933, and New Yorkers lived it as if it were all fun and games. The forbidden fruit is so much sweeter...

Ironically, the culminating moment of New York's golden age, attested to by the construction of the tallest skyscrapers in the world in Midtown (the Chrysler Building, the RCA Building at Rockefeller Center, the Empire State Building), coincided with the worst financial catastrophe ever experienced in human history at the Stock Exchange on Wall Street, which abruptly ended a period of prosperity that had gone uninterrupted since 1865. On Black Friday, October 25, 1929, stocks plummeted, bankrupting many investors and businesses. Ruined brokers threw themselves from the roof of the Stock Exchange building or, more elegantly, smashed themselves up in their Rolls-Royces. New York, which had been the hub of the financial world since 1918, dragged the economy of the entire West down with it to a depth from which it would not emerge until the beginning of the Second World War in 1939.

New York: Cultural Capital

Around 1930, the population of New York reached seven million. American workers flooded into the Big Apple in the hope of finding work, but in 1933 one quarter of the New York work force was unemployed. Long lines of men and women waiting for daily bowls of soup sent a wake-up call to the New York upper crust that had been dozing in the blissful naivety of the preceding era. The upper class acquired a certain maturity and developed a sense of its social responsibilities, and New York gained a more humane image. Many palatial homes were demolished to be replaced by more practical and less ostentatious high-rise apartments. The municipal administration, at the instigation of its first mayor of Italian origin, Fiorello La Guardia, multiplied efforts to lessen the effects of the crisis (construction of social housing and schools, development of the beltways and the international airport). In addition, the World's Fair was held in 1939 to commemorate the 150th anniversary of the inauguration of George Washington on the steps of Federal Hall.

At the same time, the art world was blossoming. As early as the 19th century, rich collectors had made French Impressionists known throughout the United States. The Armory Show of 1913 introduced America to the Fauvists and Cubists. Local artists based in Manhattan were only really discovered after 1930 when new museums and art galleries began to appear all over the city (Whitney, Guggenheim, Museum of Modern Art, etc.), creating a forum for their work. The popularity of theatrical numbers and musical productions on Broadway, as well as the rise in New York radio stations and magazines heard and read by the whole of the American population, made New York the capital of American culture from then on.

The early part of the Second World War was like a gift from heaven for New York, as cultural riches were transferred from Europe to America. These were concentrated in the Big Apple, which also served as a refuge for European intellectuals. Jewish immigration, which had slowed considerably over the 1920s, was renewed with the rise of Nazism. Finally, the weakening of Paris, London and Berlin after the war reinforced New York's role as a centre of economic decision-making. The establishment in 1947 of the headquarters of the United Nations on Manhattan Island confirmed the American metropolis' role as an international city in the post-war period.

The 1950s marked another period of prosperity for New York. The three major American television networks – ABC, CBS and NBC – were established and based in the city. Publicity and marketing agencies, publishing houses and large department stores created thousands of jobs in Midtown and, as the industrial sector declined, New York was transformed into a service economy. By 1960, the city's population was 7.5 million (over 16 million including the outlying areas of Long Island and New Jersey), and the early stages of the exodus to the suburbs were already apparent.

In 1964 the city hosted a second World's Fair that highlighted New York's modernity. That same year, Pennsylvania Station was razed, because the beaux-arts mastodon was perceived as outdated by authorities. The intelligentsia thought otherwise and fought to the end to save the old station. Although they were unsuccessful in this case, public pressure on municipal authorities led to the creation of the Landmarks Preservation Commission, a committee that protects heritage buildings, and the city's architectural history. The next year, a famous power outage – the blackout of November 9, 1965 – caused a mini baby-boom!

Slump and Rejuvenation

The exodus of the middle class to the suburbs weakened the fiscal base and aging infrastructure of the city. Since the Great Depression, New York had offered a number of free services to the poor. This municipal aid, usually provided by the central government as it is in Canada and in most European countries, although beneficial, pushed out the middle class and attracted the poorest people from all over the United States, with the result that in October 1975 the richest city in the world was on the brink of bankruptcy.

The massive arrival of blacks and Puerto Ricans over the course of the 1960s and 1970s again transformed the mosaïc of the city. Strong racial tensions resulted. The gap between the very rich and the very poor widened, but millionaires lived only a short distance from the starving. This overcrowdedness sent crime rates soaring.

The construction of the 110-story twin towers of the World Trade Center in 1973, and the arrival of large ships in the Port of New York for the ceremonies of the American Bicentennial in 1976 did not do much to boost the city's image. Over the course of the following decade, great numbers of Vietnamese and Korean immigrants settled in New York, creating little Asian enclaves in each of the five boroughs. In 1987, the Stock Exchange was shaken by another crisis, the "Junk Bonds" incident, and New York's fortunes hit rock bottom; from this point on the city slowly dragged itself out of the mud.

Construction work began on Battery Park City, a huge real estate complex built on the embankments near the World Trade Center. In 1989, New York elected its first black mayor, David Dinkins, who succeeded Edward Koch. Then, in 1993, Rudy Giuliani came onto the political scene with a program to clean up the city, literally and figuratively. He gave private companies control of specific parts of the city, with the result that crime is significantly down in many neighbourhoods and the city in general is reaping the benefits.

POPULATION

Where can you find 5,000 dentists and a lawyer for every 225 citizens? In New York, of course, and these figures are not exaggerated because the population of the city was 7,323,000 in 1990. The 1980 census put the population at 7,071,00, meaning that the city only grew by 3.6 percent, compared to the 9.8 percent rise in the population of the United States as a whole.

Multiculturalism

To say that New York is a cosmopolitan city is an understatement, even to the least observant visitor. About 3.5 million residents of Greater New York were born outside the United States, including 145,000 Dominicans; 75,000 Chinese; 74,000 Jamaicans; 67,000 Colombians and 58,000 Koreans. In Manhattan, 58 percent of the population is white, over 25 percent is Hispanic, over 22 percent is black, and 7 percent is Asian.

Racial mixing is more common in New York than it is anywhere else in the United States, and it is on the rise. Recent statistics from 1997 show that the population of the metropolitan region of New York has only been maintained by the arrival of hundreds of thousands of immigrants. Demographers therefore anticipate that the proportion of New Yorkers born outside the country will be well above the 26.7 percent it was in 1990.

The first colonists were Dutch. They were soon joined by the English, and even by French Huguenots, who were barred from emigrating to French colonies. In the 17th century, Sephardic Jews established communities on Manhattan Island.

Then in the 19th century, almost three quarters of all immigrants to the United States landed in New York and many of them chose to stay and establish themselves in the city. In that era, the United States opened its doors to anyone who wanted to start a new life. In fact, many Irish, English, Dutch, German and German Jewish people immigrated over a period of a century and a half.

Next came Italians, especially Calabrians and Sicilians, Eastern European Jews, Russians and other Slavic immigrants. The culture shock was enormous and assimilation was more difficult. In 1924, the United States put a ceiling on its policy, allowing only 150,000 new immigrants per year.

In the 20th century, many West Indians and Puerto Ricans, as well as numbers of African Americans from the South made New York their home. The West Side was preferred by Hispanics, while blacks took up residence in Harlem. By 1975, New York was the largest black city in the world.

The abolition of quotas in 1965 and the enactment of laws on the right to political asylum brought new faces to New York from all over the planet, especially since the fall of the Iron Curtain. Many are Latin American and Asian. Interestingly, new arrivals tend to settle in old immigrant neighbourhoods, replacing those who preceded them 10, 20, and 50 years ago as they "move on up" to more privileged areas of town or the suburbs.

New York contradicts the theory that immigrants simply assimilate into the American "melting pot". Many different languages can be heard on its streets. Since Spanish is the second-most spoken language, many Chinese people, Latin Americans and Italians would have a hard time communicating with each other in English. In fact, English is a second language in over 31% of households.

New York is home to the largest Chinatown in America, the most populous Jewish community outside of Israel, and an Italian neighbourhood, Little Italy, where life goes on as it does in Palermo. The city still has vibrant Greek and Polish communities. Irish descendants continue to form the largest ethnic group, a fact that is obvious every St. Patrick's Day. Another trend is that particular communities seem to monopolize certain economic sectors. Diamond dealers, for example, speak to each other in Yiddish.

New York still leads Los Angeles as the first American home town of immigrants.

Ethnic Division

The hidden face of New York's multiculturalism is the growing gap between the various ethnic groups that make up the city. For example, in Manhattan, the average income of a white household was $30,000 in 1990. The income of an Asian household is approximately $22,000, but the average black family income was under $15,000, and barely $10,000 for the average Spanish-speaking family. Almost 13 percent of the white population do not have a high school diploma. This figure may be a drastic 55 percent among Hispanics. One of the reasons for the last figure is that most new arrivals are Latin American and have only been in the United States for under ten years, not long enough for immigration services to properly accommodate them. Thus, in this case, it is hard to say whether they have been categorically discriminated against.

ECONOMY

There is a long love story between New York and money. The city is not only the financial centre of the United States – but of the Western World.

Half of the entire population of North America lives within 1,200 kilometres of New York, 20 percent of American foreign trade is shipped through the Port of New York, and one third of everything that leaves the country by airplane does so from a New York airport. So it comes as no surprise that almost all of the large banks, insurance companies, trust companies and brokerages are based here. Most company headquarters are located in the area around Broad Street, the location of the New York Stock Exchange – the largest stock market in the world – since it was moved from Wall Street. In fact, New York has more head offices of major companies than do the three other large American financial centres combined.

The communications and entertainment industries also form a significant part of New York's economy. The three main American television networks are based here. Local media production companies produce a good deal of the nationally broadcast radio shows and advertisements. In addition, Broadway has made its mark on theatre and the arts. New York is currently trying to become a centre for new communications technologies.

The fashion and clothing industry is another of the city's big industries, employing about 200,000 people. Other important sectors include medical equipment, graphic arts, computer science, energy, environmental protection and pharmaceuticals. And, obviously, the public service sector is huge as a result of New York's large population.

The Present Economic Situation

New York's economy was severely affected by the recession of the early 1990s. Hundreds of thousands of new jobs have made up for lost ground, but growth remains slow compared to that of the rest of the United States. There are several reasons for this economic stagnation. The population of New York is growing more slowly than that of the country in general. There is almost no space left in the city – everything has been built. Taxes, energy costs and labour are more expensive per square metre in New York than in other cities, and many Americans simply cannot afford New York's high standard of living.

A few economic indicators point to an imminent recovery in the city. Retail sales are increasing at the same rate as in other parts of the United States, but inflation is not. This makes New York a more attractive market for existing businesses and new industries. No one is cashing in more on this progress than bankers, who were severely rocked by the drop in real estate values. However, the city's recovery has not been shared by the rest of the state, where the mainstays of the economy are the secondary manufacturing sector and the state bureaucracy.

The former has been affected by increased international competition and the latter has suffered from government cutbacks in the public sector.

POLITICS

The administration of New York City rests in the hands of its mayor, who is assisted by a municipal law-making council of 51 representatives elected in proportion to each district or borough.

Throughout the city's history, the holder of the title of mayor has proven quickly to be either a thief, like William Tweed, or a *laissez-faire* administrator, like Fiorello La Guardia, who had to deal with the severe consequences of the Crash of 1929. Ex-mayor John Lindsay went down in history as the man who almost bankrupted the city in 1975 through his reckless spending, especially in the social sector. The state authorities put their feet down to avoid the worst and rebuilt the city finances.

The State of New York is administered on the same model as other American states: the governor and legislative assembly sit in Albany. The present governor is Republican George E. Pataki. Since his election in 1994, he has introduced many right-wing reforms: alleviating the fiscal burden, liberalizing trade, reducing the size of the state apparatus, increasing anti-crime measures, cutting back social programs and valorizing the family. The economic situation in the state has rebounded quite a bit in the last four years, but more because of the general prosperity in the whole country – since Democratic districts have improved as much as Republican ones, and vice-versa.

Finally, because the population of New York State is so large, it holds quite a bit of leverage in the government of the United States. It sends two senators and 31 representatives to Congress, making its interest groups better heard by the federal authorities.

ARTS

Film

At the end of the 19th century, film was invented by the Lumière brothers in Europe and Thomas Edison in the United States, precisely in Orange, New Jersey. From 1888 to 1893, Edison and his colleagues William Kennedy and Laurie Dickson experimented with film in a studio called Black Maria next to Edison's laboratory. He created 35-millimetre films for a kinetoscope, a machine that projects photographs taken at very short intervals, creating the impression of movement.

Many movie companies came and went, but gradually New York became the film centre of the United States. The city would hold this title until the end of the First World War, after the film giants of the era (the Kalem, Biograph and Vitograph companies; Edison himself; Pathé and Méliès, two European producers; and three producers from Chicago and Philadelphia) founded the Motion Picture Patents Company in 1908. Unfortunately, the union failed to create a monopoly in American cinematic production.

Later, in 1912, the Famous Players Film Company was founded. They made three-reel films that were an hour-and-a-half long (at a time when only short films were shown) and were mainly film versions of plays that starred the most famous actors of the day (James O'Neil in *The Count of Monte Cristo*, 1912; James Hackett in *The Prisoner of Zenda*, 1913; Mrs. Fiske in *Tess of the D'Ubervilles*, 1913).

The poor climate of New York and the need of more modern sets caused an exodus of film producers to more clement lands like California, Florida and Cuba, especially in winter. Slowly, the film business moved to the west coast. The avant-garde had already gotten some good reviews with critics and audiences in 1921 with the production of *Manhatta*, a film inspired by the writings of Walt Whitman, by Charles Seeler and Paul Strand. By 1922, New York produced 12 percent of American feature-length films, whereas the new capital of cinema, Hollywood, was responsible for 84 percent. At that time a number of independent ethnic filmmakers appeared on the scene, like Jewish producer Maurice Schwartz (*Broken Hearts*, 1926), and Oscar Michaux, who made *Body & Soul* (1924, with Paul Robeson) and *The Exile* (1930).

Cinema resurfaced in New York in the sound era. The Fox Film Corporation experimented with soundtracks as early as 1926, as did Fox Movie Tones (1927). Sound made up for Hollywood's sunny climate, and actors and directors began to be hired from Broadway. New York cinema once again became connected with the theatre world, because theatre actors were accustomed to playing speaking roles, whereas the stars of the silent screen didn't always have the nicest voices to go with their pretty faces. From this point on, acting would play a more important role than before, and the first success of this epoch was *Applause* (1929), by Rouben Mamoulian.

In 1937 no film was entirely shot in New York, and in 1939 the only films that were had an entirely black audience (*Moon over Harlem*, 1939). To help revive the industry, the American government went so far as to sue Paramount Pictures for monopolistic practices and gave special incentives independent film-makers to encourage their work.

Right after the Second World War, many great classics of New York cinema were made: *The House on 92nd Street* (1945), *Miracle on 34th Street* (1947), *Naked City* (1948). Then, avant-garde film-making rose from its ashes and New York became a centre for "off screen" cinema. Maya Deren and Hans Richter, among others, created some real gems of experimental film.

The 1960s fostered fiery directors with fresh ideas like Andy Warhol (*The Chelsea Girls*, 1966) and Canadian Michael Snow (*Wavelength*, 1967), who used painting and minimalist sculpture as an approach. New York-based, Filmways Studio produced Francis Ford Coppola's *The Godfather* (1971) and Woody Allen's *Annie Hall* (1977). Robert Downey (*Putney Swope*, 1969) and John Cassavetes (*Husbands*, 1970) made names for themselves as independent film-makers.

A few famous directors developed a particular love for the city of New York and used it in almost all of their works: Woody Allen (*Take the Money and Run*, 1969; *Manhattan*, 1979; *Hannah and her Sisters*, 1986; *New York Stories – (Oëdipus*

Wrecks), 1989; *Shadows and Fog*, 1992; *Manhattan Murder Mystery*, 1993; *Bullets Over Broadway*, 1994), Martin Scorsese (*Mean Streets*, 1973; *Taxi Driver*, 1976; *New York, New York*, 1977; *King of Comedy*, 1983; *The Age of Innocence*, 1993) and Spike Lee (*She's Gotta Have It*, 1986, *Do the right Thing*, 1989; *Jungle Fever*, 1991; *Malcolm X*, 1992; *Crooklyn*, 1994), and newcomers Jim Jarmusch (*Stranger than Paradise*, 1984; *Night on Earth*, 1991) and Wayne Wang (*Smoke*, 1995).

PORTRAIT

Music

Jazz

Jazz developed in New Orleans and Chicago, but New York also plays a role in the history of this musical genre, above all because it brought this folk art international recognition. Ragtime grew out of Harlem and consisted of a fast syncopated type of dancehall music (John P. Johnson and Fats Waller). In 1919, the blues broke through with the voice of Mamie Smith, and took a new turn when they were sung by vaudeville singers backed up by talented instrumentalists.

In 1924, big band leaders like Duke Ellington and Fletcher Henderson developed "swing", but New Yorkers still had trouble distinguishing tamer popular dance music from it. However, the centre of jazz activity in America moved from Chicago to New York, which incarnated the most subtle nuances of the genre. The first sign of this migration was when cornetist and trumpeter Louis Armstrong packed his bags for the Big Apple. New York's quality recording and broadcasting industry greatly changed the face of jazz, making its blend of soft, hard and rebellious tunes more acceptable and accessible to the public.

At the beginning of the 1930s, musical "duels" often broke out between the bands of Duke, Henderson, singer Cab Calloway and drummer Chick Webb. And despite the appearance of Ella Fitzgerald on the New York music scene, jazz of this decade still had a strictly functional role: it was dance and social music only. Jazz and popular music became one in 1936 with Benny Goodman and his band, although purer jazz attracted its share of listeners thanks to the likes of pianist and band leader Count

Basie who brought the talents of saxophonist *extraordinaire* Artie Shaw to the fore. Billie Holiday recorded with small combos, and mainly sang with saxophonist Lester Young during this era. Then, in 1939, Coleman Hawkins returned from a five year jaunt in France and re-recorded *Body & Soul*, the most famous jazz tune to this day. Frank Sinatra was discovered at an amateur music contest in 1935. He went on to work with the orchestras of Harry James (1939) and Tommy Dorsey (1940-42), and then pursued a solo career. He hit Broadway with *It Happened in Brooklyn* (1947) and *On the Town* (1949), but he is most famous for his trademark songs *That's Life, My Way*, and, of course, *New York, New York*.

An important movement was budding in New York at the beginning of the 1940s that would make jazz into an art form. Charlie Christian, Thelonius Monk, Bud Powell, Kenny Clarke, Max Roach, and above all saxophonist Charlie "Bird" Parker and trumpeter Dizzy Gillespie invented "Bebop", a big band but more fast-paced, obscure and technically virtuosic in style than its predecessor. Bebop quickly reached its apogee, and then Miles Davis reversed its course, abandoning the style, which he had favoured since 1939. His nonet, orchestrated by Gil Evans, produced a tempered sound that was soon dubbed "cool jazz". This form of jazz was popularized by west coast musicians, only a few of whom shared the spotlight, such as Chet Baker. The Modern Jazz Quartet made jazz a more respectable artform, and brought it closer to being classic. Dizzy Gillespie strove for a symbiosis of big band, bebop and Afro-Cuban musical styles. Hard-bop, a more rhythmic version of its close relative, took the spotlight in the last half of the 1950s. At the head of this movement were drummers Max Roach and Art Blakey, pianist Horace Silver, saxophonist John Coltrane and Miles Davis.

The year of 1959 marked an important step in the journey of jazz. Saxophonist Ornette Coleman came to New York from Los Angeles and presented a series of concerts at the Five Spot, where he and his band experimented with free jazz. This new style challenged all accepted notions of rhythm and tonality, and even the sound quality of the instruments: bebop seemed very traditional next to this irrational art. In the same era, Miles Davis, with *Kind of Blue*, tested a new genre called "modal", a rejection of the extreme up-tempo rhythms of bop and its near-frenetic harmonic sequences for synthetic harmonics, or block chords, from which new melodic numbers arose. Coltrane brought this genre to perfection on his albums *Impressions* and his masterpiece, *A Love Supreme* (1963), by using hypnotic chords and variations of chromatic melodies. He spent the last three years of his life playing with musical styles, ultimately sticking with an almost minimalist free jazz on *Interstellar Space* (1967).

During the 1970s the music of New Orleans lost some of its younger fans to rock. Recognizing this trend, Miles Davis, accompanied by Wayne Shorter, Joe Zawinul, Chick Corea, John McLaughlin, Dave Holland and Tony Williams, combined the two styles, creating "jazz fusion" (*Bitches Brew*, 1969). This new style gained ground all over the United States, but its new idols were in New York, where Pat Metheny (guitarist) and Jaco Pastorius (bassist) played beautifully together and alone. Wynton Marsalis, followed by his brother Branford, dominated the New York scene in the 1980s, performing a fiery improvisational brand of hard-bop similar to the early musical duels of Dixieland (1900-1930 and 1940) and the sublime, staccato phrasing of Coltrane or Wayne Shorter. New York was especially ripe terrain for funky experimental bands in the 1980s. Lost Tribe used an unconventional approach and the group M-Base, whose main members were saxophonist Steve Coleman (*Tao of Mad Phat*, 1993) and singer Cassandra Wilson, went back to their African-American musical roots.

Rock

New York played an important role in the development of rock and its predecessors, rock and roll and rhythm and blues. Atlantic Records produced Big Joe Turner, one of the pioneers of rhythm and blues, a style created in part by some of the musicians from the Duke Ellington is Big Band. One of its members, saxophonist King Curtis, became famous for his studio work.

In 1954, radio station WINS broadcast the first recordings of Fats Domino and Little Richard. The line that divided rock and roll from rhythm and blues was soon blurred by popular artists like Elvis Presley, Buddy Holly, Chuck Berry and Bill Haley, who amassed new fans with their blend of rhythm and blues and country music.

The 1960s gave birth to a new breed of artists eager for social change and influenced by the populist ideals of the left. Woody Guthrie and Pete Seeger appeared at Gerde's Folk City, the Bitter End and other venues, stealing fans of Bobby McGhee, Sonny Terry, Mississippi John Hurt and Muddy Waters. In 1965, tired of acoustic music, folk-singer Bob Dylan plugged in his guitar and was an instant success. Songs such as *Like a Rolling Stone* made an impact on mega-bands like the Beatles and the Rolling Stones. Nonetheless, rock remained on the sidelines until the New York radio station WOR spun the first track on the airwaves in 1966.

Thanks to the experimentation of the Beatles on albums like *Revolver*, *Rubber Soul*, and *Sgt. Pepper's Lonely Hearts Club Band*, the late 1960s led rock down new roads right into the heart of the city. Lou Reed and his band The Velvet Underground sang about drugs and sadomasochism to microtonal cello melodies, heavily distorted guitars, and a thunderous rhythm section. The Fugs and The Mothers of Invention pushed satire and anarchy to the limit, while Buddy Guy, Jimi Hendrix, Jerry Garcia and Johnny Winter played a mean guitar at Cafe Wha?.

Rock evolved into a more pretentious form during the 1970s, until a new movement came on the scene: punk rock, which could be heard at the bar CBGB-OMFUG. Bands like Television, Richard Hell and the Voidoids, Patti Smith and The Ramones gave way to British bands like The Sex Pistols and The Clash, whose popularity at the end of the decade was short-lived. Punk rock fragmented quickly into a variety of very different styles like New Wave, Noise Rock, Hardcore and Trash. Other musicians inspired by contemporary classical music and jazz fusion crossed the boundaries between styles such as punk and funk. John Cage (pianist), Naked City (John Zorn, Bill Frisell) and Music Revelation (David Murray and James Blood Ulmer) are some that stood out as much for their originality as for their ability to mesmerize audiences with their talents. Sonic Youth, who like Lou Reed sing about heroine, have been at it for over 13 years and have recorded many albums including solo projects. Singer and guitar virtuoso Ani Difranco draws inspiration from spoken word and folk, and combines these styles with a breathtaking rhythm section. But the most innovative band from the late 1980s was the black metal group Living Colour, led by guitarist Vernon Reid.

Literature

New York has attracted writers since the beginning of the colonization of America, but until the 20th century, Boston remained the literary centre of choice. Literary circles formed in Greenwich Village, which was nicknamed the "American Bohemia". This neighbourhood was attractive because of its rich literary culture and its minimal cost of living. From this simmering cultural cauldron emerged *Masses*, a magazine of art, leftist politics, literature and humour. The magazine was taken to court by the American government for its stance against the draft in the First World War. Another magazine, *Smart Set*, published the work of James Joyce and F. Scott Fitzgerald.

The authors of the 1920s were inspired by life and events the city of New York, which was in full expansion during that era. Edith Wharton wrote *The Age of Innocence* (1920), depicting the ups and downs of the elite that frequented Washington Square. F. Scott Fitzgerald penned *This Side of Paradise* (1920), which was labelled "jazz-age romanticism". Dos Passos described the panorama of lost voices and destinies that he found in New York in *Manhattan Transfer* (1925), while Fitzgerald satirized the public with *The Great Gatsby*, Dreiser with *An American Tragedy*, and Lewis with *Arrowsmith*. Hart Crane described the Brooklyn Bridge in detail in *The Bridge* (1930).

The contrasts and the vibrant side of the city inspired Dashiell Hammett's *The Maltese Falcon* (1934), which was even more successful when it was adapted for the big screen. John Steinbeck, who wrote *Of Mice and Men*, believed that everything was concentrated in New York: the population, the theatre, art, publishing – even murder. For John P. Marquand, New York was an undefinable myriad of triumphs, setbacks and memories. He met great success with the novels *So Little Time* (1943) and *Point of No Return* (1949). Anaïs Nin returned from Paris (she was born in Greenwich Village) and published *Winter of Artifice* (1939) and *Under a Glass Bell* (1944). Tennessee Williams did not have to starve to become a writer: he worked as a waiter in restaurants and read poetry in clubs. Then, in the 1940s and 1950s, he hit it big when his screenplays became successful theatrical productions, including *The Glass Menagerie* (1944) and *A Streetcar Named Desire* (1947).

Columbia University hired the Pulitzer poetry laureate of 1940, Van Doren. Some of his students included future poets John Berryman, Allen Ginsberg and Jack Kerouac. The *New Yorker* magazine sought its piece of the publishing pie and hired Truman Capote, whose excellent writing skills were apparent in his article on Marlon Brando. Another prominent New York literary figure, Arthur Miller, made a mark with *All My Sons* (1947) and *Death of a Salesman* (1949). Canadian Saul Bellow moved to New York and published a translation of *Gimpel the Fool* by I. B. Singer. Bellow furthered his career with a number of publications including *The Victim* (1947), *Seize the Day* (1956), *Herzog* (1964) and *Humboldt's Gift* (1975).

The Beat movement shifted to the Lower East Side, where the rents were lower and one could run into Allen Ginsberg on the street in the period when he published his long poem *Howl* (1957). Jack Kerouac described the habits of neighbourhood residents in *The Subterraneans* (1958), a novel that he called "spontaneous bop prose". Truman Capote, although not part of the Beat club, also lived in the neighbourhood when he wrote *Breakfast at Tiffany's* (1958) and *In Cold Blood* (1966). Following the Beat generation, authors like Mailer, who took the Pulitzer Prize twice with *The Armies of the Night* (1968) and *The Executioner's Song* (1979), redefined journalism with "novelized" news writing.

Broadway Musical Theatre

Musical theatre made its first appearance in New York in 1728 with a performance of *The Beggar's Opera* by John Gay and Johann Pepush, but the city would not become the nexus of musical theatre in the United States until 1870. Then, in 1894, the success of producer George W. Lederer's *The Passing Show*, brought a number of theatre troupes into the light: minstrel, vaudeville, comic opera, operetta and musical comedy took centre stage at the beginning of the 20th century.

George and Ira Gershwin breathed new life into musical theatre in the mid-1920s. In fact, their music was inspired by jazz whereas their satirical lyrics were composed by W. S. Gilbert. Their claim to fame was with the performance of *Of Thee I Sing* (1933). The duo Kern and Hammerstein II melded contemporary and traditional styles in *Show Boat* (1927).

The stock market crash of 1929 marked the end of an era for Broadway, and the best actors made their debuts in Hollywood, leaving New York behind. Nonetheless, some very good plays were staged, including *Fifty Million Frenchmen* (1929) and *Anything Goes* (1934), both renowned for Cole Porter's well-attuned melodies and scripts. Then social opposition burst onto the Broadway stage with Kurt Weil's anti-war *Johnny Johnson* (1936). *The Cradle Will Rock* (1938) pitted workers against capitalists and stirred controversy for Orson Welles' Mercury Theatre Company.

Rodgers and Hammerstein revived the days of cowboys and pioneers in *Oklahoma!* (1943), which met with unprecedented success. For the first time, audiences witnessed a violent death on stage and a "dream ballet" sequence by choreographer Agnes de Mille. Rodgers and Hammerstein's career sparkled thanks to their original librettos and the unforgettable musical scores they composed for shows like *Carousel* (1945), *South Pacific* (1949), *The King and I* (1951) and *The Sound of Music* (1959). Many tried in vain to reproduce this duo's magical formula, creating a whole new genre of lighter comedies.

Frank Loesser's *Guys and Dolls* (1950) told the story of gamblers and their girlfriends. Leonard Bernstein, Betty Comden and Adolph Green depicted the atmosphere of Greenwich Village in the 1930s in *Wonderful Town* (1953). One of the major works of the era, *West Side Story* (1957), was a modern-day adaptation of the very well-known story of Shakespeare's *Romeo and Juliet*, collaborated on by Leonard Bernstein (conductor), Arthur Laurents (librettist), Stephen Sondheim (lyricist) and director Jerome Robbins. Jerry Bock and Sheldon Harnick wrote a satirical version of the European operetta *She Loves Me* (1963). In 1964, they teamed up with Robbins for *Fiddler on the Roof*, one of the most famous Broadway plays.

New authors found original material to work with: for example, *Gypsy* pays tribute to stripper Gypsy Rose. Satire was also key in plays such as *How to Succeed in Business Without Really Trying* (1961). *Hair* (1968) introduced a rock soundtrack and, a first for Broadway, nude scenes. Despite the controversy he provoked, Stephen Sondheim continued to shock audiences with *Company* (1970), *Follies* (1970), *A Little Night Music* (1973), *Pacific Overtures* (1976), *Sweeney Todd* (1979), *Sunday in the Park with George* (1984), *Into the Woods* (1987), and *Passion* (1994). His work with Harold Prince led to a new musical concept based more on thoughts and images than the traditional well-defined scores. Inspired by Sondheim, director and choreographer Bob Fosse produced *Pippin* (1972) and *Dancin'* (1978), while Michael Bennet staged the famous *A Chorus Line* (1975) and *Dreamgirls*.

The 1980s left a bitter taste in the mouths of American artists. Great successes were imported from the United Kingdom, like *Cats* (1981) and *The Phantom of the Opera* (1989), both by Andrew Lloyd Webber, and *Les Misérables* (1987) and *Miss Saigon* (1991). Broadway seemed to have lost its oomph, but the arrival of these foreign productions, combined with a few new American shows, soon dissipated the clouds of doubt over Broadway's future.

Painting

By the end of the 19th century, the major trends of pictorial art in New York were very well represented by Ryder and Ralph Blakelock, who produced poetic landscapes that looked like veritable frescoes, and by Chase and Childe Hassam, who were inspired by Impressionism. The latter founded a group called Ten American Painters (1898).

In the beginning of the 20th century, artists outrightly rejected Impressionism, qualifying it as too "nice", and fully embraced realism, which perfectly reflected the Industrial Age with its "new humans". Inspired by poet Walt Whitman and by the European realist tradition, painters like George Luks, William James Glackens, John Sloan and Everett Shinn depicted leisurely activities of the working class. Opposed to the conservatism of the National Academy, Sloan and Shinn held an exhibition at the MacBeth Gallery (1908), which featured the aforementioned painters as well as Arthur B. Davies, Ernest Lawson and Maurice Pendergast. This group was known from then on as The Eight.

Semi-abstract painting and Cubism arrived in America with photographer Alfred Stieglitz, who also introduced New York artists to the work of John Marin, Abraham Walkowitz, Max Weber and Georgia O'Keefe. Joseph Stella took inspiration instead from Italian Futurism for his paintings of bathers at Coney Island and the Brooklyn Bridge.

The realist and semi-abstract painters organized the International Exhibition of Modern Art (the Armory Show), with over 1,600 paintings. Critics gave the show rather negative reviews and panned Marcel Duchamp's *Nude Descending a Staircase* (1912). In a more positive light, sculptor Gertrude Vanderbilt Whitney opened some important art galleries like the Whitney Studio (1914-17), the Whitney Studio Club (1918-28) and the Whitney Studio Gallery (1928-30), which regularly presented the paintings of Sloan, Alexander Brooks and Guy Pène du Bois. The Harlem Renaissance (1920-30) gave rise to black painters including Aaron Douglas and Charles Alston, famous for their murals that melded African-American traditions and modernism.

The Great Depression of the 1930s took its toll on artists, and the American government was forced to find work for them: in exchange for a reasonable salary, they were hired to decorate government offices, schools and radio stations with their works, and to paint public murals. In the 1930s and 1940s, the Museum of Modern Art presented a few very dazzling exhibitions which featured abstract, Cubist and surrealist painters. Duchamp returned to New York together with Yves Tanguy, Hans Hoffman, John Graham and Matta formed the New York School. They were soon joined by the masters of action-painting, Jackson Pollock and Willem de Kooning. This movement gained popularity and new members, like Elaine de Kooning, Arshile Gorky and Adolph Gottlieb.

A new form of realist painting emerged in the post-war period. Artists Yasuo Kuniyoshi and Stephen Greene drew attention to the human face by brutalizing and disfiguring its features. Meanwhile, Larry Rivers, Robert Rauschenberg and Jasper Johns played on the icons of popular culture to become the forerunners of pop art.

A great number of different styles emerged in the 1960s in New York. Andy Warhol, Roy Lichtenstein and James

Rosenquist made daily objects larger than life. The paintings of Ellsworth Kelly, Jack Youngerman and Jules Olitski were based on very simple, even minimalist shapes. The work of Helen Frankenthaler was characterized by large expanses of fine coats of colour. A politicized art movement was also born in this era. Artists like Rudolph Baranik, Leon Golub, Nancy Spero and May Stevens criticized imperialism, sexism and racism through their work and encouraged artists from various ethnic minorities, such as Emma Amos, Ida Applebroog, Luis Cruz Azaceta and Jean-Michel Basquiat, to express their talents.

Architecture

Colonial Architecture (1624-1776)

No vestiges of New York's Dutch period (1624-1665) have survived over the years, with the exception of a few streets and anglicised place names. In the British period (1665-1776), the narrow wood and red brick Dutch houses, with their characteristic stepped gables, were soon replaced by more comfortable, larger Georgian houses, which are is still common in the towns of neighbouring New England. These English-style houses disappeared from New York in their turn, victims of war, fire, and, most of all, the city's lightning-paced growth in the second half of the 19th century.

Although urban colonial architecture was practically wiped off the map, a few country houses, especially in Brooklyn and on Staten Island, survived the tidal wave of urbanization. The oldest of these are in a style called Dutch Colonial, which is characterized by Mansard roofs with upper slopes that are narrower than their lower slopes. Houses built after 1700 display more a rigorous sense of symmetry, roofs with gentler slopes, and a few elements borrowed from the classical vocabulary, such as pediments and columns (for example, the Morris-Jumel Mansion).

The Architecture of the Port City (1776-1850)

New York experienced a brief period of renewal in the late 18th century, coinciding with its elevation to the rank of capital of

Grace Church (Presbyterian)

the United States. During this period it acquired a few important landmarks, and modest colonial buildings were enhanced by expansion and renovation projects (for example the steeple of St. Paul's Chapel). Nonetheless, the Big Apple was still far from the mega-city that it is today. It was still concentrated around its port, which was becoming increasingly important. Dozens of warehouses with thick red brick walls were built on streets adjoining the docks, and some of these survive to this day in the South Street Seaport Historic District.

Other buildings from this period, in parts of the city that were villages in the first half of the 19th century, have been conserved. These neighbourhoods are characterized by narrow streets that don't follow the grid pattern of the rest of the city, and by typical Federal style row houses covered in red brick and accented with white-trimmed sash windows (for example, Greenwich Village). The Federal style, a lighter version of the British Adam style, persisted in the northeastern United States until the Civil War (1861).

Greek-Revival, which is a symbol par excellence of American democracy because of its Athenian ancestry, appeared toward 1800. It is characterized by ample columned porticos, often topped by pediments, directly inspired by ancient temples. The style was widely employed when public buildings worthy of that title (for example, Federal Hall National Memorial) began to be built. City Hall remained an exception to this trend, however. It displays very original architecture, inspired by the Louis XVI style, acknowledging the solid ties already forged between France and New York. The neo-Gothic style, which was popularly chosen for the construction of churches throughout the Western World, is evident in imposing buildings that became significant landmarks in the history of American architecture (for example, Trinity Church, Grace Church, and St. Patrick's Cathedral).

An Original Architectural Style (1850-1930)

New York high society began to flourish toward the middle of the 19th century, but despite the fact that it ultimately became one of the most affluent bourgeoisies on the planet, it experienced an acute, collective inferiority complex in relation to its European counterparts. Elites embraced Victorian fashions, successively adopting neo-Renaissance, Second Empire, and Beaux-Arts architectural styles for the construction of patrician houses, hotels, theatres, stores, and even office buildings. The first school was inspired by the Italian Renaissance (for example, the Villard houses) and the immense wealth of the Medicis; the second drew its vocabulary from the Paris of Napoleon III, reflecting the style and refinement of the French Second Empire; the third, a cousin of the second, was the product of the École des Beaux-Arts in Paris at the turn of the 20th century.

As would be expected, the New York landscape truly began to emerge when the demands of North American commercial and real estate activity prevailed over European conventions. This original character first expressed itself in cast-iron framework warehouses and stores, examples of which can still be seen along the streets of SoHo (for example, the Haughwout Building). These buildings, adorned with complex moulded metal façades, could be inexpensively constructed in just a few months. They were designed with large windows to reduce the use of gas lighting, which was a serious fire hazard. Because of the strength of the buildings' cast iron frameworks, they could accommodate the storage of large loads and the installation of heavy machinery on multiple levels.

The originality of New York architecture next manifested itself in brownstones, erected between 1850 and 1890. These tall, narrow row houses were efficient not only in their use of space, but also in terms of construction costs, since their façades were covered in a locally quarried, pinkish-brown sandstone called brownstone. This material lent its name to the vernacular housing style, which is still prevalent in Brooklyn Heights and in Manhattan's older residential neighbourhoods such as Murray Hill.

The installation of the first safe elevators after 1857, the design of solid structures that were fire-resistant and simple to build, the improvement of firefighting equipment, the increase in property values, and the concentration of development in Manhattan were all factors that contributed to the popularity of skyscrapers in New York beginning in the late 19th century. New York's panorama in 1886 presented an essentially horizontal profile dominated by the newly inaugurated Brooklyn Bridge. Twenty years later, this bridge was completely obscured behind dozens of towers reaching heights of as much as 30 stories each, and the image of the American city that still resonates today was born.

However, the race for the sky had just begun. Over the next 30 years, there was fierce competition among companies and developers for possession of the tallest building in the city and the world. New York held the record in this field without interruption until 1974, when the Sears Tower was inaugurated in Chicago.

Over the years, the exteriors of New York skyscrapers reflected the trends and fashions of the times. Builders adapted these towering buildings to styles usually associated with Venetian palaces, Flemish Beguine convents, and French chateaux like Versailles and Compiègne, sometimes with great success. Very few developers opted for entirely new forms, reflecting a sort of general conservatism. The true emancipation of the New York skyscraper would have to wait for the arrival of Art Deco. Even if this style mainly developed in France on the eve of the First World War, it attained its full maturity in New York after 1925. Characterized by multiple vertical lines and stylized geometric ornamentation, Art Deco gave the city some of its most beautiful landmarks (for example, the Chrysler Building, the Empire State Building, and Rockefeller Center), and its affection for stepped crowns was perfectly suited to a municipal ruling of 1916 that required high-rise buildings to narrow gradually toward the top so that sunshine could reach the city's sidewalks and wind tunnels along the streets could be prevented.

The Modern City (1930-)

Following the crises of the Depression and the Second World War, New York experienced a new period of prosperity. Times had changed, and old styles were outmoded. In the aim of respecting city regulations while simultaneously remaining loyal to the principles of modern architecture, New York urban planners dreamed up all sorts of solutions (the indoor garden at the Lever house, the plaza at the Seagram Building, and the broad esplanade at the World Trade Center). Ornamentation disappeared and was replaced by vast surfaces of mirrored glass (for example, Avenue of the Americas and Park Avenue between 42nd Street and 55th Street). However, New Yorkers soon tired of repetitive, rigid modernist "boxes". In 1980, they opted for a return to the brighter forms of their first skyscrapers, to which the Sony Building (the former ATT Building) is eloquent testimony. Today, New York is increasingly turning to international architecture stars like Philippe Stark and Christian de Porzamparc, who create works that, without echoing the styles of the past, possess sufficient character to differentiate them from their immediate neighbours.

SPECTATOR SPORTS

Baseball

Just like Chicago, the Big Apple is divided when it comes to America's national pastime. There are two baseball teams: the Yankees, who play most of their games in the American League, and the Mets, the majority of whose matches are against the best and worst teams of the National League. The Yankees, one of the oldest teams in baseball (1903), have won the hearts of most of the city's baseball fans with unequalled exploits. Mets fans, for their part, were deprived of baseball for a short period from 1958 to 1962: the heads of the two leagues wanted to popularize the sport on the West Coast, so the New York Giants and the Brooklyn Dodgers packed their bags for the Pacific in 1958. Outraged fans in eastern New York waited impatiently for the coming of another team to their dear city, until 1962.

The Yankees

Following the lead of the legendary Montreal Canadiens in the realm of hockey, the New York Yankees, thanks to many talented players who have donned the uniform over the years, have succeeded in winning the World Series 23 times (including 1998). The great adventure started in 1903, when Frank Farrell and Bill Devery bought the Baltimore franchise for the sum of $18,000 and moved it to New York. They baptized their club the Highlanders until 1915, when they renamed it the Yankees. During the first 17 years of their existence, the Yankees didn't break any records; they had a good team, but nothing more.

The first star to join the Yankees was Babe Ruth, who was such a legendary figure that a candy bar was named after him. In 1920, the Yankees obtained this star pitcher in a trade with the Boston Red Sox, who gained nothing from this "theft of the century". In fact, legend has it that the all-powerful gods punished the Boston franchise for trading away the greatest player of the era. Three years later, Ruth, transformed into a power hitter, led the Yankees on their first quest for the World Series. In 1922, Yankee Stadium (nicknamed "The House that Ruth Built"), became the team's home. In 1927, Babe Ruth beat his own single-season home-run record by hitting 60 homers, a record that held until 1961.

The driving principle behind the Yankees' success is that they always include at least two superstars who share the weight of media and fan pressure. In 1925, Wally Pipp, complaining of mild pain, refused to take his position at first base. Coach Ed Barrow assigned Lou Gehrig to take Pipp's place, and he ran out to the base. Gehrig was hit in the head during the game, but insisted on staying in. Wally Pipp must have kicked himself, because Gehrig wound up playing 2,130 consecutive matches, the equivalent of 13 complete seasons, a record that held until Cal Ripken of the Baltimore Orioles broke it just recently.

A new star guided the Yankees to glory: Joe DiMaggio. He drew some attention in 1941, when he hit safely in 56 consecutive games, a record that has yet to be broken. The same year, Gehrig was stricken by a mysterious disease (Amyotrophic Lateral Sclerosis, which has since been known as Lou Gehrig's Disease) and died at the age of 37 years. Gehrig's number four was the first Yankee jersey to be retired – even before Ruth's. In 1948, two months before his death, a last homage was paid to the Babe when his number three jersey was retired. He died August 16, 1948.

Another changing of the guard took place in 1951 when Mickey Mantle crossed the threshold of the Yankee organization. That same year, Joe DiMaggio announced his retirement. Mantle, the new king, was famous for his Herculean strength – in 1953, he hit a ball that flew 565 feet, or 188 metres (the fence was 400 feet, or 133 metres, from home plate!). Guided successively by DiMaggio and Mantle, the Yankees won the World Series five years in a row, from 1949 to 1953, setting another all-time record. An unprecedented event marked the history of the Yankees in 1956, when Don Larsen, a mediocre pitcher, orchestrated the only World Series perfect game in history. He faced the minimum number of hitters (27), without giving up a hit or a walk.

In 1961, a veritable duel was brewing between Mickey Mantle and a newcomer called Roger Maris. The two Yankees hit home runs at record-setting speed, threatening Babe Ruth's title for home runs in a single season. Maris surpassed Mantle in the last month of the season and in the last game of the year by hitting his 61st homer. Mantle ended the season with 54 home runs. In 1969, Mantle hung up his number seven jersey.

The 1970s saw George Steinbrenner III take the reins of the team. He invested many millions in the organization and signed free agents like Catfish Hunter, an eccentric pitcher, and Reggie Jackson, one of the best power hitters of all time. Jackson led the Yankees to their 21st World Series victory in 1977 by hitting three home runs in the last game of the series. The next year, the Yankees overcame an incredible deficit and took their 22nd championship.

During the late 1970s and early 1980s, Billy Martin, a colourful coach, was hired and fired (or quit) no fewer than five times! Eighteen years passed, the longest period of "lethargy" in franchise history, before the Yankees took their 23rd championship in 1996 thanks to a dramatic home run by Jim Leyritz, reclaiming the title of best team in the major leagues from the Atlanta Braves.

The fascination that surrounds this team, which manages to enthral its fans year after year, is clearly understandable.

The Mets

The Mets, who play their home games at Shea Stadium (☎718-507-8499), have a less exciting history than the Yankees, but it includes some brilliant moments. They made their debut in 1962 and held one of the worst records of all time: 40 victories and 120 defeats! During the 1960s, they remained at the bottom of their division until 1966 when they finished ninth, instead of tenth... The 1967 season included some more encouraging moments. New pitching recruit Tom Seaver (who was nominated to the Hall of Fame at the end of his career) made his debut with the Mets and took the Rookie of the Year title. The same year, Gil Hodges, a former star player, was hired as coach. In 1968, another rookie pitcher, Jerry Koosman, astonished the entire league by earning 19 wins, and in all the Mets only suffered 25 serious defeats. Another star pitcher, Nolan Ryan, also took his first steps and showed signs of greatness, but also of immaturity.

The miracle year came in 1969. The "Miracle Mets" beat all odds and won their first World Series. Tom Seaver was proclaimed the best pitcher in the National League and earned the Cy Young Award. Jerry Koosman's feats continued, and Cleon Jones had a batting average of .340 (.300 is considered a very good batting average). On July 9, Tom Seaver was three batters away from a perfect game, but he had to content himself with a one-hitter when Jimmy Qualls hit a single and stole the pitcher's dream. The 1969 Mets were nicknamed the Miracle Mets because they won 38 of their last 49 games of the season to reach the World Series and then beat the very strong Baltimore Orioles in five games.

During the 1970s, the Mets continued to play well, but never reached the heights of 1969. Then, in 1972, the Mets obtained stars like Willie Mays (the best outfielder of all time), Rusty Staub known to Montrealers as *"le Grande Orange"*, the "Big Orange", and Jim Fregosi (the Mets traded Nolan Ryan to the Angels for Fregosi, who didn't achieve much, while Ryan ended his career with over 5,000 strikeouts, a record that will be hard to beat...). In 1973, they finished first in their division, winning 29 of their last 43 games, but ended up losing the World Series in seven games to the Oakland Athletics.

The Mets fell apart in 1977, finishing last in their division for the first time since 1968. The team was in the process of rebuilding until the early 1980s when experienced players like Keith Hernandez and rookies like Hubie Brooks and Mookie Wilson thrilled New York fans again. Darryl Strawberry took the title of Rookie of the Year in 1983, and Dwight Gooden, also known as Dr. K, followed in his footsteps in 1984. Led by Strawberry, Gooden, Hernandez and newcomer Gary Carter, the Mets had their second moment of glory in 1986 when they won the World Series against the Boston Red Sox in seven games. Today, the Mets' star players include Mike Piazza, Todd Hundley, Carlos Baerga, Bernard Gilkey, and John Franco.

Basketball

The Knicks

In 1946, the Basketball Association of America was created, and the Knickerbockers, better known as the Knicks, formed the Eastern Division along with the Boston Celtics, the Philadelphia Warriors, the Providence Steamrollers, the Washington Capitols, and the Toronto Huskies. The Knicks won their first game, against the Huskies, by a score of 68 to 66, and already hopes were high for the team. Since the creation of the league, the Knicks and the Celtics are the only two original teams that have remained in their home cities.

During the 1950s, the Knicks participated in the NBA (National Basketball Association, a new league created in 1949-50) and reached the finals for the first time in 1950-51. The Knicks beat the Celtics and the Syracuse Nationals in preliminary rounds before confronting the Rochester Royals. They lost to the Royals in seven games, the last by a score of 79 to 75. The very first Knicks star was Dick McGuire; his number (15) was retired in 1992. In 1951-52, the Knicks lost in the finals again, this time to the Minneapolis Lakers in seven games. The next year, they suffered the same fate against the same team, this time in five games.

The 1960s were unlucky for the Knicks, who had several mediocre seasons in a row. They suffered their worst defeat in 1960, when Syracuse crushed them 162 to 100. By the end of the 1960s, though, a comeback was underway. In 1967-68, they had more wins than losses for the first time since 1958-59. The next year, rookies Walt Frazier and Phil Jackson (a former coach of the Chicago Bulls) were chosen for the NBA all-star team. Then they were traded Dave DeBusschere and finally had a solid team. The Knicks took their first title in 1969-70 when Willis Reed inspired his teammates by scoring the first two baskets of the last game on an injured leg. Reed led the Knicks to a 113-99 victory in the last game of a seven-game series against the Los Angeles Lakers.

The Knicks won their only other championship in 1972-73, ending the season with the second-best record in the league, 57 wins and 25 losses, behind the powerful Celtics, who had a near-perfect record of 68 victories and 14 defeats. The Knicks knocked out the Celtics in the semi-final round of the playoffs before confronting the Lakers, whom they defeated 102 to 93 in the fifth game of the championship series.

The 1980s, like the 1960s, were not rosy for Knicks fans. The team was in the process of rebuilding. The light appeared at the end of the tunnel when the Knicks had first pick at the 1985 draft, which allowed them to acquire a talented, seven-foot-eight-inch-tall player called Patrick Ewing. Together, Charles Oakley and Ewing inspired fear throughout the league, but never managed to dethrone the Chicago Bulls, who became almost legendary. The Knicks edged their way into the finals in 1993-94 by beating the Bulls in the semi-final round, but then lost the championship to the Houston Rockets in seven games.

The Knicks can be seen in action at Madison Square Garden
(☎465-JUMP).

Football

Like in baseball, New Yorkers have the pleasure of seeing two
professional football teams in action, the Giants and the Jets.

The Giants

The Giants, who play home games at Giants Stadium in East
Rutherford (☎201-935-8222), have been National Football
League (NFL) champions several times. The team, which has
been in the league since 1925, won the finals for the first time
in 1934 and again in 1938 under the leadership of Steve Owen.
Later, Jim Lee Howell led the team to the championship in
1956. Since the inauguration of the Super Bowl in 1967, the
Giants have won the prestigious Lombardi trophy twice. The
Giants were not confirmed "kings" of the league until 1986.
That year, Bill Parcells, who had coached the team since the
miserable 1983 season (3 wins, 112 losses, and one tie), led
the team to victory, after they achieved the best record in the
league by winning 14 of 16 regular season games. Led by
quarterback Phil Simms, receiver Joe Morris, and Lawrence
"LT" Taylor, the Giants crushed the San Francisco 49ers and
the Washington Redskins before beating the Denver Broncos in
the Super Bowl by a score of 39 to 20. In 1991, Bill Parcells
led the Giants to the Super Bowl again, this time against the
more difficult Buffalo Bills. Quarterback Jeff Hostetler and
receiver Ottis Henderson distinguished themselves, but the
game was only decided in its he last seconds when Scott
Norwood missed a 47-yard field goal and the Giants won the
game by a score of 20 to 19.

The Jets

The New York Jets, who also play home games at Giants
Stadium (☎516-560-8200), have only won the Super Bowl
once. Led by Weeb Ewbank, the Jets of 1969 and star
quarterback Joe Namath won the game in a 16-7 upset. The

Baltimore Colts had dominated the league all season, with a record of 15 wins and a single loss. Perseverance, and Namath's arrogance (he predicted his team's victory one week before the game), quieted skeptics. Since this victory, however, the Jets have been unexceptional, achieving more wins than losses, only 11 times in 28 seasons.

Hockey

New York City has two professional hockey teams, the Islanders, who play at Nassau Veterans' Memorial Coliseum (tel. 519-794-4100), and the Rangers, whose home games are held at Madison Square Garden (☎465-6000). Each has thrilled its fans by winning the prestigious Stanley Cup four times.

The Islanders

Despite their short history (they were founded in 1972), the Islanders were praised to the heavens between 1980 and 1983, when they brought the Stanley Cup to New York four times in a row. Led by fiery goalie Billy Smith, talented wingman and scorer Mike Bossy, and centre Bryan Trottier, the Islanders came within one championship of tieing the Montreal Canadiens' record for winning the Stanley Cup five years in a row. The powerful Edmonton Oilers, with the help of the best hockey player of all time, Wayne Gretzky, eliminated the Islanders in 1984, and the Canadiens held on to their title.

Since their last Stanley Cup win, the Islanders have lost much of their luster. The future looks promising, though, since many talented young players have joined the team, including the spectacular Zigmund Palffy, defence man Bryan Berard, and goalie Tommy Salo.

The Rangers

The Rangers are without question New Yorkers' favourite team. New York hockey fans quickly fell in love with them. In their first 16 years in the league, the Rangers missed the playoffs only once. Moreover, in 1928, only two years after they joined the league, the Rangers defeated the Montreal Maroons against all odds in the Stanley Cup finals. They won the Stanley Cup three times in the early years of the league, in 1928, 1933, and 1940. The team won more than their share of games, and Madison Square Garden became a meeting place for the city's elite. In total, however, the Rangers have won the prestigious trophy only four times in 72 years. Although New Yorkers adore them, the Rangers, one of the six original National Hockey League (NHL) teams, have caused their fans quite a bit of worry over the years.

In 1972, Vic Hadfield electrified Madison Square Garden by becoming the first Ranger to score 50 goals in one season. A new team of players, notably including Anders Hedberg, Ulf Nilsson, Ron Greschner, Phil Esposito, Barry Beck, and John Davidson, reached the finals in 1979, to be eliminated by the Montreal Canadiens in five games.

Ecstatic Rangers fans had to wait until 1994 for a saviour to take them to the "promised land". This saviour, Mark Messier, led them with a strong arm. He scored three hat tricks (three games in which he scored three goals) and the winning goal of the seventh and last game against the Vancouver Canucks.

In 1998, the Rangers ended one of their worst seasons, even with team members Wayne Gretzky and Pat Lafontaine, who suffered several concussions. Adam Graves, an important element of the 1994 dream season, seemed worn out, while goalie Mike Richter, who just signed a five-million-dollar-a-year contract (!), had the worst season of his career.

PRACTICAL INFORMATION

I nformation in this section will help visitors better plan their trip to the "Big Apple".

The **area code** for New York is **212**. This area code encompasses all of Manhattan. For the other boroughs, dial 718, followed by the seven-digit telephone number.

ENTRANCE FORMALITIES

Travellers from Canada, the majority of western European countries, Australia and New Zealand do not need visas to enter the United States. A valid passport is sufficient for stays of up to three months. A return ticket and proof of sufficient funds to cover your stay may be required. For stays of more than three months, all travellers, except Canadians and citizens of the British Commonwealth, must obtain a visa ($120 US) from the American embassy in their country.

Caution: as medical expenses can be very high in the United States, travel health insurance is highly recommended. For more information, see the section entitled "Health" (p 79).

CUSTOMS

Foreigners may enter the United States with 200 cigarettes (or 100 cigars) and duty-free purchases not exceeding $400 US, including personal gifts and 1 litre of alcohol (the legal drinking age is 21). There is no limit on the amount of cash you are carrying, though you must fill out a special form if you are carrying $10,000 US or more. Prescription medication must be placed in containers clearly marked to that effect (you may have to present a prescription or a written statement from your doctor to customs officials). Meat and its by-products, all kinds of food, grains, plants, fruits and narcotics cannot be brought into the United States.

For more detailed information, contact:

United States Customs Service
1301 Constitution Avenue Northwest, Washington, DC 20229, ☎(202) 566-8195.

GETTING TO NEW YORK CITY

By Plane

Air Canada offers four daily scheduled flights between Montreal and New York (La Guardia Airport).

From Europe, Air France offers several daily flights (8 to 10) between Paris and New York; Sabena provides three flights a day to New York. From Geneva, several weekly flights are offered by Swissair, with a stopover in Zurich or Brussels. Some flights leave directly from Zurich.

The following airlines have offices at one of New York's three airports (or at all three) and in downtown Manhattan: **Air Canada** *(15 West 50th St., ☎1-800-776-3000)*, **Air France** *(120 West 56th St., ☎1-800-237-2747)*, **American Airlines** *(18 West 49th St., ☎1-800-433-7300)*, **British Airways** *(530 5th Ave., ☎1-800-247-9297)*, **Continental Airlines** *(100 East 42nd St., ☎1-800-525-0280)*, **KLM** *(437 Madison Ave.,*

☎1-800-374-7747), **Swissair** *(608 5th Ave.,* ☎1-800-221-4750),* **TWA** *(1 East 59th St.,* ☎1-800-221-2000),* **United Airlines** *(100 East 42nd St.,* ☎1-800-241-6522),* **USAirways** *(101 Park Ave.,* ☎1-800-428-4322).*

John F. Kennedy International Airport (JFK)

The John F. Kennedy International Airport (JFK) *(☎718-656-4520 or 244-4444)* has nine terminals, that form in a circle. A third of U.S.-bound international flights land here: this is one of the busiest airports in the United States. The **International Arrivals Building** receives most international flights from carriers such as Air France and Northwest Airlines. British Airways, Delta Airlines, American Airlines and TWA have their own terminals. The Delta terminal also welcomes flights from Swissair and Sabena. The airport is located about 24 kilometres southeast of downtown Manhattan. Note that there are **foreign exchange offices**, with varying business hours, in each of the terminals.

Most car-rental agencies have a branch at the airport: **Avis** *(☎1-800-331-1212),* **Budget** *(☎1-800-527-0700),* **Dollar** *(☎1-800-800-4000),* **Hertz** *(☎1-800-654-3131),* **Thrifty** *(☎1-800-367-2277).*

The easiest and cheapest way of getting downtown is unquestionably by subway (one ticket: $1.50). Take the blue courtesy bus (free) from any of the airport's air terminals (every 10 to 15 minutes) for the **Howard Beach-JFK Airport** subway station. Once there, take the **A train**, which runs through lower Manhattan (1 hour), then heads north, stopping at Washington Square, 34th Street-Penn Station, 42nd Street-Port Authority and 59th Street-Columbus Circle.

The **Carey Airport Express Coach Bus** *(☎1-800-284-0909)* takes passengers straight to Grand Central Station and to the Port Authority Terminal for $13. Buses also stop at about thirty downtown hotels. They leave every 30 minutes between 5am and 1am, and take 45 to 75 minutes to reach Manhattan's JFK Airport.

Gray Line Air Shuttle *(☎212-315-3006 or 1-800-451-0455)* provides minibus service between 7am and 11pm from JFK

Airport to a few hotels on the island of Manhattan. Fare: $14 from JFK to downtown Manhattan, $16.50 from downtown to JFK.

A (yellow) **taxi** between the airport and downtown Manhattan will cost you $30 to $40. The ride generally takes 40 to 60 minutes, but traffic jams often cause further delays. **Limousine** services are also available, including those of **Olympia Limousine** *(☎212-992-1200)* and **Imperial Limousines** *(☎212-229-9292)*, for $50.

La Guardia Airport

Located 13 kilometres southeast of Manhattan, **La Guardia Airport** *(☎718-476-5000 or 533-3400)* handles flights from the United States, Canada and Mexico only. To get from one of the five terminals to another, take the courtesy bus that runs between them every 15 minutes, from 6am to 11:30pm. Each terminal has a foreign exchange office (with varying business hours) as well as a few information desks (1st floor of the Main Terminal and in each of the three major terminals).

For $9, the **Carey Airport Express Coach Bus** *(☎1-800-284-0909)* takes you to Grand Central Station in 40 minutes. The bus stops at the train station every 20 to 30 minutes. You can then take the shuttle to the Port Authority Bus Terminal, located at 8th Avenue and 42nd Street.

You can also opt for the **Gray Line Air Shuttle** *(☎212-315-3006 or 1-800-451-0455)*, a minibus that can drop you off anywhere you like between 23rd Street and 63rd Street.

A **taxi** from the airport to downtown Manhattan costs $20 (plus tolls)on average.

Newark Airport

This third airport *(☎201-961-2000)*, located 26 kilometres southwest of Manhattan in the state of New Jersey, mainly receives Continental Airlines' international flights, at terminals B and C. A courtesy bus connects the airport's various terminals in 10 minutes. The foreign exchange office is in terminal B, and the information desks at the arrivals level of terminals A and B. Terminal C also has an information desk, at gate B.

To reach Manhattan from the airport, **Bus NJ Transit** *(☎201-762-5100)* runs to the Port Authority Bus Terminal every 15 minutes, from 6am to 1am. The ride takes 30 to 60 minutes, depending on traffic. Fare: one way $7, return $12.

Olympia Trail Express *(☎212-964-6233)* is another option. For only $7, you can go to either **Grand Central Station**, **One World Trade Center** *(West St.)* or **Penn Station**. Departures every 20 minutes, from 6:15am to midnight (8:45pm for the World Trade Center). The **Gray Line Air Shuttle** service (see p 62) is also available from Newark Airport, for $20.

Taking a **taxi** is the costliest option. The fare from the airport to downtown Manhattan ranges from $40 to $50.

By Car

From Montreal, take Autoroute 15 Sud toward the American border. Once past the border, this highway turns into the I-87, which runs right to New York City. From Toronto, take the Queen Elizabeth Way to Niagara Falls, then switch to the Buffalo-bound US62, followed by the eastbound I-90 to Syracuse. Proceed until you reach the junction of the I-87 South (right near Albany), which runs to New York City. From Boston, take the I-95 straight to the Big Apple. If you are coming from the southern United States, the North I-95 runs straight to New York City.

By Bus

Besides by car, the bus is the best way to get from one city to another in the United States. Efficient and inexpensive, bus service covers most of the country.

For schedules and destinations contact **Greyhound** *(☎402-341-1900 or 1-800-231-2222)*.

Quebecers and Canadians can buy tickets from **Voyageur** in Montréal *(☎514-842-2281)* or **Greyhound** in Toronto *(☎416-393- 7911)*.

Smoking is forbidden on most lines. In general, children 5 years and under travel for free. Travellers over 60 are eligible for special discounts. Animals are not permitted on board.

By Train

In the United States, the train is not always the cheapest way travel, and it is certainly not the fastest. It can be interesting, however, for long distances, as it is very comfortable (try to get a seat in a dome car to take advantage of the scenery). To obtain schedules and destinations, contact Amtrak, the main transport company of the American rail network *(toll-free in North America, ☎1-800-872-7245)*. To reach the New York AMTRAK office, dial ☎582-6875. By Internet: www.amtrak.com.

AMTRAK offers various passes that can save you a great deal of money as you travel to New York and nearby regions. The **North American Rail Pass**, in conjunction with **VIA Rail**, allows you to explore over 900 destinations throughout Canada and the United States for up to 30 consecutive days of travel. This pass costs $645 US ($450 US in the off-peak season). You can also opt for the **Northeastern North America Rail Pass** and, for $400 US ($300 US in the off-peak season), visit the entire northeastern coast of the United States and Canada from Detroit, Michigan, in the west, to Newport News, Virginia, in the south, and up to Gaspé in southeastern Quebec. At $195 US ($175 US in the off-peak season), the best-value pass is unquestionably the **Northeast Rail Pass**, which is good for 15 consecutive days of travel along the northeast coast, by way of such places as Virginia Beach, Philadelphia, New York City, Niagara Falls and Montreal. The 30-day pass goes for $230 US ($215 US in the off-peak season). The **East Rail Pass** allows travellers to visit the entire east coast of the United States as well as southern Quebec and Ontario. For $250 US ($205 US in the off-peak season), you can travel up the Atlantic coast from Miami to Montreal.

By taking the *Twilight Shoreliner* night train, you can make your way from Boston to Virginia Beach via Williamsburg, Virginia. As of 1999, the **Northeast Corridor High-Speed Train** will run from Boston to New York City every hour, and depart twice an hour from New York City to Washington, DC. These trains will be able to reach speeds of up to 240 km/h and transport as many as 301 passengers.

AMTRAK trains leave from **Penn Station** (☎582-6875), located on 33rd Street, between 7th and 8th Avenues. **Grand Central Station** (*42nd St.*, ☎736-4545) only serves New York's suburbs.

EMBASSIES AND CONSULATES

United States Embassies and Consulates Abroad

Australia
Embassy: Moonah Place, Canberra, ACT 2600, ☎(6) 214-5600.

Belgium
Embassy: 27 Boulevard du Régent, B-1000 Brussels, ☎(02) 512-2210, ≈(02) 511-9652.

Canada
Embassy: 2 Wellington Street, Ottawa, Ontario, K1P 5T1, ☎(613) 238-5335, ≈(613) 238-5720.

Consulate: Place Félix-Martin, 1155 Rue Saint-Alexandre, Montréal, Québec, H2Z 1Z2, ☎(514) 398-9695, ≈(514) 398-9748.

Consulate: 360 University Avenue, Toronto, Ontario, M5G 1S4, ☎(416) 595-1700, ≈(416) 595-0051.

Consulate: 1095 West Pender, Vancouver, British Columbia, V6E 2M6, ☎(604) 685-4311.

Denmark
Embassy: Dag Hammarskjölds Allé 24, 2100 Copenhagen Ø, ☎(35) 55 31 44, ≈(35) 43 02 23.

Germany
Embassy: Clayallee 170, 14195 Berlin, ☎(30) 832-2933, ✉(30) 8305-1215.

Great Britain
Embassy: 24 Grosvenor Square, London W1A 1AE, ☎(171) 499-9000, ✉(171) 491-2485.

Italy
Embassy: Via Vittorio Vérito, 11917-121 Roma, ☎(06) 467-41, ✉(06) 610-450.

Netherlands
Embassy: Lange Voorhout 102, 2514 EJ, Den Haag, ☎(70) 310-9209, ✉(70) 361-4688.

Spain
Embassy: C. Serrano 75, Madrid 28001, ☎(1) 577-4000, ✉(1) 564-1652, Telex (1) 277-63.

Sweden
Embassy: Strandvägen 101, 11589 Stockholm, ☎(08) 783 53 00, ✉(08) 661 19 64.

Switzerland
Embassy: 93 Jubilam Strasse, 3000 Berne, ☎31-43-70-11.

FOREIGN CONSULATES AND DELEGATIONS IN NEW YORK

Australia
630 5th Ave., New York, NY 10111-0100, ☎408-8400.

Belgium
1330 Avenue of the Americas, New York, NY 10022-6601, ☎586-5110.

Canada
1251 Avenue of the Americas, New York, NY 10020-1628, ☎596-1628, ✉596-1790.

Denmark
1 Dag Hammarskjold Plz., New York, NY 10017-2201, ☎(212) 223-4545.

Germany
460 Park Ave., New York, NY 10022-1906, ☎308-8700 or 572-5600.

Great Britain
845 3rd Ave., New York, NY 10022-6601, ☎745-0202.

Italy
690 Park Avenue, New York, NY 10021-5009. ☎737-9100.

Netherlands
1 Rockefeller Plaza, New York, NY 10020-2094, ☎246-1429.

Spain
150 East 58th St., New York, NY 10155-0099, ☎355-4080.

Sweden
1 Dag Hammarskjold Plz., New York, NY10017-2201, ☎751-5900.

Switzerland
655 5th Ave., New York, NY 10022-5303, ☎758-2560.

TOURIST INFORMATION

For all tourist information contact:

New York Convention and Visitors Bureau
229 West 42nd Street, New York, NY 10019, ☎397-8222 or 1-800-692-8474, ⌁245-5943.

New York State Tourist Bureau
1515 Broadway Avenue, 52nd Floor, ☎225-5697.

Guided Tours

Why not explore Central Park by bicycle with one of the guided tours offered by the **Central Park Bicycle Tour Company** *(tours depart from Columbus Circle;* ☎*541-8759)*. Their excursions vary in length and bicycle rentals are included in the cost.

Circle Line *(departure from Pier 83, corner of 42nd and 12th Ave.,* ☎*563-3200)* ferries make a round trip of Manhattan Island, so passengers can get a comprehensive view of downtown New York. From the ship's deck you will be able to admire Midtown's skyscrapers, the Statue of Liberty, Brooklyn Bridge and other sights.

Discover New York Tours *(*☎*439-1049 or 935-3960)* are organized by the Municipal Art Society, a hundred-year-old institution known for its professionalism. Its walking tours deal mainly with architecture and history, and last two to three hours.

Discover New York from the air with **Helicopter Flight Services** *(depart from 60th St. Heliport, corner of 60th and York Ave.,* ☎*355-0801 or 1-888-933-5969,* ⇌*355-0950, copterny@sprintmail.com)*. Even if the prices seem high *($70 to $120, depending on the route)*, the 12 to 20 minute excursions are definitely worth it, especially on clear days.

For a bird's-eye view of Manhattan Island, nothing surpasses beats **Liberty Helicopter Tours** *(departures from the heliport, corner of 30th St. and 12th Ave. or from Pier 6 in Lower Manhattan,* ☎*967-6464 or 487-4777,* ⇌*487-4781)*. You can even film the panorama while listening to the pilots' commentary. Prices range from $64 to $150 per person, depending on the route.

Since London's transport commission decided to sell its old double-decker buses, it has had no difficulty finding buyers, because several guided tours of New York have extensively adapted these vehicles to their new vocation. In good weather, you can sit outside on the top deck. When it rains, most people sit in the lower level which is covered and heated. If you buy a special pass you can get off the bus at your leisure to explore an area in more detail on foot before continuing the tour on the next bus. **New York Apple Tours** *(☎944-9200 or 1-800-876-9868, ⇌944-8290)* offer this type of tour. You can buy your ticket at several hotels or on board the buses.

Besides their traditional 90-minute cruise around New York's harbour, the **New York Sightseeing Cruises** *(departures from Pier 78, corner of 12th Ave. and 38th St.; ☎201-902-8700 or 1-800-533-3779, ⇌201-223-4387)* offer several cruises on the Hudson River, enabling you to take in the wooded riverbanks of this majestic waterway. Some itineraries even have stops at various points so that you can visit some of the large estates that once belonged to New York celebrities.

The **Scoozi Tours NYC** *(☎714-4504, ⇌753-4718)* offer guided walking tours off the beaten track. Among their themes are the "Harlem Gospel Walk" and the "Star Walk" (which visits the sites of famous movie-shoots) are especially popular. Departure points vary, depending on which tour you choose.

Seaport Liberty Cruises *(departures from Pier 16 on South Street Seaport, ☎630-8888, www.seaportliberty.com)* will take you on an hour-long cruise around New York Bay. From the ship's deck, you can admire the southern tip of Manhattan Island, the Statue of Liberty and Ellis Island.

With **The Discovery Tour** *(departs from Victor's Sportsworld; 489 5th Ave., ☎763-8051)* allow you to discover Harlem and the Bronx from different perspectives (gospel, jazz, restaurants, theatre, etc.). The visit is by bus... or by plane; the choice is yours.

The Real New York *(departures from Columbus Circle; ☎718-652-3702)* take you to the hidden nooks and crannies of Harlem and the Bronx, by bus or on foot.

```
┌─────────────────────────────────────────────────┐
│                                                 │
│   FINDING YOUR WAY AROUND THE CITY              │
│           AND ITS SURROUNDINGS                  │
│                                                 │
└─────────────────────────────────────────────────┘
```

General Orientation

Finding your way around New York City is relatively easy. The city is criss-crossed by a network of streets and avenues almost always intersecting at right angles. This grid is systematically composed of streets that run east-west intersecting avenues or boulevards that run north-south. New York City addresses always bear the designations "East" or "West", so you know which neighbourhood the street runs to: Any address east of Fifth Avenue is designated "East" (for example, 255 East 93rd Street), while any address west of Fifth Avenue is indicated as "West" (for example, 35 West 42nd Street). For addresses on thoroughfares running north-south, consult the box on p 71, which will tell you at the corner of which arteries you can find an address.

By Public Transportation

New York City Transit (☎718-330-1234) operates the New York City subway and its 469 stations, which makes it the world's most extensive subway system. The subway (or **Metropolitan Transit Authority** or **MTA**) fare is $1.50. There are 25 transfer points. If you venture north of Manhattan (Queens, Brooklyn and the Bronx), you will notice that the subway runs outside (and not underground). These are known to New Yorkers as "**El**" trains, an abbreviation of "Elevated Rapid Transit Train". For safety reasons, avoid taking the subway between 11pm and 7am, even though it runs 24 hours a day. If you hate crowds, avoid rush hours when the subway is completely overloaded.

Buses, though slower than the subway, are safer, more pleasant and comfortable. Bus fare is $1.50 during rush hours and $1 during off-peak hours. You can also pay the fare with a subway token. If you need to take more than one bus to reach your destination, request a transfer from the bus driver, but do not expect your smile to be reciprocated

Avenues

Amsterdam Avenue	
250	72nd Street
550	86nd Street

Broadway	
100	Fulton
600	Houston
700	4th Street
1000	23rd Street
1400	39th Street
1600	51st Street
2000	68th Street
2090	72nd Street

Central Park West	
1	60th Street
115	72nd Street

Columbus Avenue	
260	72nd Street
550	86th Street

Lexington Avenue	
63	25th Street
461	45th Street
659	55th Street
1004	72nd Street

Madison Avenue	
30	25th Street
300	42nd Street
500	52nd Street
1000	78th Street

Park Avenue	
101	40th Street
300	49th Street
345	50th Street
520	60th Street
760	72nd Street

Park Avenue South	
75	10th Street
251	20th Street
440	30th Street

West End Avenue	
250	72nd Street
525	86th Street
740	96th Street

York Avenue	
1116	60th Street
1308	70th Street
1510	80th Street

1st Avenue	
224	14th Street
428	25th Street
616	35th Street
802	45th Street
1100	60th Street
1344	72nd Street

2nd Avenue	
139	8th Street
440	25th Street
638	35th Street
846	45th Street
1140	60th Street
1392	72nd Street

3rd Avenue	
120	14th Street
300	23rd Street
715	45th Street
1010	60th Street
1254	72nd Street

5th Avenue		8th Avenue	
50	12th Street	80	14th Street
150	20th Street	400	30th Street
350	34th Street	600	40th Street
500	42nd Street	925	55th Street
800	61st Street		
910	72nd Street	9th Avenue	
		42	14th Street
6th Avenue		350	30th Street
(Avenue of the Americas)		550	40th Street
50	Canal	850	55th Street
250	Houston		
400	8th Street	10th Avenue	
800	28th Street	60	14th Street
1063	40th Street	350	30th Street
1370	55th Street	650	45th Street
		850	55th Street
7th Avenue			
63	14th Street	11th Avenue	
262	25th Street	28	14th Street
600	43rd Street	200	24th Street
865	55th Street	600	45th Street
		800	55th Street

STREETS

(numbers begin on 5th Avenue)

EAST SIDE

♯10	Madison Avenue
♯100	Park Avenue
♯140	Lexington Avenue
♯200	3rd Avenue
♯300	2nd Avenue
♯400	1st Avenue
♯500	York Avenue

WEST SIDE

♯100	6th Avenue
♯200	7th Avenue
♯300	8th Avenue
♯400	9th Avenue
♯500	10th Avenue
♯600	11th Avenue

UPPER WEST SIDE

♯200	Columbus Avenue
♯300	Amsterdam Avenue
♯400	West End Avenue

The Subway

Be forewarned: you're likely to be surprised and disconcerted the first time you look at a map of the New York City subway system. To the untrained eye, it looks like nothing more than a tangle of numbers, letters and randomly intersecting coloured lines. The first time you actually enter a subway station, you're sure to be discombobulated, especially if it happens to be rush hour, when people are shouting all over, the employees in the token booths are in a foul mood and the regulars are on a mission to make their way through the crowds of commuters in record time. Try not to spend too long examining the mugshots on wanted signs in some stations; you'll stick out as a tourist.

Yes, the subway can be dirty and poorly ventilated, but it can also be incredibly clean, depending on the line or even the particular station. It is also remarkably efficient – and inexpensive – if you manage to figure out how it works. Don't expect to master the maze right away, but with a little patience and logical reasoning, you'll get your bearings after a few days.

A few words of advice:

There is always a detailed map near the token booth. Incidentally, the employees who work in these booths often look bothered, are generally less than eager to offer assistance and don't like to provide change for bills over $10. To avoid waiting in line, buy a few tokens at a time.

Before you blindly climb aboard the first train you see, you should be aware that there are two kinds of trains, local and express. Local trains stop at all stations, express trains only at the major ones. Each train has a sign at the front indicating which kind it is.

Though the subway operates 365 days a year, 24 hours a day, there is not always someone present to sell you a token at night, so you might want to keep a few extra on hand. If you don't, make sure to look at the light at the mouth of the station: red means the token booth is closed, green that there is an employee on duty.

PRACTICAL
INFORMATION

By Car

Like in many other major cities, driving is neither the most efficient nor the most pleasant way of getting around in New York City. The many traffic jams and the heavy traffic will make driving a waste of your time, at least in the downtown area. We therefore strongly advise you to explore New York on foot and, for greater distances, resort to the efficient public transportation, or take one of the city's countless taxis.

If you still wish to rent a car, keep in mind that several agencies require their clients to be at least 25 years of age and be a major credit-card holder. Here are a few car-rental agencies with offices in downtown New York City:

AAMCAR
315 West 96th Street, ☎222-8500 or 1-800-722-6923.

Avis
217 East 43rd Street (between 2nd and 3rd Avenues), ☎1-800-230-4898.

Hertz
222 East 40th Street (at East Gate Plaza), ☎486-5060.

National Tilden
21 East 12th Street, ☎620-4894.

Things to Consider

Driver's License: As a general rule, foreign drivers' licenses are valid in the United States. Take note that certain states are linked by computer to provincial police services in Canada and that a ticket issued in the United States is automatically transferred to your file in Canada.

Driving and the Highway Code: Signs marked "Stop" in white against a red background must always be respected. Some stop signs are accompanied by a small sign indicating "4-way". This means that all vehicles must stop at the intersection. Come to a complete stop even if there is no apparent danger. If two vehicles arrive at the same time, the one to the right has the right of way. Otherwise, the first car to the intersection has the right of way.

Traffic lights are often located on the opposite side of the intersection, so make sure to stop at the stop line, a white line on the pavement before the intersection.

Turning right on a red light after a full stop is permitted, unless otherwise indicated.

When a school bus (usually yellow) has stopped and has its signals flashing, **you must come to a complete stop, no matter what direction you are travelling in**. Failing to stop at the flashing signals is considered a serious offense, and carries a heavy penalty.

Seat belts must be worn at all times.

There are no tolls on the highways, except on most Interstate highways, indicated by the letter I, followed by a number. Interstate highways are indicated by a blue crest on a white background. The highway number and the state are written on the sign. "Interstate" is written on a red background at the top of the sign.

The speed limit is 55mph (88kph) on most highways. These signs are rectangular with a black border, white background and black writing.

The speed limit on Interstate highways is 65 mph (104 kph).

Red and white triangular signs with the word "Yield" under them indicate that vehicles crossing your path have the right of way.

The speed limit is indicated by square signs with a white background, and "Speed Limit" and the maximum speed underneath are written in black.

A round, yellow sign with a black X and two Rs indicates a railroad crossing.

Gas Stations: Because the United States produces its own crude oil, gasoline prices are less expensive than in Europe; gas is also less expensive than in Canada, due to hidden taxes north of the border. Self-serve stations will often ask for payment in advance as a security measure.

Table of distances (km/mi) Via the shortest route								© ULYSSES
Example: The distance between New York and Syracuse is 411km/255mi. 1 mile = 1.62 kilometres 1 kilometre = 0.62 miles								
						Albany (NY)	Albany (NY)	
					Buffalo (NY)	477/296	Buffalo (NY)	
				Montréal (QC)	643/399	363/225	Montréal (QC)	
			New York (NY)	611/379	634/393	252/156	New York (NY)	
		Philadelphia (PA)	176/109	740/459	619/384	376/233	Philadelphia (PA)	
	Pittsburgh (PA)	497/308	626/388	983/609	350/217	761/472	Pittsburgh (PA)	
Plattsburgh (NY)	1004/622	635/394	506/314	104/64	664/412	259/161	Plattsburgh (NY)	
Syracuse (NY)	429/266	584/362	415/257	411/255	411/255	244/151	236/146	Syracuse (NY)
Toronto (ON)	411/255	552/342	524/325	827/513	823/510	542/336	172/107	638/396	Toronto (ON)
Wash. (DC)	920/570	587/364	844/523	405/251	224/139	382/237	949/588	631/391	582/361	Washington (DC)

By Taxi

A great many taxis roam the streets of New York City. Most of the time, all you have to do is raise your arm to hail one. We have nevertheless listed the numbers of a few taxi companies for your convenience.

New York City's yellow and black taxis are easy to spot and can be an affordable means of transportation if there's a group of you, since up to four passengers are permitted. The meter starts at $2, then goes up 30¢ for every fifth of a mile. After 10 p.m., a 50¢ surcharge is added to the total fare. You might land a driver who doesn't know how to get where you want to go, so make sure that you always have detailed information about your final destination (for instance, 27th Street, between Madison and Park Avenue). A 10-15% tip for the driver is standard.

Carmel Car & Limo Service
☎666-6666.

City Ride Car & Limo
☎861-1000 or 1-800-248-9743.

Highbridge Car Service
☎927-4600.

Tel-Aviv Car & Limo Service
☎777-7777 or 1-800-222-9888,
(credit cards accepted).

Uptown Taxi
☎304-4400.

NYC Taxi and Limousine Commission
☎302-TAXI.

League of Mutual Taxi Owners
☎947-3380.

The following is a list of New York City's major taxi stands:

● right outside the Port Authority Bus Terminal *(8th Ave., between West 41st St. and West 42nd St.)*;

● at Penn Station *(at 7th Ave. and West 32nd St.)*;

● at Penn Station *(at 8th Ave. and West 33rd St.)*;

● at the Grand Central Terminal *(at Vanderbilt Ave. and East 42nd St.)*;

● at Peter Minuit Plaza, adjacent to the Staten Island Ferry terminal;

● at the Citycorp Center *(Lexington Ave., between West 53rd St. and West 54th St.)*.

On Foot

A city is generally best appreciated on foot, and New York City is no exception. Walking thus remains the best way to experience the rich melting pot that is the American megalopolis, to enjoy its many public squares or do some window shopping. This guide comprises some twenty tours through the Big Apple's various districts, most of which are on foot. So if you're heading to New York City, be sure to bring your walking shoes...

By Bicycle

New York City is not exactly designed for cyclists: traffic is heavy and often a mess, and bicycle paths are few and far between.

Nevertheless, when traffic is lighter, on weekends for example, it is possible to explore the city by bike (remember to wear your helmet!). You can take the 3.6-kilometre path around Central Park (closed to traffic Monday to Thursday from 10am to 3pm and 7pm to 10pm; Fridays from 10am to 3pm and 7pm until 6am Monday). More leisurely cyclists can head to Riverside Park (between 72nd and 110th Streets). Another good place to go on the weekend is on the deserted streets of Wall Street. Finally, the paths of Prospect Park, in Brooklyn, are just the place for weekend excursions.

INSURANCE

Cancellation Insurance

Your travel agent will usually offer you cancellation insurance upon purchase of your airline ticket or vacation package. This insurance allows you to be reimbursed for the ticket or package deal if your trip must be cancelled due to serious illness or death. Healthy people are unlikely to need this protection, which is therefore only of relative use.

Theft Insurance

Most residential insurance policies protect some of your goods from theft, even if the theft occurs in a foreign country. To make a claim, you must fill out a police report. It may not be necessary to take out further insurance, depending on the amount covered by your current home policy. As policies vary considerably, you are advised to check with your insurance company. European visitors should take out baggage insurance.

Life Insurance

Several airline companies offer a life insurance plan included in the price of the airplane ticket. However, many travellers already have this type of insurance and do not require additional coverage.

Health Insurance

This is the most useful kind of insurance for travellers, and should be purchased before your departure. Your insurance plan should be as complete as possible because health care costs add up quickly. When buying insurance, make sure it covers all types of medical costs, such as hospitalization, nursing services and doctor's fees. Make sure your limit is high enough, as these expenses can be costly. A repatriation clause is also vital in case the required care is not available on site. Furthermore, since you may have to pay on the spot, check your policy to see what provisions it includes for such situations. To avoid any problems during your vacation, always keep proof of your insurance policy on your person.

HEALTH

Vaccinations are not necessary for people coming from Europe or Canada. On the other hand, it is strongly suggested, particularly for medium or long-term stays, that visitors take out health and accident insurance. There are different types, so it is best to shop around. Bring along all medication, especially prescription medicine. Unless otherwise stated, the water is potable throughout New York state.

PRACTICAL
INFORMATION

SAFETY AND SECURITY

Unfortunately, American cities are not always the safest. This does not mean, however, that you should spend your trip barricaded in your hotel room.

Upon arriving, simply inquire about which neighbourhoods are to be avoided, no matter what the time of day. By taking the necessary precautions, there is no reason to worry about your safety. If, however, you are unlucky, remember to dial **911** for all emergencies.

As a general rule, it is best to avoid riding the New York subway alone early in the morning or very late at night. The same holds true for the city's big parks (Central Park, etc.), which you should also steer clear of after dark, unless some event or other spectacle drawing large crowds is being held.

The business district, known Wall Street, is a virtual ghost town after office hours. Wandering there alone in the evening or at night is not recommended. Also to be avoided come nightfall are Spanish Harlem (northwest of Central Park) and Little Italy (southeast of downtown). Venturing to the northern part of the city without a guide is not recommended, by day as well as by night.

To avoid potential problems, it is always better to opt for a taxi after nightfall, unless you are very familiar with the neighbourhood you plan to visit.

CLIMATE

To understand New York's humid and temperate climate, you have to pay attention to the humid direction of the wind. If it is blowing from the west, it generally means dry weather for the city. The Appalachian mountain range creates an effective barrier between the Atlantic coast and the American midwest. Most of the humidity contained in the winds from the plains condenses and precipitates as either rain or snow when it reaches these mountains. On the other hand, nothing stands in the way of the hot, humid air that travels from the Gulf of

Mexico, in the south, right up to New York. This humidity, along with that of the warm Gulf Stream in the Atlantic, are strong contributing factors to the storms, hurricanes and snowstorms which hit the region. This is particularly true when these hot and humid winds meet up with a mass of arctic air. The friction between the two air currents creates violent winds and heavy precipitation.

The humidity and heat of the Atlantic Ocean have, however, have a beneficial effect since they temper the intense summer heat and the deadly cold of winter. This is no insignificant fact in a city where the mercury can rise to 40°C in the summer and drop to -25°C in the winter.

The following chart gives you an idea of the temperature and precipitation in New York City.

Careful: the chart gives you the averages, and it is wise to take them with a grain of salt when packing your bags. To begin with, it will be warmer in the streets at noon than along the shore at midnight. Also, there have been numerous bizarre weather phenomena in recent years that are completely at odds with the statistics. El Niño has no particular regard for tourists...

PRACTICAL INFORMATION

	Precipitation (cm / in)	Average temperature (°C / °F))
January	8.1 / 3.19	0 / 32
February	7.9 / 3.11	0.8 / 33.4
March	10.7 / 4.21	5.2 / 41.3
April	9.7 / 3.81	11.2 / 52
May	9.7 / 3.81	17 / 62.6
June	8.1 / 3.19	21.9 / 71
July	9.7 / 3.81	25 / 77
August	10.2 / 4	24 / 75.2
September	9.4 / 3.7	21 / 70
October	8.6 / 3.38	14.2 / 57.5
November	10.4 / 3.93	8.3 / 47
December	9.7 / 3.81	2.6 / 36.5

You should also note that during the winter, some precipitation falls as snow. To get an idea of the levels of precipitation, consider that snow takes up about ten times more space than rain. For example, if New York experiences a particularly cold December with average precipitation, Time Square will be covered with about 97 cm of snow before it rings in the New Year.

One last climatological phenomenon specific to Manhattan is worth mentioning. The office towers built here are artificial obstacles to the wind's circulation. This can result in unexpected gusts and updrafts when the wind surges between the skyscrapers. This can be especially unpleasant if you are wearing a hat or carrying an umbrella.

When to Visit New York?

All in all, the transitional seasons (spring or fall) are the most pleasant time of year to visit New York City.

Summers tend to be very hot and humid. The nights can be uncomfortable, since the temperature can soar to 34°C. The winters are quite long and sometimes icy. Usually, however, the temperature rarely drops below zero.

PACKING

Since New York is a four-season destination, what you bring will depend on when you plan to visit.

As winters are cold, be sure to pack a warm sweater, gloves, hat and scarf. Don't forget your warmest winter coat and your boots.

It can be extremely hot in the summer. Bring T-shirts, loose blouses, light pants, shorts and sunglasses. You may need a light jacket or sweater for evenings.

During the spring and fall, you'll need a sweater, a jersey, and a scarf – and don't forget an umbrella!

For all seasons (except winter), light, flexible and comfortable shoes are essential to explore all the different parts of the city.

MAIL AND TELECOMMUNICATIONS

Post Offices

You can purchase stamps not only at any post office, but also at major hotels. Mail is collected on a daily basis.

Post offices are generally open Monday to Friday, from 9:30am to 5:30pm (sometimes until 8pm on Thursday), and Saturday, from 10am to 2pm. New York City's main post office is located at 421 8th Avenue *(☎967-8585)* and open 24 hours a day. There is another post office at the Franklin Roosevelt Station *(☎330-5549)*, located at 903 3rd Avenue, at 55th Street. You can also drop off your mail on the main floor of the Rockefeller Center (610 Fifth Avenue) between 9:30am and 5:30pm.

Telecommunications

The phone system in the U.S. is extremely efficient. Coin-operated pay phones or those that accept credit cards or pre-paid phone cards are easy to find. **The area code for New York is 212.** This guide generally omits the area code in telephone listings in order to save space. Unless otherwise indicated, remember that all telephone numbers are preceded by 212. In the region just outside of Manhattan, the area code is 718.

Throughout the guide, you may notice phone numbers preceded by 1-800 or 1-888. These are toll-free numbers, which are generally accessible from all over North America.

To call New York from elsewhere in North America, dial 1-212 and then the seven-digit number you are trying to reach. To call New York from Belgium and Switzerland, dial 1-12-212, and then the number you are trying to reach.

Some Useful Numbers

Emergency . . . . ☎911
Crime Victim's Hotline . . . . ☎577-7777
Gay and Lesbian Switchboard . . . . ☎777-1800
AAA Motorclub . . . . . . ☎1-800-262-6327 or 757-2000

To call other places in North America from New York, dial 1 then the area code then the seven-digit number you are trying to reach. To call Belgium, dial 011-32, the area code, then the number. To call Switzerland, dial 011-41, the area code and the number.

It is sometimes cheaper to call long-distance by using the direct access numbers below to contact an operator in your home country:

United States
AT&T: ☎1-800-CALL ATT
MCI: ☎1-800-888-8000

British Telecom Direct
☎1-800-408-6420 or 1-800-363-4144

Australia Telstra Direct
☎1-800-663-0683

New Zealand Telecom Direct
☎1-800-663-0684

Moreover, most hotels are equipped with phones in each room, as well as fax machines. Keep in mind, however, that it can be more expensive to call from your hotel than from a phone booth.

MONEY AND BANKING

Money

The monetary unit is the dollar ($), which is divided into cents
(¢). One dollar = 100 cents.

Bills come in one, five, 10, 20, 50 and 100 dollar
denominations; and coins come in one- (penny), five- (nickel),
10- (dime) and 25-cent (quarter) pieces.

Dollar and fifty-cent coins exist, as does a two-dollar bill, but
they are very rarely used. Virtually all purchases must be paid
in American currency in the United States. Be sure to get your
travellers' cheques in American dollars. You can also use any
credit card affiliated with an American institution like Visa,
MasterCard, American Express, Interbank, Barclay Bank, Diners'
Club and Discovery. **Please note that all prices in this guide are
in American dollars.**

Banks

Banks are open Monday to Friday from 9am to 3pm.

Banks can be found almost everywhere, and most offer the
standard services to tourists. Most automatic teller machines
(ATMs) accept foreign bank cards so that you can make direct
withdrawals from your account (check before to make sure you
have access) and avoid the potentially high charges of using a
real teller. Most machines are open at all times. Cash advances
on your credit card are another option, although interest
charges accumulate quickly. Money orders are a final
alternative for which no commission is charged. This option
does, however, take more time. The easiest and safest way to
carry your money, however, is with travellers' cheques.

Exchange Rates

$1 CAN	= $0.64 US	$1 US	= $1.55 CAN
1 £	= $1.64 US	$1 US	= 0.61 £
$1 Aust	= $0.58 US	$1 US	= $1.73 Aust
$1 NZ	= $0.49 US	$1 US	= $2.03 NZ
1 guilder	= $0.49 US	$1 US	= 2.03 guilders
1 SF	= $0.66 US	$1 US	= 1.50 SF
10 BF	= $0.27 US	$1 US	= 37 BF
1 DM	= $0.56 US	$1 US	= 1.80 DM
100 pesetas	= $0.66 US	$1 US	= 152 pesetas
1000 lire	= $0.56 US	$1 US	= 1,774 lire
1 Euro	= $1.10 US	$1 US	= 0.91 Euro

Exchanging Money

Several banks readily exchange foreign currency, but almost all charge a **commission**. There are exchange offices that do not charge commission, but their rates may be less competitive. These offices often have longer opening hours. It is a good idea to **shop around**.

In addition to the main floor counters of the international-flight terminals in New York's three airports (see p 61), there are several foreign exchange offices in the downtown area:

Chase Manhattan Bank
158 West 14th Street;
at 23rd Street and 6th Avenue,
71 West 23rd Street,
245 Fifth Avenue.

Thomas Cook
29 Broadway;
317 Madison Avenue, at 42nd Street,
157 West 57th Street,
1590 Broadway, at 48th Street.

American Express
Bloomingdale's, at 59th Street and Lexington Avenue, ☎705-3171.

American Express
374 Park Avenue, ☎421-8240.

TAXES AND TIPPING

Taxes

An 8.25% sales tax is automatically added to all purchases in New York.

The hotel tax is 13.25%.

Tipping

Tipping applies to all table services, that is in restaurants or other places in which customers are served at their tables (fast food service is therefore not included in this category). Tipping is also compulsory in bars, nightclubs and taxis.

The tip is usually about 15% of the bill before tax, but varies, of course, depending on the quality of service. The tip is not included in the bill; you must calculate it yourself and leave it on the table for the waiter or waitress.

BUSINESS HOURS AND PUBLIC HOLIDAYS

Business Hours

Stores

They are generally open Monday to Wednesday from 10am to 6pm, Thursday and Friday from 10am to 9pm, and Sunday from noon to 5pm. Supermarkets close later or, in some cases, are open 24 hours a day, seven days a week.

PRACTICAL INFORMATION

Holidays and Public Holidays

The following is a list of public holidays in the United States. Note that most stores, government offices and banks are closed on these days.

New Year's Day: January 1

Martin Luther King Jr.'s Birthday: third Monday of January

President's Day: third Monday of February

Memorial Day: last Monday of May

Independence Day (American national holiday): July 4

Labor Day: first Monday of September

Columbus Day: second Monday of October

Veterans Day: November 11

Thanksgiving Day: fourth Thursday of November

Christmas Day: December 25

CALENDAR OF EVENTS

The following is a list of the biggest annual events held in New York City. Please contact the organizers of the various festivities for the exact dates, which vary from year to year.

January

New Year's Eve: Dec. 31st: virtually the whole city gathers in Times Square for the countdown to the new year; at midnight, an 8-kilometre marathon in Central Park is also organized (☎364-3456).

Chinese New Year: following the lunar calendar, Chinese New Year falls on a different date every year. The first day of the year is celebrated in Chinatown with a dazzling array of fireworks (☎619-4785).

February

Black History Month: the third Monday of January, namely Martin Luther King Day, marks the beginning of citywide activities relating to the history of African-American culture. **Harlem's Schomburg Center for Research in Black Culture** (☎491-2200) can provide you with more information.

March

Saint Patrick's Day Parade: on March 17, New York City's Irish community fêtes its patron saint with great pomp and ceremony, and has been doing so for 200 years now. A big parade takes place along Fifth Avenue.

April

Avignon/New York Film Festival: takes place during the last week of April and features the latest productions by French and American independent film-makers. This festival actually combines two events, namely the *Avignon/New York Film Festival*, in Manhattan, and the *Rencontres Franco-Américaines*, in Avignon, France. The festival's main objective is to transcend cinematographic boundaries through the contemporary; it also attempts to generate a critical stance through discussion between film-makers, critics and the audience. There is nothing Hollywoodish about this festival. On Internet: www.francetelecom.com.

May

International Food Fair: 9th Avenue is literally overrun by a hungry crowd who have come to sample dishes from various countries, at kiosks set up between 42nd and 57th Streets.

This fair takes place in mid-May, on the weekend preceding Memorial Day, and officially heralds the beginning of summer.

June

Change Your Mind Day: philosophical debates hosted by Tibetan monks in Central Park (☎360-2756).

JVC Jazz Festival (☎787-2020).

Lesbian and Gay Pride Week: comes out at the end of June. The NYC Gay Pride Parade is one of the biggest events of its kind in the world, along with those of San Francisco and Toronto, and can draw as many as 1,000,000 people.

Met in the Parks: every year, in June, the Metropolitan Opera gives concerts in various New York parks.

Museum Mile Festival: on the second Tuesday of June, the nine museums on Upper 5th Avenue welcome art lovers free of charge from 6pm to 9pm.

New York Shakespeare Festival: plays performed at this festival often feature big silver-screen stars (☎861-7277).

Toyota Comedy Festival (☎903-9600).

Welcome Back to Brooklyn Celebration: concerts, plays and much more are featured all summer long (☎718-855-7882, ext. 52).

What is Jazz? Festival (☎219-3006).

July

Outdoor Concerts: In July and August, the New York Philharmonic and Metropolitan Opera give concerts at Central Park and other parks in the city (☎360-3456).

Independence Day: on the 4th of July, Macy's department store organizes a fireworks display near the East River. The whole city is in a festive mood and a multitude of activities are offered to revellers.

Lincoln Center Events: shows and events, several of which are free, are held at the Lincoln Center (☎875-5108).

August

Greenwich Village Jazz Festival (☎929-5149).

Harlem Week: the foremost African-American district in the country remembers its roots (☎427-3317).

September

Caribbean Day: Labor Day gives rise to the biggest event of the year, as a huge crowd takes to the streets of Brooklyn *(Eastern Parkway or Grand Army Plaza subway station,* ☎625-1515).

Jazz at Lincoln Center: the event's artistic director, trumpet player Wynton Marsalis, is given carte blanche (☎875-5599, *www.jazzatlincolncenter.org*).

New York Film Festival (☎875-5600).

New York is Book Country Festival: a great rare-book fair takes place on 5th Avenue, between 53rd and 57th Streets, one weekend in mid-September.

US Open Tennis Tournament: this tournament, the third Grand Slam, takes place in Flushing Meadows every year; the women's and men's finals are held on Labour Day weekend.

October

New York City Marathon: some 25,000 runners take part in this 42-kilometre marathon, organized by the New York Road Runners Club (☎1-800-697-7269).

New York is Book Country Festival: a great rare-book fair takes place on 5th Avenue, between 53rd and 57th Streets, one weekend in mid-September.

US Open Tennis Tournament: this tournament, the third Grand Slam, takes place in Flushing Meadows every year; the women's and men's finals are held on Labour Day weekend.

October

New York City Marathon: some 25,000 runners take part in this 42-kilometre marathon, organized by the New York Road Runners Club (☎1-800-697-7269).

Halloween Parade: in Greenwich Village, a very noisy and rambunctious crowd races down 6th Avenue to a street party on Christopher Street, where they celebrate far into the night.

November

Thanksgiving Day Parade: Organized by the Macy's department store on the last Thursday of November, this huge parade proceeds along Broadway, from 72nd Avenue to Herald Square.

December

Christmas Windows: the 5th Avenue shop windows of **Barney's**, **Lord & Taylor**, **Macy's** and **Sak's Fifth Avenue** are skilfully decorated during the Christmas season.

Rockefeller Day Christmas Tree Lighting: A huge Christmas tree is erected at Rockefeller Center on the Tuesday following Thanksgiving, and a number of special events and concerts are then broadcast by Radio City Music Hall (☎632-3975).

 ACCOMMODATIONS

No matter what your budget or preferences, this guide has a place for you to lay your head. Remember that rooms are harder to come by and more expensive in summer. Travellers planning to visit New York during this lovely season should therefore reserve in advance.

The "Accommodations" chapter in this guide presents a vast selection of hotels, organized by area and price, from the least expensive to the most expensive. The prices given are those for the high season (summer); therefore, if you are planning to visit during another period of the year, ask about reductions. Prices are for one room, double occupancy. Budget hotels *(less than $70 per night)* are usually clean and satisfactory, but very modest. The advantages of mid-range hotels *($70 to $120)* vary with their location, though the rooms are generally larger. Those in the mid-to-high range *($120 to $200)* offer spacious rooms and attractive lobbies; most have restaurants, shops and a bar. Finally, luxury hotels *(more than $200)*, reserved for those for whom money is no object, are the best in the city. Note that there is an additional 13.25% tax on all New York hotel rooms, as well as a $2 surcharge per night.

Note that reductions are often available on weekends. Business people constitute the majority of hotel clients in New York. As their numbers diminish on weekends, special packages are offered to the general public. Don't hesitate to inquire about such promotions when making your reservations.

Bed & Breakfasts are also available in New York City. These establishments often offer accommodation in beautifully decorated old houses. They generally comprise less than 12 rooms. For information and reservations, contact Adobe Bed and Breakfast *(PO Box 20022, New York, NY 10021, ☎472-2000)*.

 RESTAURANTS

The "Restaurants" chapter in this guide describes dining establishments in each part of New York in order of price, from the least to the most expensive. Places at the bottom of the price scale *($)*, where the bill should come to no more than about $15, the atmosphere is informal, the service quick, and the clientele local. In mid-range restaurants *($$)*, where a meal is still affordable between $15 and $24, the ambiance is more

$ *less than $15*
$$ *between $15 and $24*
$$$ *between $25 and $34*
$$$$ *more than $34*

BARS AND DANCE CLUBS

Some establishments have cover charges, particularly when there is a band. Tipping the doorperson is not mandatory and thus left to your discretion; should you decide to do so, tips are appreciated. It is, however, standard practice to leave a 10% to 15% tip (see p 87) for your drinks. Depending on what type of liquor license they hold, New York's bars, nightclubs, dance clubs and "afterhour" clubs can stay open until anywhere between 4am and 7am.

Note that the legal drinking age is 21.

CHILDREN

New York City has many different leisurely activities for the whole family. Children will especially enjoy the **Children's Museum of Manhattan** *(212 West 83rd St., ☎721-1223)* (see p 256), as well as the **Intrepid Sea-Air-Space Museum** (see p 280). You can also visit Central Park's **Children's Zoo** (see p 215) as well as that of the Bronx, which is much bigger. The Big Apple Circus performs at the Lincoln Center. At Madison Square Gardens, the Ringling Bros and Barnum & Bailey Circus dazzles children of all ages in May and June.

It's raining outside and the kids are bored? No problem! Check out **Rain or Shine** *(Mon to Fri 9am to 6pm, Sat and Sun 10am to 6pm; 115 East 29th St., ☎532-4420),* where children aged one to six can have a great time. A large selection of games to entertain the young ones can be found in this enormous space. Children must be accompanied by their parents.

HANDICAPPED TRAVELLERS

All buildings and government institutions provide services for the disabled by law. Restaurants advertize if their establishment is wheelchair accessible. Should you have any questions, contact the municipal department in charge of services to the physically handicapped (☎788-2830). The SATH (Society for the Advancement of Travel for the Handicapped) organization can also be of help (347 5th Ave., Suite 610, ☎447-7284).

WOMEN TRAVELLING ALONE

Women travelling alone in New York City should not encounter any problems, even though the subway might seem dangerous. In fact, the crime rate is higher in the streets than it is in the subway cars. If you feel unsafe anyway, just enter the driver's compartment in the middle of the train. Change compartments if some shady-looking character bothers you. Whistling, catcalls and propositions are common; it is wiser to ignore them and stare straight ahead as you continue on your merry way.

SENIOR CITIZENS

Senior citizens can get special rates for museum access, prescription drugs and hotel rooms. Seniors 65 years of age or over with proof of I.D. are entitled to a free transfer with the purchase of a token. For reduced travel rates and other information, contact the **American Association of Retired Persons** (601 E Street NW, Washington, DC 20049, ☎1-800-424-3410), the most important senior-citizens organization in the United States.

GAY AND LESBIAN LIFE

Gay and lesbian life in New York City is vibrant, especially in Greenwich Village and Chelsea in Manhattan, and Jackson Heights, in Queens. **The Lesbian and Gay Community Services Center** (208 West 13th Ave., ☎620-7310) deals with social and

Gay Pride

Thirty years after Stonewall, the Gay Pride Parade draws such a high level of participation that it seems to take over the entire city, making difficult to imagine gay life in 1969.

It was in this year that Stonewall marked a turning point in the history of homosexuality. Stonewall is the name of a bar that still exists, where one night in June 1969, the police tried to carry out one of their routine and abusive raids. On that night, rather than undergo arbitrary arrest without resistance, the police were met with a defensive clientele. The patrons succeeded in detaining the police in the bar. Before help arrived, Greenwich Village, already a very gay district, mobilized to create a situation that had never before been seen, proclaiming their right to be different in the streets. But the repressive arm of power struck back. Three nights of rioting ensued, signalling the birth of the gay civil rights movement which soon spread throughout the world.

The Gay Pride Parade commemorates this event and is held in New York on the last Sunday of June, as the finale of a week of events celebrating and advancing the cause of gays, who continue to be victims of discrimination in all countries of the world, including the most democratic ones.

The parade begins at noon at the corner of 5th Avenue and 52 Street, and heads south and then west towards Greenwich Village. More than 250,000 people march in the street, and 300,000 spectators gather on the sidewalks to express their support of gay rights, or simply to take in the show. And what a show it is! The organization places groups that are under-represented in society at the head of the parade, such as lesbians on motorcycles, who usually lead the parade, or Amerindians. Thus, you get the impression that all the nations of the world are marching by, before giving way to various organizations, lobby groups, and even political parties. Towards the end of the parade, you can even see a large contingent of gay police officers, who receive a warm round of applause from the crowd.

The whole city is involved in the parade which underlines the fact that the gay community is here to stay and that it is as diverse as any society can be; it also affirms that it's O.K. to be gay and affirm your difference.

The organizers have deliberately chosen a festive tone for this parade, even though it is highly political, advocating for gay rights.

legal issues, serving no less than 5,000 people a week. **The Gay and Lesbian Switchboard *(☎777-1800)* is an information service that operates 24 hours a day and provides information about activities going on in the city. Volunteers staff the

The World Trade Center: Twin Peaks.
- *T. B.*

A face that needs no introduction – that of the Statue of Liberty.
- *New York Convention & Visitors Bureau*

Two of the bridges spanning the East River.
- *Tibor Bognar*

phones from noon to midnight. For advice concerning blood tests for the HIV virus and other health issues, contact **Gay Men Health Crisis** *(☎807-6664)* or **Community Health Project** *(☎675-3559)*. Victims of abuse can get in touch with **The Anti-Violence Project** *(☎807-0197)* day and night.

TIME DIFFERENCE

New York is 6 hours behind Europe and 3 hours ahead of the west coast of North America. New York is in the same time zone as Montreal, Toronto and Washington (Eastern time zone). Remember that the United States spans several time zones.

DRUGS

Recreational drugs are against the law and not tolerated (even "soft" drugs). Anyone caught with drugs in their possession risks severe consequences.

ELECTRICITY

Voltage in the United States is 110 volts and 60 cycles., the same as Canada; to use European appliances, you must have a transformer/converter

Electrical plugs are two-pinned and flat; you can find adapters in New York, or purchase them at a travel boutique or bookshop before your departure.

MEDIA

Newspapers

The Big Apple's two major dailies are *The New York Times* and *The Wall Street Journal*. The former is the biggest daily in the country (with the largest staff and number of foreign

PRACTICAL INFORMATION

correspondents), while the latter mainly caters to businesspeople.

Also worth mentioning among the daily papers published in New York City are the tabloidish *Daily News*, and the *New York Post*, a rather poor knock-off of a famous English newspaper. *The New Yorker*, a seventy-year-old and once respectable publication, is now more sensationalist, to the bitter disappointment of its long-time readers.

The Village Voice, a free weekly issued every Wednesday, also offers a great overview of New York City's cultural life. Inside, you'll find nightlife listings, a host of news articles, concert reviews and the must-see shows. Also worth picking up is *Where New York*, available in hotels, which has an abundance of information about the various cultural events held in and around the city.

Another weekly, *Time Out*, which saw the light of day in 1995, has an excellent section on activities in the gay and lesbian community.

Radio

The WNYC-AM (820) channel is the national public radio network's local station. Classical-music lovers can tune in to 93.9 (WNYC) or 96.3 (WQXR) on the FM dial, whereas 100.3 (WHTZ) is for rock fans. At least five stations play classic rock. For jazz, turn to 88.3 FM (WBGO); for soul, tune in to 107.5 (WBLS), and for hip-hop or rap, check out 97.1 (WQHT). If you like a little bit of everything, 89.9 (WKCR) and 90.1 (WFMU) will satisfy your listening needs.

Television

It goes without saying that the major American television networks, namely CBS, NBC, ABC and FOX, are available a metropolis like New York City. Cable television gives further viewing with dozens of specialty stations, including the continuous news network, CNN; the ESPN sports network; the

MTV rock and pop video channel; and HBO, which presents special events as well as a number of films.

WEIGHTS AND MEASURES

The United States use the imperial system:

Weights
1 pound (lb) = 454 grams (g)
1 kilogram (kg) = 2.2 pounds (lbs)

Linear Measure
1 inch = 2.2 centimetres (cm)
1 foot (ft) = 30 centimetres (cm)
1 mile = 1.6 kilometres (km)
1 kilometres (km) = 0.63 miles
1 metre (m) = 39.37 inches

Land Measure
1 acre = 0.4 hectare
1 hectare = 2.471 acres

Volume Measure
1 U.S. gallon (gal) = 3.79 litres
1 U.S. gallon (gal) = 0.83 imperial gallon

Temperature
To convert °F into °C: subtract 32, divide by 9, multiply by 5
To convert °C into °F: multiply by 9, divide by 5, add 32

EXPLORING

New York is a complex city that takes everything to extremes, including its size. Full of contrasts, it is bursting with an electric energy – and with 7.7 million inhabitants, not counting the 16 million living in its suburbs, New York is the largest urban conglomeration in the United States. The Big Apple, as the city is often called, is made up of five buroughs. Manhattan, named after the island on which it is located, is the largest of these, and also the best known. It lies at the heart of the megalopolis and is one of the quintessential symbols of America. Most tours in this guide cover this area, and allow you to discover both the famous landmarks and the hidden corners in this city of a thousand faces.

New York is best discovered on foot, so don't hesitate to explore its streets and avenues, all of which stretch over several kilometres. It is also a treat to visit the observation decks on some of the taller buildings, from which you can admire the lofty skyscrapers which are often difficult to appreciate fully from the street level. Also, getting away from the crowded streets (a walk through Central Park, or taking a ferry around the bay of New York, etc.) allows you to get an overview of the downtown area. Finally, you should also venture down some of the main avenues (Broadway, Times

Square, Fifth Avenue, Park Avenue, etc.) in the evening, to take in the impressively lit buildings.

Since 1990, the municipal administration, in collaboration with the private sector, has spared no effort in making New York cleaner and safer. The complete transformation of Times Square from a disreputable place into a familial area in under ten years is the most noticeable achievement of this change. Everywhere, buildings' façades are being cleaned, and attractive boutiques are opening in otherwise deserted spaces. Garbage collectors, hired by the owners of properties along certain arteries, empty garbage cans and clean up the paper and other refuse that continually litters the sidewalks. Most significantly, New Yorkers, sick and tired of their reputation as being surly and rude, are becoming increasingly welcoming and polite!

TOUR A: WALL STREET AND THE FINANCIAL DISTRICT ★ ★ ★ (one day)

In the glorious era of steamships, ladies in mink and immigrants in rags crossed their respective bridges over New York Bay and were struck by the sight of the mural of skyscrapers that spirals out from Wall Street at the southern tip of Manhattan Island. This shimmering New York façade, a symbol that defines America, seems almost unreal in the mists of early morning. From solid ground, this imposing concentration of tall towers and bank headquarters, which has turned this rather confined area into the foremost financial district in the world, looks like the prow of a giant ship pushing into the sea. The few buildings erected before 1850 that survived the burgeoning prosperity of the early decades of the 20th century are like tiny, fragile jewels tucked among mastodons and serve as reminders that this is the oldest section of the city. Even though it is far from Midtown and its big hotels, this tour ranks first because of the abundance of historical information it provides and the fundamental symbolism it conveys. It also affords a better grasp of the geography of New York since it offers expansive views over the Hudson and East Rivers and the New Jersey and Long Island (Brooklyn) coasts from vantage points in Battery Park and from the observation deck of the World Trade Center. We recommend that you visit this area on a weekday, between 10am and 4pm, since many of the attractions mentioned are

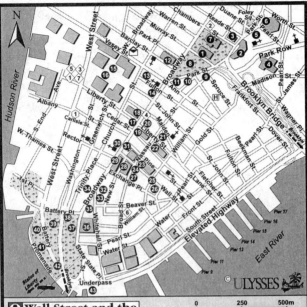

Ⓐ Wall Street and the Financial District

0	250	500m
0	750	1500ft.

● ATTRACTIONS

1. City Hall
2. Municipal Building
3. Surrogate's Court
4. Police Headquarters
5. Police Headquarters
6. New York County Courthouse
7. Tweed Courthouse
8. City Hall Park
9. Statue of Benjamin Franklin
10. Potter Building
11. Park Row Building
12. Woolworth Building
13. St. Paul's Chapel
14. AT&T World Headquarters
15. World Trade Center
16. Top of the World
17. Liberty Plaza Park
18. One Liberty Plaza
19. Marine Midland Bank
20. Chamber of Commerce of the State of New York
21. Federal Reserve Bank of New York
22. Chase Manhattan Bank
23. Federal Hall National Memorial
24. Statue of George Washington
25. Wall Street
26. Citibank
27. Morgan Guaranty Trust Company
28. New York Stock Exchange
29. Irving Trust
30. Trinity Church
31. American Surety Building
32. Standard Oil Building
33. Museum of American Financial History
34. Cunard Building
35. Bowling Green
36. National Museum of the American Indian
37. Battery Park
38. Netherlands Memorial Flagpole
39. Hope Garden
40. Castle Clinton National Monument
41. Statue of Giovanni da Verrazano
42. East Coast Memorial
43. Staten Island Ferry

◯ ACCOMMODATIONS

1. Marriot Financial Center Hotel

◇ RESTAURANTS

1. Cellar in the Sky
2. Ellen's Café and Bake Shop
3. Greenhouse Café
4. McDonald's
5. The Greatest Bar on Earth
6. Wall Street Kitchen and Bar
7. Windows on the World

closed after 4pm and on weekends. It is worth noting that admission to a number of these sights is free.

The tour begins in front of New York City Hall, on Murray Street east of Broadway, in the middle of City Hall Park. By subway, take Train 4 or Train 6 to the Brooklyn Bridge/City Hall Station, or take Train N or Train R to City Hall Station. Buses M1 (weekdays only), M6, M9, M15 and M103 all serve the City Hall area.

The offices of the mayor of New York and his staff are located in elegant **City Hall ★★** *(free; Mon to Fri 10am to 4pm; Murray St., ☎788-3000)*, a building designed in 1803 by French architect Joseph-François Mangin who, a few decades earlier, helped Jacques-Ange Gabriel build Place de la Concorde in Paris. New York City Hall, many times threatened by the wrecking ball, is a marvellous combination of Louis XVI and Federal period influences. A delicately shaped, elliptical entrance hall accesses the City Council Chamber, and a curving staircase ascends to the Governor's Room, formerly the quarters of the state governor on visits to the city, where exhibition galleries have been laid out. Some of the furniture on display was used by George Washington, the first president of the United States, when New York was still the national capital. City Hall's diminutive size, relative to that of the sprawling city over which it governs, is a sign of its age: in the era of the building's construction, the Big Apple was but a modest town – City Hall marked its northern border!

A large group of buildings was added behind City Hall in the second half of the 19th century to meet the municipal government's growing need for office space. This ensemble, known as the Civic Center, is dominated by the **Municipal Building ★** *(northeast of City Hall, straddling Chambers St.)*, an imposing 40-story skyscraper that houses various administrative departments. The building is crowned by a gilded statue by Adolph Weinman called *Civic Fame*, although a newlywed couple would be just as fitting an ornament, since this building very much resembles a wedding cake. Necessitated by the creation of Greater New York in 1898, which effectively doubled the city's population, construction of the Municipal Building began in 1907. Its abundance of columns and obelisks is evocative of student designs submitted to a contest held by Paris's École des Beaux-Arts at the turn of the 20th century. Another beaux-arts flight of fancy, conceived in 1905 to house the municipal archives, faces the Municipal Building. This building is now occupied by the **Surrogate's Court ★** *(31 Chambers St.)*, which deals exclusively with wills and cases of estate succession. Two sculpture arrangements, symbolizing New York in the Colonial and Revolutionary periods, stand on either side of the entrance, and the top of the façade's colonnade is lined with statues of former governors and mayors of New York by Philip Martigny. It is worth stepping into the courthouse to admire its exuberant hall clothed in marble and mosaic. A few other interesting buildings can be seen north and east of these last two: Police Headquarters, a modern structure that can be reached from the carriage entrance of the Municipal Building; the **United States Courthouse ★** *(40 Center St.)*, a federal court building crowned by a golden, pyramidal roof; and the **New York County Courthouse ★** *(on Foley Sq.)*, which you may recognize from its countless film appearances – a colossal, hexagonal building that houses the state court.

Construction work on **Tweed Courthouse** *(52 Chambers St.)* began in 1858. The project took over 20 years to complete, required extravagant expenditures and managed to exceed its initial four-million-dollar budget by ten million dollars. The building is an excellent illustration of the generalized corruption that reigned in city politics in the days of Tammany Hall when William Marcy "Boss" Tweed (1823-1878) acted as mayor. This former courthouse now serves as an annex in back of City Hall.

Cross City Hall Park to the intersection of Broadway and Park Row.

Tweed Courthouse and City Hall both stand in **City Hall Park ★**, a patch of green hemmed in on all sides by skyscrapers, which provides a slightly set back view of the tops of the area's very ornate and numerous buildings. The park was laid out on the site of a British gallows where the fate of captured American Revolutionaries was meted out, including that of Nathan Hale, in whose honour a monument was erected at the corner of Murray Street and Broadway. Buildings have encroached on the park on many different occasions, but, with the exception of the aforementioned two, all have disappeared to make way for trees. One of these is worth mentioning though: the Vanderlyn

EXPLORING

Panorama was a circular structure, erected in 1818, on the walls of which was affixed a painting of the gardens of Versailles that is now housed at the Metropolitan Museum of Art (see p 235).

Some of New York's oldest skyscrapers line Park Row. In the 19th century, these contained the offices of many of the city's great newspapers, including *The Herald*, *The Sun*, *The Times*, *The Tribune* and *The World*. The 16-story World Building, which launched the great skyscraper-building battle in 1890 – a race for the heavens that has yet to slow – used to stand behind the statue of Benjamin Franklin . To the south stands the stunning Potter Building *(38 Park Row)* of 1883, which has an exterior of red terracotta shaped into complex mouldings. The **Park Row Building** *(15 Park Row)* was the tallest skyscraper in the world when it was inaugurated in 1899.

The west side of Broadway is dominated by the impressive, 60-story, neo-Gothic, terracotta mass of the **Woolworth Building ★★** *(233 Broadway)*, which had its turn as the tallest building on the planet between 1913, the year it was completed, and 1931, when the Empire State Building (see p 174) was finished. Nicknamed the "Cathedral of Commerce", it was built to house the headquarters of Woolworth, a family retail business that unfortunately closed the doors of the last of its 1,465 discount stores in 1997 after 117 years in operation. The building was inaugurated by President Woodrow Wilson who pressed a button in his office in the White House, thereby illuminating the 80,000 light bulbs that decorated it for the occasion. Originally, the Woolworth Building was equipped with its own power plant. A visit to the entrance hall, the Skyros marble walls of which support vaults covered in brilliantly shining glass and gold mosaics, is a must. The sculpted figures on the capitals include Cass Gilbert, the building's architect, and Frank Woolworth, who financed the 13.5-million-dollar project in cash; the former is depicted holding a scale model of the structure in his arms, and the latter is shown counting coins.

Walk south on Broadway.

The delicate silhouette of **St. Paul's Chapel ★★**, built in 1766 by Thomas McBean of Scotland, appears on the right. This is the oldest church in New York and one of only a few extant

Colonial buildings on Manhattan Island. Modelled on 18th-century London churches, this Anglican chapel (the term "Episcopal" has been in use since the American Revolution) bears an Ionic portico under which stands a monument to General Montgomery, who died in Québec during the American invasion of 1775. Curiously, the rectangular chapel is reached by way of the sanctuary, which was modified in 1787 by Pierre Charles L'Enfant. George Washington's pew is in the row on the right. The actual façade of St. Paul's Chapel, surmounted by an elegant bell tower that was added in 1796, opens onto a little, shady cemetery that is the burial place of various military men, including F. M. Bechet, Sieur de Rochefontaine, a general in the army of Louis XVI.

Leave the cemetery enclosure on the Fulton Street side.

At the corner of Broadway and Fulton Street is the former **AT&T World Headquarters** ★ *(195 Broadway)*, constructed between 1915 and 1922. This corporation, which for a long time reigned supreme in the American telecommunications industry, has moved its head office several times since the construction of this enormous "layer cake". A look at the building's marble lobby, supported by austere Doric columns, is a must.

Walk west on Fulton Street, cross Church Street, and then turn left to reach the World Trade Center.

Next to the twin towers of the **World Trade Center** ★★★ *(west of Church St., between Liberty and Vesey Sts.)*, which are each 110 stories (411 metres) tall, the other skyscrapers in the financial district seem like miniatures despite their more than respectable heights. This three-million-square-metre complex attracts some 50,000 workers daily, making it one of the largest office spaces on the planet. It is home to the World Trade Center of New York, which supervises similar organizations located around the world. These consist of facilities designed to promote international trade by centralizing all of the services necessary for business transactions between people of different nations. The adjacent buildings, on the perimeter of the plaza, house U.S. Customs of the Port of New York; the Commodities Exchange Center, where, notably, petroleum products are traded; and exhibition halls in which huge commercial fairs are held. Beneath the brick plaza, a

EXPLORING

regional train station, an underground shopping mall and a vast parking lot have been laid out on multiple levels. On February 26, 1993, a bomb that had been hidden in a truck parked in the middle of this lot exploded, killing six people and injuring hundreds more. This attack on the World Trade Center led to more stringent security standards in many of New York's large buildings.

The WTC was built between 1966 and 1973 by architects Emery Roth & Sons and Minoru Yamasaki (1912-1986). A bronze sculpture by German artist Fritz Koenig entitled *Globe* adorns the centre of the immense plaza. Large aluminum lines separating the building's windows, which seem to scale the heavens, are discernable as you approach the towers. These two skyscrapers are true miracles of engineering – no pillars interrupt the surface areas of their floors. To the right of the **North Tower** *(1 World Trade Center)* is **North Bridge** *(every day 6am to midnight)*, which leads to the World Financial Center in Battery Park City (see the Battery Park City tour, p 131). The New York Port Authority, co-owner of the building, has laid out two observation decks for visitors at the top of the South Tower, one indoors and one outdoors, both of which offer simply breathtaking, panoramic views of the city that extend all the way to New Jersey and the Atlantic Ocean. In addition to the glassed-in observation area on the 107th floor and the open-air platform on the 110th floor (the highest of its kind anywhere in the world; open in fair weather only), **Top of the World** ★★★ *($10; &; every day, Oct to May 9:30am to 9:30pm, Jun to Sep 9:30am to 11:30pm; 2 World Trade Center, ☎323-2340, www.wtc-top.com)* offers snack bars, souvenir shops and three movie theatres that present films for high-altitude thrill-seekers. Also, a son et lumière show is presented on the roof in the evening, weather permitting. Self-guided tours are available at the information counter. Tickets must be purchased at the kiosks on the mezzanine, where there are also a tourist office and a counter that sells discounted, last-minute tickets for Broadway shows (TKTS). As for the famous restaurant Windows on the World, it is located on the 107th floor of the North Tower (see p 108). Take note that all visitors must pass through a metal detector.

Return to Church Street and proceed southward. Turn left on Liberty Street. You will come to the network of winding streets of Old New York, etched in the medieval tradition of Dutch and British cities.

To your right is **Liberty Plaza Park** *(at the corner of Liberty St. and Broadway)*, a little granite square planted with trees and a meeting place for chess players. This semi-public space was created by developers behind the black skyscraper at **One Liberty Plaza** to allow for the transfer of air rights. Designed by architects Skidmore, Owings and Merrill in 1974, the building displays a sturdy steel structure – a veritable advertisement for the U.S. Steel Corporation, the company that financed the project. Today it houses the New York headquarters of the Bank of Nova Scotia.

Cross Broadway to Nassau Street, which has been converted into a pedestrian mall between Maiden Lane and Beekman Street).

On the little square of the **Marine Midland Bank** *(140 Broadway)*, another Skidmore, Owings and Merrill project (1967), there is a 1973 sculpture by Isamu Noguchi entitled *Cube*. The former **Chamber of Commerce of the State of New York** *(65 Liberty St.)* comes next – a 1901 beaux-arts folly that is now dwarfed by the skyscrapers surrounding it.

The long façade of the **Federal Reserve Bank of New York ★★** *(free admission; free guided tours by appointment; 33 Liberty St., ☎720-6130)* cuts diagonally across the axis of Liberty Street. The 1924 building, modelled on an Italian Renaissance fortified palace by architects York and Sawyer (who are also responsible for the Royal Bank on Rue Saint-Jacques in Montreal), protects one of the largest gold reserves in the world. Many countries store their gold here, safe from political tumult; when one country reimburses another it is a simple matter of moving a few ingots from pile to pile. Manhattan banks also make use of this reserve, which was created in 1913 under the Wilson administration as a method of stabilizing economic fluctuations. There are a dozen such establishments in all, spread throughout the United States. Get a look at the complicated wrought-iron and bronze decoration, the creation of artist Samuel Yellin, around the building's entrance and in the hall. Visitors can take a 45-minute guided tour of the Federal Reserve Bank, which includes the main vault, in a basement five stories under the street level, in which the gold

EXPLORING

is safe-housed. Space on these tours is limited; it is necessary to make reservations at least one month in advance by telephoning the Public Information Department. Tickets are then sent by mail. Tours leave at 10:30, 11:30, 1:30 and 2:30, Monday through Friday. All personal belongings (handbags, cameras, etc.) must be left at the entrance and all visitors must pass through a metal detector.

Return to Nassau Street and walk south toward Wall Street.

The 60-story tower of the **Chase Manhattan Bank** *(1 Chase Manhattan Plaza)*, another accomplishment of architects Skidmore, Owings and Merrill (1960), stands on the left. At its foot is Jean Dubuffet's *Group of Four Trees* (1972), a large, twisted sculpture in white and black fibreglass that is representative of the artist's later work.

Pause at the corner of Nassau and Pine Streets before entering Federal Hall National Memorial through its secondary entrance on Pine.

In 1653, the residents of New Amsterdam had a *Stadt Huys*, in which the burgomasters of the city's first municipal government held debates. In 1701, the English erected New York's second city hall on the east side of Nassau Street, between Pine and Wall Streets. In 1789 this Georgian building was transformed by Pierre Charles L'Enfant into the first American Capitol, a function it served for the brief period when New York was the capital of the United States. At this point, the building was renamed Federal Hall. (L'Enfant is better known for his design of the city of Washington, which epitomizes the concepts of 18th-century French urbanism.) On April 30, 1789, George Washington gave his inaugural speech from the balcony of Federal Hall, thereby taking office as the first President of the United States, and shortly thereafter, Congress met for the first time in this same building.

Despite its historical significance, Federal Hall was demolished in 1812. Between 1834 and 1842, a customs house went up on its site: a beautiful Greek Revival building by Ithiel Town and Alexander J. Davis, vaguely inspired by the Parthenon in Athens. Since 1955, the site has been home to the **Federal Hall National Memorial ★** *(free; Mon to Fri 9am to 5pm; 26 Wall St., ☎264-8711)*, a little museum that relates the historic events that unfolded here through the centuries with the aid of models and short films. Guided tours are offered every hour. The wear and tear of over a century is evident in slight depressions in the marble floor of the rotunda where clients stood in front of the semi-circular counters of customs officers, traces of which are also apparent along the walls of the room. It is also possible to visit the old vaults in the building's basement, in which the nation's silver was stored when the U.S. Sub-Treasury occupied the premises (1862-1925).

Leave the Federal Hall National Memorial via the main entrance on Wall Street. From the top of the steep staircase, there is a famous view of Trinity Church to the west and of the Stock Exchange to the south.

A **statue of George Washington**, sculpted by John Quincy Adams Ward in 1833, sits enthroned in the middle of the staircase – this figure is a veritable treasure to Americans, whose patriotism never flags.

Wall Street ★★★ *(between Broadway and South St.)*: its name is synonymous with colossal fortunes and ambitious brokers; the banks that control the world economy line its pavement; and here it is, right underfoot! This little stretch of road, which is rather narrow in comparison to the size of the buildings around it, was opened in 1699 on the site of the enclosing wall that marked the northern border of New Amsterdam – hence its name – and remained a principally residential artery for the duration of 18th century. The first banks appeared in the area around 1820; one hundred years later, Wall Street would surpass London to become the most important financial district on the planet.

EXPLORING

The double colonnade of **Citibank ★★** *(55 Wall St.)*, which occupies the former Merchant's Exchange, built in 1836 by architect Isaiah Rogers, is visible to the east. This was one of the first buildings constructed specifically for the purposes of commerce and business on Wall Street. Rogers' original plans actually correspond to the bottom Ionic colonnade. The second Corinthian one was superposed on the first in 1907 to enlarge the bank, which had by then occupied the whole building. A quick peek at the banking hall by McKim, Mead and White is well worthwhile: its marble columns support a coffered ceiling topped by a glass dome, the whole creating a spectacular effect.

On September 16, 1920, a bomb hidden in a truck exploded in front of the headquarters of the **Morgan Guaranty Trust Company** *(23 Wall St.)*, killing 33 passers-by and injuring 200 others, but sparing J. P. Morgan Jr., the target of the attack. Traces of this incident are visible on the walls of the 1913 building, which still houses the bank founded by John Pierpont Morgan.

Many people hold the misconception that the **New York Stock Exchange** ★★ is situated on Wall Street: in reality, the market's tall, neoclassical portico looks out over Broad Street. This is the saint of saints of high finance, the business world's sacred ground, where the shares of almost all of the large multinationals are traded. The most important stock exchange in the world was founded in 1792; in those days merchants met under a tall tree. The exchange did not obtain a written charter until 1817, hence the confusion over its date of origin. In October 1929, the New York Stock Exchange was the arena of the worst financial catastrophe of the modern era. Wednesday the 23rd, stocks crashed; Thursday the 24th panic set in; Friday the 25th, "Black Friday", the economy of the western world crumbled – it would take 10 years for the market to recover from these three short days. Ruined brokers and businessmen flung themselves from the balcony; some even leapt from the rooftop, to be sure not to miss their mark. The Stock Exchange was built in 1903 by George B. Post, who was at the time applying the finishing touches to his Montreal Stock Exchange. Its façade, covered in white marble from Georgia (U.S.), displays an admirable Corinthian portico surmounted by a pediment decorated with a sculpted allegory symbolizing Commerce created by artists John Quincy Adams Ward and Paul Bartlett. The New York Stock Exchange is open to visitors during the week, permitting "mere mortals" to witness the perpetual chaos that reigns on its famous floor from a balcony designed for this very purpose. The Stock Exchange also possesses an interpretive centre that explains the activities of the market. It is recommended to arrive at the visitors' entrance, to the left of the colonnade, before two o'clock to reserve a spot in the visitors' gallery before the markets close.

If the Empire State Building is New York's best-known Art-Deco skyscraper, the **Irving Trust Building** ★ *(1 Wall St.),* on the other hand, is by far the city's most elegant example of this style. Its pure lines and slender profile – mirroring the silhouette of a great lady in evening wear – are the 1932 creation of architects Voorhees, Gmelin and Walker. Its gold- and red-toned lobby is also worth a quick look. The best view of the top of the tower is from the western end of Trinity Church Cemetery, on the other side of Broadway.

Trinity Church ★★ *(free; Mon to Fri 7am to 6pm, Sat and Sun 8am to 4pm; corner of Broadway and Wall St., ☎602-0800)* manages to block off the view down Wall Street, even if nowadays this Anglican church is overshadowed by the many skyscrapers that surround it. Founded in 1697, Trinity Parish is the oldest in New York. The present temple, designed in the neo-Gothic style by Richard Upjohn between 1839 and 1846, is the third to occupy this site. The building is considered one of the crowning accomplishments of 19th-century American religious architecture and served as the model for numerous churches across the continent. Its 85-metre steeple was the tallest structure in the city until 1889. Even more remarkable though are its beautiful bronze doors, designed by Richard Morris Hunt, which depict scenes from the Bible (main entrance) and from the history of the United States (southern aisle). These were donated by the Astor family, as was the Caen-stone main retable, which was added in 1876 (Frederick Clarke Withers, sculptor). To the right of the sanctuary is the Chapel of All Saints (1913), as well as a small museum that displays the original charter accorded to Trinity Parish by English King William III in 1697. The remains of various historic figures, including Robert Fulton, who invented the steamboat with Jouffroy d'Abbans and is credited with the legendary submarine *Nautilus*, lie in the cemetery, which opened in 1681 and extends out from either side of the church.

Take a moment to look around at the buildings neighbouring the cemetery.

The architect of the Château Frontenac in Quebec City, Bruce Price, also designed the **American Surety Building** ★ *(100 Broadway)* in 1894. Now occupied by the powerful Bank of Tokyo, this office tower, which was for a time the tallest in the world, marked an important development

EXPLORING

in the history of this type of construction. The first steel-framed skyscraper in New York, it was also innovative for adopting the principal of tripartite façade composition (base, shaft, crown). Up until this point, architects had contented themselves with stacking story upon story, modifying the decor every two or three levels to break up the monotony. The goddesses depicted on the building's Ionic portico are the work of J. Massey Rhind.

Return to Broadway and continue southward (turn right on exiting the church by the main door).

The **Standard Oil Building** ★ *(26 Broadway)* was once the headquarters of the richest oil company in America (Standard Oil later became Mobil Oil, which has its main offices in Midtown); today it is occupied by Standard & Poor's, the distinguished agency that ascribes credit ratings to the various nations of the world. Designed by Carrère and Hastings in 1922, the complex shape of this tower, which hugs the curb of Broadway at its foot and orients itself toward the network of avenues in its upper section, greatly accentuates the Lower Manhattan skyline. From above, it looks like the product of a Romantic imagination that took great pleasure in designing it as an abode for the gods. The ground floor of the Standard Oil Building houses the minuscule **Museum of American Financial History** *(free admission; Mon to Fri 11:30am to 2:30pm, 26 Broadway, ☎908-4110)*, which recounts the ascension of New York to its present-day status as financial capital of the world. The reason for the museum's early closing time is a mystery.

Across the street from the Standard Oil Building is the **Cunard Building** *(25 Broadway)*, which housed the head offices of the transatlantic navigation company Cunard Line until 1975. Founded in 1840 by Samuel Cunard, who was originally from Nova Scotia, Canada, the company was famous for owning such notable ships as the *Titanic*, the *Queen Mary* and the *Queen Elizabeth II*. Since the advent of freight airplanes, however, the shipping business has been in decline. The building's great vaulted booking hall, where passengers purchased tickets to Europe, remains intact, even if it now contains but a simple post office.

Broadway begins its long trek to the northern tip of Manhattan at the edge of a tiny oval park called **Bowling Green** *(corner of*

Broadway and Whitehall St.), the oldest green space in the city, dating from 1733. As indicated by its name, it was originally used for lawn bowling. The fence that encloses it dates from 1772. The poured bronze sculpture of a plumpish bull, the creation of Italian artist Arturo DiModica, was moved to Bowling Green after the artist illegally deposited it in front of the Stock Exchange in the weeks following the Crash of 1987. Traditionally, the bull connotes an active stock market on the upswing, while the bear represents a steady or declining market. The animal depicted here has all the necessary qualifications of a symbol of productivity...

A visit to the **National Museum of the American Indian** ★★ *(free; ♿; every day 10am to 5pm, Thu to 8pm; 1 Bowling Green, ☎668-6624)* of the Smithsonian Institute is a must, if only to admire the great elliptical room at the centre of the building which housed U. S. Customs from 1907 to 1973. Luckily, its marble counters and the superb mural paintings on its vault which depict scenes of the Port of New York (Reginald Marsh, 1937), were preserved when architect Cass Gilbert's beaux-arts "palace" was converted into a museum of native history and culture. The exhibits now displayed here illustrate the traditions and daily lives of the first nations of the Americas. The George Gustav Heye collection is an assembly of more than one million artifacts acquired by this New York millionaire between 1900 and 1905 from all over the Americas, including objects from as far and wide as Peru and British Columbia by way of the Nevada desert. The museum offers craft workshops and presents dance performances that bring the collection to life and set it in a contemporary context. Visitors can also meet native storytellers and attend sacred ceremonies (telephone ahead of time for the calendar of events). The participation of various aboriginal nations in the museum's programming is significant. On the way out, take note of the sculpted allegories on the façade representing, from left to right, Asia, America, Europe and Africa, executed by Daniel Chester French.

Come into Battery Park at the entrance facing the circular building of Castle Clinton at the corner of Battery Place and State Street.

The contrast between the narrow streets and canyons of beige-stone skyscrapers that make up a large part of this

EXPLORING

neighbourhood, and the immense expanse of green and blue that suddenly opens up on the shore of New York Bay at **Battery Park** ★ ★ is striking. In 1693, a battery of 92 cannons, the park's namesake, was established here on the southern point of Manhattan Island. This fortification, which also included the old Dutch fort of New Amsterdam, was known as Fort George until it was razed during the reconstruction of the city after the American Revolution. Its high earthen ramparts served as levees in the bay and helped create the landscape that is now the park. From the promenade along the water's edge there is a view of Ellis Island and the Statue of Liberty (see p 117). Governor's Island, an American Coast Guard base that closed in 1998, is visible on the left.

The **Netherlands Memorial Flagpole** greets visitors at the entrance to Battery Park. It marks the spot of a plaque commemorating the purchase of Manhattan Island by the Dutch in 1626. On the way to Castle Clinton, you will cross **Hope Garden**, a rose garden that was inaugurated in 1992 in memory of AIDS victims.

The **Castle Clinton National Monument** ★ *(free; &; every day 8:30am to 5pm; in Battery Park, ☎344-7220)* is an old circular brownstone fort erected in 1812 to defend the Port of New York against the threat of British attack. At first it was situated about 100 metres from the shore and completely surrounded by water. The structure was given the name of the mayor of the day, De Witt Clinton. Later, having outlived its military use, the island-fort was transformed into a concert hall and linked to Manhattan by a footbridge. It was here that an aging Lafayette was received with great pomp and that soprano Jenny Lind, "the Swedish Nightingale", put on her triumphant performance of 1850. Next, the building was converted into a processing centre for new immigrants, a function it served until the infrastructure on Ellis Island was completed, and was permanently linked to Manhattan. In 1896, the structure was again modified to house the Aquarium of New York. Today it serves as a ticket office for the ferries to Ellis Island and the Statue of Liberty (passengers board from the promenade along the bay) and displays a small exhibition retracing the building's eclectic past. Guided tours of the fort and the park that now surrounds it leave every hour.

A **statue of Giovanni da Verrazano** by Ettore Ximenes (1909) stands to the east of the fort. Even though he never set foot on Manhattan Island, this legendary Italian explorer is considered to have "discoverered" New York while in the service of French King Francis I. A little further along is the **East Coast Memorial**, a monument to American merchant marines who died in the Atlantic during the course of the Second World War. It comprises eight granite steles encircling a golden eagle.

What could be more enjoyable, or more appropriate to top off this stroll back through Lower Manhattan's history, than a short boat ride, complete with salty sea breezes, re-creating the mythical feeling of arriving at the Port of New York by steamship. You can relive this experience by boarding the **Staten Island Ferry ★★★** *(free; 24 hrs/day, every 30 min, every 15 min during rush hour, every hr after 11pm; at the southern end of State St., at the end of Broadway, ☎727-2508)*, which docks at the Staten Island Ferry Terminal, Battery Park's eastern neighbour. This ferry serves the most rural of New York's five boroughs. As the boat leaves the dock, there is a diminishing view of the skyscraper neighbourhood of Wall Street – the effect is spectacular. Passengers salute the Statue of Liberty on the way to Staten Island. If you return immediately, the whole trip takes about 45 minutes.

To return to Midtown by subway, take Train 1 (toward 242 St./ Van Cortland Park) from the South Ferry Station, Train 4 or 5 (toward Woodlawn or Dyre Ave.) from Bowling Green Station, or train N or R (toward Ditmars/Astoria Ave. or Continental Ave.) from Whitehall St./South Ferry. Buses M1, M6, and M15 also serve the Battery Park area.

EXPLORING

TOUR B: THE STATUE OF LIBERTY AND ELLIS ISLAND ★★★ (half a day)

The statue of Liberty was the first to greet the millions of immigrants to the United States before they reached Ellis Island, where their fate was once decided. Would they be permitted to set foot on the New World or be sent back to their native lands?

The two small islands in Upper New York Bay, on which the immigration centre and the Statue of Liberty were built in the late 19th century, are now veritable national shrines as well as great symbols of freedom to visitors from all over the world. The number of Americans whose ancestors passed through Ellis Island between 1892 and 1954 is estimated at 120 million, or approximately 40% of the United States' current population!

Ellis Island and Liberty Island — on which the Statue on Liberty was erected — are easily accessible by ferry from the piers at Battery Park. You may visit one or both of the islands, as you prefer. Long waiting periods are generally to be expected, however, as the islands are very popular tourist sites.

The best way to reach the piers of the Statue of Liberty/Ellis Island ferries is by subway. Get off train 1 at the South Ferry station or the N or R trains at the Bowling Green station. Tickets include admission to both islands and their facilities and can be purchased at the Castle Clinton (round, stone-built structure, see p 116) in Battery Park, then take one of the ferries leaving Manhattan every half-hour.

During the War of American Independence (1775-1783), the French directly contributed to the creation of the United States by deploying their army along the coasts of the future country. This action, though often perceived as a move in favour of freedom from British colonial rule, was also a tactical operation by King Louis XVI meant to weaken England. Whatever the underlying reason, the French intervention would create lasting bonds of friendship between the United States and France. Today, the **Statue of Liberty** ★★★ *(everyday 9:30am to 5pm; tickets sold at Castle Clinton in Battery Park, departures every half hour; Liberty Island, ☎363-7620, ferry information ☎269-5755)* is the foremost symbol of this friendship between the two countries.

To commemorate the centenary of American independence, obtained in 1776, Parisian sculptor Frédéric Auguste Bartholdi (1834-1904), who is also accredited with the *Lion of Belfort* (France), designed a statue without precedent in the art world. He in fact planned to graft 300 copper sheets to an iron structure, designed by engineer Gustave Eiffel, which he would fashion into a grand lady and officially name *La Liberté éclairant le monde* (Liberty Enlightening the World). He suggested that this colossal work of art be presented to the United States as a token of friendship between the two nations. After finding a

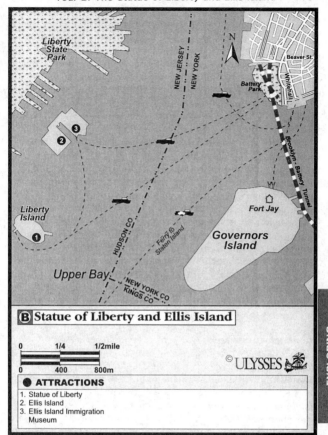

B Statue of Liberty and Ellis Island

| 0 | 1/4 | 1/2 mile |
| 0 | 400 | 800m |

© ULYSSES

● **ATTRACTIONS**
1. Statue of Liberty
2. Ellis Island
3. Ellis Island Immigration
   Museum

EXPLORING

site in New York Harbor, Bartholdi set to work in 1874, creating the figure whose serene demeanor and determined gaze were modelled on his mother's. The statue's bust, on which the American Declaration of Independence rests, and raised arm holding aloft the torch of liberty soon emerged from his studio in the *17e arrondissement* (administrative district). A bronze scale model of the project — 11 metres high itself — was later set up in Paris, at the foot of the Pont de Grenelle.

Meanwhile, the United States was busy building the pedestal for the statue. A former star fort, erected for the War of 1812, was used as a base for the embossed stone structure, designed by architect Richard Morris Hunt, on which a poem by Emma Lazarus extolling the virtues of the United States as the "land of the free", was engraved. After several financial and technical difficulties, the Statue of Liberty was finally unveiled with great pomp and ceremony on October 28, 1886. The statue underwent extensive restoration work from 1983 to 1986, giving it back its original lustre.

The Statue of Liberty stands 92 metres above sea level, or as high as a 25-story building. Eiffel's metallic structure alone measures 46 metres in height. The statue also boasts a museum, at the base of the pedestal, which chronicles the monument's history. The museum leads to the statue's three observation levels: the Promenade (2nd floor), where the queue is the shortest, the top of the pedestal (10th floor), which is easily accessible by elevator, and the statue's crown. To reach the latter platform, which can only accommodate two people at once, you must climb 22 stories. It takes about 2 to 3 hours to reach the top. The effort is well worth the wait, however. The ascent is not recommended for those subject to claustrophobia or a fear of heights. The same is true for people with heart trouble and the elderly.

Get back on the ferry, which then heads to Ellis Island.

Well before becoming an independent country, the United States had welcomed a number of Europeans, victims of ethnic and religious persecution. In the 17th century, the *Mayflower* pilgrims initiated a wave of immigration that would reach its peak between 1840 and 1925. Also migrating to the U.S. were many of the world's poor in search of a better economic future and the "American dream". After occupying the Castle Clinton for several decades, the immigration centre was set up on **Ellis Island ★★** *(everyday 9:30am to 5pm; tickets sold at Castle Clinton in Battery Park, departures every half hour; the ferry first stops at the Liberty Island pier before proceeding to Ellis Island; recorded message ☎363-3200 or 363-7620, ferry service information ☎269-5755)* in 1892. Closed in 1954, the vast complex has since been converted into a museum on US immigration.

After disembarking on Ellis Island, you will walk under a long glass awning (Beyer Blinder Belle, architect, 1989) to the

Registry Room of the Main Building (Boring and Tilton, architects, 1900). Though designed along contemporary lines, the awning is reminiscent of the original one, long since gone. The Great Hall, as it was called, whose ceiling is graced with Gustavino tiles, is the room where immigrants were inspected and processed by doctors and customs officers who could easily spot the sick ones from the balustrade up above. Those who were rejected on either medical or other grounds were taken to another part of the island, while their families and other immigrants looked on in panic. Ellis Island is consequently known as the "Island of Tears" to many.

Spread throughout the Registry Room are the exhibition rooms of the **Ellis Island Immigration Museum** ★ *(everyday 9:30am to 5pm, closed Christmas day; Ellis Island, ☎363-3200)*, which recount the history of the island and American immigration. Upon exiting the Main Building, you will notice a group of abandoned buildings covered in greenery on the other side of the pier. This was formerly the infectious diseases hospital, where several hundreds of thousands of people died. Finally, the cement wall demarcating the island is coupled with a long bronze plaque on which the names of several hundreds of thousands of immigrants who successfully passed through Ellis Island are engraved.

Take the ferry back to Battery Park.

 ## TOUR C: SOUTH STREET SEAPORT ★
(4 hours)

Before Wall Street financiers took over in the mid-19th century, shipowners and importers controlled the New York economy. They were clustered in the city's old port district, on the banks of the East River, along South Street, hence the name South Street Seaport. Among the vestiges of this era, now dwarfed by gigantic office towers, the most vital is definitely the Fulton Fish Market, which is still in operation. West of the market lies the South Street Seaport Historic District, a collection of old warehouses and shops that have been restored and converted into museums and galleries under the banner of the South Street Seaport Museum. The area is also home to a number of pubs and renowned fish and seafood restaurants, some of which have been open for over a century. The streets here have been closed to traffic and transformed into pleasant pedestrian malls extending onto piers moored with old sailboats. A sort of outdoor maritime museum, South Street Seaport is the perfect place to explore if you've had enough of the choruses of car horns and sirens in Midtown Manhattan. Once the heart of New York, South Street Seaport has ironically become one of the city's most atypical neighbourhoods – so much so that you sometimes feel like you're somewhere in New England. This tour offers a chance to admire the area's red-brick architecture and take in some lovely views of Brooklyn Heights and the Brooklyn Bridge.

The tour starts on State Street, in front of Battery Park. To get there by subway, take trains 4 or 5 to the South Ferry station. The last stop on the M1, M6 and M15 bus routes is also nearby. For a description of Battery Park, see p 116.

New York Unearthed ★ *(free admission; changing schedule; 17 State St., ☎748-8628)* is part of the South Street Seaport Museum, which is actually a collection of small museums highlighting various aspects of the city's history and everyday life in Lower Manhattan. This interpretation centre displays artefacts found during archaeological excavations carried out on urban construction sites (for a water main, a new building, etc.) – everyday objects from different eras, from prehistorical times up to the 1950s. Visitors can watch the curators restoring recent acquisitions in the workshop.

● ATTRACTIONS

1.	New York Unearthed	14.	Morgan Bank
2.	Shrine of St. Elizabeth Bayley Seton	15.	Manhattan Bank
3.	Our Lady of the Rosary Church	16.	RMS Queen Elizabeth Monument
4.	Broad Street	17.	Front Street
5.	Fraunces Tavern Museum	18.	South Street Seaport Historic District
6.	Vietnam Veteran's Plaza	19.	South Street Seaport Museum
7.	South Street	20.	Seamen's Church Institute
8.	First Precinct Station House	21.	Fulton Market Building
9.	India House	22.	Bogardus Building
10.	Statue of Abraham de Peyster	23.	Schermerhorn Row Block
11.	Delmonico's	24.	Fulton Fish Market
12.	Seligman Brothers Building	25.	Pier 17 Pavillion
13.	Seamen's Bank for Savings Headquarters		

◯ ACCOMMODATIONS

1.	Best Western Seaport Inn
2.	Manhattan Seaport Suites

◇ RESTAURANTS

1.	Bridge Café	6.	Sequoia
2.	Carmine's	7.	Sloppy Louie's
3.	Fraunces Tavern Restaurant	8.	The Yankee Clipper
4.	Fulton Café	9.	Zigolini's Lavazza
5.	Paris Café		

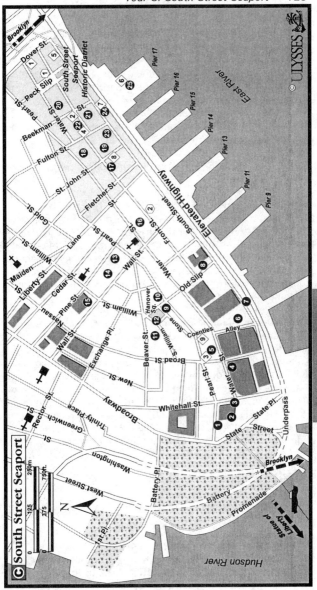

C South Street Seaport

Hudson River

East River

Elevated Highway

South Street Seaport Historic District

South Street

Pier 17
Pier 16
Pier 15
Pier 14
Pier 13
Pier 11
Pier 9

Dover St.
Peck Slip
Pearl St.
Beekman St.
Fulton St.
St. John St.
Fletcher St.
Gold St.
William St.
Maiden Lane
Liberty St.
Cedar St.
Pine St.
Nassau
Wall St.
Exchange Pl.
New St.
Broadway
Trinity Place
Greenwich St.
Rector St.
Whitehall St.
State Street
State Pl.
Battery Pl.
Washington
West Street
St. Pl.
Battery Promenade
Water St.
Front St.
Pearl St.
Lane
St.
Beaver St.
Hanover Sq.
S. William St.
Stone St.
Coenties Alley
Coenties Slip
Broad St.
Pearl St.
Water St.
Old Slip

Brooklyn

Statue of Liberty

Underpass

EXPLORING

© ULYSSES

N

0   125   250m
0   375   750ft.

The **Shrine of St. Elizabeth Bayley Seton** *(free admission; every day noon to 6pm; 7 State St., ☎269-6865)* is dedicated to the founder of the Sisters of Charity. The building, the former home of James Watson, is the only survivor of the many mansions that lined State Street and Broadway in the late 18th century. The right part of the house, in the Federal style, was built in 1793, while the left part, fronted by a peculiar colonnade that follows the curve of the street, was added in 1805. **Our Lady of the Rosary Church** *(8 State St.)*, on the north side of the house, is also part of the shrine.

Turn left on Water Street, then left on Broad Street and right on Pearl Street.

Broad Street *(between South and Wall Streets)* was laid out on the embankments of a canal modelled on the waterways of Amsterdam, dug by the Dutch around 1650. Due to its questionable usefulness – after all, the island of Manhattan already had kilometres of shoreline – and its stagnant waters, the canal was not destined for success. The road that superseded it in 1676 was unusually wide for the time, hence its name.

The **Fraunces Tavern Museum** ★ *($2.50; Mon to Fri 10am to 4pm, Sat noon to 4pm; 54 Pearl St., ☎425-1778)* is an obligatory stop for anyone retracing the various chapters of the American Revolution. Laid out on the second and third floors of the Fraunces Tavern (see p 320), this museum displays objects that once belonged to George Washington – including one of his teeth. Visitors will also find a recreation of the dining room where he bade farewell to his officers at the end of the War of Independence (December 4, 1783). The building itself is a reconstruction (1907) of a house built in 1719 for a Huguenot by the name of Étienne de Lancey. Samuel Fraunces, a black West Indian, opened his famous tavern in 1762, before becoming Washington's butler.

Turn right on Coenties Alley then walk across Water Street to the Vietnam Veterans Plaza.

The **Vietnam Veterans Plaza** *(at the corner of Coenties Alley and Water Street)* lies between two huge office complexes, where Coenties Slip was once located. There used to be several such slips, small artificial bays designed to shelter ships from bad weather, perpendicular to Water Street, but they were all filled in the second half of the 19th century. In the center of the plaza, there is a monument to the soldiers, both living and dead, who fought in the Vietnam War. Moving excerpts from letters and recordings sent by the soldiers to their family and friends have been engraved in blocks of glass in this work by William Britt Fellows, Peter Wormser and Joseph Ferrandino. A small amphitheatre completes the ensemble.

In the centre of 55 Water Street, there is a staircase leading to a raised square, at the foot of which lies **South Street** *(between State and Dover Streets)*. This waterfront street, for which the neighbourhood is named, was once lined with the biggest import-export companies in the United States. It's a sorry sight today, squeezed between outsized office towers and Franklin Delano Roosevelt Drive (FDRD), an elevated expressway. Tied to the pier straight ahead is an amazing, white hospital ship, which is still in operation. Also visible, on old piers, are the New York heliport and some indoor tennis courts under what looks like an inflated tent. The silhouettes of the old-fashioned buildings in the lovely Brooklyn Heights neighbourhood can be seen in the distance.

Head back to Water Street, turn right and stop at the corner of Old Slip.

At the south end of Old Slip, you'll see the **First Precinct Station House** *(100 Old Slip)* of the New York Police Department (NYPD), erected in 1911. This little gem, in the Italian Renaissance Revival style, has been converted into private offices.

Turn left to visit Hanover Square.

India House *(1 Hanover Sq.)* is an earlier example of the Italian Renaissance Revival style. Built in 1854, this brownstone housed the Cotton Exchange back when New York had a near monopoly on the exportation of cotton produced on the great plantations of the southern U.S., to the great displeasure of New Orleans merchants. It is now a private club and a restaurant. India House faces onto Hanover Square, which is graced with a **statue of Abraham de Peyster**, a wealthy Dutch importer who lived in New York back when it was New Amsterdam (George Bissel, 1896).

EXPLORING

Continue to William Street.

The triangular building at the corner of William Street has been a depressing sight ever since **Delmonico's** *(56 Beaver St.)*, to which it was home for nearly a century, closed in the 1980s. The restaurant was one of the oldest in New York and had been the most prestigious in town up until the 19th century. Wall Street millionaires swore by its oyster dishes and turtle soup. John Delmonico, a native of Switzerland, opened his famous business a few steps from here in 1831. Known as the first real French restaurant in New York (which now has hundreds), Delmonico's moved into these quarters in 1891. The columns of the portal were supposedly brought from Pompei by Mr. Delmonico himself.

The old **Seligman Brothers Building** *(1 William St.)*, on the left, is an unique skyscaper designed in the Italian Baroque Revival style. This lovely edifice by Francis Kimball (1907) features rusticated ashlar finishings and rounded pediments perfectly suited to the Banca Commerciale Italiana, to which it is now home. The water tower is cleverly concealed on the corner.

Turn right on Beaver Street and continue to Wall Street. The maze of narrow streets in this area serves as a reminder that you are in the heart of what was once New Amsterdam. Looking west on Wall Street, you can enjoy the traditional vista of Trinity Church (see p 277).

The rusticated stone of the old **Seamen's Bank for Savings Headquarters** *(74 Wall St.)*, erected in 1926, contrasts attractively with the ashlar, glass and metal of the neighbouring buildings. The bas-relief over the archway at the entrance bears witness to the edifice's original use. To the west stands the massive, 52-story **Morgan Bank** *(60 Wall St.)*, built in 1988 according to a design by architect Kevin Roche. It visually competes with the pyramidal roof of the neo-Gothic tower that once served as the headquarters of the **Manhattan Bank** *(40 Wall St.)*.

Turn right on Wall Street, then left on Water.

In front of Pine Street, you'll see a small glass cage containing the letters Q and E in bronze. These were taken from the prow of the *RMS Queen Elizabeth*, an ocean liner that went down off

Hong Kong in 1972. The **RMS Queen Elizabeth Monument** pays homage to the ship and its passengers. The neighbouring sculpture, entitled *Disk and Slab*, is the work of artist Yuyu Yang (1973).

Turn right on John Street (Burling Slip) and cross Front Street. You are now entering the South Street Seaport Historic District.

In this part of Lower Manhattan, Pearl Street, Water Street, **Front Street** and South Street have taken turns being the waterfront artery on the East River, as the embankments have been filled in bit by bit since the time of the Dutch. The business district is now nearly twice its original size. Front Street ran right along the banks of the river for the entire first half of the 18th century, hence its name.

After the opening of the Erie Canal (1825) finally made it possible to transport merchandise to the heart of the North American continent, New York became the largest port in the United States. A huge transhipment complex was added to the little fishing port founded on the banks of the East River in the 17th century. All this activity centred around South Street, which soon acquired the nickname "Street of Ships", after the forest of masts around the piers along its east side. However, the advent of power-driven, heavy-tonnage boats at the end of the 19th century caused port activities to shift over to the banks of the Hudson River, on the west side of Manhattan. Deeper than the East River, this big waterway permanently supplanted South Street after 1914. When the local fishing industry started losing ground to New England, it was the last nail in the neighbourhood's coffin. The red-brick warehouses, three-quarters abandoned, were torn down one by one to make way for the big office towers of the business district.

Fortunately, a small group of New Yorkers succeeded in saving a few local buildings, almost all of them clustered around the fish market, thus creating what later became the **South Street Seaport Historic District** ★★ *(between Maiden Lane and Dover St., and from the East River piers to Pearl St.)*, protected by the New York Landmarks Preservation Commission since 1977. These architecture buffs sold the air rights of the smaller buildings so they could be transferred to properties farther south, thus allowing for the construction of the colossal towers we saw earlier along Water Street.

EXPLORING

The money collected from these sales went to pay for the ongoing restoration of 11 blocks of old warehouses and the establishment of the **South Street Seaport Museum** ★★ *($6; Apr to Sep, every day 10am to 6pm, Thu until 8pm; Oct to Mar, Wed to Mon 10am to 5pm, closed Tue; in 17 different places in and around the historic district, ☎748-8600, cruise schedule ☎748-8786, ⌐ 748-8610, www.southstseaport.org).* This institution, founded in 1967 thanks to the efforts of Peter Stanford, aims to familiarize the public with the history of New York's old port. It includes conventional galleries, as well as sailboats tied up at the piers along South Street, which may be toured and even offer short cruises. The museum also hosts all sorts of activities (demonstrations of 19th-century working methods, treasure hunts, etc.). It is designed to be interactive, especially where children are concerned. Tickets may be purchased anywhere in the historic district, so you can start your tour wherever you wish – simply show your ticket at each attraction. The various parts of the museum are described below, but have not been numbered on the map to avoid over-crowding of the area.

The **Norway Galleries** *(171 John St.)*, in the A.A. Low Building (once occupied by a company that imported Chinese merchandise), presents temporary exhibitions on pirates, the pearl trade and other maritime subjects. In the neighbouring building, to the north, tots can learn about history and navigation at the **Children's Center** *(165 John St.)*.

Go back to Front Street. Take a right and walk to Fulton Street, which has been turned into a pleasant pedestrian mall covered with paving stones. Turn left.

The **Titanic Memorial Lighthouse** *(at the corner of Fulton and Water Streets)* is dedicated to those who died when the supposedly unsinkable ship hit an iceberg and foundered. Many of the victims were New Yorkers. The lighthouse originally stood atop the old Seamen's Church Institute at Coenties Slip (1913), and a black ball used to slide down its wall to tell sailors at the port when it was noon.

Head north on Water Street.

Ocean liners are the focal point at the **Whitman Gallery** ★ *(209 Water St.)*, which retraces the romantic history of transatlantic liners and their passengers through a lovely collection of old posters and model ships. Next door, **Bowne and Company, Stationers** *(211 Water St.)*, a late 19th-century printing works, shows visitors how a printing press from that era operated. You can even help make your own little souvenir. Lovely greeting cards are also sold on the premises. Immediately to the north, the **Melville Gallery** *(213 Water St.)* presents exhibitions of artwork inspired by ships and the sea.

Cross Beekman Street.

The **Seamen's Church Institute ★ (20)** *(241 Water St.)* is a boarding house and social club for sailors passing through town. Founded on a small boat in 1834, it was originally just a simple chapel where shady characters would gather. After relocating to a building at Coenties Slip and then another in front of Battery Park, the Seamen's Church Institute moved into its present quarters on Water Street in 1993. Lovely model sailboats made by seamen are displayed in a room on the ground floor.

Head back to Beekman Street and turn left, then take a right on Front Street.

On the left, you'll see the **Fulton Market Building ★** *(at the corner of Fulton and Front Streets)*. A reconstruction of the old public market that stood here until 1948, it was erected in 1983, thus filling in an unsightly gap in the historic district. The new building has some pleasant outdoor cafes, as well as a workshop where small crafts are built.

The austere metal-frame building on the northwest corner of Fulton Street is a reconstruction of the **Bogardus Building** *(15 Fulton St.)*, which was built in 1848 at the corner of Washington and Murray Streets. Its demountable façade, designed by James Bogardus, was the most daring piece of architecture of its time in the United States.

Turn left on Fulton Street.

The best preserved group of buildings in the South Street Seaport Historic District is the **Schemerhorn Row Block ★** *(2-18 Fulton St.)*, a block of old warehouses bounded by Fulton, Front and South Streets. These red-brick buildings, erected in

EXPLORING

1811, are reminiscent of the architecture of Boston, Massachusetts and Portland, Maine. The **Museum's Visitors' Center and Store** *(12-14 Fulton St.)* sells lovely items related in one way or another to sailing (books, models, postcards, etc.).

As you make your way towards the sailboats tied up at Pier 16, you might find yourself wondering if the elevated expressway that mars the view will one day be destroyed. As of yet, however, you have no choice but to walk under it to reach the piers, where, on your left, you'll see the main building of the **Fulton Fish Market ★**, the largest fish market in North America. This place comes alive just before 11pm then winds down around 8am, Sunday through Thursday. Huge trucks from New England, New Brunswick and Nova Scotia arrive at night to unload their cargo of fish and seafood, sold mainly to wholesalers. The South Street Seaport Museum offers early morning guided tours of the market during the summer, enabling visitors to see the merchants in action. If you go, watch out for the vehicles coming and going and make sure not to get in anyone's way!

Children will be fascinated by the collection of old boats at the South Street Seaport Museum. Three of these ships, permanently docked here, may be toured. The biggest is the **Peking ★**, a four-master which was built in 1911 and was among the last sailing cargo ships launched in the early 20th century. Its neighbour, the **Wavertree** (1885), a three-master from Southampton, England, was acquired by the museum in 1996. The **Ambrose**, on the other side of Pier 16, is a lighthouse boat built in 1908. All three ships have seen better days and are currently being restored, a process that will take several years. While on board, make sure to keep a close eye on the little ones, as there are open hatches on the various decks, as well as rusted machinery with sharp edges. The museum has three other ships that offer short cruises on the East River *($16 per person)*: the **Pioneer ★**, an 1885 schooner, the **Lettie G. Howard**, built in 1893 and protected by the National Historic Landmarks Commission, and the tugboat **W.O. Decker**, used only for private cruises. The boats operated by Seaport Liberty Cruises Harbor Excursions are tied up at the end of Pier 16 (see p 69). The small building near Pier 15 is the **Maritime Crafts Center ★**, a workshop where you can watch artisans carving figureheads and model boats. They will gladly answer any questions you might have.

Go to Pier 17 and walk all the way to the end.

The **Pier 17 Pavillion** ★★, built by a Boston company, is a shopping centre with lots of souvenir shops and a number of restaurants with large outdoor seating areas. The tip of the pier offers a classic view of the East River, Brooklyn Heights and the Brooklyn Bridge. If you turn around, you also can admire the skyscrapers of the business district.

To reach the nearest subway station, walk up Fulton Street to William Street. The station bears the name of the intersection and is served by trains 2, 3 and 4. For those who'd prefer to stay above ground, the M15 runs along Water Street.

TOUR D: BATTERY PARK CITY ★ (two hours)

Truly a city within a city, Battery Park City was built in 1979 west of the financial district, on vast embankments jutting into the Hudson River, which were created when the basins that separated the steamboat docks were filled in. After mulling over many proposals, including some that were outright utopian, the Port Authority, which owned the land, chose to emulate traditional New York architecture and urban planning by constructing a complex of apartment towers and urban parks that is evocative of Riverside Drive and Central Park.

Battery Park City is bordered by a long riverside promenade that allows New Yorkers to have direct contact with the water and to benefit from magnificent views over the wide river, a too rare commodity in this extremely dense, inward-looking city. And, in this unique case, no highway mars pedestrian access to the shore. Because of the wealth of these media in Battery Park City, this tour is almost entirely dedicated to the art and architecture of the two last decades of the 20th century.

The tour begins on the plaza of the World Trade Center (for a description of the WTC, see p 107). Walk along the right side of North Tower (1 World Trade Center) to North Bridge, which leads to the World Financial Center's Winter Garden. To reach the departure point of the tour, go down to the Cortland Street/World Trade Center subway station (served by the

EXPLORING

1 train), or to the World Trade Center station, the southern terminus of the E train. The best bus route is the M10.

On the way to Battery Park City, pause on North Bridge, which spans West Street and offers a view on the right of an imposing brown brick building that stands out from its neighbours. This is the **Barclay-Vesey Building ★** *(140 West St.)*, the first Art Deco skyscraper in North America, designed in 1923 by the very talented Voorhees and Gmelin. This building, originally erected for the New York Telephone Company, influenced the conception of high rises for the next two decades, especially with its terraced volumes, its many vertical lines and its pre-Columbian-accented geometric motifs.

North Bridge opens onto the World Financial Center's impressive **Winter Garden ★★**. This vast glassed-in atrium, planted with 16 Washington Robusta palms, is a 40-metre-high, vaulted semi-public space surrounded by shops and restaurants. Its main staircase frequently serves as an amphitheatre for cultural events (concerts, circuses, dance performances, etc.) organized by the Arts and Events Program of the WFC. The Winter Garden was immortalized on film in a famous scene featuring a drunken writer played by Bruce Willis in *The Bonfire of the Vanities*.

Exit at the other end of the atrium which opens onto the esplanade of Battery Park City.

Three of the four grey granite towers of the **World Financial Center ★**, which regroups businesses closely connected to the New York Stock Market, are visible on either side of Winter Garden. The tower on the right *(1 World Financial Center)* houses the head offices of Dow Jones & Company, the famous brokerage that gave its name to the New York Stock Market index; the dome-crowned skyscraper *(2 World Financial Center)* is the world headquarters of Merrill Lynch; while the tallest of the three, the one topped by a pyramidal roof *(3 World Financial Center)*, is the global headquarters of American Express. The ensemble was constructed by architect Cesar Pelli in 1984.

The towers of the WFC hem in **North Cove ★**, a sort of artificial bay that shelters a sailing harbour for the luxury yachts of New York millionaires. Many works of art have been

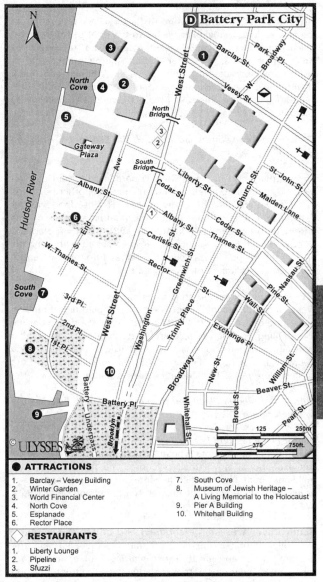

D Battery Park City

EXPLORING

● **ATTRACTIONS**

1. Barclay – Vesey Building
2. Winter Garden
3. World Financial Center
4. North Cove
5. Esplanade
6. Rector Place
7. South Cove
8. Museum of Jewish Heritage – A Living Memorial to the Holocaust
9. Pier A Building
10. Whitehall Building

◇ **RESTAURANTS**

1. Liberty Lounge
2. Pipeline
3. Sfuzzi

integrated into the architecture of Battery Park City, such as the two stainless-steel piles visible to the right of North Cove. These sculptures, simply called *Pylons*, are the work of American artist Martin Puryear (1995). Another creation closer by features extracts of poems by Walt Whitman and Frank O'Hara inscribed in bronze and affixed to the gate that separates us from the bay. This last work was realized by sculptor Siah Armajani in 1986.

Skirt North Cove southward to reach the Esplanade along the Hudson.

The southern part of North Cove is bordered by the Gateway Plaza residential complex, which precedes the other buildings in Battery Park City by a few years (1979). Up next, the **Esplanade** ★★ is without doubt the greatest success of this enormous urban project. Created in 1985 by urban planners Cooper, Eckstut and Associates, it is equipped with benches and street lamps, reproducing the street furniture in Central Park, along a distance of 1.5 kilometres.

The strange colonnade that pops up like a mirage at the western end of Albany Street is actually a sculpture of reddish aggregate by Ned Smyth (1987). *The Upper Room* symbolizes a crumbling Egyptian temple and in its centre is a long table specially designed for chess players. A little further along is the *Rector Gate* by R. M. Fisher (1988), a work worthy of Fritz Lang's *Metropolis*. This "door" accesses Rector Place.

Turn left on Rector Place and then right on South End Avenue to reach South Cove.

Rector Place *(around Rector Park)* is surrounded by tall towers full of luxury apartments whose sale prices are only rivalled by the exceptional views their balconies and patios offer. The buildings' brick construction accented by multiple recesses is very much evocative of the Prewar Apartments on Central Park West.

South Cove ★★ *(at the southern end of South End Ave.)* symbolically unites the city and nature, the past and the present, water and earth. These marriages of opposites are represented by groups of rocks, plants, metallic structures, and logs that recall old piers. Dreamed up by three creative minds that work in different media, sculptor Mary Miss, architect Stanton Eckstut, and landscape architect Susan Child, this sprawling environmental artwork was inaugurated in 1988.

Starting in the 17th century, New York was home to a large Jewish community that would grow with succeeding waves of anti-Semitic persecution throughout the world. Thousands of Jews, fleeing the tzarist pogroms in Russia, established themselves here at the end of the 19th century, making this American metropolis the largest Jewish city in the world. These waves of immigration were followed by Jews escaping the Nazi regime beginning in 1933, often leaving behind family members who would perish a few years later in Hitler's death camps. The **Museum of Jewish Heritage – A Living Memorial to the Holocaust** ★★ *($7; &; Sun to Wed 9am to 5pm, Thu 9am to 8pm, Fri 9am to 2pm, closed Sat and on Jewish holidays; 18 First Pl., ☎968-1800)* retraces the journey of the Jewish community in the 20th century on a global scale. The museum building, inaugurated in 1997, is the work of architects Kevin Roche, John Dinkeloo and Associates. Its hexagonal form is evocative of the six million Jews who died in concentration camps during World War II. On the ground floor, objects from the daily lives of the various Jewish communities of Europe and the Americas are displayed. The second level is dedicated to the Holocaust, presented through the testimonials of survivors of the tragedy (not for the fainthearted). Finally, the third level deals with the creation of the State of Israel and the evolution of the Jewish community in the United States after the war.

Skirt the museum along the Hudson River walkway.

From the Esplanade, the Statue of Liberty is visible in New York Bay. Closer to shore are three environmental sculptures. The first, *Ape & Cat (At the Dance)*, a figurative representation in poured bronze of a cat and an ape dancing on the grass from 1993, reflects the intimacy of a couple that is sought by so many millions of New Yorkers. It is the work of Jim Dine, who is better known as one of the apostles of 1960s Pop Art. The second sculpture was created in 1996 by British artist Tony Cragga and is entitled *Resonating Bodies*. The work consists of two bronze pieces that resemble a lute and a tuba. Waves of energy disturb the surfaces of the two "instruments". The third sculpture is a major work by French-born sculptor Louise Bourgeois, an eccentric ultra-perfectionist who is hard to peg

EXPLORING

down and who has lived in New York for over 50 years. Her sculpture for Battery Park City, made up of six groups of bronze hands set at the edge of the water, is entitled *The Welcoming Hands* and evokes the reception offered to immigrants from around the world by New Yorkers throughout the course of history.

Head to Battery Place, which runs along Battery Park.

The **Pier A Building** *(corner of Battery Pl. and West St.)*, at the very southern tip of Battery Park City, is the last vestige of the old warehouses that were dotted all along the circumference of Manhattan Island in the 19th century. This pier and the various structures on it were erected in 1886. The public clock tower was added in 1919 as a memorial to sailors who died in the First World War.

Battery Place is dominated by the beaux-arts bulk of the **Whitehall Building** *(17 Battery Pl.)*, built between 1902 and 1910. The shadows and winds caused by this enormous "pile of stones" motivated municipal authorities to endorse an alternative to its tall vertical walls that push straight up into the sky. So developed the terraced high rise, which minimized whirlwinds and maximized sunshine on surrounding sidewalks.

For a description of Battery Park, see p 116 in the Financial District tour. To return to Midtown by subway, take train 1 (toward 242 Street/Van Cortland Park) at the South Ferry station, or trains 4 or 5 (toward Woodlawn or Dyre Avenue) at the Bowling Green station, or trains N or R (toward Ditmars/Astoria or Continental Avenues) at the Whitehall St./South Ferry station. Buses M1, M6 and M15 also serve the Battery Park area.

TOUR E: CHINATOWN, LITTLE ITALY AND THE LOWER EAST SIDE ★ (4 hours)

Since its foundation, New York has been known as a cosmopolitan city that regroups people of various ethnic and linguistic origins. While the various northern European ethnic groups who settled here in the 17th and 18th centuries lived side by side fairly easily, it was another story for the more culturally divergent groups who came over in the tidal waves of

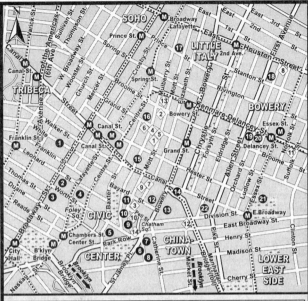

E | Chinatown, Little Italy and the Lower East Side

0   250   500m
0   750   1500ft.

© ULYSSES

EXPLORING

● ATTRACTIONS

1.	TriBeCa	11.	Museum of Chinese in the Americas
2.	New York Life Insurance Company	12.	Edward Mooney House
3.	Jacob K. Javits Federal Office Building	13.	Confucius Plaza
		14.	Manhattan Bridge
4.	NYC Health and Sanitation Departments	15.	Mulberry Street
		16.	New York City Police Headquarters
5.	Chatham Towers	17.	Old St. Patrick's Cathedral
6.	Shearith Israel Graveyard	18.	The Bowery
7.	St. James Catholic Church	19.	Orchard Street
8.	Mariner's Temple	20.	Lower East Side Tenement Museum
9.	Mott Street	21.	Essex St. and Hester St.
10.	Church of the Transfiguration	22.	Eldridge Street Synagogue

◇ RESTAURANTS

1.	Caffè Palermo	8.	Katz
2.	Caffè Roma	9.	Mandarin Court
3.	Chinatown Ice Cream Factory	10.	Mueng Thai
4.	Ferrara's	11.	Ratner's
5.	Florio's Grill & Cigar Bar	12.	Triple Eight Palace
6.	Il Palazzo	13.	Umberto's Clam House
7.	Jing Fong Restaurant	14.	Vietnam

immigration of the 19th century. Tension and rejection, along with the natural urge to stay among one's own in a new environment, engendered the creation of ethnic neighbourhoods throughout the city. Among the first of these were Chinatown, Little Italy and the Lower East Side, which developed next to each other on either side of Canal Street.

Chinatown, New York's traditionally Chinese sector, occupies a limited area around its main artery, Mott Street, but the growing Chinese community is now spreading into Little Italy to the north and the Lower East Side to the east. The neighbourhood's exotic fruit stands set on narrow sidewalks, its many restaurants and its Far East gift shops make it very popular with tourists and with the entire New York Asian community, for whom it is a weekend meeting place. Chinese New Year, on the first full moon after January 20, is celebrated here with a great many fireworks and multicolored dragons.

Little Italy is now pretty much limited to Mulberry Street; the rest of the city's traditionally Italian neighbourhood has been absorbed into Chinatown. But this road is lined with a multitude of restaurants equipped with outdoor patios that attracts crowds of suburban New Jerseyites on Saturday nights. The perpetually festive atmosphere that reigns on this modest, flag-lined alley peaks between September 10 and 19 every year when the festival of San Gennaro (St. Januarius) is celebrated. This religious festival in homage to the patron saint of Naples is the pretext for the organization of a colourful festival that highlights Italian cuisine.

The Lower East Side has evolved into a mixed neighbourhood. The tens of thousands of Jews who once lived here started to desert the area in 1950, but precious bits of evidence of their bygone way of life remain. In the last two decades of the 19th century, 1.4 million Jews fled persecution in Poland and Russia. Almost half of them settled in the Lower East Side, bringing with them various Eastern European traditions that notably gave birth to what is now commonly perceived as American cuisine: hot dogs, hamburgers, smoked meat sandwiches, bagels, pickles, and so on.

This tour combines visits to Chinatown, Little Italy and the Lower East Side, beginning at the corner of Broadway and Canal Street, which is served by three subway stations all called "Canal Street". These are on the J, N, R and 6 train lines. Buses M1 and M6 travel south on Broadway and stop at the intersection of Canal Street.

Before venturing into Chinatown, walk south on Broadway for a glimpse at a few beautiful examples of the iron-framework architecture of **TriBeCa**. This 19th-century warehouse district roughly forms a triangle south of Canal Street – its name is short for "Triangle Below Canal Street". The buildings on its cross streets (White, Franklin, Leonard) are rife with ornamentation cast right into the iron inspired by the Italian Renaissance style. The main concentration of buildings with this feature is in SoHo (see p 143).

The former headquarters of the **New York Life Insurance Company** ★ stand at 346 Broadway. Designed by the architectural firm of McKim, Mead and White in 1898, the building is crowned by an elegant public clock and is unusually long, extending all the way to Lafayette Street.

Turn left on Worth Street.

On the right appears the hulking mass of the **Jacob K. Javits Federal Office Building** *(26 Federal Plaza)*, which houses, unsurprisingly, the New York offices of the federal government as well as the US Customs Courthouse, which hears cases related to international trade.

The **NYC Health and Sanitation Departments** *(125 Worth St.)* building is in the vast Civic Center complex, which is actually part of the Financial District (see p 102). It was created in 1935 in a purified Art Deco style not unlike that favoured by the dictatorships of the era, and it houses, among others, the offices of the agency responsible for domestic trash collection – no mean feat in a city like New York.

The tour skirts Foley Square and then reaches the front of **Chatham Towers** *(corner of Worth St. and Baxter St.)*, one of the city's most successful public housing projects of the 1960s. The buildings' rough-concrete construction makes them an archetypical example of modernist Brutalism.

Turn left on Mott Street. An optional excursion to the oldest Jewish cemetery in the United States is possible: continue

EXPLORING

along Worth Street to Chatham Square, the centre of which is graced by a monument to Chinese-American heroes of the World Wars, then turn right onto St. James Place.

The Jews of Spain and Portugal were expelled from the Iberian Peninsula when the last Moorish territories there were recaptured by the Catholic sovereigns Ferdinand and Isabella in 1492. Many of the exiled sought refuge in Spanish and Portuguese colonies in the Americas, but they were outcast in turn from these territories and ultimately reached New York in the middle of the 17th century. The only existing legacy of this era is the **Shearith Israel Graveyard ★** *(55 St. James Pl.)*, a tiny Sephardic Jewish cemetery that opened in 1683. Although it closed in 1828, it still encloses a few tombstones, making it the oldest Jewish cemetery in the United States.

Two neoclassical churches erected in the image of the temples of antiquity stand on the little streets that hem in the cemetery. These are **St. James Catholic Church** *(32 St. James St.)*, built in 1837, and **Mariner's Temple** *(12 Oliver St.)*, a Baptist church from 1844 that serves the Chinese community.

Return to Mott Street to resume the main tour (if you have opted for the detour above).

Once on **Mott Street ★★**, the tour truly penetrates the heart of New York's Chinatown. This is a little like a trip down memory lane because this part of Chinatown has changed very little since the turn of the century. Today, Mott Street is home to many shops and restaurants that attract Chinese-American families on weekend outings; only the medicinal herb dealers evoke the aura of mystery that once enveloped the area.

The **Church of the Transfiguration** *(25 Mott St.)* seems lost amid the hustle and bustle of Chinatown. This little Chinese Catholic church was designed in the neo-Gothic style in 1801, which makes it one of the earliest examples of this type of architecture in North America.

The small **Museum of Chinese in the Americas ★** *($3; Tue to Sun noon to 5pm; 70 Mulberry St., ☎619-4785)*, housed upstairs in an former school, recounts the adventuresome history of Chinese emigration to the New World.

Turn right on Bayard Street.

Edward Mooney House *(18 Bowery)*, a small Georgian residence built in 1785 that is the oldest existing row house on Manhattan Island, is set on the Bowery (see p 142) between Bayard and Pell Street. In an amusing coincidence it was originally built for a horse breeder and it now serves as a betting office for the races at the New York Tracks.

Turn left on Bowery.

The east side of the Bowery is occupied by the immense complex called **Confucius Plaza** *(between Chatham Sq. and the on ramps to the Manhattan Bridge)*, in front of which sits a statue of the famous philosopher who was the namesake of this 1975 institutional and residential development.

The construction of the **Manhattan Bridge** ★★ *(east of Bowery, at the end of Canal St.)* in 1905 greatly disrupted daily life for Lower East Side residents, but on the other hand it endowed this neglected sector of the city with a grandiose monument. The new suspension bridge over the East River also alleviated the heavy flow of traffic on the Brooklyn Bridge, located a few hundred metres to the south. The triumphal arch at the entrance to the bridge is the work of architects Carrère and Hastings. It is a beaux-arts horseshoe-shaped structure, the central section of which echoes the configuration of Porte Saint-Denis in Paris. The arch celebrates the 1898 merger of the cities of Brooklyn and New York and presents itself as the "entrance gate" to the borough of Brooklyn across the river.

Turn left on Canal Street and then right on Mulberry Street.

Ironically, the **New York City Police Headquarters** ★★ *(240 Centre St.)* was once located in Little Italy, two steps from Mulberry Street. The building, which has since been transformed into luxury apartments, was put up in 1909 in the English neo-baroque style, and it displays such refined elegance that it is easy to forget that this architectural achievement was meant for police officers. The police department left the premises in 1973, moving to offices closer to city hall.

Turn right on Broome Street to return to Mulberry Street, then go north by turning left.

EXPLORING

Before St. Patrick's Cathedral on Fifth Avenue (see p 178) could be completed, the modest **Old St. Patrick's Cathedral ★** *(260 Mulberry St.)* housed the seat of the Catholic bishopric of New York. It was built in 1815 by Joseph-François Mangin, who is also credited with the design for New York City Hall. This biracial architect – a rarity in the era – had great talent. His cathedral is typical of the very first neo-Gothic buildings, combining neoclassical shapes and medieval decoration. Its interior was redone in 1868 following a fire. The fact that the former seat of the church in New York was placed under the protection of Patrick, the patron saint of Ireland, is testament to the strong presence of Irish Catholics in the area before the massive arrival of Italians beginning in 1880.

Turn right on East Houston Street. Cross the Bowery and then turn right on Orchard Street. The tour leaves Little Italy now for the Lower East Side.

The **Bowery** *(between Park Row and Houston St.)* follows the country lane that once led to the family farm of Peter Stuyvesant, the last governor of New Amsterdam (1647-1664). His farm, or *bouwerij* in Old Dutch, occupied a vast parcel of land north of Houston Street. The Bowery was urbanized at the very beginning of the 19th century and quickly became New York's first red-light district. It was home to many taverns, brothels, and theatres specializing in tasteless vaudeville and "scenes" featuring young people in their barest apparel – nude dancing was not invented yesterday!

New immigrants to New York traditionally established themselves in the Lower East Side before relocating to other parts of the city or moving to other cities. Those who stayed longest in this stopover area were Jews, and as a consequence the neighbourhood is mostly marked by their culture. At the beginning of the 20th century, this was one of the most densely populated neighbourhoods in the world. For many decades, its narrow, dark tenement apartments were the only world poor families would know.

Shortly after their arrival, immigrants often had to part with the last of their personal possessions (jewellery, clothing, and so-on) to pay the rent, so they would go down to **Orchard Street** *(between East Houston and Canal St.)* and pawn these objects in the shops there. Today, a motley assembly of stores that attract bargain-hunting New Yorkers share the commercial space on this artery.

A visit to the **Lower East Side Tenement Museum** ★ *($8; guided tours only; Tue to Fri 1:30pm, 2:30pm and 3:30pm, Sat and Sun every hr between 11am and 4pm; 97 Orchard St., ☎431-0233)* brings to light the lifestyle of these late 19th-century immigrants, exposing the spaces, joys and pains of their experiences. Set up in partially restored former tenements, the museum re-creates the daily life of this period through exhibitions and animators in period costume.

Continue south on Orchard Street, then turn left on Broome Street and right on Essex Street.

The intersection of **Essex Street** and **Hester Street** formed the heart of the Jewish neighbourhood in the Lower East Side at the beginning of the 20th century. A few representative shops, which sell such religious paraphernalia as kippas and menorahs, are still to be found here.

Turn right on Canal Street then left on Eldridge Street, which adjoins the on ramps to the Manhattan Bridge.

Once one of the largest synagogues in the New World, the Congregation K'hal Adath Jeshurun Synagogue, better known as the **Eldridge Street Synagogue** ★ *(admission charge; guided tours only; Tue to Thu 11:30am and 2:30pm, Sun every hr between 11am and 4pm; 12 Eldridge St., south of Canal St.)*, occupies an 1887 building designed by the Herter Brothers in a half-Romanesque, half-Moorish style that reflects its ties to both the Sephardic and Ashkenazi communities.

Head back to Canal Street and turn left to return to the departure point of the tour. Take note that the M1 bus travels north on Lafayette Street (the first street west of Mulberry). To continue sightseeing in the area see the SoHo tour, p 143.

EXPLORING

 TOUR F: SOHO ★   (2 hours)

Nowhere else in the world will you find a more impressive collection of buildings with cast-iron façades than in tiny SoHo (from "**So**uth of **Ho**uston Street"). Erected between 1850 and 1890, these amazing Renaissance-Revival edifices were originally clothing factories. Since the 1970s, however, they have been filled art galleries, furniture designers and fashionable restaurants. These businesses are among the best examples of the American avant-garde in the fields of industrial design, visual arts and dining. In the last century, the area was nicknamed "Hell's Hundred Acres" because of the inhuman working conditions in the factories here. Declared a Landmark District in 1973 and renamed, more flatteringly, the Cast Iron District, it has since become one of the most attractive neighbourhoods in downtown Manhattan.

Our tour of SoHo starts at the corner of Broadway and West Canal Street, at the exit of the Canal Street subway station (N and R trains). You can also get there by taking the M1 bus, which runs along Broadway for part of its route. Head west on West Canal Street then turn right onto Greene.

Walking up **Greene Street** ★★ *(between West Canal St. and Prince St.)*, you can admire a number of façades made of cast iron, a material that made it possible to create elaborate designs at low cost and also reduce the risk of fire. Furthermore, because the interior structure is partially braced by cast-iron pillars, machinery that would have been too heavy for wooden pillars to support could be installed on any floor. Most of the façades along Greene Street are in the Italian Renaissance Revival style, characterized by projecting cornices and multiple entablatures supported by rows of small columns set between the openings.

Turn right on Prince Street.

When you get to **Prince Street** ★ *(between West Broadway and Broadway)*, you'll see the façade of a building depicted in trompe-l'œil on the side of #112-114 Prince Street (Richard Haas, 1975), to the left. Over the years, this lovely work of art has become a veritable symbol of SoHo's renaissance.

Turn right on Broadway.

The **Guggenheim Museum SoHo** ★★ *($6; Wed to Fri and Sun 11am to 6pm, Sat 11am to 8pm; 575 Broadway, at the corner of Prince, ☎423-3500)* is an offshoot of the famous

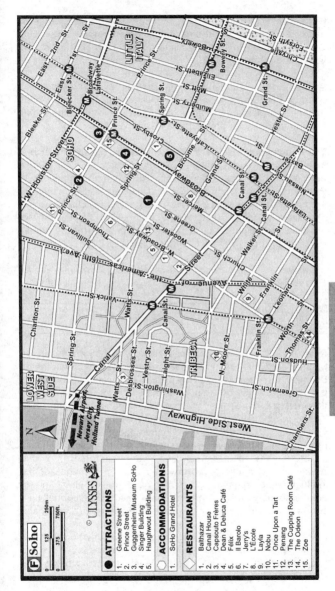

F Soho

0 125 250m
0 375 750ft.

© ULYSSES

● **ATTRACTIONS**
1. Greene Street
2. Prince Street
3. Guggenheim Museum SoHo
4. Singer Building
5. Haughwout Building

⬡ **ACCOMMODATIONS**
1. SoHo Grand Hotel

◇ **RESTAURANTS**
1. Balthazar
2. Canal House
3. Capsouto Frères
4. Dean & Deluca Café
5. Félix
6. Il Barolo
7. Jerry's
8. L'Ecole
9. Layla
10. Nobu
11. Once Upon a Tart
12. Penang
13. The Cupping Room Café
14. The Odeon
15. Zoe

Guggenheim Museum on Fifth Avenue (see p 230), which is devoted almost exclusively to contemporary art. The Guggenheim SoHo, set up inside an old 19th-century store, was inaugurated in 1992.

A little farther south, the **Singer Building** ★ *(561 Broadway)* was the first Singer sewing machine factory. Its façade, with its metal, glass and terracotta curtain wall, was truly revolutionary for its time (Ernest Flagg, 1904).

The **Haughwout Building** ★ *(488 Broadway)* boasts one of the loveliest cast-iron façades in SoHo. It is also one of the oldest buildings in the area, dating from 1857. Once completed, it was equipped with the world's first safe passenger elevator. This invention, developed by an American named Elisha Graves Otis, revolutionized architecture by making it possible to increase the height of buildings without making office clerks huff and puff on the stairs all day.

To return to the starting point of the tour, continue down Broadway to Canal Street.

TOUR G: GREENWICH VILLAGE ★★
(3 hours)

New York City was once localized on the southern tip of Manhattan Island; the remaining territory was mostly farmland. Between the farms were a few peaceful hamlets dominated by the bell towers of their respective Anglican churches. Greenwich Village – pronounced "gren-itch" and not "green-witch" (this is how real New Yorkers pronounce it!) – was one of these hamlets. Founded in about 1730 on the site of a former Algonquin village, which later became a small Dutch market town, Greenwich was integrated into the American metropolis a century later. Several vestiges of its independence remain, of which the most eloquent is unquestionably its network of roads, laid out diagonally in contrast with that of avenues and streets in other boroughs.

Since 1850, Greenwich Village has been synonymous with a certain individualistic bohemian lifestyle, as opposed to the "communal" bohemia of theatre people that has beset the Upper West Side. Writers, painters and sculptors were the first to settle here, following in Edgar Allan Poe and Mark Twain's footsteps. During the Roaring Twenties, penniless artists took up residence here at patron and sculptress Gertrude Vanderbilt Whitney's instigation, she who would later found the beautiful American art museum bearing her name (see p 225). After 1950, beatniks gathered in Greenwich-Village coffee-houses, which then compared to those of Saint-Germain, in Paris. During the same period, the Village saw the advent of the gay revolution, which swept across North America during the seventies. These days, Greenwich Village is no longer considered the main homosexual hub of New York City, a role partially taken over by Chelsea (see p 153). The lightning increase in the price of houses, combined with the omnipresence of suburbanites in the restaurants and bars, has profoundly changed the look of the district's narrow streets.

The tour of Greenwich Village begins at the corner of Fifth Avenue and West 14th Street. The starting point is easily reached by subway (Union Square/14th Street Station, where the N, R, 4 and 6 trains stop; 14th Street Station, where the F train stops) or by bus (routes M1, M2, M3, M5 and M6). You can also get here on foot from the hotels in Midtown, by walking down Fifth Avenue to West 14th Street.

Take Fifth Avenue, heading south.

The **Forbes Magazine Galleries** ★★ *(free admission; ᵺ; Tue to Sat 10am to 4pm; 62 Fifth Ave., at West 12th St., ☎206-5549)*, on the same premises as the magazine itself, display press tycoon Malcolm Forbes' personal collection. By no means conventional, this interesting collection consists of more than 500 toy boats, thousands of tin soldiers on their respective battlefields, as well as beautiful eggs encrusted with gems, created by Carl Fabergé for Tsar Nicholas II.

Adjacent to a little garden, the **First Presbyterian Church** ★ *(48 Fifth Ave.)* Is like a breath of fresh air on this compacted stretch of Fifth Avenue. An attractive cast-iron gate leads to the Gothic Revival structure, erected in 1846 after architect Joseph Wells' design. The Presbyterian Church, the established church of Scotland, was founded in 1559 by reformer John Knox.

Its neighbour, the **Church of the Ascension** ★ *(36 Fifth Ave.)* is of episcopal denomination (American Anglican). It was designed by architect Richard Upjohn (1841). The inside of the church, remodeled by architects McKim, Mead and White in 1889, is adorned with a retable by Augustus Saint-Gaudens as well as a mural and stained-glass windows by John La Farge.

Turn right on West 10th Street to see a lovely group of row houses clad in brownstone (brownish-pink sandstone), typical of New York City. The set of houses, nicknamed "English Terrace Row" (20-38 West 10th St.), was designed by engineer James Renwick Jr. in 1858.

As you stroll onto 6th Avenue (Avenue of the Americas), you will notice the different orientation of the network of streets in the old part of Greenwich Village. Before us stands the massive High-Victorian-Gothic structure of the **Jefferson Market Library** ★ *(425 6th Ave.)*. Built in 1877, this former multi-functional building (courthouse, fire station, public market) was converted to a branch of the New York Public Library in 1967, thus becoming one of the first Victorian-building recycling projects in the United States.

Cross 6th Avenue to take Christopher Street, which runs slantwise, south of the Jefferson Market Library.

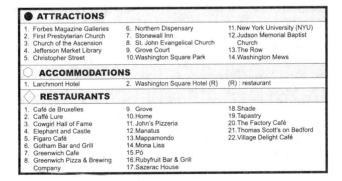

● ATTRACTIONS

1. Forbes Magazine Galleries	6. Northern Dispensary	11. New York University (NYU)
2. First Presbyterian Church	7. Stonewall Inn	12. Judson Memorial Baptist
3. Church of the Ascension	8. St. John Evangelical Church	Church
4. Jefferson Market Library	9. Grove Court	13. The Row
5. Christopher Street	10. Washington Square Park	14. Washington Mews

◯ ACCOMMODATIONS

1. Larchmont Hotel	2. Washington Square Hotel (R)	(R) : restaurant

◇ RESTAURANTS

1. Café de Bruxelles	9. Grove	18. Shade
2. Caffé Lure	10. Home	19. Tapastry
3. Cowgirl Hall of Fame	11. John's Pizzeria	20. The Factory Café
4. Elephant and Castle	12. Manatus	21. Thomas Scott's on Bedford
5. Figaro Café	13. Mappamondo	22. Village Delight Café
6. Gotham Bar and Grill	14. Mona Lisa	
7. Greenwich Cafe	15. Pó	
8. Greenwich Pizza & Brewing	16. Rubyfruit Bar & Grill	
Company	17. Sazerac House	

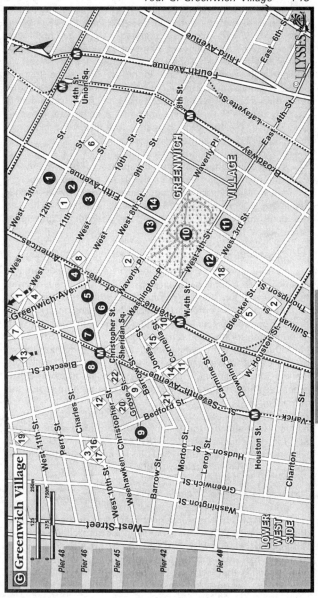

Christopher Street ★ *(between 6th Ave. and the piers along the Hudson River)* is closely associated with the gay revolution of the 1960s, which allowed a certain gay lifestyle to flourish in the cities of North America. A "place of pilgrimage" for homosexuals throughout the world, it has since lost its anti-establishment side to become, with the passing years, little more than a small street lined with bars and restaurants mainly catering to the "Saturday-night crowd". A somewhat amusing coincidence: the first cross street on the left was nicknamed "Gay Street" over a century ago.

The medical clinic of the **Northern Dispensary** *(165 Waverly Pl.)* was founded as early as 1827 by an association of doctors anxious to improve sanitary conditions in Greenwich Village. The austere Georgian-style red-brick building, which still houses the clinic, has occupied this triangular site along Christopher Street since 1831.

On June 27 of 1969, the New York City police force carried out another one of its many raids on gay establishments in order to enforce "public morality" (sic). This time, they targeted the **Stonewall Inn** *(53 Christopher St.)*, which had opened its doors in the 18th century. The place had been frequented by the gay community since the fifties. That night, fed up with being beaten for no good reason, the patrons of the Stonewall Inn fought back with stones and fists, to the great surprise of the police, who were forced to retreat. The Stonewall riots marked the beginning of gay liberation throughout North America. The bar currently bearing the same name is not the original inn.

As you continue up the street, you will catch sight of the **St. John Evangelical Church** *(81 Christopher St.)*, a small Lutheran church erected in 1821. Its façade was redone in the Romanesque Revival style in 1886.

Turn left on Bedford Street.

In New York City, where the incessant noise of the traffic can drive you crazy, a private, quiet and verdant cul-de-sac like **Grove Court** ★ *(southwest of Bedford St.)* is a real luxury. Its fortunate residents inhabit a group of houses with brick and wood façades that were erected between 1820 and 1850.

Memorial Arch

Return to Bedford Street. Turn left on Barrow Street and right on Bleecker Street, which boasts several restaurants. Finally, turn left on Cornelia Street then right on West 4th Street, which leads to beautiful Washington Square Park.

Laid out in 1824, **Washington Square Park ★★** *(at the south end of Fifth Ave.)* is a major landmark in this part of the city. The symbol of a certain enlightened middle class, this public garden has been featured in numerous movies, including *Barefoot in the Park*, starring Robert Redford. The Memorial Arch, situated directly in line with Fifth Avenue, is the park's main monument. Designed by architects McKim, Mead and

White, the triumphal arch was erected in 1889 to commemorate the centenary of George Washington's investiture. The park should be avoided come nightfall.

The **New York University (NYU)** campus, to the east and south of Washington Square, gives this part of Greenwich Village, which borders on the East Village (see p 156) and SoHo (see p 143), a certain Latin-Quarter quality. However, though this semipublic university was founded back in 1832, its campus is rather modern and rambling.

The **Judson Memorial Baptist Church ★** *(55 Washington Sq. S.)* overlooks the south side of Washington Square Park. Its archaic Romanesque Revival architecture is the work of McKim, Mead and White (1892). The interior is graced with stained-glass windows by John La Farge and low reliefs by Herbert Adams and Augustus Saint-Gaudens. Also of note is that the campanile adjacent to the church now houses student's quarters!

Cross Washington Square Park to reach Washington Square North.

The lovely series of houses appropriately nicknamed **The Row ★** *(1-25 Washington Sq. N.)*, which line the north side of the park, was raised between 1829 and 1833. Its red-brick façades and Ionic portals have attracted a number of New-York personalities over the years. In fact, these houses were once inhabited by such celebrities as writer John Dos Passos and painter Edward Hopper. Author Henry James, whose grandmother lived in one of the houses facing the park, would later write the best novel to deal with life in Greenwich Village. He quite simply chose to entitle it *Washington Square*.

Go back up Fifth Avenue to the start of the tour.

Behind the patrician houses facing the park are service alleys similar to those in London. The **Washington Mews ★** *(east of Fifth Ave., between Washington Sq. N. and West 8th St.)* are lined with old stables that were converted into luxurious accommodations much prized by New Yorkers. Nearby towers the massive pyramidal structure of 1 Fifth Avenue, an Art-Deco-style apartment building (1929), whose upper floors afford magnificent views of the city. If you know someone living there, get yourself invited for dinner...

 | TOUR H: CHELSEA ★ (1 hour)

The area that extends south from West 14th Street to West 23rd Street, between Fifth Avenue to the east and the Hudson River to the west, is a hodgepodge of row houses, shops, warehouses and factories. Though it was labelled Chelsea in the mid-18th century, it is still suffering from something of an identity crisis. After being the opera and theatre district for a brief period, it was home to the fledgling American film industry until the movie-makers headed off to the sunnier climates of California. Since the heyday of disco, big nightclubs have been coming and going here, their rise and fall reflecting the various trends in New York nightlife. Many cater to the gay community, which is no longer concentrated only in Greenwich Village.

This tour starts at the corner of 14th Street and Sixth Avenue (Avenue of the Americas), just opposite the 14th Street subway station served by the F train. The other 14th Street station, served by the 1, 2 and 3, is located nearby. Those who prefer the bus can take the M5 or the M6.

Head north on Sixth Avenue.

St. Francis Xavier Church ★ *(30 West 16th St.)* has a strange, Jesuit-style Baroque-Revival façade with a deep, arched portico. The church was built in 1882 by the prolific Brooklyn architect Patrick C. Keely, who, in the course of his long career, designed about a hundred Catholic churches throughout the United States and Canada (another example being the Église du Gesù on Rue Bleury in Montréal).

The lovely glazed terra cotta facade of the old **Siegel-Cooper Department Store** ★ *(616 Sixth Ave.)* is sure to catch your eye as you walk by (DeLemos and Cordes, architects, 1895). The building bears witness to the days when Sixth Avenue was known as Fashion Row, due to the many stores clustered along it between West 14th Street and West 23rd Street. Make sure not to confuse Fashion Row with Ladies' Mile, which was located between Broadway and 6th Avenue.

EXPLORING

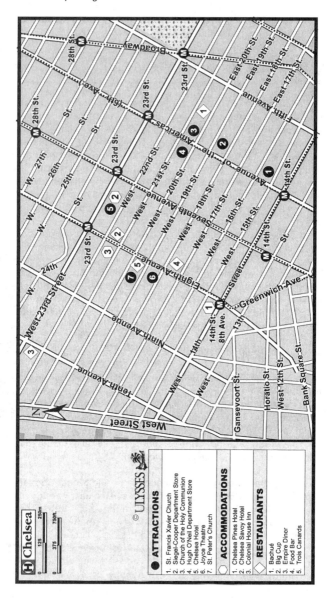

Chelsea

0   125   250m
0   375   750ft.

© ULYSSES

● **ATTRACTIONS**

1. St. Francis Xavier Church
2. Siegel-Cooper Department Store
3. Church of the Holy Communion
4. Hugh O'Neil Department Store
5. Chelsea Hotel
6. Joyce Theatre
7. St. Peter's Church

◇ **ACCOMMODATIONS**

1. Chelsea Pines Hotel
2. Chelsea Savoy Hotel
3. Colonial House Inn

◇ **RESTAURANTS**

1. Bachué
2. Big Cup
3. Empire Diner
4. Food Bar
5. Trois Canards

The former members of the congregation of the **Church of the Holy Communion** *(47 West 20th St., at the corner of Sixth Ave.)* must have rolled over in their graves when this Episcopal church became one of the most fashionable discotheques in New York in the mid-1970s. The Limelight, a gay club, now occupies the premises. Designed by Richard Upjohn, the church was built in 1846.

Could it be that the most impressive cast-iron facade in New York is not in SoHo? Perhaps. The old **Hugh O'Neil Department Store ★** *(655 Sixth Ave.)*, erected in 1875, is at least as lovely as the finest buildings in the Cast Iron District. It is shown off to great advantage in the evening, thanks to some strategic lighting.

Turn left on West 23rd Street.

The **Chelsea Hotel ★** *(222 West 23rd St.)* is more famous for its guest list than its architecture, which is nonetheless very attractive, with its cast-iron balconies adorned with a sunflower pattern, typical of the Queen-Anne style. This 12-story hotel, built in 1884, has been a home away from home – for years in some cases – for such notables as writers Arthur Miller, Tennessee Williams and Jack Kerouac, who wrote his famous novel *On the Road* here. Singers Bob Dylan, Joni Mitchell and Sid Vicious have also stayed at the Chelsea Hotel; Sid Vicious even committed suicide in one of the rooms – after killing his girlfriend. Charming, isn't it?

Turn left on Eighth Avenue.

The **Joyce Theatre** *(175 Eighth Ave., at West 19th)*, erected in 1942, was originally a movie house. Its Art-Moderne façade was restored when the building was converted into a theatre specializing in modern dance.

On West 20th Street, you'll find **St. Peter's Church** *(344 West 20th St.)*. This former parish of Trinity Church (see p 277) is one of the oldest extant Gothic Revival churches in New York (1836).

To return to the starting point of the tour, turn left on West 16th Street and continue to Sixth Avenue. This will give you a chance to see one of Chelsea's residential streets.

EXPLORING

TOUR I: EAST VILLAGE ★ (2 hours)

In New York, as in big cities the world over, neighbourhoods go in and out of fashion, with each one's time in the limelight usually lasting about 20 years. In general, a handful of little-known artists, penniless restaurateurs and enterprising shopkeepers move into a rundown part of town where the rents are cheap. After a few years, they attain a certain level of success, thereby attracting more well-to-do artists to the area. Hip bars and luxury boutiques start opening up and prices rise. At that point, the "pioneers" take flight. The East Village, located, as indicated by its name, east of Greenwich Village, is presently undergoing this metamorphosis from a neglected neighbourhood to a trendy area.

Of course, the East Village had a history before its commercial renaissance in 1985. In fact, in a previous life, this neighbourhood was a hub of economic and artistic activity. In the first half of the 19th century, a portion of the New York bourgeoisie moved into the area, building lovely Greek Revival houses along its shady streets. Just when they had started to establish quality cultural institutions, however, they picked up and left, moving farther north, onto Fifth Avenue. Warehouses and factories soon sprang up, and the immigrant communities of the Lower East Side (see p 136) spilled over into this area. Before long, Jewish, Polish, Italian and Irish enclaves had developed amidst the row houses. Around 1965, the East Village became the stomping ground of New York hippies. Times change and so do hairstyles, and starting in 1980, the area was invaded by punks. Today, the East Village is home to an intricate mosaic of recent immigrants (Albanians, Puerto Ricans, Russians, Serbs, etc.), drag queens wearing inch-thick makeup and poli-sci students doing everything in their power to renounce their New Jersey upbringing.

Our tour of the East Village starts at the corner of East Houston Street and Lafayette Street, which is easy to reach from any of the nearby subway stations (Broadway/Lafayette Station, served by the B, D and F trains; Prince Street Station, served by the N and R trains; Bleecker Street Station, served by the 6). As for buses, the M1, M5, M6 and M21, which run along Broadway and Houston Street, all stop nearby.

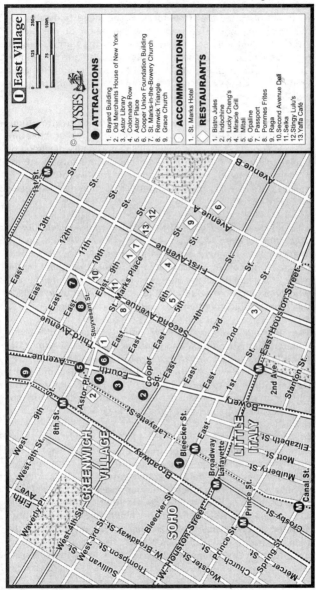

© ULYSSES

East Village

N

0   125   250m

0   75   150ft.

● ATTRACTIONS

1. Bayard Building
2. Old Merchants House of New York
3. Astor Library
4. Colonnade Row
5. Astor Place
6. Cooper Union Foundation Building
7. St. Marks-in-the-Bowery Church
8. Renwick Triangle
9. Grace Church

⬡ ACCOMMODATIONS

1. St Marks Hotel

◇ RESTAURANTS

1. Bistro Jules
2. Indochine
3. Lucky Cheng's
4. Miracle Grill
5. Mitali
6. Opaline
7. Passport
8. Pommes Frites
9. Raga
10. Second Avenue Deli
11. Selka
12. Stingy Lulu's
13. Yaffa Café

EXPLORING

It should be noted that Houston is pronounced "Howston" in this instance, not "Hewston," like the name of the city in Texas. Lafayette Street, was named after the famous French general – prepare yourself! – Marie-Joseph-Paul-Yves-Roch-Gilbert Motier de La Fayette (1757-1834), a friend of Benjamin Franklin's who helped the American colonists gain independence from Great Britain.

The **Bayard Building** *(65 Bleecker St.)*, just off Lafayette Street, is one of the few examples of the Chicago School architecture in New York. It is also the only building in the city designed by Louis Sullivan (1898). Considered one of the fathers of the modern skyscraper, Sullivan was one of the first architects to design curtain walls made of lightweight materials like glass and terra cotta.

The **Old Merchants House of New York** *(admission fee; Sun to Thu 1pm to 4pm; 29 East 4th St., ☎777-1089)* is an old mansion that is now open to the public. A fully furnished, Federal-style house, it was built in 1832 for a merchant by the name of Joseph Brewster. However, it was the Tredwell family, who lived here from 1835 to 1933, that truly left their mark on this house, which contains many of their belongings.

The first public library in New York was built with funds donated by the fur-trader and financier John Jacob Astor. The **Astor Library** *(425 Lafayette St.)*, which opened in 1853, was converted into a theatre around 1970. Its collections were incorporated into those of the New York Public Library in the early 20th century. Make sure to take a look at the Germano-Romanesque architecture of the building, which is made of reddish stone.

Almost right across the street, you'll see the remains of the prestigious **Colonnade Row ★** *(428-434 Lafayette St.)*, originally named La Grange Terrace, after the Marquis de La Fayette's chateau in France. The four remaining houses (there were once nine), built in 1933, are fronted by a lovely marble Corinthian colonnade, which made this the most sophisticated architectural ensemble of its kind in the United States at the time. "Commodore" Cornelius Vanderbilt, one of the richest men in North America in the 19th century, used to live here.

In 1849, **Astor Place** was still the heart of the cultural scene in New York. In those days, several theatres faced onto the triangular public "square", including the opulent Astor Place Opera. There was fierce competition amongst both actors and patrons of the arts. However, the poverty-stricken populace living in the areas south of East Houston Street took a dim view of the ostentatious display taking place just a few blocks from their homes. Then, on the night of May 10, terrible riots broke out when two actors, one American, the other British, performed in the same play in two different theatres. More a form of social catharsis than a real political conflict, these riots, which claimed 34 lives, plunged the neighbourhood into rapid decline. Today, Astor Place is a shapeless space whose main attraction is a replica of one of the first cast-iron entryways to the New York subway. Like the Paris metro, which has lost many of its original entrances designed by Guimard, New York was divested of all its metal entryways in the 1950s and 1960s which were designed by Heins and La Farge between 1902 and 1906.

Turn right on Astor Place, which turns into St. Marks Place (East 8th St.).

The gloomy **Cooper Union Foundation Building** ★ *(41 Cooper Sq., at the corner of Astor Pl. and East 7th St., ☎254-6374)*, faced entirely with brownstone, was built in 1859. Its interior structure is partly made of steel beams and was considered a real innovation at the time. Originally a technical college for the working classes, the building was erected by American steel magnate Peter Cooper. Abraham Lincoln delivered his famous speech on the rights of blacks here, in this cradle of social change, in 1860. Courses and conferences are still held here on a regular basis.

Walk eastward along St. Marks Place, then turn left on Second Avenue.

Here in this quintessentially urban setting, it is quite a surprise to discover a charming little rustic church surrounded by greenery. **St. Marks-in-the-Bowery Church** ★ *(Second Ave. and East 10th St.)* was built in 1799 on the site of a private chapel owned by the family of the last Dutch governor of New Amsterdam, Peter Stuyvesant. Stuyvesant's tomb can still be

EXPLORING

found in the tiny adjoining cemetery. The cast-iron portico in front of the church entrance was added in 1858.

Take a left on East 10th Street.

West of the church stands one of the loveliest groups of brownstones in New York. These tall, narrow row houses form **Renwick Triangle** ★ *(at the corner of Stuyvesant and East 10th)*, named after architect James Renwick, who designed them in 1861. They were built by Peter Stuyvesant's great grandson on the site once occupied by his great-grandfather's farm (which burned down in 1778).

Turn right on Broadway.

Grace Church ★★ *(800 Broadway)* and its rectory were designed in a flamboyant style that makes them two of the most interesting examples of Gothic Revival architecture in the United States. Designed in 1843 by the engineer James Renwick, Jr., who was only 24 at the time, the church was modelled on the English churches of Augustus Welby Pugin. The polychrome interior could use a little freshening up but boasts lovely stained-glass windows. Tom Thumb was married here in 1863.

Continue northward on Broadway to East 14th Street. If you head south instead, you'll be back at the starting point of the tour in a few minutes.

 TOUR J. THE SQUARES ★★ (4 hours)

The four square-parks around which the New York bourgeoisie congregated in the first half of the 19th century lie right in the middle of New York City, between Lower Manhattan and Midtown. Though long since forsaken, their trees have survived, bringing a breath of fresh air to what is now a densely built neighbourhood where green spaces are few and far between. The tour of these squares includes the quiet enclave of Gramercy, around the park of the same name, where a number of New York personalities have lived over the years. Greek Revivalist houses from 1840, done up by artists, many of whom have settled here, still grace the area. New types of businesses (software designers, dating agencies, art restoration studios), which cannot afford Midtown rents, have moved into offices lining the avenues, thus encouraging the growth of restaurants and fashion boutiques. Though there are few famous monuments here, the tour of these squares makes for a pleasant walk in the heart of the city.

The tour begins in front of the Flatiron Building, located at the intersection of Broadway and Fifth Avenue, at 23rd Street. Get off at one of the three "23rd Street" subway stations, where the 1, F, N and R trains stop. The M1, M2, M3 and M5 buses also stop in the area.

What was once known as the Fuller Building has been renamed the **Flatiron Building** ★★ *(175 Fifth Ave.)* due to its triangular shape, which recalls that of an old iron, or flatiron. Highly prized by photographers, its dramatic profile was designed by architect Daniel H. Burnham (1902), one of the intellectual leaders of the Chicago School. It was the first high-rise building to be erected outside the Wall Street district. The structure boasts decorative bossage inspired by Italian *palazzo*, as well as a lovely cast-iron entrance on the corner of the façade. Police officers were once posted here to chase away men who came to take advantage of the draught created by the skyscraper and get a glimpse of women passers-by's legs, briefly exposed as their skirts were raised by the gusts of wind.

Cross East 23rd Street and follow Madison Square Park to Madison Avenue.

Madison Square Park ★ *(from Fifth Ave. to Madison Ave., between East 23rd St. and East 26th St.)* was created in 1842 on the site of a common grave. The green expanse planted with stately trees is transected by paths bordered by long continuous benches, typical of New York City. Legend has it that members of the Knickerbocker Club, once located nearby, had invented baseball here around 1845. Among the many statues adorning the park, that of Admiral **David G. Farragut** *(on Fifth Ave., facing 25th St.)* stands out from the pack, both by its pedestal, which foreshadowed *art nouveau* (Stanford White, architect, 1881), and by its body, created by the most celebrated sculptor in New York at the time, Augustus Saint-Gaudens.

EXPLORING

The headquarters of the **Metropolitan Life Insurance Company** ★★ *(1 Madison Ave.)* once occupied this 50-story tower, later moving into the former Pan Am Building on Park Avenue. The company's former skyscraper, the work of French architect Napoléon Le Brun, held the title of tallest building in the world from 1909, the year of its inauguration, to 1913, when the Woolworth Building near City Hall was completed. At night, the upper part of the building is illuminated by powerful floodlights, giving this gargantuan campanile a magical appearance. Sadly, the original interior decor was obliterated during drastic renovations, in 1964.

Take Madison Avenue, heading north.

At the corner of East 25th Street stands the majestic neoclassical building of the **Appellate Division Courthouse of the New York State Supreme Court** ★ *(35 East 25th St.)*, which hears New York County's civil and criminal cases.

● ATTRACTIONS

1.	Flatiron Building	15.	The Gramercy
2.	Madison Square Park	16.	The 36 Gramercy Park East
3.	Metropolitan Life Insurance Company	17.	Block Beautiful
		18.	Irving Place
4.	Appellate Division Courthouse of the New York State Supreme Court	19.	17 Hotel
		20.	Stuyvesant Square Park
5.	Indifference to Injustice is the Gate to Hell	21.	St.George's Episcopal Church and Parish House
6.	New York Life Insurance Company	22.	Friends Seminary
7.	69th Regiment Armory	23.	Energy Museum
8.	Federation of Protestant Welfare Agencies	24.	Consolidated Edison Company Building
9.	Calvary Church	25.	The Palladium
10.	Gramercy Park	26.	Union Square Park
11.	3 and 4 Gramercy Park West	27.	Union Square Theatre and the New York Film Academy
12.	National Arts Club		
13.	The Players	28.	Ladies' Mile
14.	The Brotherhood Synagogue	29.	Theodore Roosevelt Birthplace

○ ACCOMMODATIONS

1.	Gramercy Park Hotel	2.	Gershwin Hotel

◇ RESTAURANTS

1.	52 Irving Place	10.	Naturally Tasty
2.	Blue Water Grill	11.	News Bar
3.	Bouchon	12.	Noodles on 28
4.	Brasserie les Halles	13.	Souen
5.	Café Journal	14.	The Parlour Café
6.	Café Spice	15.	Turkish Kitchen
7.	Cena	16.	Union Square Café
8.	Luna Park	17.	Verbena
9.	Union Square Open Market	18.	Zen Palate

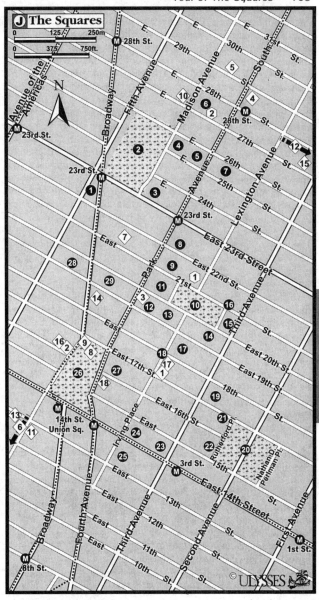

Designed by James Browne Lord in 1896, the building is adorned with several allegorical sculptures, including those of *Wisdom* and *Force*, positioned in several places around the entrance. North of the small courthouse stands a white marble sculpture, gracing the side of a building, entitled ***Indifference to Injustice is the Gate to Hell***. Created by Feigenbaum (1990), this monument in memory of Holocaust victims bears a three-dimensional reproduction of the plan of the Auschwitz concentration camp as it appeared on August 25 of 1944. On the southeast corner of Madison Avenue and 26th Street once stood Leonard Jerome's residence, which comprised a ballroom and even a theatre where Mr. Jerome's mistresses would sing and dance. His unfortunate lawful wife ended up leaving him to settle in London with their two young daughters. One of them, Jennie Jerome, would later wed Lord Randolph Churchill. They would choose to name their now famous son Winston.

The head offices of the **New York Life Insurance Company ★★** *(51 Madison Ave.)* occupy two entire quadrilaterals. This other major insurance company had a skyscraper built whose neo-Gothic exterior conceals a neoclassical interior (Cass Gilbert, architect, 1928). The building was erected on the site of the former Madison Square Garden, a theatre, arena and hanging-gardens complex designed in 1890 by Stanford White, of the famed architectural firm, McKim, Mead and White. White was a notorious Don Juan. He had a pied-à-terre in the vicinity, where he installed a swing hanging from red velvet ropes, particularly enjoyed by one of his mistresses, Evelyn Nesbit Thaw. In 1906, during a society evening held on the roof of Madison Square Garden, the lovely Evelyn's lawful husband, Harry Thaw, killed White with a gunshot to the head, causing a huge scandal still talked about today.

Go through the central corridor of the New York Life Insurance Company to Park Avenue South. Head south.

Behind the buildings on the east side of Park Avenue South (between East 25th Street and East 26th Street) stands the enormous bulk of the **69th Regiment Armory** *(68 Lexington Ave.)*, which hosted the famous Armory Show in 1913. This was a momentous exhibition of painting and sculpture, which would introduce the American public to European fauvism and cubism. At the time, the big museums were singularly uninterested in these "daubs" of Picasso, Vuillard, Duchamp and others. As its name suggests, the hall of the 69th Regiment Armory normally serves as a military arms depot.

Cross 23rd Street, which, for some, marks the end of Midtown.

The **Federation of Protestant Welfare Agencies** ★ *(281 Park Ave. S.)* is housed in an interesting and eclectic grey-stone building whose façade is a successful blend of neo-Romanesque and Flemish Renaissance styles (1894). Right next door is the **Calvary Church** *(273 Park Ave. S.)*, an Anglican (episcopal) church erected in 1848 by James Renwick Jr., to whom we are also indebted for St. Patrick's Cathedral (see p 186).

Turn left on East 21st Street, then right on Gramercy Park West, opposite Gramercy Park.

A marsh the Dutch had named *Krom Moeraije* (small tortuous marsh) lay here in the 18th century. The British would later distort its name into "Gramercy". Property developer Samuel Ruggles purchased the land in 1831, laying out a lovely park on the drained marsh, designing it in the image of London square-parks, in order to attract wealthy residents. The operation was success, on both a commercial and urban development level. **Gramercy Park** ★★ *(at the south end of Lexington Ave., between 20th St. and 21st St.)* has the distinctive feature of having remained, since its inauguration, a private park surrounded by a gate to which only wealthy residents have a key. The district extending around the park is one of the most charming in New York City.

Two row houses from 1846 (Alexander Jackson Davis, architect), at **3 and 4 Gramercy Park West**, boast magnificent cast-iron porticos similar to those in New Orleans.

Turn left on East 20th Street, also known as Gramercy Park South.

Founded in 1898, the **National Arts Club** ★ *(admission fee; visit by appointment only; 15 Gramercy Park South, ☎475-3424)* aims to make American visual arts known and appreciated. Prior to 1930, New York artists were scorned by the establishment, which gave preference to European academic painters and sculptors. This private club managed to change

EXPLORING

things by awarding medals and organizing exhibitions. Among its members are wealthy collectors and renowned artists. In the beginning of the 20th century, the club was one of the few to admit men and women as equals. The club has been set up in the former residence of one-time New York governor, Samuel J. Tilden, since 1906. This building is the work of architect Calvert Vaux, who designed the fountains in Central Park. Vaux employed a polychromatic and High Victorian Gothicizing architecture, harmoniously combining pinkish brownstone and black polished granite (1884). Inside, you can admire beautiful stained-glass windows created by John LaFarge and Donald MacDonald, a master glass-worker from Boston, as well as long galleries, where paintings and sculptures donated to the club by some of its members are exhibited. A 13-story building housing artists' studios has been erected at the back to put up visiting artists (entrance on 19th Street). The façade of the National Arts Club was made famous by Woody Allen's comedy, *Manhattan Murder Mystery*, in which Alan Alda and Diane Keaton are seen sitting at the window during a wine tasting.

Actor Edwin Booth acquired a house in Gramercy Park in 1888 to make it a private club where actors could relax between theatre performances. **The Players ★** *(admission fee; visit by appointment only; 16 Gramercy Park S., ☎475-6116)* still occupies this house, built in 1845, to which Stanford White added a large porch as well as a pair of Italian Renaissance-style gas street lamps. Notable among its features are library with a collection of books on the theatre, as well as more than 5,000 plays. This library is open to serious researchers, by appointment. Other highlights include the billiard table on which Mark Twain played (in the middle of the Grill Room), the elevator in which Sarah Bernhardt was stuck for over an hour in 1911 and Edwin Booth's set of rooms on the first floor. A monument paying tribute to the latter, which was set up in the middle of Gramercy Park in 1918 (Edmond T. Quinn, sculptor), can be seen from the porch.

East of Irving Place is **The Brotherhood Synagogue** *(28 Gramercy Park S.)*, housed since 1975 in the Quakers' former Friends Meeting House, built in 1859. A few interesting buildings give out on Gramercy Park East, including the distinctly Victorian **The Gramercy ★** *(34 Gramercy Park E.)*, erected in 1883, and its neighbour, **The 36 Gramercy Park**

East, a tall, white terracotta Gothic Revival structure fronted by two authentic armoured suits saluting passers-by.

Return to Irving Place; head south.

The section of 19th Street between Irving Place and 3rd Avenue is considered one of the loveliest streets in New York City. Nicknamed **Block Beautiful ★**, it was entirely restored during the twenties.

Irving Place *(between Gramercy Park and East 14th St.)* was named thus in honour of New York essayist and historian Washington Irving (1783-1859), whose bust, for that matter, can be seen in front of the High School of the same name (Beer, sculptor, 1885). The author of *The Sketchbook of Goeffrey Crayon* lived his last years in the Gramercy district.

Turn left on East 17th Street and continue to Rutherford Place.

Time magazine was born at 141 East 17th Street. A little farther on stands the peculiar **17 Hotel** *(225-229 East 17th St.)*, built around 1885, where Mrs. Hauss took refuge in Woody Allen's comedy, *Manhattan Murder Mystery* (Hotel Waldron).

Turn right on Rutherford Place, which follows the west side of Stuyvesant Square Park.

In 1836, Peter G. Stuyvesant, heir to an old Dutch family from New York and direct descendent of the last governor of New Amsterdam, donated part of his land to the borough provided that it lay out a park here. **Stuyvesant Square Park ★** *(between Rutherford and Nathan D. Perlman Places, from East 15th St. to East 17th St.)* is actually made up of two distinct public squares, separated by 2nd Avenue. In the middle of the one bordering Rutherford Place stands a statue of governor Peter Stuyvesant, the work of Gertrude Vanderbilt Whitney (1936). The huge Beth Israel Medical Center complex (a Jewish hospital) is visible from the opposite side of the other park.

St. George's Episcopal Church and its **Parish House ★★** *(at Rutherford Pl. and East 16th St.)* was once a well-off parish that brought together several illustrious members of the New York bourgeoisie. Behind the neo-Romanesque church of 1856

EXPLORING

looms the Parish House, an embossed brownstone built in 1888, almost as monumental as the church itself.

On the other side of East 16th Street is the **Friends Seminary ★** *(at East 16th St. and Rutherford Pl.)*, founded by the Quakers in 1786. The utmost simplicity of the red-brick Meeting House (1860) reflects the strict principles of the sect, founded in England in the 17th century. Its official name is the Religious Society of Friends. Over the years, other buildings were added in the back to form a block that is now a private school for girls and boys (accommodating 570 students). The school remains the property of the Society of Friends. It has been turned into an modern, experimental establishment offering New York children anthropology, foreign language, 3D computer-design classes and more.

Turn right on East 15th Street, left on 3rd Avenue and right again on East 14th Street.

The **Energy Museum ★** *(free admission; ♿; Tue to Sat 10am to 5pm; 145 East 14th St., ☎460-6244)* is owned by the Consolidated Edison Company. This interactive museum explains the operation of the company's thermal power stations, which supplies part of New York with electricity. Among the things to be learned here is that New York City was the first place in the world, in 1883, to have an underground power supply.

The headquarters of the **Consolidated Edison Company Building ★** *(4 Irving Pl.)* are right next to the museum. You will need to stand back a bit, however, in order to fully appreciate the architecture. Its tower, created by architects Warren and Wetmore in 1926, comprises a beautiful clock overlooking the East Village, to the south. At night, the floodlit tower of "Conn Ed", as New Yorkers call it, is revealed in all its splendour.

The Palladium *(126 East 14th St.)*. The mega-discotheque opened in 1985 in a former silent movie house built in 1926. Visiting the place is a must, even for those not particularly keen on dancing, if only to admire the interior decor created by Japanese architect Arata Isozaki and French designer Andrée Putman.

Follow East 14th Street westward. Turn right on Union Square East (Park Avenue South).

Four times a week (Monday, Wednesday, Friday and Saturday) during the summer months, the west side of **Union Square Park ★★** *(between Broadway and Park Ave. S., from East 14th St. to East 17th St.)* is transformed into a fruit and vegetable market, giving this highly urban setting a lively, rural character. The public square was laid out in 1830 to lure wealthy New Yorkers who wanted a quieter environment to set up house in. From 1854, however, the square rather became a theatre and popular entertainment district. It could almost be considered the "Times Square" of the time. The Academy of Music, which occupied the site of Consolidated Edison's main branch, was inaugurated that year. In the beginning of the 20th century, two subway lines were dug under the square, obliging engineers to raise the park. At that time, Union Square Park became a meeting place for leftists who distributed communist tracts and delivered fiery speeches here. A crowd gathered here on August 22, 1927, awaiting the sentence to be pronounced upon anarchists Sacco and Vanzetti. When the two were sentenced to death, a riot broke out during which several demonstrators were killed. Over the course of the thirties, May-Day (May 1st) and Labor-Day (September 1st) celebrations would attract millions of people. Unfortunately, frequenting of the park declined from 1960, leaving the whole place to drug dealers, who ruled the park until the place was spruced up in 1986. A **statue of Lafayette** (1876) by Frédéric-Auguste Bartholdi, creator of the *Lion of Belfort* and the famous Statue of Liberty, occupies a place of honour at the park's entrance. It was given to the United States by France during the hundredth-anniversary celebrations of American independence.

The **Union Square Theatre** and **New York Film Academy** *(at Union Sq. E. and East 17th St.)* are housed in the last "sanctuary" of the Tammany Society. This private school turns out film directors and technicians.

Turn left on East 17th Street, then right on Broadway.

The part of Broadway stretching from Union Square Park to Madison Square Park was once nicknamed **Ladies' Mile ★★** due to the many clothing stores that lined the street. Women of polite society would arrange to meet here to go shopping for

EXPLORING

a few hats. This was before the high-class boutiques moved to Fifth Avenue, in Midtown (from 1920). Several buildings that housed 19th-century shops still remain. Their ground floors now accommodate furniture and antique shops, while the upper floors are occupied by design studios and art galleries. Some of these buildings sport lavish Second Empire architecture, characterized by high sloping ceilings wreathed with cast-iron crests *(881-887 and 901 Broadway)*.

On East 20th Street, admirers of Theodore Roosevelt, the only American president originally from New York City, have restored the house in which he was born in 1858. The **Theodore Roosevelt Birthplace** *(admission fee; Wed to Sun 9am to 4pm; 28 East 20th St., ☎260-1616)* opened its doors in 1923. Artifacts that belonged to the president and his family are displayed here.

Visitors can return to this tour's point of departure by following Broadway, heading north. The Chelsea tour begins in the vicinity.

TOUR K: FROM THE EMPIRE STATE BUILDING
TO THE UNITED NATIONS ★★★ (half a day)

Little remains of the posh residential neighbourhood that lay on either side of 34th Street in the mid-19th century. Starting in 1920, the mansions that stood here were destroyed to make way for skyscrapers – and not just any skyscrapers. This tour includes some of the most famous buildings not just in New York but in the world. As we make our way across the island of Manhattan, you'll see different types of local buildings, including two train stations, a museum, apartment buildings and a department store. Furthermore, some of the streets you'll be walking along are veritable stars of the silver screen; we all remember *Miracle on 34th Street*, and Fifth Avenue, Park Avenue and 42nd Street have all appeared in scores of films. To top it all off, why not pay a little visit to the various foreign delegations that line the halls of the permanent headquarters of the United Nations, located on the shores of the East River?

This tour starts at the corner of Seventh Avenue and West 32nd Street. To get there by subway, take train 1, 2 or 3 to the Penn Station/34th Street station; by bus, take the M4, M10 or M34.

New Yorkers are still mourning the loss of their beloved **Pennsylvania Station** *(on the west side of Seventh Avenue, between West 31st St. and West 33rd St.)*, levelled in 1963. Its demolition stirred up a great deal of controversy, thus leading to the creation of the Landmarks Preservation Commission, which has since enabled New York City to protect heritage buildings from the wrecking ball. Enormous "Penn Station", as New Yorkers affectionately still refer to it, was built between 1906 and 1910. Piranese's most fanciful drawings were realized, in stone, in this enormous building designed by McKim, Mead and White. Behind its long, neoclassical colonnade lay a huge hall topped by a vaulted, steel-framed skylight. Behind that, there was a waiting room inspired by the Baths of Caracalla in Rome. All this was replaced by the present station, an underground monstrosity whose central mall and sinister corridors evoke images of the Communist empire. Photographs of the old station adorn the pillars of the new building, lest we forget that an error of the same magnitude could be made today. A project to turn the former central post office (behind Penn Station) into a train station is presently under consideration. Ironically, it is a neoclassical building designed by none other than McKim, Mead and White.

Madison Square Garden *(admission fee; guided tours hourly Mon to Sat 10am to 3pm, Sun 11am to 3pm; on the west side of Seventh Avenue, between West 31st and West 33rd streets, ☎465-MSG1)*, a gigantic masonry cylinder, rises up above Pennsylvania Station. This 20,000-seat sports stadium is home to the Rangers, New York's hockey team, as well as a venue for pop concerts. Founded in 1874 by circus producer P.T. Barnum, the Garden used to face onto Madison Square, hence its name (see p 161).

Across the street stands the hulking, gloomy-looking **Pennsylvania Hotel**, immortalized in the song *Pennsylvania 6-5000*, whose title refers to the hotel's old telephone number. In the 1930s, this 3,000-room establishment was home base for Glen Miller and Benny Goodman's big bands.

Head north on Seventh Avenue, then turn right on West 34th Street.

The **Garment District** lies between Broadway and Ninth Avenue, from 25th Street to 40th Street. Millions of garments and other cloth items (bedspreads, bath towels, etc.) are manufactured in the skyscrapers here. During the day, the area is buzzing with activity, making it one of the most picturesque parts of the Big Apple. Watch out, though, or someone will run you over with a rack of dresses!

According to its owners, **Macy's** *(151 West 34th St.)* is the biggest department store on earth. Though it's true that this 10-story store, with its 200,000 square metres of floor space, sells everything imaginable, from rattan furniture to Russian caviar to tap shoes, claims of that kind are always tricky. Macy's is known for its parade featuring Santa Claus, which takes place on Broadway every year on Thanksgiving (late November). Most of the department stores in New York used to be located around 34th Street. Macy's has survived, but Gimbel's and Altman disappeared in the 1980s. The former was destroyed to make way for a shopping mall, and the latter was converted into a school.

The offices of *The New York Herald* used to face onto tiny, triangular **Herald Square** *(at Broadway and Sixth Ave., at West 34th St.)*. Though the *Herald* is gone, a lovely public clock in

● ATTRACTIONS

1.	Pennsylvania Station	10.	Grand Central Terminal (R)
2.	Madison Square Garden	11.	Chrysler Building
3.	Pennsylvania Hotel	12.	Mobil Building
4.	Garment District	13.	Daily News Building
5.	Macy's	14.	Ford Foundation Building
6.	Herald Square	15.	United Nations Headquarters
7.	Empire State Building	16.	Delacorte Geyser
8.	Murray Hill		
9.	Morgan Library	(R): Restaurant	

◯ ACCOMMODATIONS

1.	Best Western Manhattan	8.	Howard Johnson Hotel on 34th
2.	Herald Square Hotel	9.	Jolly Madison Towers Hotel
3.	Hotel Bedford	10.	Morgans (R)
4.	Hotel Deauville	11.	Murray Hill East Suite
5.	Hotel Metro	12.	Murray Hill Inn
6.	Hotel Pennsylvania	13.	Quality East Side
7.	Hotel Wolcott	(R): Restaurant	

◇ RESTAURANTS

1.	Boby Van's	4.	Morgan Court Café
2.	Chez Laurence	5.	Piccolino's
3.	Ipanema	6.	Spot

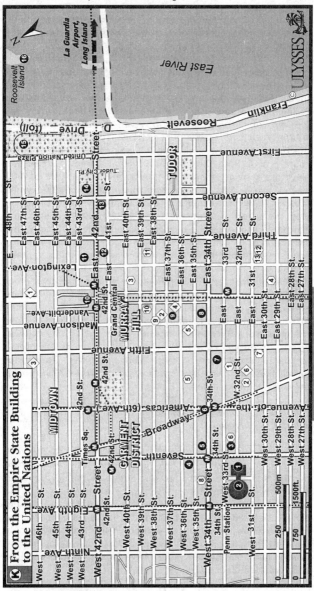

EXPLORING

the centre of the square bears witness to its presence here. Nearby stands a statue of Minerva by Antonin Jean Charles (1895).

It would be easy to walk right past the most famous skyscraper in New York without realizing it. Many a visitor has done just that, because the upper portion of the **Empire State Building ★★★** *(admission fee for observation decks; every day 9:30am to 11pm; 350 Fifth Ave., at West 34th St., ☎736-3100)* is not visible from its base. The ultimate symbol of the Big Apple (New York is the "Empire State") nonetheless soars proudly into the Manhattan sky (381 m). Sixty-seven elevators provide access to the private offices on its 102 stories. From 1931, when it was inaugurated, to 1972, when the first tower of the World Trade Center was completed, it was the tallest skyscraper in the world (Shreve, Lamb and Harmon). This Art-Deco building, scaled by King Kong, is the starting point of many guided tours of the city. Its mast was originally intended to be a mooring tower for dirigibles. Make sure to go up to one of the public observation decks. One is an open-air platform on the 86th floor, the other a glassed-in room on the 102nd floor; the panoramic view of Manhattan and its surroundings is breathtaking, particularly at night. Two special-effects cinemas have recently been added on the second floor: the **New York Skyride** *(admission fee; ♿; every day 9am to 11pm, ☎244-4721)*, which takes visitors on a fascinating simulated aerial tour of New York, and the **Transporter** *(admission fee; every day 9am to 11pm; ☎244-4721)*, which presents documentaries.

Continue eastward on 34th Street. Cross Fifth Avenue, then turn left on Madison.

Murray Hill ★ *(from East 34th St. to East 41st St., east of Fifth Ave.)* is a residential enclave whose peaceful atmosphere contrasts sharply with the nonstop action on the neighbouring streets. Named after Robert Murray, whose house stood at the top of the hill in the 18th century, it is still home to the old New York "aristocracy", who consider the Upper East Side too nouveau riche. The streets of Murray Hill are lined with lovingly restored brownstones dating from 1850, as well as several dozen carriage houses that have been converted into comfortable homes.

Morgan Library

The **Pierpont Morgan Library** ★★ *($5; ⅙; Tue to Fri 10:30am to 5pm, Sat 10:30am to 6pm, Sun noon to 6pm, free guided tours Mon to Fri 2:30pm; 29 East 36th St., ☎685-0610)* is justly considered the jewel of Murray Hill. Financier Pierpont Morgan's (1837-1913) former private library, which adjoins his house, has been open to the public since 1924. A small building designed by McKim, Mead and White (1906), it houses a remarkable collection of early printed books, rare editions, notebooks, drawings, prints, paintings and sculptures of undeniable historic value. As you make your way through its seven rooms, which are panneled with magnificent woodwork, you will be able to admire numerous etchings by Rembrandt, three Gutenberg bibles, the original handwritten manuscript of Dickens's *A Christmas Carol*, letters penned by Voltaire and musical scores handwritten by Bach, Mozart and Beethoven. If big museums wear you out, the Morgan Library will be right up your alley.

Head east on East 36th Street. Turn left on Park Avenue South then right on East 42nd Street.

Grand Central Terminal ★★ *(East 42nd St. and Vanderbilt Ave.)* faces straight down Park Avenue South. Warren and Wetmore, whose other credits include the Ritz-Carlton hotel in Montreal, designed this mammoth station in 1903 for the New York Central Railway Company. The building you see is just the

EXPLORING

tip of a gigantic iceberg: 80% of the station is underground. This East Coast terminus, which took a decade to build, was designed so that passengers could be brought right into the heart of New York without causing too many headaches for local residents. Some 60 tracks stretch through tunnels under Park Avenue, north and south of the station. Big buildings on piles (hotels, office towers, apartment buildings, etc.) stand above the tracks on either side of the avenue (see Park Avenue Tour, p 193). Grand Central was one of the most ambitious projects of the early 20th-century City Beautiful movement, which favoured large perspectives and broad avenues. The station, a beaux-arts gem, is topped by a clock surrounded by mythical figures sculpted by Jules Coutan (for more information on the old Pan Am Building behind the station, see p 197). The entrance under the 42nd Street overpass leads to the main hall, which has an incredible ceiling decorated with the signs of the Zodiac (Paul Helleu and Whitney Warren).

Back on East 42nd Street, you'll see a number of well-known buildings, including the famous **Chrysler Building** ★★★ *(lobby open Mon to Fri 8am to 5pm; 405 Lexington Ave., at 42nd St.)*, definitely the most distinctive Art-Deco skyscraper in New York. This 77-story building, erected in 1929 by auto manufacturer Walter P. Chrysler (William Van Alen, architect), is known mainly for its top, which features a sunburst motif and corners adorned with gargoyles shaped like the radiator caps used on Chrysler cars back then. The interior of the ground floor is decorated with murals from the old showroom, depicting planes and factories. The Art Deco style was the first decorative movement to use ornamentation that reflected the modern world.

Across the street stands the **Mobil Building** ★ *(150 East 42nd St.)*, which was built in 1956 and houses the offices of Mobil Oil, the multinational oil company and worthy heir of Standard Oil. It is faced with panels of embossed stainless steel.

The **Daily News Building** ★★ *(220 East 42nd St.)* was even more revolutionary for its time (1930) and set the style for skyscrapers for the next three decades. Designed by Raymond Hood, it features simple vertical lines and setbacks (in accordance with municipal regulations). Its lobby, which contains a huge globe, kindled the imagination of the man who created Superman. It is interesting to compare this building to the McGraw-Hill Building (see p 204), which is located on the same street, dates from the same year and was designed by the same architect but has primarily horizontal lines.

Be sure to make a short detour to the pretty indoor garden in the **Ford Foundation Building** ★ *(321 East 42nd St.)*, designed in 1967 by Kevin Roche. The building houses the offices of a private foundation established by the Ford automobile company to support various charitable organizations.

Walk under the overpass of the Tudor City residential complex, then turn left on First Avenue, renamed United Nations Plaza here. The visitors' entrance to the United Nations is located at East 46th Street.

After the League of Nations failed to prevent World War II, another international organization was established in 1946 with the aim of preserving world peace. Today, 185 countries from all five continents are members of the United Nations. The UN headquarters was originally supposed to be located in Geneva, but European cities fell out of the running after billionaire John D. Rockefeller donated this piece of land on the banks of the East River to the organization. The **United Nations Headquarters** ★★★ *($7; &; children under 5 not permitted, guided tour required, tours start every half-hour; Mar to Dec every day 9:15am to 4:45pm; Jan and Feb, Mon to Fri 9:15am to 4:45pm; at the corner of First Ave. and 46th St., ☎963-7713)*, erected between 1947 and 1952, was designed by a committee of 12 architects representing the various member countries. These included Wallace K. Harrison (U.S.A.), Le Corbusier (France) and Oscar Niemeyer (Brazil). There are four main buildings in the complex. From left to right, you'll see the domed General Assembly Building; the slender, 39-story Secretariat Building and the Hammarskjöld Library. The Conference Building, which contains the meeting rooms of the Security Council and the Economic and Social Council, is partly hidden by the Secretariat Building.

The United Nations occupies an international zone that is not, strictly speaking, American territory. It is guarded by a separate police force and has its own postal service, just like the Vatican. Visitors must enter through the bronze doors of the General Assembly Building, donated by Canada in 1950 (Ernest Cormier, architect). Guided tours, offered in a number of

EXPLORING

languages, provide a chance to admire the many works of art given to the UN over the years. From the end of September to mid-December, it is also possible to attend a meeting of the General Assembly, where the fate of humanity is discussed.

Upon exiting the United Nations, head to the gardens on the banks of the East River.

At the east end of the plaza, in front of the General Assembly Building, stands *Peace* by sculptor Antun Augustincic of the former Yugoslavia. From the lovely rose garden that runs along the riverbank, you can see the **Delacorte Geyser** *(at the southern tip of Roosevelt Island)*, which spurts up alongside the Roosevelt Memorial.

The quickest way back to the starting point of the tour is to hop on the M42, which runs west on 42nd Street. Get off at the corner of Seventh Avenue, then catch the M10.

 TOUR L: FIFTH AVENUE ★★★ (one day)

Fifth Avenue, which shares its status as the best-known street on the planet with Paris's Champs-Élysées, could be considered the showcase of the American metropolis. The avenue, whose name can also be written in the more banal form "5th Avenue", is home to some of the New York's most beautiful monuments as well as all sorts of luxurious stores, and thus attracts more tourists than any of the other 13 avenues running up and down the island of Manhattan.

In the second half of the 19th century, after the Astor Place riots drove wealthy New Yorkers out of Lower Manhattan (1849), Fifth Avenue became the elegant main residential artery of the American upper class. Its denizens would stroll along it after church on Sunday afternoons, decked out in their finest attire. They would go all out on Easter Sunday, which marks the beginning of spring in New York, and thus introduced the ongoing tradition of the Easter Parade. In those days, Fifth Avenue was studded with palatial homes, almost all of which were destroyed after 1925 to make room for the skyscrapers that flank the street today. This tour focuses on the densest part of Fifth Avenue, between 42nd and 59th Streets, where a wide variety of buildings can be found (shops, offices, private clubs, hotels, churches and museums).

The tour starts on the steps of the New York Public Library, located on Fifth Avenue, facing down 41st Street. Trains B, D and F serve the 42nd Street/Bryant Park subway station on 6th Avenue. For those who prefer the bus, the M1, M2, M3, M4 and M5 all stop in front of the building.

The **New York Public Library** ★★★ *(free admission; &; free guided tours at 11am and 2pm; Mon to Sat 10am to 6pm; on the west side of Fifth Ave., between 40th and 42nd streets, 10018-2788, ☎930-0800, http://www.nypl.org)* is a huge Beaux Arts palace built in 1911 according to plans by Carrère and Hastings. Despite its name, the library is actually a private institution devoted to research, and relies heavily on donations from New York's elite. With several million volumes in its collection, it rivals the Library of Congress in Washington. The books cannot be taken out and must therefore be consulted on the premises. The rooms, restored between 1983 and 1988, are worth a quick tour, starting with the lobby, which is covered in Vermont marble. Behind the lobby are the library shop and the vast Gottesman Exhibition Hall (also a reading room), topped by a magnificent coffered oak ceiling carved by the cabinetmaker Maurice Grière. On the top floor, the McGraw Rotunda is ringed with mural paintings on the theme of reading, executed during the economic crisis of the 1930s. It gives access to the Edna Barnes Salomon Room, which contains old paintings of important figures in the history of New York, as well as rare books and pieces of furniture, including Charles Dickens's desk. Before leaving, make sure to take a look at the sumptuous Public Catalog Room (on the other side of the McGraw Rotunda) and the Main Reading Room, which is over 80 metres long.

Bryant Park ★★ *(between Fifth Ave. and 6th Ave., from 40th to 42nd St.)*, one of the city's loveliest public gardens, lies behind the library. It's hard to believe that this haven of peace and serenity in the heart of Midtown was a hangout for drug addicts and prostitutes until 1993. Thanks to the cleanup efforts of the municipal government, this green space, surrounded by stone balustrades and graced with lovely rows of sycamores, has recovered its dignity. Restaurants and cafés with charming outdoor seating areas have even opened here.

EXPLORING

The park, named after poet William Cullen Bryant, is reminiscent of those found in Europe, with beige rock paths, metal chairs and a luxuriant carpet of ivy.

There are a few interesting buildings around the park, including the old **American Radiator Building** *(40 West 40th St.)*, designed by Raymond Hood and André Fouilhoux (1924). Its stepped crown evokes the Art-Deco style, while its brick walls contrast sharply with the gilded terracotta ornamentation at the top. The old **Beaux Arts Studios** *(80 West 40th St.)*, at the corner of 6th Avenue, date from 1901. The building contains a whole series of split-level artist's studios, each with a large, north-facing window to let in natural light.

Walk back to Fifth Avenue and head north.

In this forest of skyscrapers, it would be easy to overlook the small **Manufacturers Hanover Trust** *(510 Fifth Avenue)* building, located at the corner of 43rd Street. Nevertheless, this sober-looking steel and glass structure, designed by Skidmore, Owings and Merrill in 1954, completely revolutionized the

● ATTRACTIONS

1.	New York Public Library	14.	Rockefeller Center	27.	Old Gotham Hotel
2.	Bryant Park	15.	St. Patrick's Cathedral	28.	St. Regis Hotel
3.	American Radiator Building	16.	Villard Houses	29.	Fifth Avenue Presbyterian Church
		17.	Cartier Jeweller's		
4.	Beaux Art Studios	18.	Swing Street	30.	Sony Building
5.	Manufacturers Hanover Trust	19.	Museum of Television and Radio	31.	IBM Building
				32.	Trump Tower
6.	Century Association	20.	CBS	33.	Harry Winston
7.	Harvard Club	21.	St. Thomas Church	34.	Tiffany & Co.
8.	New York Yacht Club	22.	Museum of Modern Art	35.	Crown Building
9.	Fred French Building	23.	James Goodwin House	36.	Solow Building
10.	Little Brazil	24.	Rockefeller Apartments	37.	BergdorfGoodman
11.	Diamond Row	25.	The American Craft Museum	38.	Grand Army Plaza
12.	Charles Scribner's Sons			39.	General Motors Building
13.	Saks Fifth Avenue	26.	University Club	40.	Plaza Hotel

◯ ACCOMMODATIONS

1.	Big Apple Hostel	5.	Plaza	9.	The Mansfield
2.	Hotel Iroquois	6.	Quality Hotel and Suites at Rockefeller Center	10.	The Peninsula New York
3.	New York Hilton and Towers			11.	The Shoreham
		7.	Royalton	12.	The Warwick Hotel
4.	New York Palace	8.	The Algonquin Hotel		

◇ RESTAURANTS

1.	Bryant Park Café	8.	Garden Café	15.	Nirvana
2.	Bryant Park Grill	9.	Istana	16.	Rainbow Room
3.	Burger Heaven	10.	La Bonne Soupe	17.	Seryna
4.	Cirque 2000	11.	La Côte Basque	18.	Trump Tower Café
5.	Croissant & Gourmet	12.	Lucky's Bar & Grill	19.	Via Brazil
6.	Fashion Café	13.	Micheal's		
7.	Fresco	14.	Motown Cafe		

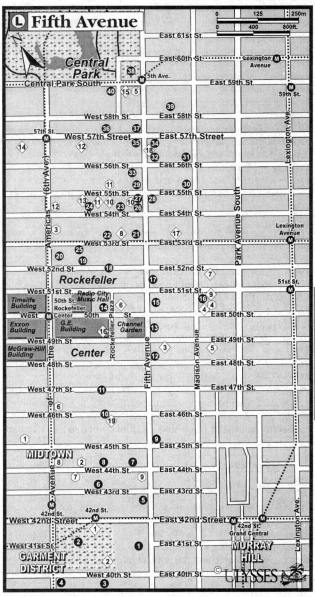

architecture of banks. Its disconcerting simplicity and even more importantly, its interactive relationship with the street (the safe is right in the window) changed the way banking institutions were built, making them more welcoming to the average consumer. In fact, the only people who might have been intimidated by this new style of architecture were thieves.

Most of the private clubs in New York are located on the cross streets of Midtown, near Fifth Avenue. For example, you'll have to take a detour onto West 43rd Street to admire the handsome façade of the **Century Association** ★ *(7 West 43rd St.)*. Erected in 1891, this was one of the first Beaux Arts buildings in America (McKim, Mead and White). The members of this club come from different walks of life but all share an interest in the arts.

Go back to Fifth Avenue and continue northward, then turn onto West 44th Street to see two other clubs.

First, you'll spot the **Harvard Club** ★ *(27 West 44th St.)*, a private club for graduates of Harvard University (Cambridge, Massachusetts). The building was designed in the Georgian Revival style, whose combination of beige stone and red brick is perfectly suited to the spirit of the school. A little farther along, you can admire the façade of the **New York Yacht Club** ★★ *(37 West 44th St.)*, whose windows, shaped like sterns of ships in Louis XIV's fleet, seem to be afloat on a raging sea. This Beaux Arts flight of fancy (Warren and Wetmore, 1899) is topped with a wooden pergola once used for outdoor receptions. In the evening, from the street, when the lights are on inside, you can see the large room displaying miniature replicas of the racing yaughts owned by members of this prestigious institution.

Back on Fifth Avenue, continue northward to Rockefeller Center.

On the way, you'll pass the gilded bronze entrance of the **Fred French Building** *(551 Fifth Ave.)*, built in 1927 in a style combining Art Deco with the taste for the exotic that characterized Hollywood during the great era of silent films (notice the unicorns and the Babylonian-looking winged lions on the portal). This entrance is now protected by the New York Landmarks Preservation Commission.

New York Yacht Club

In this chic, reserved part of New York, it is always surprising to come upon **Little Brazil** *(46th St., between Fifth and 6th avenues)*, a section of 46th Street that is crammed with Brazilian shops and restaurants. Small Brazilian flags fly over the street, lending this part of Midtown a carnival-like atmosphere all year round.

Some visitors will be even more amazed by **Diamond Row ★** *(47th Street, between Fifth and Sixth avenues)*, where the city's diamond merchants are clustered. Most of the jewellery stores here belong to Hasidic Jewish families. You'll find yourself staring wide-eyed at window displays containing brooches, watches and necklaces of up to $100,000 dollars apiece. The jewellery is removed from the display cases at night, and most of the shops are closed on Saturday, the Jewish Sabbath. It is estimated that 80% of the diamonds and other precious stones that enter North America pass through Diamond Row.

Particularly noteworthy among the lovely stores on Fifth Avenue is the façade of the old **Charles Scribner's Sons** *(597 Fifth Ave.)* bookstore, now a Benetton clothing store. Behind the display window, with its ironwork structure, lies a

EXPLORING

vaulted space designed by Ernest Flagg in 1913. The new tenants have made judicious use of the premises, which have been placed under a preservation order by the city. A little farther along stands **Saks Fifth Avenue** *(611 Fifth Ave., see p 394)*, one of the most elegant department stores in New York. All the big names in fashion are represented here in a tasteful, sober decor.

Rockefeller Center ★ ★ ★ stretches from 49th to 52nd Street, west of Fifth Avenue. This vast architectural ensemble, a veritable city within a city, consists of 19 tall buildings linked by a network of underground passageways lined with shops, known as **The Concourse**. An estimated 250,000 people come to work here each weekday. The headquarters of many communications-related businesses (book and magazine publishers, record companies, television networks, advertising agencies and marketing firms), Rockefeller Center is also New York's most popular attraction. The oldest buildings in the complex were erected during the economic crisis of the 1930s by the visionary millionaire John D. Rockefeller, Jr. Over the following decades, they exerted a considerable influence on urban planning in the western part of the world. Clad in a harmonious blend of flat limestone and aluminum appliqués, the buildings have a delicate sophistication rarely found in skyscrapers built during the inter-war period.

The first buildings you'll see upon arriving at Rockefeller Center are **La Maison de la France** and the **British Empire Building**, which contain several shops selling French and British products respectively. These two edifices are separated by the famous **Channel Gardens**, thereby mimicking the geography of Europe. These narrow gardens, redesigned periodically by various New York landscape artists, lead to the **Sunken Plaza**, a huge outdoor terrace, which is crowded with tables of surrounding restaurants during summer and is transformed into a romantic skating rink in winter. Towering over the plaza is an enormous **gilded statue of Prometheus** (Paul Manship, 1934), the Titan who, according to Greek mythology, stole fire from the gods and gave it to man. Every year, an immense Christmas tree twinkling with lights is erected here, to the delight of both young and old.

Rising up in the background is the old **RCA Building** *(30 Rockefeller Plaza)*, renamed the GE Building a few years

Gilded statue of Prometheus

ago. This slender, 70-story Art-Deco tower, inaugurated in 1933, is Raymond Hood and André Fouilhoux's masterpiece. Its pure vertical lines, representing a new form of classicism, made quite a splash at the time. The lobby is adorned with a series of frescoes on the theme of human progress, executed by the Spanish painter José Maria Sert. The 65th floor of the RCA Building is home to the famous **Rainbow Room** *(see p 346)*, a chic restaurant-cum-cabaret with a spectacular view of Midtown. The RCA Building is also the national headquarters of the **NBC television network** *($8.50; guided studio tours every 15 min; Mon to Fri 9:30am to 4:30pm; 30 Rockefeller Plaza, Room IM48 10112, ☎664-7174)*. At night the building is shown off to magnificent advantage by powerful spotlights.

Walk across the Channel Gardens, around the Sunken Plaza and into the GE Building. Go downstairs for a short stroll through The Concourse, then exit onto 6th Avenue, also known as the Avenue of the Americas.

The marquee of the legendary **Radio City Music Hall** *($12; guided tours every hour; every day 10am to 4pm; 1260 Ave. of the Americas, ☎632-4041, www.radiocity.com)*, rimmed with red neon lights, dominates the northeast corner of 50th Street and 6th Avenue. The tour of this other famous section of Rockefeller Center starts in the Grand Foyer, whose ceiling is covered with 24-carat gold leaf. This hall gives access to a huge, 6,000-seat amphitheatre, the home of the Rockettes,

EXPLORING

those high-kicking dancers known for their perfect synchronization. Over the years, their Christmas show, the Radio City Christmas Spectacular, has become an American tradition. Many American movies have premiered at Radio City Music Hall since it opened in 1932. Every year, a number of gala events broadcast to television viewers all over the world are held here, such as the Grammy Awards (for music), the Tony Awards (for theatre), the Emmy Awards (for television) and the MTV Awards (for music videos). It is not unusual to see crowds of young people outside hoping to catch a glimpse of their favourite stars. The huge theatre, designed by Edward Durrell Stone and Donald Deskey, is one of the most important examples of streamlined Deco in North America. It also boasts one of the best-known electric organs in the world, the Mighty Wurlitzer.

In 1938, workers were finally given the go-ahead to start dismantling a segment of the elevated railway (or "el") that had been disfiguring 6th Avenue since the 19th century and blocking the westward expansion of Rockefeller Center. It wasn't until the end of World War II and the boom of the 1960s, however, that a new section of the huge complex finally went up on 6th Avenue, part of which was renamed the Avenue of the Americas for the occasion (only visitors use this name; real New Yorkers still say 6th Ave.). The buildings dating from that period include, from left to right: the **McGraw Hill Building** *(1221 6th Ave.)*, which houses the offices of a major publishing house; the **Exxon Building** *(1251 6th Avenue)*, headquarters of the multinational oil company; and the **Time-Life Building** *(1271 6th Avenue)*, designed in 1959 by Harrison and Abramovitz for the publishing house of the same name.

Take 50th Street back to Fifth Avenue.

There are still more noteworthy parts of Rockefeller Center on Fifth Avenue, including the **Palazzo d'Italia**, where several Italian shops are clustered, and the **International Building** (1935), in front of which is an imposing bronze **statue of Atlas** holding up the world (Paul Manship, 1935).

Soaring skyward across from Rockefeller Center are the spires of **St. Patrick's Cathedral** ★★★ *(Fifth Ave. and 50th St., ☎753-2261)*. A Catholic cathedral, the seat of the archbishopric of New York, it was erected by the large Irish community that settled in the metropolis in the middle of the 19th century, fleeing the misery in their native land (St. Patrick, of course, is the patron saint of Ireland). Though dwarfed by the surrounding skyscrapers, the flamboyant neo-Gothic-style building, is nonetheless impressive, with its towers rising 101 metres above Fifth Avenue and its 124-metre-long nave. Designed by James Renwick, Jr., the cathedral was begun in 1858 but wasn't completed until 30 years later. Particularly noteworthy inside are the 7,800-pipe organ, the gilded baldachin over the Italian marble high altar, and the 60 stained-glass windows from Chartres, as well as the exquisite Lady Chapel, added to the back of the chancel in 1906. St. Patrick's is open to the public during the day, except during religious ceremonies. High Mass starts at 10:15 on Sunday.

Walk to Madison Avenue, behind the cathedral.

Madison Avenue is one of the best vantage points from which to view the cathedral. You can see how complex the apse is and admire the symmetry of the archbishop's palace and its southern equivalent, which houses the presbytery. Across the street stands a group of six brownstones, designed like a single, U-shaped, Renaissance Revival palace around a pretty inner court, which is now part of the New York Palace Hotel. The **Villard Houses** ★★ *(451-455 Madison Ave.)*, designed by McKim, Mead and White in 1884, made the architects stars in their field. They were built for Henry Villard, a journalist and railroad magnate. In 1980, the houses at the back of the court were destroyed to make room for the hotel. Only the façades were preserved, along with a few decorative elements, which now grace the lobby. The two houses facing onto Madison Avenue have met with a happier fate. The one on the right is home to Le Cirque 2000 (see p 346); the one on the left, to the **Urban Center**, which has a big bookstore specializing in architecture and urban planning.

Go back to Fifth Avenue and turn right.

North of 50th Street, the shops on Fifth Avenue become even more luxurious. **Cartier** *(651 Fifth Ave.)*, the French jewellery store, has its New York branch here, in the former mansion of millionaire Morton Plant, built in 1905.

The section of 52nd Street between Fifth and 6th Avenues was renamed **Swing Street** in 1979, due to the many jazz clubs that were located here in the 1930s. Granite plaques inlaid into the sidewalk pay tribute to jazz greats like Dizzy Gillespie, Billie Holiday and Sarah Vaughan. This block is also home to the **Museum of Television and Radio** ★ *($6; ♿; Tue to Sun noon to 6pm; 25 West 52nd St. 10019, ☎621-6600)*, established by William S. Paley, founder of **CBS** (Columbia Broadcasting Society), one of the major American television networks, whose headquarters is located right nearby in a black-granite skyscraper designed in 1965 by Finnish-born architect, Eero Saarinen *(51 West 52nd St.)*. The museum is actually a huge audio-visual library with recordings of 60,000 radio and TV shows. Comfortably ensconced in one of 96 armchairs, headphones in place, you can sit back and enjoy your favourite episodes of *I Love Lucy*.

At the corner of Fifth Avenue and 53rd Street stands the lovely **St. Thomas Church** ★★★ *(1 West 53rd St. 10019, ☎757-7013)*, an Episcopal church whose neo-Gothic architecture strongly influenced the design of religious edifices in North America in the years following its inauguration in 1914. Its architect, Bertram Grosvenor Goodhue, succeeded in building a majestic church on a cramped site. Particularly noteworthy among the many sculptures on the façade are the four medallions surrounding the central rose window, which represent the attributes of the Evangelists: the buffalo for St. Luke, the eagle for St. John, the lion for St. Mark and the angel for St. Matthew. Upon entering the building through the big portal on Fifth Avenue, you will be struck by the noble, pious atmosphere inside. Your eyes will be immediately drawn to the retable, made of Dunville stone, a veritable pantheon of saints sculpted by Lee Lawrie; St. Thomas is shown kneeling before Christ over the high altar. Take a look at the stone vault overhead and, beneath it, the big stained-glass windows in intense shades of blue, made by the Whitefriars atelier in London. The sporadic vibrations you'll feel through the floor are not caused by the fires of hell but rather by the E and F trains of the subway.

The **Museum of Modern Art** ★★★ *($9; ♿; Thu and Sat to Tue 10:30am to 6pm, Fri 10:30am to 8:30pm, closed Wed.; 11 West 53rd St., ☎708-9480, ☞708-9889, www.moma.org)*, commonly referred to as MoMA, is located on West 53rd

Street. This extraordinary museum was founded in 1929 by a group of enlightened art patrons led by Mrs. John D. Rockefeller Jr. Through exhibitions of paintings, sculptures, photographs, furniture and architectural drawings, it highlights the creative endeavors of daring artists of the modern era (1880 to the present day). Many landmarks of modern painting hang here, including Van Gogh's *Starry Night*, Monet's *Water Lilies*, Picasso's *Les Demoiselles d'Avignon* and Dali's *The Persistence of Memory*. The museum also houses a large film library, founded in 1935. Selections from its collection of 10,000 films are shown regularly in two theatres in the basement. At the back of the lobby, visitors can relax in the lovely **Abby Aldrich Rockefeller Sculpture Garden**, a tranquil spot in the heart of Midtown. Refreshments are available at the Garden Café (see p 343). The MoMA shop, for its part, sells lovely reproductions of modern design classics. It takes at least half a day to see the entire museum, so we recommend making a separate trip here on another occasion.

Through the gates of the Sculpture Garden, you'll see an interesting row of buildings whose façades look out onto 54th Street. Among these are the **James Goodwin House** *(9-11 West 54th St.)*, which is actually two brick houses. Designed by McKim, Mead and White in 1897, the Goodwin House marked the beginning of the revival of colonial American architecture that occurred at the turn of the 20th century. The **Rockefeller Apartments** *(17 West 54th St.)*, to the left, is a handsome modern building distinguished by its semicircular oriel windows (André Fouilhoux, 1936).

The nearby **American Craft Museum ★** *($5, &; Tue to Sun 10am to 5pm; 40 West 53rd St., ☎956-3535)* displays 20th-century pottery, collages, furniture, etc. and offers courses on the various techniques used by artisans.

Go back to Fifth Avenue and continue north to 54ᵗʰ Street.

The **University Club ★★** *(closed to the public; 1 West 54th St.)* is reminiscent of the most sumptuous palaces of Florence and Rome. It's a private club that only admits graduates of 18 renowned American universities, whose crests, sculpted by Daniel Chester French, can be seen between the little half-storey windows. Inside, there are dining rooms, sitting rooms, a bar, a long vaulted library, a hairdressing salon and about 20 rooms for visiting members from outside New York City. Another masterpiece by McKim, Mead and White (1899), this building bears witness to the immense wealth amassed by certain New Yorkers in the late 19th century.

The old **Gotham Hotel ★** (see p 300) *(2 West 55th St.)* stands alongside the University Club and echoes its design. The Gotham and its rival, the **St. Regis Hotel ★**, across the street on Fifth Avenue, were both built during the *belle époque* and are very ornate inside.

In 1875, St. Patrick's Cathedral was nearing completion and the first Anglican church in Midtown went up. Not wanting to be left out, the Presbyterians built the **Fifth Avenue Presbyterian Church ★★** *(705 Fifth Ave.)*, made of brownstone from Belleville, New Jersey. Over the entrance, there is an interesting mosaic with all sorts of symbols in it, including a circle representing the Earth, in a triangle representing the Holy Trinity. The interior, covered with dark, neo-Gothic woodwork, is laid out around the pulpit normally reserved for the altar; the sermon plays a more important role than the Eucharist in Presbyterian services. The lovely stained-glass windows were executed by John C. Spence of Montreal.

Take 55th Street east to the entrance of the atrium of the Sony Building.

The North American subsidiary of the Sony empire has moved into the former headquarters of AT&T (the American Telephone and Telegraph Company). The **Sony Building ★★** *(free admission; Sony Plaza every day 8am to 6pm, museum Tue to Sat 10am to 6pm, Sun noon to 6pm; 550 Madison Ave. 10022, ☎833-8100)*, the standard-bearer of 1980s postmodernism, was designed by Philip Johnson and John Burgee in 1984. Its silhouette, shaped like a Chippendale highboy topped by a broken pediment, revolutionized the way skyscrapers were designed in North America. In its atrium, renamed **Sony Plaza**, you can meet a friendly robot eager to chat with visitors. The **Sony Wonder Laboratory**, next to the atrium, is a museum with interactive exhibits filled with gadgets that will entertain both children and adults and familiarize them with high technology and communications.

Leave the atrium through the 56th Street exit.

On the other side of 56th Street, you'll see the bamboo-filled atrium of the **IBM Building** *(590 Madison Ave.)*. Designed as a revolutionized public space in the early 1980s, this indoor garden has aged poorly. Since its inauguration, IBM Buildings with similar bamboo gardens have been erected all over the world.

Go back to Fifth Avenue and turn right.

Real-estate magnate Donald Trump, whose marriages and divorces have been the topic of front-page stories in all the tabloids, made his own contribution to the urban landscape of Fifth Avenue by building a tall office tower atop the five-story shopping centre that replaced the Bonwit-Teller department store. He humbly named the result the **Trump Tower ★** *(every day 9am to 6pm; 725 Fifth Ave.)*. Inside, the public spaces are covered with pink Italian marble, and the counters are plated with 22-carat gold. The central atrium, adorned with a waterfall, gives access to a series of meandering corridors lined with shops. You'd better have deep pockets if you plan on buying something in this shopping mall for millionaires. If heights make you dizzy, don't take the escalators up to the two tiny gardens laid out on the roofs of the building's overhangs. The one on level four offers a good view of the Sony Building.

In her famous song, *Diamonds Are a Girl's Best Friend*, Marilyn Monroe enumerates a whole list of prestigious jewellery stores on Fifth Avenue. The most exclusive of them all is definitely **Harry Winston** *(at the corner of 56th St.)*, whose emerald and ruby necklaces, glittering behind tiny, square display windows, are worth a small fortune. Not just anyone can enter this well-guarded fortress ("Talk to me, Harry Winston, tell me all about it").

You won't have any trouble getting into **Tiffany & Co. ★★★** *(727 Fifth Ave. 10022, ☎755-8000)*, which has four floors of luxury items (the escalators are at the back). This company, whose name is synonymous with sparkling diamonds, was founded by Charles Lewis Tiffany in 1837. In 1867, Tiffany won a gold medal for his silverware at the World's Fair in Paris, enabling him to become the official silversmith of 17 European monarchs. Ten years later, the Tiffany Diamond, the largest yellow diamond in the world at an original weight of 287 carats, was discovered in the mines of Kimberley, South Africa.

EXPLORING

In 1886, Tiffany invented claw settings for stones on rings, which soon became the norm all over the world. Around the same time, Charles Tiffany's son, Louis Comfort Tiffany, became artistic director of the company. A pioneer of art nouveau, he created beautiful jewellery shaped like plants and insects; luminous stained glass windows and splendid lamps that collectors fight over at auctions and antique sales. Since the 19th century, Tiffany has also been designing magnificent silver trophies for various sports events, such as the US Open (tennis) and the Superbowl (Vincent Lombardi Trophy for football). Tiffany & Co. also made the rings awarded to the members of the Toronto Blue Jays baseball team when they won the World Series (1992). Paloma Picasso has been the head of the design department since 1980. Tiffany moved into its current location in 1840, a building vaguely Art Deco in style. Audrey Hepburn can be seen gazing dreamily into its windows in *Breakfast at Tiffany's*.

The Playboy empire's New York offices are headquartered in the **Crown Building** ★ *(730 Fifth Ave.)*, a beige brick tower with lavishly gilded ornamentation. It is worth craning your neck to admire its fanciful top.

The big, 50-story edifice with the curved façade that dominates the urban landscape of West 57th Street is the **Solow Building** ★ *(9 West 57th St.)*, designed by Skidmore, Owings and Merrill. It is partially occupied by the offices of real-estate developer Sheldon Solow.

Continue up Fifth Avenue to Grand Army Plaza, which opens onto the soothing greenery of Central Park.

The luxury department store **Bergdorf-Goodman** *(754 Fifth Ave.)* occupies two buildings on either side of Fifth Avenue, north of 57th Street (see p 393). The one of the west side was built in 1928 on the site of the mansion of Cornelius Vanderbilt II, who was the richest man in the world at the end of the 19th century. With over 60 rooms, his home was a veritable palace in the French Renaissance Revival style and looked out onto a main courtyard in front of Grand Army Plaza.

Grand Army Plaza ★ *(Fifth Ave. and Central Park S.)* marks the end of the commercial part of Fifth Avenue and the beginning of the institutional and residential section that runs along the

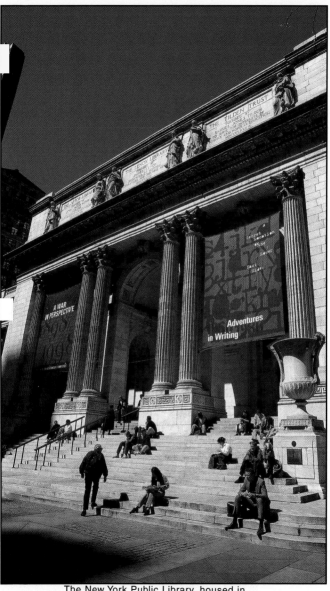

The New York Public Library, housed in
an enormous Beaux-Arts building from 1911
built by Carrère and Hastings. - *T. B.*

The Empire State Building towers over this part of Manhattan's urban jungle.
- *T. B.*

The South Street Seaport district has become a sort of open-air maritime museum and the least "New York" in character, with more of a New England feel.
- *T. B.*

east side of Central Park. The centre of the square, known simply as "the plaza" by New Yorkers, is occupied by the **Pulitzer Memorial Fountain** (see Pulitzer House, p 223), topped by a statue of Pomona, the goddess of abundance (Karl Bitter, 1912). On the north side, there is a gilded equestrian statue of **General William Tecumseh Sherman**, who died in New York in 1891 (Augustus Saint-Gaudens, 1903). A career soldier, Sherman won many victories against the South during the Civil War. Coach drivers offer carriage tours of Central Park from Grand Army Plaza.

The **General Motors Building** *(767 Fifth Ave.)*, the New York headquarters of the largest American automobile manufacturer, stands east of the plaza. This 50-story building was erected in 1968 on the site of the Savoy Hotel.

More fortunate than its neighbour, the **Plaza Hotel** ★★ *(west of Grand Army Plaza)* has withstood tremendous pressure from real-estate developers. It has become a Hollywood star of sorts, thanks to the many scenes that have been shot on the premises. You can see it in *Plaza Suite*, *Crocodile Dundee* and *Home Alone II*, to name a few. All this exposure has made the Plaza world-famous. The building, covered with glazed white brick, was erected in 1905 in the German Renaissance style (Henry J. Hardenberg). Make sure to go inside and have a look at the luxurious Palm Court and the opulent black-veined, white marble corridors leading to the famous Oak Bar (see p 383), where you can admire a mural painting of Cornelius Vanderbilt II's mansion, mentioned above.

Before continuing northward on Fifth Avenue, you might want to do the tour of the Upper East Side, which starts at Grand Army Plaza. The plaza is also the starting point of the Central Park tour. To get back to 42nd Street, take any of the buses heading back down Fifth Avenue (M1, M2, M3, M4 or M5).

TOUR M: PARK AVENUE AND SURROUNDINGS ★★ (3 hours)

Midtown East, so-called because it is east of Fifth Avenue, is an area dominated by the headquarters of international manufacturing companies, most of them installed in the lofty, glass and steel skyscrapers of Park Avenue. At the end of the

EXPLORING

19th century, Park Avenue was nothing more than a horrible trench run through by railroad tracks that connected to Grand Central Terminal at 42nd Street (see From the Empire State Building to the United Nations, p 170). The thoroughfare that is so renowned today was laid down over this gulley between 1903 and 1913, but it is amusing to know that a big ditch is actually at the root of Park Avenue's exceptional prestige. The neighbourhood became immediately fashionable and elegant upper-class homes were built here. Many of these later gave way to tall office towers in Midtown East, south of 60th Street, and luxury apartment buildings on the Upper East Side, between 60th Street and 96th Street.

Midtown is New York's second business district. Since the Wall Street financial district was constrained to a limited area, it was imperative that a new nucleus of skyscrapers develop in another part of New York. Because of the characteristics of the ground between Canal Street and 23rd Street, tall buildings could not be built there, so, beginning in 1925, this new centre was created in Midtown, and Manhattan Island acquired its famous profile marked by these two groves of skyscrapers, one at its southern tip and the other right in the middle, near Central Park. It is strongly recommended to avoid visiting this neighbourhood at office quitting time, around 5pm, when a generalized and very unpleasant sort of chaos predominates.

The tour begins across from Bloomingdale's at the exit from the 59th Street/Lexington Avenue subway station, which is served by the 4, 6, N and R trains and buses M101, M102 and M103.

Paradoxically situated on the edge of the Upper East Side, New York's poshest neighbourhood, **Bloomingdale's** *(740 Lexington Ave.)* foremost targets a middle-class clientele (see p 394). In the tradition of large Parisian stores, this huge department store is laid out in a series of more or less well-connected buildings from different eras. Its Lexington Avenue façade is a sober Art Deco design from 1930 that attempts to unify the whole.

Take Lexington Avenue southward.

The curving shape of the building known simply as **135 East 57th Street** *(corner of Lexington Ave. and 57th St.)*, designed by Kohn Pedersen Fox, the architects behind the IBM-Marathon tower in Montreal, is typical of 1980s post-modernism. The

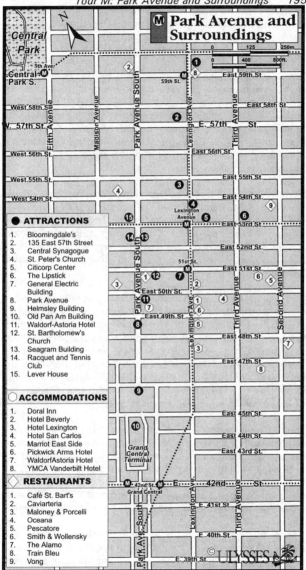

M Park Avenue and Surroundings

ATTRACTIONS

1. Bloomingdale's
2. 135 East 57th Street
3. Central Synagogue
4. St. Peter's Church
5. Citicorp Center
6. The Lipstick
7. General Electric Building
8. Park Avenue
9. Helmsley Building
10. Old Pan Am Building
11. Waldorf-Astoria Hotel
12. St. Bartholomew's Church
13. Seagram Building
14. Racquet and Tennis Club
15. Lever House

ACCOMMODATIONS

1. Doral Inn
2. Hotel Beverly
3. Hotel Lexington
4. Hotel San Carlos
5. Marriot East Side
6. Pickwick Arms Hotel
7. WaldorfAstoria Hotel
8. YMCA Vanderbilt Hotel

RESTAURANTS

1. Café St. Bart's
2. Caviarteria
3. Maloney & Porcelli
4. Oceana
5. Pescatore
6. Smith & Wollensky
7. The Alamo
8. Train Bleu
9. Vong

EXPLORING

© ULYSSES

open peristyle on the corner is especially remarkable and a
perfect illustration of the echoing of antiquity that is
characteristic of some post-modern works.

The **Central Synagogue** ★ *(free; Mon to Thu noon to 2pm;
652 Lexington Ave.)*, of the Ahawath Chesed Shaar
Hashomayim congregation, was erected in 1870 by the first
famous Jewish architect in New York, Henry Fernbach. Its
"minarets" and its Moorish arches are evidence of the
popularity of Middle Eastern forms in synagogue construction
in the later half of the 19th century. Its polychrome interior is
worth a quick peek.

In contrast to the eclecticism and mass of the Central
Synagogue, **St. Peter's Church** ★ *(corner of Lexington Ave.
and 54th St.)* is disarmingly simple. This Lutheran church was
rebuilt in 1976 as part of the Citicorp project described below.
Its bay window directly overlooks the tent-shaped sanctuary
and provides a view of a group of sculptures by Louise
Nevelson.

Tiny St. Peter's is nestled at the foot its big neighbour, **Citicorp
Center** ★ *(corner of Lexington Ave. and 53rd St.)*, a 68-story
skyscraper built in 1977 by Hugh Stubbins and Emery Roth &
Sons. Its slanted top, which originally was supposed to hold
solar panels, has become an icon of the late modernism of the
1970s, when architects were attempting to fragment the
traditional box-shape of the skyscraper. The building's exterior
is covered in polished aluminum and the tower sits on four
enormous piles, freeing up space at street level.

The red tower visible to the east down 54th Street, lovingly
nicknamed **The Lipstick** ★ *(885 3rd Ave.)* by New Yorkers, is
without question one of the most original skyscrapers of the
1980s (John Burgee and Philip Johnson, architects, 1986). At
once amusing and elegant, complex and pure, it is composed
of three telescoping ovals creating the impression that it would
grow taller if someone twisted it at the base, just like a lipstick!

The refined details of the **General Electric Building** ★★
(570 Lexington Ave.) make it an exceptionally rich work. Built
in 1931 for the RCA Victor record and electric appliance
company, the thin tower designed by Cross & Cross skilfully
combines Art Deco and neo-Gothic elements. Especially

remarkable are the aluminum lightning bolts in its bas-reliefs, a not too abstract symbol of electricity. It is worth a little meander to the middle of the long interior hall, and the suspicious looks of building staff, to admire its neon-light-accented decor.

Turn right on 49th Street to reach Park Avenue.

Park Avenue ★★★ exudes a sense of incredible space and grandeur. This prestigious avenue stretches from Union Square north into Harlem. It is interrupted along the way by Grand Central Terminal, to which are annexed the Helmsley and Pan Am Buildings, the whole creating a splendid view from the south. The central islands that divide the avenue, once huge and grassy, have unfortunately been reduced significantly to ease the flow of car traffic.

The **Helmsley Building** ★ *(230 Park Ave.)* is the focal point on the Park Avenue landscape. Erected in 1928 to house the offices of the Grand Central Railway Company, the powerful train company founded by Cornelius "the Commodore" Vanderbilt in the 19th century, it possesses two large arcades on its ground floor that allow automobiles to access the station situated behind it. At night, the top of the Helmsley Building is embellished by skilful lighting that emphasizes the complex ornamentation of its crown.

The profile of the upper floors of the former **Pan Am Building** ★ *(200 Park Ave.)*, erected in 1963, is visible above the Helmsley Building. The headquarters of the defunct airline today house the offices of Metropolitan Life, the largest life insurance company in North America. This building is probably the best-known symbol of 1960s New York, thanks to its octagonal form, conceived by the founder of Bauhaus, Walter Gropius, and to its numerous appearances in the films of that era.

Take Park avenue north.

In 1897, a dispute between the queen of New York high society, Caroline Astor, and her brother-in-law and neighbour, William Waldorf Astor, incited the latter to demolish his home and erect in its place a huge hotel that he named The Waldorf, in the hope of causing maximal disturbance in the until then peaceful neighbourhood. Rather than raise a white flag,

EXPLORING

Caroline Astor's family put up another hotel next to The Waldorf, this one twice the size, and called it The Astoria. A few months later, the two branches of the family were reconciled and the two establishments at the corner of Fifth Avenue and 34th Street merged to become the Waldorf-Astoria, the largest hotel in the world. In 1931, the Fifth Avenue buildings were torn down to make way for the Empire State Building and the **Waldorf-Astoria Hotel ★** *(301 Park Ave.)* moved into a 59-story Art-Deco mastodon of over 1,800 rooms. The hotel of choice for crowned heads and political personalities has a separate entrance on 50th Street that leads directly to its tall towers of luxuriously furnished apartments in which such notables as John F. Kennedy, Henry Kissinger and the Duke of Windsor have stayed. Follow in the footsteps of most of the monarchs of the 20th century by taking a stroll on the long lobby promenade.

Very beautiful **St. Bartholomew's Church ★★★** *(between 50th St. and 51st St.)* was one of the first prestigious buildings to go up on Park Avenue once it was laid out over the New York Central railroad tracks. This temple was designed in 1916 by the American champion of neo-Gothic churches, Bertram Grosvenor Goodhue, who also built pious St. Thomas Church on Fifth Avenue (see p 188). His mandate here included the integration of a Romanesque portal donated by the Vanderbilt family, which was designed by McKim, Mead and White for an earlier church in 1909, and he made the exceptional choice of elevating the entire structure, in a Byzanto-Romanesque flavour. The result remains spectacular despite the construction of skyscrapers all around the temple in the decades that followed. Its exterior walls, in salmon-pink brick and grey Indiana limestone, conceal an interior that is particularly rich for the Episcopalian Church. The porphyry and Sienna marble choir, complemented by the mosaics of artist Hilary Maiere, set the tone. The dome, added in 1927, is comprised of a tangle of ducts that are actually part of the 12,442-pipe electro-pneumatic Aeolian-Skinner organ, the largest instrument of its kind in New York. The chapel off the principal nave, nicknamed "the children's chapel", adopts the more sober vocabulary of the earliest Christian churches. It is worthwhile to take a stroll through the square adjoining the church for a detailed view of its dome.

Prohibition, the law that made it illegal to sell liquor in the United States, was adopted in 1919, sparking the opening up of a gigantic black market in the distillation and distribution of spirits. To position himself in this market, Canadian Sam Bronfman bought the Seagram & Sons distillery and, over the course of the 1920s, established his headquarters in Montreal, where he supervised the shipment of his alcohol over the border. The abolition of prohibition in 1933, far from harming the company, propelled it to new heights of success because the quality of its products had become renowned despite their temporarily illicit character. At the beginning of the 1950s, Sam Bronfman wanted to ensconce Seagram's presence in the American metropolis. His daughter, Phyllis Lambert, then an architecture student, protested against his conservatism and demanded that this building make a splash. At her instigation, the **Seagram Building** ★★ *(375 Park Ave.)* was erected in 1956 according to the plans of the intellectual leader of the Bauhaus movement, Ludwig Mies van der Rohe. Its design rejected the principal of terracing, preponderant in New York since 1916, in favour of a tower set back on a plaza. Its heavy bronze shell and the purity of its lines have made it one of the most important monuments of modern architecture in the world.

Across from the Seagram Building stands the **Racquet and Tennis Club** *(370 Park Ave.)*, erected in 1918 in the style of an Italian Renaissance palace by the architectural firm of McKim, Mead and White. This is one of seven private clubs where the sport of rackets, or racquetball, is still practised in North America. Since they could not play tennis, 18th-century English nobles incarcerated in debtor's prison created a game in which the object was to hit a hard ball against the prison wall. The club also has a room laid out for the even rarer sport of court tennis, a game played by Louis XIV in the court of Versailles.

All of the great cities of the world now boast mirrored-glass buildings in which people can check their reflections before important meetings. **Lever House** ★★ *(390 Park Ave.)* is the doyen of these mirror-curtained towers. Built in 1952 by Skidmore, Owings and Merril, it is elevated on a podium that surrounds a charming garden in a design very much influenced by the thinking of Le Corbusier. It houses the headquarters of the Lever company, a skin-care and domestic-cleaning product manufacturer.

To return to the tour departure point, turn right on 55th Street and left on Lexington Avenue.

TOUR N: TIMES SQUARE AND BROADWAY ★★ (4 hours)

Broadway weaves its way up and across the island of Manhattan, intersecting diagonally with a number of avenues. At 7th Avenue and 43rd Street, the intersection forms a tiny, unimpressive triangle identified by a small sign reading "Times Square". The offices of the New York Times used to face onto this triangle, hence its name, which has unofficially come to designate the shapeless sea of asphalt extending as far as 48th Street.

Somewhat depressing during daytime, like a dark television in the corner of someone's living room, Times Square becomes a magical place after dark, when its huge neon signs light up.

● ATTRACTIONS

1.	Old Knickerbocker Hotel	16.	Lyceum Theatre
2.	New Victory Theatre	17.	Church of St. Mary the Virgin
3.	Ford Center for the Performing Arts	18.	Times Square Visitor's and Transit
4.	New Amsterdam Theatre		Information Center
5.	Port Authority Bus Terminal	19.	Palace Theatre
6.	Old McGrawHill Building	20.	Duffy Square
7.	The St. James and the new Helen Hayes	21.	TKTS
	Theatre	22.	Morgan Stanley Headquarters and Ethel
8.	The Majestic, Broadhurst, and Shubert		Barrymore Theatre
	Theatres	23.	LuntFontanne Theatre
9.	Shubert Alley	24.	Brill Building
10.	Music Box Theatre	25.	Winter Garden Theatre
11.	The Booth, Plymouth, Royale and Golden	26.	Roseland
	Theatres	27.	Broadway Theatre and the Ed Sullivan
12.	Times Square		Theatre
13.	One Times Square	28.	Arts Student League Building
14.	Marriott Marquis Hotel and the Marquis	29.	Carnegie Hall
	Theatre	30.	Alwyn Court Appartments
15.	Old Paramount Building		

◯ ACCOMMODATIONS

1.	Best Western Woodward	6.	Millenium Broadway
2.	Casablanca Hotel	7.	Novotel New York
3.	Crowne Plaza Manhattan	8.	RIGHA Royal Hotel
4.	Hotel Edison	9.	The Paramount
5.	Milford Plaza Ramada	10.	Westpark Hotel

◇ RESTAURANTS

1.	Becco	8.	Le Max
2.	Bernadin	9.	Petrossian
3.	Carnegie Deli	10.	Restaurant Charlotte
4.	Figaro	11.	Russian Samovar
5.	Hour Glass Tavern	12.	Stage Deli of New York
6.	JeanLafitte	13.	The Daily Soup
7.	Le Marais	14.	Zen Palate

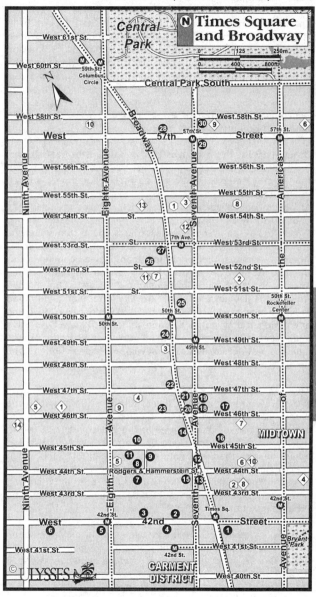

The neighbouring streets are lined with theatres (about 40 in all), which present not only big Broadway musicals but also lesser-venue plays and dance shows. In 1995, over 9.5 million tickets were sold here. Between 6th and 9th Avenues, the streets are also studded with some 250 restaurants of all different kinds, as well as about 30 hotels ranging from seedy rooming houses to luxury accommodations. Every year on December 31, nearly half a million people pack onto Times Square to kick off the New Year.

Up until 1993, this area was best avoided after dark. It was teeming with pickpockets and other malefactors. In between the theatres, there were scores of strip clubs and peep shows. Prostitutes, both male and female, hung about on the sidewalks propositioning passersby, and drug dealers used the telephone booths as offices. However, thanks to a major cleanup effort, Times Square has metamorphosed at a speed that would be impossible anywhere else but in New York. Nowadays, typical American families, toddlers in tow, can be seen coming out of the Disney store at around 11pm, loaded up with stuffed animals. Fans of the film *Midnight Cowboy*, starring John Voight and Dustin Hoffman, are likely to feel their blood pressure shoot up at the sight. Local authorities are doing everything in their power to improve Times Square's negative image and attract tourists from all over with a barrage of eye-catching advertisements. The developers cut straight to the point: "Times change."

The area is extremely dense, and you sometimes have to cross the narrow streets right in the middle of an intersection (be careful not to get run over by the limousines whizzing by) to admire the part of the theatres above their marquees, which usually extend over the sidewalk. To make your life simpler, avoid touring the area between 5pm and 8:30pm, when theatre-goers pack into local restaurants to wolf down a meal then line up on the sidewalk waiting to be let into the shows, completely blocking the way for pedestrians, who have no other choice but to walk in the street.

The Times Square and Broadway tour starts at the intersection of 7th Avenue and 42nd Street, near the various exits of the Times Square/42nd Street subway station, served by the N, R, 1, 2, 3 and 7 trains. The M10 bus, which runs up and down the island of Manhattan, also stops here.

Unlike the present-day theatres, most of which are located on cross streets, the first "Broadway" theatres faced right onto the artery for which they were named. They were clustered on this side of Times Square, around the old Metropolitan Opera House (demolished) erected in 1883, down by 39th Street. This theatre was built by people who had been rejected by the Academy of Music, an institution that prided itself on handpicking its audience. Revenge is sweet: the Metropolitan Opera was an immediate success, forcing its rival theatre to shut down after three miserable years of decline.

The sole survivor from that era is the former **Knickerbocker Hotel** *(1466 Broadway)*, which was built in 1906 and has been converted into offices. Its Louis XIII facing, a blend of beige stone and red brick, bares witness to the popularity of the Parisian Beaux-Arts style in this area in the early 20th century. Enrico Caruso, who sang regularly at the neighbouring opera house, kept rooms here.

Take West 42nd Street west, toward 8th Avenue.

Forty-second Street is almost as famous as Broadway. Its name calls to mind the great American musicals of the 1920s and 1930s. The **New Victory Theatre ★** *(209 West 42nd St.)* was built in 1900 by Oscar Hammerstein, one of the first theatre managers to set up business in this area, known in the 19th century as Long Acre. Up until then, it had been home to carriage-builders and stables for horses used to pull taxis. The New Victory had its heyday in the 1920s, then later fell into disuse and was a porno theatre up until 1993. Completely restored in 1995, it now presents children's shows (circuses, marionette shows, etc.), thus epitomizing the drastic turnaround Broadway has undergone in the 1990s, nearly a century after the first theatres opened here.

The **Ford Center for the Performing Arts ★** *(213 West 42nd S.)*, inaugurated in 1997, is a 1,840-seat theatre adorned with decorations from two historic theatres, the Apollo (not to be confused with the theatre of the same name in Harlem), where singer Ethel Merman performed for years, and the Lyric, where Irving Berlin's musical *Coconuts*, starring the Marx Brothers, was first presented. These two theatres, whose original façades look onto 43rd Street, now open onto 42nd Street, where the main entrance of the Ford Center is located.

EXPLORING

Just across the street from the aforementioned theatres, the **New Amsterdam Theatre** ★★ *(214 West 42nd St.)* was built in 1903 according to a design by Herts and Tallant. Its interior is one of the few examples of Art Nouveau in North America. The New Amsterdam was beautifully restored in 1996 by Disney after 14 years of neglect. Those fortunate enough to get inside can admire the rose and peacock patterns on the ceiling, the proscenium lights shaped like clusters of grapes and the oval former smoking room, surrounded by heavy columns that look straight out of some Germanic tale from the Middle Ages.

At the corner of 8th Avenue stands the gloomy, massive **Port Authority Bus Terminal**, which has an unsettling air about it. It is here, at this gigantic tiered terminal, that all buses to New York arrive (see p 62). Rising up behind it is the old **McGraw-Hill Building** ★ *(330 West 42nd St.)*. This greenish tower, erected in 1931, was one of the first modern skyscrapers in the United States. Designed by the talented Raymond Hood, it features a curtain wall made up of a series of horizontal, stepped bands containing alternating panels of glass and terra cotta.

Turn right on 8th Avenue, then right again on 44th Street, renamed Rodgers & Hammerstein Street, between 8th Avenue and Broadway.

You are now in the heart of the largest collection of theatres in the world. On the south side of the street stand the **St. James** *(246 West 44th St.)* and the new **Helen Hayes Theatre** *(240 West 44th St.)*; on the north side, the **Majestic** *(247 West 44th St.)*, where the musical *South Pacific* first opened, the **Broadhurst** *(235 West 44th St.)* and the **Shubert** *(225 West 44th St.)*, where the famous musical *A Chorus Line* ran for 15 years, from 1975 to 1990.

Take Shubert Alley, which runs alongside the theatre of the same name, to 45th Street.

Actors and actresses hoping to get a role in a Broadway show used to spend lots of time in **Shubert Alley**. They sometimes had to wait for hours at production companies like the Shubert Organization before being allowed a brief audition for some blasé producer.

In 1988, the New York Landmarks Preservation Commission added 28 Broadway theatres to its list of protected buildings. Among these was the **Music Box Theatre** ★ *(239 West 45th Street)*, whose lovely Georgian Revival façade was designed in 1921 by the great American theatre specialist, architect Howard Crane. The Music Box was built by the prolific Russian-American composer Irving Berlin (1888-1989), who wrote the musicals *Top Hat* and *On the Avenue*, as well as about a thousand popular songs, including *Easter Parade*, *White Christmas* and *Cheek to Cheek*. Berlin owned the theatre right up until he died – nearly 68 years, a record in the industry. Across from the Music Box stand the **Booth** *(222 West 45th St.)*, the **Plymouth** *(236 West 45th St.)*, the **Royale** *(242 West 45th St.)* and the **Golden** *(252 West 45th St.)*.

Take 45th Street east to the centre of Times Square.

Despite the crowds, the hubbub and the glitter and glare, a visit to **Times Square** ★★★ is an essential part of any trip to New York. Of course, you won't find beauty and elegance here, but rather American consumerism in one of its purest and most frenzied forms. Make sure to come back in the evening if you tour the area during daytime, as the difference between day and night is truly dramatic at Times Square!

To the south, you'll see **One Times Square** *(at the intersection of Broadway and 7th Ave.)*, a triangular building that was once the headquarters of *The New York Times*. The inauguration of the building on December 31, 1904 was marked by noisy fireworks, and thus was born the famous tradition of ushering in the New Year at Times Square. After undergoing some unfortunate modifications in 1966, the building was modernized once again to house the offices of the Time-Warner company. Hanging on its north side is a huge TV screen, the Panasonic Astrovision, on which NBC broadcasts all its shows. Also on the building is the famous Dow Jones Zipper, a narrow horizontal screen with the stock prices running across it.

The first giant neon signs on Times Square went up in 1916. Advertisers soon started coming up with imaginative ways to compete for the attention of passers-by, installing mechanical movements to make the legs of the stars featured on the signs move, adding waterfalls to imitate the sound of a famous soft drink or sending out smoke rings from a huge metal cigarette.

EXPLORING

The 1986 construction of the enormous **Marriott Marquis Hotel** *(1535 Broadway)* led to the demolition of two historic theatres, the old Helen Hayes and the Morosco, thereby mobilizing public support for the preservation of old Broadway theatres. To make up for this wrongdoing, developer John Portman built the **Marquis Theatre**, whose rounded form can be seen at the foot of the giant, 1877-room hotel. The hotel lobby, which extends from the 8th floor to the top, is not to be missed.

Cross Broadway, then turn around for a better view of the west side of Times Square.

The old **Paramount Building** *(1501 Broadway)*, to the southwest, was built by the production company of the same name in 1926. The tower, equipped with a clock and topped by a black ball that used to light up, quickly became a symbol of Times Square.

Make a small detour east on West 45th Street to see an important theatre.

The Baroque Revival **Lyceum Theatre ★** *(149 West 45th St.)*, graced with one of the loveliest façades in the area, captures the essence of the *belle époque*. It was built in 1903 by Herts and Tallant.

Go back to 7th Avenue and head north, then make a short detour onto 46th Street to admire a church façade.

In the middle of the block, amidst all the theatres and hotels, a vision will rise up before you. The **Church of St. Mary the Virgin ★** *(145 West 46th St.)* is a member of the Free Church movement, where Mass is celebrated in Latin. The ample use of incense during the long, complex ceremonies has earned the church the nickname Smoky Mary. The neo-Gothic building, begun in 1895 by architect Napoléon Le Brun, is the oldest steel-frame church in the world.

Go back to 7th Avenue and continue northward.

Detailed maps of the area are available at the **Times Square Visitor's and Transit Information Center ★★** *(free admission; every day 9am to 9pm; 1560 Broadway, ☎768-1560, www.times-square.org)*, which also presents an exhibition on the history of Times Square and its paramour, 42nd Street. The center offers free guided walking tours of the theatre district every Friday at noon.

The **Palace Theatre** *(1564 Broadway)* is one of the only Broadway theatres whose entrance is actually on Broadway and not on one of the cross-streets. Since its construction in 1913, it has hosted performances by such celebrities as Sarah Bernhardt and Houdini. The musical *La Cage aux Folles* also played here for many years.

At the corner of Broadway and 46th Street, a tiny, triangular space known as **Duffy Square** is struggling to find itself a place in the sun. Actually, all New Yorkers think of it as part of Times Square. The bronze statues of George Cohan (1878-1942), author of the famous song *Give My Regards to Broadway*, and Father Francis Duffy (1871-1932), confessor of actors and writers, stand amidst the crowds of people who come here to buy theatre tickets at the booth at the Times Square Theatre Center, better known as **TKTS** *(no credit cards or cheques; two- to three-hour wait to purchase tickets; Mon and Tue and Thu and Fri 3pm to 8pm, Wed and Sat 10am to 2pm and 3pm to 8pm, Sun 11am to 7pm; Broadway and 47th St.)*, in the north part of the square. If you've got a lot of patience, you can purchase tickets for the most famous shows on Broadway here. These tickets, sold at discount prices (often 50% off), are for same-day shows. There is another TKTS booth in Lower Manhattan, inside 2 World Trade Center *(Mon to Fri 11am and 5pm, Sat 11am to 3pm)*, which not only has the advantage of being protected from bad weather but is also less of a zoo.

Turn left on 47th Street, cross 7th Avenue then turn right on Broadway and continue for 10 blocks to 57th Street.

A multimedia sign providing all sorts of financial information (stock prices, currency values, etc.) was installed on the **New Morgan Stanley Headquarters** *(1585 Broadway)* in 1995. Behind this building stands the **Ethel Barrymore Theatre** *(243 West 47th St.)*, where *A Streetcar Named Desire* was first produced in 1947, with Marlon Brando in the starring role. Theatre buffs will no doubt want to backtrack to admire the entrance of the **Lunt-Fontanne Theatre ★** *(205 West 46th St.)*, designed by Carrère and Hastings (1910). It was here that *The*

EXPLORING

Sound of Music was presented for the first time, before being expertly adapted for the screen.

Tin Pan Alley, the legendary street of American lyricists and composers, has actually existed in several different places, the most recent being the space in front of the **Brill Building** *(1619 Broadway)*, which is home to a number of music publishers.

The **Winter Garden Theatre** *(1634 Broadway)*, across from the new Paramount building *(1633 Broadway)*, hosted the world premiere of the musical *West Side Story*. The building, erected in 1911, is completely covered with signs, so none of its original architecture is visible.

The **Roseland** *(239 West 52nd St.)* is a huge dance hall that looks like something out of Fellini's *Ginger and Fred*. Bands playing everything from ballroom music to South American samba perform in a deco-meets-1950s decor. In the lobby, the dancing shoes of a number of celebrities, including Ginger Rodgers and Gene Kelly, are on view in a simple display case.

The 1765-seat **Broadway Theatre** *(1681 Broadway)* is one of the biggest Broadway venues. It was here that Anthony Quinn played in *Zorba the Greek* and *Evita* brought audiences to their feet. On the other side of 53rd Street stands the **Ed Sullivan Theatre** *(1697 Broadway)*, which is actually a big television studio that is open to the public. This is where the famous *Late Night with David Letterman* show is broadcast live.

Turn right on 57th Street.

The **Arts Student League Building** *(215 West 57th St.)*, now an art school, was built in 1892 as the American Fine Arts Society, a private club for informed collectors.

Carnegie Hall ★★ *(free admission to the museum, $6 for the guided tour; museum Thu to Tue 11am to 4:30pm, guided tours Mon, Tue, Thu and Fri 11:30am, 2pm and 3pm; 154 West 57th St., museum: ☎903-9629, guided tours: ☎903-9790)* is justly considered a musical shrine in the United States. Any artist who succeeds in performing within these hallowed walls is immediately consecrated. Many memorable events in the history of music and song have taken place here, including the inaugural concert, conducted by Tchaikovsky himself (1891), the premiere of Dvorak's Symphony no. 9 ("From the New World"), Isaac Stern's magnificent violin recitals, Judy Garland's final performances (one of which can be heard on a fantastic record) and the Beatles' first North American concert (1964). We should add that up until Avery Fisher Hall was built at Lincoln Center (see p 257), Carnegie Hall was the home of the New York Philharmonic Orchestra, conducted for many years by Arturo Toscanini. The façade, which bears little resemblance to the architecture of the neighbouring theatres, has often been ironically compared to a 19th-century brasserie. The concert hall itself, restored between 1986 and 1991, is known for its outstanding acoustics. It is surrounded by studio apartments for stage artists. Dancer Isadora Duncan and actor Marlon Brando are among the luminaries to have slept beneath this roof. Behind the building stands a narrow office tower designed by Cesar Pelli in 1989. A small museum documents all sorts of other highlights in the history of Carnegie Hall.

Head north on 7th Avenue.

At the corner of 58th Street, you'll find what just might be the world's most ornate apartment building. Every square inch of the **Alwyn Court Apartments ★★** *(180 West 58th St.)* is faced with terracotta decorated with elaborate, Renaissance-style mouldings of crowns, salamanders and various other emblems. The ground floor is occupied by a famous Russian restaurant, Petrossian (see p 354), which offers access to a tall and very narrow central courtyard. The space used to be somewhat gloomy until the surrounding walls were adorned with a mural by Richard Haas in 1985.

For a break from the concrete and the crowds, we recommend winding up your tour with a visit to Central Park, where you can relax on a bench. There is a park entrance just a few metres north, at the corner of 7th Avenue and Central Park South (West 59th Street). To return to the starting point of the tour, take the N or R train toward Brooklyn (95th Street-Bay Ridge; Stillwell Avenue-Coney Island) at the 57th Street station (at the corner of 7th Avenue).

EXPLORING

TOUR O: CENTRAL PARK ★ ★ ★ (3 hours)

In 1856, the city councilors of New York decided to set aside a large, rectangular piece of land (340 hectares) in the upper part of Manhattan in order to create a huge city park. It was thanks to this wise decision that Central Park came into being two years later. For the next 20 years, the park was laid out according to the plans of landscape architect Frederick Law Olmsted (1822-1903) and British architect Calvert Vaux (pronounced "Vox", 1824-1895). Olmsted, considered the father of North American landscape architecture, also designed Brooklyn's Prospect Park and Montréal's Parc du Mont-Royal, among others.

Central Park is the only real expanse of greenery in Manhattan. On hot July days, when the city streets become suffocating, this shady green space is a true blessing. It also offers an all too rare opportunity to get away from all the skyscrapers of the neighbouring areas. Visitors can enjoy a variety of athletic activities in the park (horseback riding, tennis, in-line skating, etc.) or simply stroll along the paths, which are lined with rows of Art-Nouveau benches.

When visiting Central Park, it is necessary to take a few basic precautions. Don't go in the park after dark (the only way to visit the park safely at night is to climb aboard a horse-drawn hansom cab at Grand Army Plaza and have the driver take you for a ride along the main paths). If you are going to the northern part of the park, north of the Jacqueline Kennedy Onassis Reservoir, it is better to do so in small groups of three or four people, even during the day. This last piece of advice does not apply to this tour, which focusses on the southern part of the park.

Our tour of Central Park starts at the park entrance at the corner of Central Park South and Grand Army Plaza. If you are travelling by subway, get off at any of the nearby stations (the Fifth Avenue Station, served by the N and R trains; the East 59th Street/Lexington Avenue Station, served by the 4 and 6 trains or the West 57th Street Station, served part-time by the B and Q trains). It is also possible to get there by taking one of the scores of buses heading south down Fifth Avenue or north

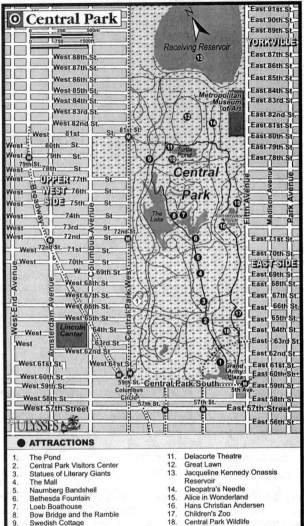

● ATTRACTIONS

1.	The Pond	11.	Delacorte Theatre
2.	Central Park Visitors Center	12.	Great Lawn
3.	Statues of Literary Giants	13.	Jacqueline Kennedy Onassis
4.	The Mall		Reservoir
5.	Naumberg Bandshell	14.	Cleopatra's Needle
6.	Bethesda Fountain	15.	Alice in Wonderland
7.	Loeb Boathouse	16.	Hans Christian Andersen
8.	Bow Bridge and the Ramble	17.	Children's Zoo
9.	Swedish Cottage	18.	Central Park Wildlife
10.	Belvedere Castle		Conservation Center

◇ RESTAURANTS

1.	Tavern on the Green

*up Madison Avenue (M1, M2, M3, M4 or M5); get off at the
corner of East 59th Street (Central Park South).*

Once on the other side of the low stone wall that separates
Central Park from the heavy traffic on the surrounding streets,
follow the path to **The Pond** ★, to the west. The Midtown
skyscrapers are reflected in this charming, meandering body of
water, a popular meeting place for lovebirds.

After running along the east side of the pond, the path leads to
The Dairy, which used to sell milk produced by the herd of
cows that once grazed in the park. The small, neo-Gothic
building, designed by Calvert Vaux, is now the **Central Park
Visitors Center** *(Tue to Sun 11am to 5pm; at the corner of East
Dr. and Transverse Rd. No. 1, ☎794-6564)*, where you can pick
up a detailed map of the park.

*Walk across Transverse Road Number 1 and Center Drive to the
entrance to The Mall.*

Statues of several literary giants guard the entrance to The
Mall. William Shakespeare (John Quincy Adams War, sculptor,
1870) stands here, along with the Scottish poet Robert Burns
(John Steel, sculptor, 1880) and his compatriot, the poet and
historical novelist Sir Walter Scott (John Steel, 1872).

The Mall ★ offers one of the only classical perspectives in
Central Park. This wide, symmetrical promenade was laid out
by Calvert Vaux in order to satisfy the more traditional tastes
of certain 19th-century New York decision-makers. Olmsted,
with his love for the natural and the rustic, would have been
happy with a few paths among the trees, as evidenced by the
park he laid out on Mont Royal, in Montréal, where he was
permitted to do as he pleased. Be that as it may, The Mall is
still one of the most elegant places in the park.

The **Naumberg Bandshell**, halfway up The Mall, is an outdoor
stage where brass bands and chamber music ensembles
perform. Many of the concerts are in the evening, offering
visitors another opportunity to view the park safely after
nightfall – provided you follow the crowds to the exits
afterward.

Bow Bridge

At the north end of The Mall, there is a staircase leading to the **Bethesda Fountain ★★**, where you'll find a paved terrace and a lovely arch made of carved sandstone (Emma Stebbins, sculptor, 1870). The fountain was named after a legendary pool in Jerusalem to which an angel had given healing powers, hence the winged angel at the top.

The Bethesda Fountain looks onto The Lake and the **Loeb Boathouse ★** *(along East Dr., at East 75th St.; rentals every day 11am to 5pm, avoid coming on weekends and holidays: boats ☎517-2233, bicycles ☎861-4137)*, where bicycles and boats may be rented. Inside the boathouse, there is a restaurant that has outdoor seating during warm weather. Going for a leisurely row around the lake in Central Park is one of the most romantic things you can do. New Yorkers love to relax this way, soaking up the striking contrast between the bucolic setting of the park and the wall of skyscrapers in the background.

Head left on the path that runs around the lake. Walk across the iron bridge and follow the paths through The Ramble without losing sight of the water.

The **Bow Bridge** and **The Ramble ★★** are two of the most photographed features of Central Park. The cast-iron Bow Bridge, which has appeared in many a movie, spans the narrowest part of the lake (Calvert Vaux, architect, 1860). The

Ramble, for its part, is a stretch of land strewn with rocks and clusters of trees and bushes. It is easy to lose your way in the maze of paths here.

Walk across Transverse Road Number 2 and head for Belvedere Castle.

Along the way, on your left, you'll see the lovely Shakespeare Garden, which contains plants mentioned in Shakespeare's plays, as well as the **Swedish Cottage**, a Scandinavian-looking structure that serves as a marionette theatre *(shows at 10:30am and noon, ☎988-9093)*.

Belvedere Castle ★★ is a weather station disguised as Sleeping Beauty's castle. Its terrace offers an interesting view of The Great Lawn and the buildings of the Upper West Side. The Castle, an extremely eclectic piece of architecture, was designed by Calvert Vaux. Shakespeare plays are regularly presented at the nearby **Delacorte Theatre** *(schedule of performances available at the Central Park Visitors Center, see above)*.

When you live in a two-room apartment in a 30-story building, running around on **The Great Lawn ★★★** is a delightful pleasure. Standing in an open space like this, almost right in the geographic centre of the island of Manhattan, makes you aware of what an incredible luxury empty space is in a city as dense as New York, and also awakens you to the high level of urban planning underlying the city's apparent disorder. This vast, treeless lawn was laid out in 1929 on the site of the Croton Reservoir, which supplied the island of Manhattan with drinking water in the 19th century. During the economic crisis of the 1930s, the area was taken over by jobless New Yorkers, who turned it into a shanty town derisively named Hooverville in an ironic tribute to Herbert Hoover, the president at the time. Since the 1960s, The Great Lawn has been the scene of several huge rock concerts that have gone down in entertainment history, one example being Simon and Garfunkel's 1981 show.

At the other end of The Great Lawn is the Central Park reservoir, long known as the Receiving Reservoir. It shed that rather banal name to become the **Jacqueline Kennedy Onassis Reservoir** in 1994, following the death of the former first lady.

The pool was dug in 1862 to increase the capacity of the Croton Reservoir. The jogging track that runs around it is very popular with New York runners. The entire north portion of Central Park lies beyond the reservoir.

Walk along the south edge of The Great Lawn toward the back of the Metropolitan Museum of Art, visible between the trees (see p 235).

Before reaching the road that runs past the museum, make a brief detour to the left to see **Cleopatra's Needle ★**, a famous Egyptian obelisk that dates from about 1450 BC and once stood, with its twin, in front of a temple in Heliopolis. The two monuments were moved to Alexandria in the 12th century BC and renamed after Cleopatra. Later, the colonial government of Egypt gave one to Great Britain and the other to New York City. The former was erected on the Victoria Embankment in London in 1878, while the latter has been standing in Central Park since 1881.

Follow the road that runs in back of the museum, then turn right on the path that leads back to Transverse Road Number 2.

One the many monuments and sculptures adorning this part of Central Park is a lovely statue of **Alice in Wonderland** by Jose de Creeft, whose creation is faithful to Lewis Carroll's famous book. A bit farther south stands a bronze statue of another famous story-teller, **Hans Christian Andersen**, the Danish author of such tales as "The Emperor's New Clothes" and "The Ugly Duckling" (George Lober, sculptor, 1956).

Before reaching the main Central Park zoo, you'll walk past the **Children's Zoo**, which is guaranteed to be a hit with the kids. It is home to small farm animals that you can see up close.

The entrance to the **Central Park Wildlife Conservation Center ★★** *(admission fee; &; Apr to Oct, every day 10am to 5pm; Nov to Mar, 10am to 4:30pm; Fifth Ave. and 64th St., ☎861-6030)* is adorned with a fanciful musical clock activated hourly by metal animals. On the other side of the gate, behind the ticket counters, lies an urban zoo inhabited by polar bears, monkeys and sea-lions, among other creatures. The walkways are shaded by lovely pergolas. On the left stands The Arsenal,

EXPLORING

which was built in 1848 and now serves as the New York City Department of Parks and Recreation Headquarters. Though much smaller than the Brooklyn and Bronx zoos (see p 283 and 285), the **Central Park Zoo** is an interesting place for foreign tourists to visit, due to its location, right in the heart of Manhattan.

Before returning to the starting point of the tour, walk along the path that runs past the zoo. All sorts of artists, booksellers, musicians and vendors sell their wares between the zoo and Grand Army Plaza, offering everything from worthless junk to one-of-a-kind works of art.

TOUR P: THE UPPER EAST SIDE ★★
(one day)

New York City was founded in 1624. Its elite has since changed neighbourhoods several times, gradually moving north through Manhattan Island. After occupying the area surrounding Bowling Green for close to two hundred years, the bourgeoisie briefly settled in what is now the TriBeCa district, before congregating around Gramercy Park and Union Square toward the middle of the 19th century. The Astor Place Riots prompted them to move again, this time to Fifth Avenue and Murray Hill, around 34th Street. The queen of New York City's high society, Caroline Astor, would then initiate another northward migration, from 1895 on, by moving to the east side of Central Park, known today as "the Upper East Side". This district, where the elite of the city settled for good (though nothing is truly definite when it comes to New York City) is populated by fabulously wealthy financiers, very recognizable politicians, exiled aristocrats, successful intellectuals and world-famous stars (actors, writers, singers, etc.).

Since the beginning of the 20th century, the Upper East Side has attracted not only the American elite, but also that of the world over. Russian countesses driven out by the Bolsheviks, Japanese billionaires weary of Nipponese rigidity, Arab princes lured by the Western way of life, not to mention the many French expatriates who put down roots in the American metropolis over the years... All gather in the district's restaurants, private nightclubs and exclusive boutiques, before retiring to their townhouses and apartments gracing the

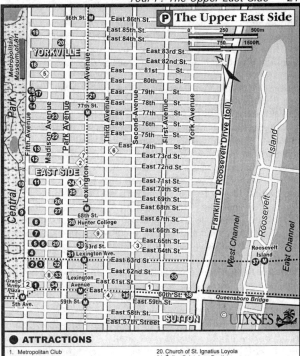

P The Upper East Side

● ATTRACTIONS

1. Metropolitan Club
2. Fifth Avenue Synagogue
3. Old Ernesto Fabbri House
4. Old Edward J. Berwind House
5. Old Marshall Orme Wilson House
6. Wildenstein & Company
7. Temple Emmanuel
8. Old Harris Fahnestock House
9. 7th Regiment Monument of the New York National Guard
10. Richard Morris Hunt Memorial
11. Frick Collection
12. Lycée Français de New York
13. Pulitzer House
14. French Consulate
15. New York University Institute of Fine Arts
16. French Embassy: Cultural Services
17. Old Isaac Fletcher House
18. Old Benjamin Duke House
19. 3 East 84th Street
20. Church of St. Ignatius Loyola
21. Église Saint-Jean-Baptiste
22. Whitney Museum of American Art
23. Hotel Carlyle
24. Asia Society
25. Union Club
26. Italian Consulate General, Instituto Italiano di Cultura, Spanish Institute, Percy Pyne House
27. Council on Foreign Relations
28. 7th Regiment Armory
29. Franklin Delano Roosevelt House
30. Richard M. Nixon House
31. Central Presbyterian Church
32. Colony Club
33. Christ Church
34. Grolier Club
35. Abigail Adams Smith Museum
36. Roosevelt Island Aerial Tramway
37. Roosevelt Island
38. Queensboro Bridge

○ ACCOMMODATIONS

1. Bridge Apartments
2. Hotel Pierre

◇ RESTAURANTS

1. Blanche's Organic Take-Away and Juicebar
2. Café Word of Mouth
3. China Fun
4. Contrapunto
5. E.A.T.
6. EJ's Luncheonette
7. House of Health
8. Sofia's Fabulous Grill
9. The Sign of the Dove

EXPLORING

neighbourhood's streets and avenues. You guessed it, the Upper East Side is the poshest residential district in New York City. Nicknamed "The Gold Coast" by many, the area boasts magnificent private mansions and wonderful museums.

The tour of the Upper East Side thus constitutes a pleasant stroll in one of the city's most elegant and peaceful districts. Central Park skirts Fifth Avenue over half the distance, on the left as you head back up. It was necessary to split up the famous "Museum Mile", however, to make the outing something more than a simple tour of museums. By heading back down toward Midtown, you can enjoy window-shopping along "Miracle Mile", which stretches from 59th Street to 79th Street along Madison Avenue (known as "Mad" to habitués), where the priciest luxury boutiques in the city are concentrated. You can then make a detour onto "Lex" (that's right, Lexington Avenue) in order to contemplate a few lesser-known monuments.

The tour of the Upper East Side begins opposite Grand Army Plaza and can be combined with that of Fifth Avenue (see p 178). To reach the starting point, take one of the many buses (M1, M2, M3, M4, M5) going north along Madison Avenue or south along Fifth Avenue. You can also take the subway, and get off at one of the stations near Grand Army Plaza (trains N and R: Fifth Avenue Station; trains 4 and 6: East 59th Street/Lexington Avenue Station; trains B and Q run part time to West 57th Street Station)

From Grand Army Plaza, you will discern the neo-Gothic crown of the Sherry Netherland Hotel, which is similar to that of Hotel Pierre, located a little farther north. Between the two lurks the **Metropolitan Club** ★ *(1 East 60th St.)*, designed in 1895 by architects McKim, Mead and White, to whom we are also indebted for the Club Mont-Royal on Sherbrooke Street in Montréal. At night, you can admire the Renaissance ceilings of this posh private club's salons from the sidewalks of Fifth Avenue. Also worth beholding is its façade, on 60th Street, lined with a bronze gate that opens onto a narrow main courtyard.

Leisurely stroll back up Fifth Avenue to 84th Street while admiring the buildings described below.

North of East 62nd Street, Fifth Avenue trades its shops and hotels for a series of luxury high-rise apartment buildings. These are graced with canvas canopies, beneath which stands a liveried doorman, ready to open a lady or gentleman's limousine door. Diplomatic missions, research institutes, churches and a few museums brighten up this homogeneous whole. A small foray onto 62nd Street allows you to see the **Fifth Avenue Synagogue** *(5 East 62nd St.)*, built in 1956, whose stone façade is punctuated by bizarre windows shaped like cats' eyes. A little farther east stands the old **Ernesto Fabbri House** ★ *(11 East 62nd St.)*, designed in 1900 in the Italianesque Beaux-Arts style, notably characterized by colossal cartouches that support the second floor's small windows. Behind the thick of Central Park is The Arsenal, or the New York City Department of Parks and Recreation Headquarters.

The old **Edward J. Berwind House** *(2 East 64th St.)* was built in 1902 for the world's biggest coal-mining baron. Similar mansions once lined Fifth Avenue from 34th Street to 90th Street, but most were razed after 1920, as the district's population grew increasingly denser. Another residence on 64th Street worthy of attention is the old **Marshall Orme Wilson House** ★ *(3 East 64th St.)*, whose high sloping roof recalls those of Second-Empire Parisian mansions (Warren and Wetmore, architects, 1903). A little farther, you can see the **Wildenstein & Company** building *(19 East 64th St.)*, which houses a famous art gallery that was founded in Paris in 1875. The talent of its designer, Horace Trumbauer, is recognized throughout the United States, and this despite the fact that he has never taken an architecture course in his life!

The northeast corner of Fifth Avenue and 65th Street was once occupied by legendary Caroline Astor's "palace." She who reigned supreme over New York City's high society and who had instigated the bourgeoisie's move to the Upper East Side hosted a grand ball here every year. On the guest list were the 400 people who made up, according to her own criteria, the *crème de la crème* of the "upper crust". Needless to say, those who were rejected hardly cared for this woman, who was said to be particularly capricious. The **Temple Emmanuel** ★★ *(free admission; Sun to Thu 10am to 5pm; 840 Fifth Ave., ☎744-1400)* was built on the site of the Astor house in 1929. The huge Byzanto-Romanesque synagogue, which can

EXPLORING

Marshall Orme Wilson House

accommodate up to 2,500 souls, reminds us that New York City has the largest Jewish population in the world. The temple's beautiful stained-glass windows depict the Tables of the Law.

Farther north stands the old **Harris Fahnestock House** *(15 East 66th St.)*, which was Imelda Marcos' main shoe warehouse throughout the seventies. The spouse of Filipino dictator Ferdinand Marcos had a compulsive habit of buying countless pairs of shoes during her trips to the United States.

On the west side of Fifth Avenue stands the **7th Regiment Monument of the New York National Guard** *(at East 67th St.)*, which honours the regiment's soldiers who fought during the Great War (Karl Illva, sculptor, 1927). A little higher on Fifth Avenue, the **Richard Morris Hunt Memorial** *(at East 70th St.)* is one of the all-too-rare monuments raised in memory of the architect (Daniel Chester French, sculptor; Bruce Price, architect, 1898). Richard Morris Hunt (1827-1895) was the first American graduate of the École des Beaux-Arts in Paris. In the 1860s, he popularized French styles in the United States, before becoming the darling of the American bourgeoisie from 1880 onward.

The main entrance of the **Frick Collection** ★★★ *($5; ♿, no children under 10 allowed; Tue to Sat 10am to 6pm, Sun 1pm to 6pm; 1 East 70th St., ☎288-0700)* is on East 70th Street and not Fifth Avenue, as one might assume. This exceptional art museum is set up in billionaire Henry Clay Frick's former residence. His neo-Louis XVI-style "palace" (Carrère and Hastings, architects, 1914) is one of the only remaining homes from the golden age of New York City that is open to the public. A great collector, Frick bequeathed his house and countless works of art to the City of New York in 1919. After a few extensions and modifications, the building opened its doors in 1935. The extraordinarily rich collection, which consists of sculptures and paintings, is supplemented by numerous pieces of antique furniture produced by the best English, French and Italian cabinetmakers distributed throughout the residence's various rooms. These are graced with beautiful Louis XV- and Louis XVI-style woodwork. When visiting the museum, it is best to follow the numbering of rooms appearing on the map supplied at the entrance.

Among the paintings to be admired in the South Hall (room 5) are Goya's *Don Pedro*, François Boucher's *Madame Boucher*, Renoir's *Mother and Children* and, above all, two of Vermeer's major works, *Girl Interrupted at Her Music* and *Soldier and Laughing Girl*. Moreover, because there are only about thirty authentic Vermeers left in the world, these two works by the painter from Delft assembled in the same room are priceless treasures. Beneath these magnificent paintings are Louis XVI-style furnishings, including a chest of drawers and a writing desk made by Riesener for queen Marie Antoinette's state apartments in the Palais des Tuileries. The Boucher Room (8), for its part, features eight panels with the arts and sciences as their theme, which Madame Pompadour commissioned François Boucher to do for the library in her château at Crécy (1750). Famous British paintings, including Hogarth's *Miss Mary Edwards* and Gainsborough's *The Mall in St. James Park*,

EXPLORING

grace the four walls of the old dining room (9). The Fragonard Room (11) is, as its name indicates, devoted to painter Jean-Honoré Fragonard. Four of the 10 decorative panels from the "The Progress of Love" series, integrated into the room's woodwork, were commissioned by Madame du Barry for her château at Louveciennes

Hanging on the walls of the Living Hall (room 12) are two of Hans Holbein's greatest paintings: *Sir Thomas Moore* and *Thomas Cromwell*. Also worthy of contemplation here is El Greco's beautiful *Saint Jerome*, placed above the chimney. This room also boasts a view of the formal garden right outside its windows, which open onto Fifth Avenue. In the library (room 13) are two outstanding paintings by Turner (*Fishing Boats Entering Calais Harbour* and *Mortlake Terrace*) as well as busts of *Louis XV Enfant*, by Coysevox, and the *Grand Dauphin*, by Girardon. The North Hall (room 14) notably comprises Ingres' *The Comtesse d'Aussonville*, Bernini's *Head of an Angel* and Houdon's *Marquis de Miromesnil*.

Your bedazzlement will reach its peak when you enter the West Gallery (room 15), where paintings such as Turner's *The Harbour of Dieppe*, Véronèse's *Allegory of Wisdom and Strength* (this work once belonged to the Duke of Orléans), Rembrandt's *The Polish Rider* and the museum's third Vermeer, entitled *The Letter* (or *Lady with her Maidservant*), are displayed. At the west end of this gallery is the Enamel Room (16), where beautiful paintings by Piero della Francesca and magnificent, 16th century Limoges enamels are displayed. In the centre of the Oval Room (17), located at the other end of the large gallery, Houdon's terracotta, *Diana the Huntress*, occupies a place of honour. Particularly noteworthy in the East Gallery (room 18) are Van Dyck's *James, Seventh Earl of Derby, His Lady and Child*, Degas' *The Rehearsal* and David's *Comtesse Daru*. Finally, Manet's remarkable *La Corrida* and Coysevox's bust of architect *Robert de Cotte*, are on display in the winter garden.

Resume your walk along Fifth Avenue, heading north.

Living in the "70's" (between East 70th and East 78th Streets, from Fifth Avenue to Lexington Avenue) is the tops! You can't do any better than this in the United States, except perhaps to own a house in Beverly Hills, California. But as slightly snobbish

New Yorkers are wont to maintain quite plainly, the West Coast is so naff! The Beaux-Arts style, which graces the mansions at numbers 7 and 9 of 72nd Street, is perfectly suited for the **Lycée Français de New York** ★, which now occupies the two buildings. The one on the left, crowned with a pavilion roof, was built in 1899 for Oliver Goul Jennings, while the one on the right, punctuated with volutes, was formerly the property of H. T. Sloane (Carrère and Hastings, architects, 1894).

The famous Pulitzer Prize, awarded every year since 1917 to a skilled writer or journalist, was named thus in homage to New York press tycoon Joseph Pulitzer (1847-1911), whose enormous house is still on 73rd Street. One of architects McKim, Mead and White's most original works, the **Pulitzer House** ★ *(9 East 73rd St., not open to the public)* has since been converted into an apartment building.

North of the **French Consulate** *(934 Fifth Ave.)* is the **New York University Institute of Fine Arts** ★ *(1 East 78th St.)*, which occupies James Duke's former "palace". The American cigarette king, owner of the powerful American Tobacco Company, insisted Horace Trumbauer take his inspiration for the house from the Hôtel Labottière, in Bordeaux. As its name indicates, the place is now an institution that offers art courses (art history, art restoration, drawing, etc.).

The **French Embassy Cultural Services** ★ *(972 Fifth Ave., north of East 78th St.)* are set up in patron and sculptress Gertrude Vanderbilt Whitney's former residence, designed by architects McKim, Mead and White in 1903. The discovery of a Michelangelo statue in its entrance hall in 1995 was widely publicized. Exhibitions on France and its territories are organized here periodically.

At the corner of Fifth Avenue and East 79th Street stands the old **Isaac Fletcher House** ★★ *(2 East 79th St.)*, whose neo-Gothic profile is modeled on the French mansions of the Middle Ages, particularly the Hôtel Jacques-Cœur in Bourges. A relic of the distant past built in the middle of the 20th-century city, the residence is a great historicist success by architect Cass Gilbert.

Facing the main entrance to the Metropolitan Museum of Art (see p 235), the old **Benjamin Duke House** ★ *(2 East 82nd St.)*

is clad in a mixture of pink brick and beige stone, lending the place a Louis-XIII-style look (1901). Particularly noteworthy is the very *belle-époque*, cast-iron oriel window, on the west end of the façade. Lest we forget, all these houses were originally single-family dwellings...

Turn right on 84th Street. Cross Madison Avenue, then turn right on Park Avenue.

The small apartment building at **3 East 84th Street** was designed by architect Raymond Hood in 1928. Its vertical lines and Art-Deco, pressed-metal spandrels were the basis for many buildings of the same kind erected throughout North America.

As you head east, you will suddenly end up on Park Avenue, whose exceptional width is attributed to the trains still running underground. To the north, the long asphalt ribbon seems to disappear beneath the horizon, while to the south, it runs right to the former Pan Am Building (see p 197) in the distance. The large apartment buildings from the roaring twenties that line the avenue over several kilometres eclipse the numerous, though imposing churches found on certain street corners. The **Church of St. Ignatius Loyola** ★★ *(980 Park Ave., at East 84th St.)* is the Jesuits' main church in New York City. Built between 1895 and 1898, the structure had its interior entirely covered in Siena marble and Venitian mosaïcs for the next two decades. Visitors will also notice several Society of Jesus devices (two stars framing a crescent moon topped by the letters *IHS: Iesus Hominum Salvatore*, which means "Jesus is man's salvation") placed throughout the church. Jacqueline Bouvier-Kennedy-Onassis' former parish — her funeral was held here in 1994 — also comprises the Our Lady of Montserrat sanctuary, adorned with a medieval Madonna, and the Irish chapel, St. Laurence O'Toole, in the basement.

Head south along Park Avenue, toward Midtown. Turn left on East 79th Street, then right on Lexington Avenue.

In July of 1810, Quebecer Gabriel Franchère left Montreal to settle in New York City with several of his compatriots. He had just been hired to manage millionaire John Jacob Astor's fur trading empire, the Pacific Fur Company. Franchère's journey, made by bark canoe down the Richelieu and Hudson rivers, is recounted by American writer, Washington Irving. In 1850,

Franchère founded the *Société Saint-Jean-Baptiste* in New York, modeled on that of Montreal. This organization is a cultural association whose aim is to preserve the French language in North America. In its heyday, circa 1900, New York City's French-Canadian community was over 20,000 strong and mostly centred in Yorkville and the Upper East Side. The French-Canadian Catholic Saint-Jean-Baptiste parish was founded in 1882, on Father Cazeneuve's instigation. It would be followed by the *Académie Villa-Maria des Soeurs de la Congrégation Notre-Dame*, the *École Saint-Jean-Baptiste des Frères Maristes* and the *Hôpital de la Miséricorde* of the nuns of the same name. The current **Église Saint-Jean-Baptiste ★** *(at Lexington Ave. and East 79th St.)* was built in 1912. Its Indiana-limestone, neo-Baroque façade, the work of Italian architect Nicolas Serracino, is somewhat reminiscent of that of the Église Saint-Jean-Baptiste in Montreal. The parish, containing a relic of St. Anne, has been run by the *Pères du Saint-Sacrament* since 1900.

Head south along Lexington Avenue. Turn right on East 75th Street, then left on Madison Avenue.

Only the rich shop on Madison Avenue, which boasts dozens of luxury boutiques that do their utmost to dazzle the district's wealthy clientele. In the midst of these shops is the strange building of the **Whitney Museum of American Art ★★** *($8; ♿; Wed and Fri to Sun 11am to 6pm, Thu 1pm to 8pm; 945 Madison Ave., at East 75th St., ☎570-3676, www.echonyc.com/~whitney)*, designed like a modern-day fortress by architect and furniture designer Marcel Breuer in 1966. Breuer also built the Unesco headquarters in Paris. The "Whitney", as it is commonly known by, is an interesting private museum dedicated to 20th-century American art. It was founded by Gertrude Vanderbilt Whitney in 1931 to promote the work of American artists who were shunned until then by New York's bourgeoisie in favour of European artists. The museum's collection includes paintings such as Robert Henri's *L'enfant rieur*, Edward Hopper's *Seven A.M.*, George Tooker's *The Subway* and Willem de Kooning's *Woman and Bicycle*.

North of the museum, the façade of the **Hotel Carlyle** *(on the east side of Madison Ave., between East 76th and East 77th Streets)* will catch your eye. American presidents Truman and Kennedy stayed here on their trips to the city.

EXPLORING

Head south along Madison Avenue to admire a few of the shop windows lining the main thoroughfare. Then take a left on 70th Street to return to Park Avenue.

The **Asia Society** ★ *(admission fee; ᵬ; Tue, Wed, Fri and Sat 11am to 6pm, Thu 11am to 8pm, Sun noon to 5pm; 725 Park Ave., at 70th St., ☎517-6397)* is actually a private museum featuring John D. Rockefeller III's personal collection of Asian art, which was bequeathed to the institution in 1976. Among the artifacts on display are Hindu temple pieces, exquisite Chinese vases as well as Japanese screens painted with exceptional skill.

Follow Park Avenue toward Midtown (south).

English architectural styles hold pride of place on the stretch of Park Avenue between East 67th and 70th Streets. On the east side is the **Union Club** *(701 Park Ave.)*, designed by architects Delano & Aldrich, in 1932. The impressive building, designed to house New York City's oldest private club (the Union Club was founded back in 1836) adopts an English-conservative, neo-Baroque style. The west side of the avenue, for its part, is lined with a lovely group of old neo-Georgian homes. South of the **Italian Consulate General** *(690 Park Ave.)*, located in the Davidson House built in 1916, is the **Instituto Italiano di Cultura** *(686 Park Ave., south of 69th St.)*, where New Yorkers can study Italian culture. The institute is set up in the Sloane House, erected in 1919. Its Spanish counterpart, the **Spanish Institute** *(684 Park Ave.)*, occupies the neighbouring house, designed by architects McKim, Mead and White in 1926 for the Filley family. The latter residence was saved from demolition by marchioness De Piedrablanca de Guana Cuevas, née Rockefeller, in the mid-sixties. On the corner of East 68th Street, you can admire the stately **Percy Pyne House** ★ *(680 Park Ave.)*, built in 1911. Nikita Khrushchev, the former communist leader of the USSR, settled here during his controversial trip to the United States in September 1959, at the time when the building housed the Soviet UN delegation. Finally, the **Council on Foreign Relations** ★ *(60 East 68th St.)* is set up in the prodigious Harold Pratt House, which modestly attests to architects Delano and Aldrich's great talent. The international organization has successfully preserved this English-style, Italian Renaissance Revival mansion, originally built for one of the owners of the Standard Oil Company.

The red-brick walls of the **7th Regiment Armory** ★ *(Park Ave., between 66th and 67th streets)* stretch from Park Avenue east to Lexington Avenue. The military barracks' interior was designed by Louis Comfort Tiffany (1883) (see p 192), which probably makes it the least Spartan of all such buildings in the United States.

Admirers of erstwhile American presidents should make a point of taking East 65th Street, where two presidents have resided. To the west of Park Avenue is the **Franklin Delano Roosevelt House** *(49 East 65th St.)*, where FDR lived a cloistered life for two years following a bout of poliomyelitis, while to the east of the prestigious avenue stands the **Richard M. Nixon House** *(142 East 65th St.)*, where "Mr. Watergate" spent the last years of his life.

The **Central Presbyterian Church** ★ *(593 Park Ave., at 64th St.)* was John D. Rockefeller's parish before he decided to have his "own" church built in Morningside Heights (see Riverside Church p 265). Both structures, for that matter, adopt the same Flemish neo-Gothic style, thus revealing the personal tastes of Rockefeller, who paid for the construction of both churches out of his own pocket.

The **Colony Club** *(51 East 62nd St.)* is yet another of architects Delano and Aldrich's neo-Georgian marvels (1916). The resident women's club was founded by New York millionaires' spouses.

Bertram Grosvenor Goodhue's business associate, Ralph Adams Cram, another American medievalist, designed the **Christ Church** ★ *(520 Park Ave.)*. Though the Methodist church looks like something right out the last crusade, it was nevertheless built in the years preceding World War II.

Most of the French-speaking world is familiar with Grolier encyclopaedia. The **Grolier Club** *(47 East 60th St.)* is a private club for those interested in the art of bookbinding, something that also fascinated the Jean Grolier de Servières, Viscount of Aguisy, a French nobleman and ardent bibliophile, born in Lyons (1479-1565).

Turn left on 60th Street, left again on 3rd Avenue, then right on 61st Street.

EXPLORING

Facing the enormous pillars of the Queensboro Bridge (described below), the **Abigail Adams Smith Museum** *(admission fee; Tue to Sun 11am to 4pm, closed in Aug; 421 East 61st Street, between York and 1st Ave., ☎838-6878)* looks very fragile. This small ashlar-stone building, built in 1799, is the oldest in the district. It was converted into a museum in 1939 by the Colonial Dames of America, after having served consecutively as a cowshed behind the home of Abigail Adams, daughter of American president John Adams, a country inn and a school.

Retrace your steps and take 2nd Avenue, heading south.

To end this tour on a high note, why not observe the distance covered from above in the **Roosevelt Island Aerial Tramway ★★** *($2; avoid the morning and evening rush hours; departures every 15 minutes from 6am to 2am; 2nd Ave., at 60th St., ☎832-4543)*. This cable car runs from Manhattan to **Roosevelt Island**, in the middle of the East River. The very long and narrow island comprises thousands of dwellings — this is where "Main Street, NYC." is — as well as several huge hospitals. The short (return) trip allows passengers to contemplate the silhouettes of Midtown's skyscrapers, the East River's West Channel and the impressive structure of the **Queensboro Bridge ★★**. As its name indicates, the cantilever bridge, built in 1909 by engineer Henry Hornbostel and architect Gustav Lindenthal, links Midtown Manhattan to the borough of Queens. Particularly noteworthy are its Art-Nouveau-style spiky pinacles.

Return to the starting point by heading west along 59th Street.

TOUR Q: CARNEGIE HILL AND YORKVILLE ★★ (one day)

The hill that rises up north of East 86th Street once offered a sweeping view of the environs. Andrew Carnegie, the king of steel, was the first moneyed New Yorker to take an interest in this part of Manhattan, back when squatters still lived here. He built a magnificent house on the hill, and the entire area was named after him. East of Carnegie Hill lies the former village of Yorkville, the locality favoured by New York's German and Hungarian communities in the late 19th century. There are still

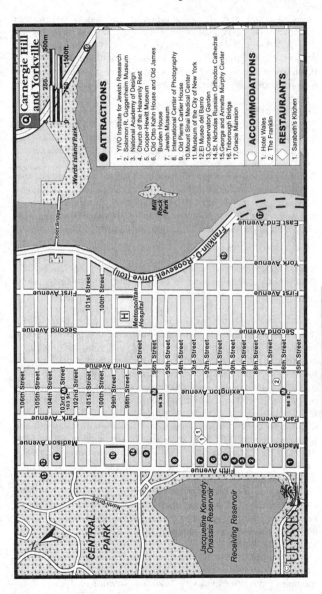

Q Carnegie Hill and Yorkville

● ATTRACTIONS

1. YIVO Institute for Jewish Research
2. Solomon R. Guggenheim Museum
3. National Academy of Design
4. Church of the Heavenly Rest
5. Cooper-Hewitt Museum
6. Old Otto Kahn House and Old James
   Burden House
7. Jewish Museum
8. International Center of Photography
9. Old Pierre Cartier House
10. Mount Sinai Medical Center
11. Museum of the City of New York
12. El Museo del Barrio
13. Conservatory Garden
14. St. Nicholas Russian Orthodox Cathedral
15. George and Annette Murphy Center
16. Triborough Bridge
17. Gracie Mansion

◇ ACCOMMODATIONS

1. Hotel Wales
2. The Franklin

◇ RESTAURANTS

1. Sarabeth's Kitchen

EXPLORING

many German and Hungarian businesses along the former Hauptstrasse, which became East 86th Street after World War II. Museum Mile, which runs up Fifth Avenue, starts around 60th Street, so our itinerary includes all sorts of fascinating museums. We have only allotted time for two of the nine museums described, however; the choice is yours.

This tour starts at the corner of 86th Street and Fifth Avenue. The nearest subway station is the 86th Street Station, served by the 4 and the 6, which run under Lexington Avenue. The intersection is also on the M1, M2, M3 and M4 bus lines.

The **Yivo Institute for Jewish Research** *(on the southeast corner of Fifth Ave. and East 86th St.)* is a private research facility devoted to the Yiddish culture of Eastern European Jews. It occupies the former home of Mrs. Cornelius Vanderbilt, a Louis-XIII-style mansion designed by Carrère and Hastings in 1916.

Walk up Fifth Avenue and take a look at the huge Jacqueline Kennedy Onassis Reservoir in Central Park (on the left), which supplies the city's drinking water (see p 214).

For many years, the ingenious Frank Lloyd Wright (1867-1959), the enfant terrible of American architecture, took a keen interest in helical structures. After warming up with an automobile observatory and planetarium, he spent 15 years working on the plans for a museum based on the same concept. This private institution would house copper magnate Solomon R. Guggenheim's extraordinary collection of modern art. Despite Guggenheim's death in 1949 and the grumblings of various conservative circles, the **Solomon R. Guggenheim Museum** ★★★ *($8; ♿; Sun to Tue 10am to 6pm, Fri and Sat 10am to 8pm, closed Thu; 1071 Fifth Ave., at 88th St., ☎423-3500)* was finally inaugurated in 1959 and quickly became a classic of modern American architecture. This strange-looking building, made of reinforced concrete, consists of a long platform topped by a sort of giant teacup. In 1991, a 10-story rectilinear addition (Gwathmey Siegel) adapted from Wright's plans was built onto the back of the museum to provide more space for exhibitions.

To view the interior from the most dramatic angles, tour the museum from the top down. Take the elevator to the top floor,

Solomon R. Guggenheim Museum

then walk down the spiral ramp past such well-known paintings as Franz Marc's *Yellow Cow*, Cézanne's *Watchmaker* and *Bathers* and Picasso's *Accordionist* and *Harlequins*. You'll also find important works by Braque, Chagall, Kandinksy, Klee, Léger, Modigliani and Mondrian. The impressionists and post-impressionists are also well-represented in major pieces by Manet, Pissarro, Renoir, Toulouse-Lautrec and Vuillard.

The **National Academy of Design** ★ *($5; &; Tue to Thu and Sat and Sun noon to 5pm, Fri noon to 8pm; 1083 Fifth Ave., ☎369-4880)*, an old, private philanthropic society, was founded in 1825 by Samuel Morse, the inventor of the telegraph. It hosts temporary exhibitions devoted to the work of American architects, painters and graphic artists.

A little farther up Fifth Avenue stands the Episcopal **Church of the Heavenly Rest** *(at 90th St.)*, a late neo-Gothic building whose design reveals an Art-Deco influence (Mayers, Murray and Philip, 1929). The lovely Madonna on the pulpit was sculpted by Malvina Hoffman.

The **Cooper-Hewitt National Design Museum ★★** *($5; ♿; Tue 10am to 9pm, Wed to Sat 10am to 5pm, Sun noon to 5pm; 2 East 91st St., ☎860-6868)* is part of the Smithsonian Institution, based in Washington, D.C. The museum is housed in the restored Andrew Carnegie Mansion, designed in 1899 by Babb, Cook and Willard, whose other credits include the Quebec Bank-New York Life building on Place d'Armes in Montréal, regarded as that city's first skyscraper (1888). The huge, 64-room, polychrome mansion stands just as it did in the early 19th century, in the midst of a lovely garden surrounded by a cast-iron and stone fence. The museum's collection includes pieces from all over the world and from all different eras, offering a panorama of the decorative arts, from 4th-century China to France during the Age of Enlightenment and Georgian England.

North of the Carnegie Mansion stands the former **Otto Kahn House ★** *(1 East 91st St.)*, built in 1918 for the banker after whom it was named. Designed by Cass Gilbert, it is a Renaissance Revival building reminiscent of the Palazzo della Chancelleria in Rome. It is now occupied by the Convent of the Sacred Heart, like its neighbour, the former **James Burden House** *(7 East 91st St.)*, built in 1905 (Warren and Wetmore) for the founder of the American Machine and Foundry Company.

The **Jewish Museum ★** *($7; ♿; Sun to Mon and Wed to Thu 11am to 5pm, Tue 11am to 8pm, closed Fri and Sat; 1109 Fifth Ave., at 92nd St., ☎423-3200)* is set up inside the former residence of the Warburg family, a Gothic Revival mansion built in 1908. Its permanent exhibition, entitled "Culture and Continuity: The Jewish Journey", traces the history of the Jewish people through artifacts from the Middle East and Europe. The museum also presents temporary exhibitions of works by Jewish artists and hosts concerts and conferences on Jewish culture.

The **International Center of Photography ★** *($5; Tue 11am to 8pm, Wed to Sun 11am to 6pm; 1130 Fifth Ave., at 94th St., ☎860-1777)* took over the Willard Straight House from the National Audubon Society. This American neo-Georgian house, whose multiple oculi reveal the influence of British architect Christopher Wren, is one of the most elegant brick buildings in the entire city (Delano and Aldrich, 1914). The centre presents interesting exhibitions of old and contemporary photographs from its enormous collection.

On your way past East 96th Street, you might want to take a look at the old **Pierre Cartier House** *(15 East 96th St.)*, built in 1915 in the French Renaissance style. Pierre Cartier, a member of the famous family of Parisian jewelers, lived here for many years.

If you would like to learn more about the history of the Big Apple, pay a visit to the Museum of the City of New York, located on Fifth Avenue, north of 103rd Street (see below). To continue the main tour, turn right on East 97th Street.

North of 98th Street, you'll reach the **Mount Sinai Medical Center** *(on the east side of Fifth Ave., between East 98th and East 102nd streets)*, the most prestigious Jewish hospital in New York. Since its inauguration in 1904, many major medical breakthroughs have been made here.

The **Museum of the City of New York ★★** *($5; ♿; Wed to Sat 10am to 5pm, Sun 1pm to 5pm; 1220 Fifth Ave., north of East 103rd St., ☎534-1672)* is a gold mine for anyone wishing to learn more about New York, its history, its urban development and its population. Among many other things, visitors will find a lovely model of New Amsterdam in 1660 and entire rooms from demolished New York mansions, such as the opulent sitting room from the W.K. Vanderbilt House and billionaire John D. Rockefeller's peculiar bedroom.

El Museo del Barrio ★ *($4; Wed to Sun 11am to 5pm; 1230 Fifth Ave., north of East 104th St., ☎831-7272)*, on the other side of East 104th, is located at the north edge of Carnegie Hill, where East Harlem – also known as Spanish Harlem, due to its large Latino, and more specifically Puerto Rican, population – begins. This "neighbourhood museum", which serves as a link between the prestigious institutions on Museum Mile and the more modest houses to the north, highlights the culture of the Antilles in general and Puerto Rico in particular through conferences, art exhibitions and shows.

The **Conservatory Garden ★★** *(every day 6am to 5pm; on the west side of Fifth Ave., entrance at East 105th St.)*, on the edge of Central Park, is a charming, rectilinear garden that

EXPLORING

combines French and Italian traditions. Its entrance gate is from the former residence of Cornelius Vanderbilt II, king of the American railroad.

Double back on Fifth Avenue to return to the main tour. Head east on East 97th Street.

Towering above East 97th Street are the onion domes of the **St. Nicholas Russian Orthodox Cathedral ★** *(15 East 97th St.)*, erected in 1902. Back in the days of Soviet socialism, this church was the seat of the exiled Russian orthodox clergy. Its many colours make it lively.

Turn right on Park Avenue, then left on East 90th and continue east to York Avenue.

Many of the first reinforced concrete structures built in the early 20th century have been demolished without much opposition. Consequently, numerous examples of this daring architecture have vanished forever. The city's old asphalt plant, designed by Ely Jacques Kahn and Robert Allan Jacobs in 1944, faced the same fate until a group of citizens saved it from the wrecking ball. Its architects drew their inspiration from the dirigible hangars designed by Eugène Freyssinet for Orly airport, outside Paris. The building, shaped like a parabola, has since been converted into a community, cultural and sports centre and renamed after two donors who provided generous support for the project. The **George and Annette Murphy Center** *(York Ave. and 90th St.)* is surrounded by a park with a view of Mill Rock Island, in the middle of the East River, and Ward's Island, on which a number of psychiatric hospitals are located. East of the latter, you'll see one of the four roadways of the **Triborough Bridge** (1936), which, as indicated by its name, runs over three of New York's five boroughs – Manhattan, Queens and the Bronx.

Head south on York Avenue. Turn right on East 89th, then cross East End Avenue to reach Gracie Mansion.

Before becoming the official residence of the Mayor of New York in 1942, **Gracie Mansion ★** *(admission fee; guided tours only, reservations required; mid-Mar to mid-Nov, Wed 10am, 11am, 1pm and 2pm; East End Ave. and East 88th St., in Carl Schurz Park, ☎570-4751)* served for many years as the

Museum of the City of New York (now located on Fifth Avenue; see p 233). This lovely colonial house, surrounded by long wooden porches, was built in 1799 for Scottish-born merchant, Archibald Gracie.

To return to the starting point of the tour, take East End Avenue to East 86th Street and turn right.

TOUR R: THE METROPOLITAN MUSEUM OF ART ★★★ (two days)

If our rating system allowed us to add a fourth star to one of the tours of New York, it would certainly be granted to the Metropolitan Museum of Art, one of the three biggest art museums in the world. And, if there is one museum worth visiting in the North America, it is this one! Because the place is so vast, it is virtually impossible to cover the entire museum in one visit. Thus, we decided to map out a tour of most of the major works on display here — its "highlights", as it were — in two days or thereabouts. Keep in mind, however, that, unlike a city's buildings, the works of art on display in a museum are easily subject to change, according to curators' tastes.

The Metropolitan Museum of Art was founded in 1870 by a group of art lovers and local collectors who wanted to make the American public more aware of the beauty of art and its educational benefits. Ten years later, the museum took up its current location, in Central Park. The first eclectic and polychromatic buildings, designed by Calvert Vaux in 1880, were soon embellished by Richard Morris Hunt's imposing Beaux-Art entrance (1895) on Fifth Avenue and by the sober side wings of McKim, Mead and White (1906). A major expansion project was undertaken in 1971. It was carried out under the leadership of architects Kevin Roche and John Dinkeloo, to equip the "Met" (not to be confused with the "Met" of the Lincoln Center Metropolitan Opera House) with modern spaces, flooded with an abundance of natural light. Pleasant interior courtyards have been laid out between the galleries, offering visitors a welcome respite from the barrage of masterpieces.

In addition to its rich and varied collections of more than 2 million works of art (paintings, sculptures, woodwork, furniture,

EXPLORING

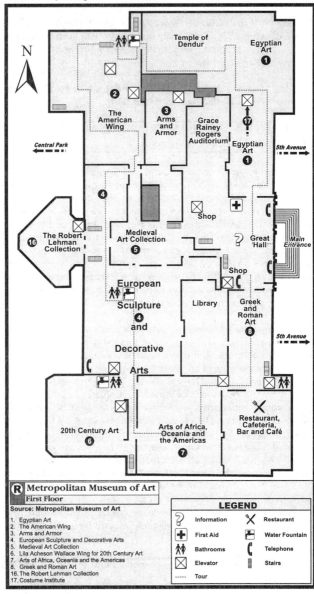

N

Central Park ◄ - - - -

5th Avenue - - - ►

5th Avenue - - - ►

Temple of
Dendur

Egyptian
Art ❶

❷

The
American
Wing

❸
Arms
and
Armor

Grace
Rainey
Rogers
Auditorium

Egyptian
Art ❶

❶❼

❹

The Robert
Lehman
Collection
❶❻

Medieval
Art Collection
❺

Shop

Great
Hall

Main
Entrance

European

Sculpture

and

Decorative

Arts

Library

Shop

Greek
and
Roman Art
❽

20th Century Art
❻

Arts of Africa,
Oceania and
the Americas
❼

Restaurant,
Cafeteria,
Bar and Café

Ⓡ Metropolitan Museum of Art
First Floor

Source: Metropolitan Museum of Art

1. Egyptian Art
2. The American Wing
3. Arms and Armor
4. European Sculpture and Decorative Arts
5. Medieval Art Collection
6. Lila Acheson Wallace Wing for 20th Century Art
7. Arts of Africa, Oceania and the Americas
8. Greek and Roman Art
16. The Robert Lehman Collection
17. Costume Institute

LEGEND

? Information   ✗ Restaurant

✚ First Aid   🖼 Water Fountain

🚺🚹 Bathrooms   (Telephone

⊠ Elevator   ▮ Stairs

- - - - Tour

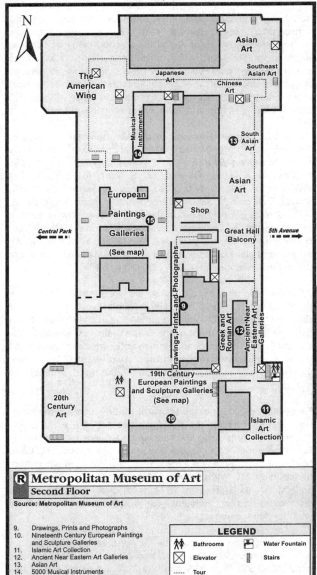

N

The American Wing

Japanese Art

Asian Art

Southeast Asian Art

Chinese Art

Musical Instruments

South Asian Art

Asian Art

European Paintings Galleries (See map)

Shop

Great Hall Balcony

Central Park

5th Avenue

Drawings, Prints and Photographs

Greek and Roman Art

Ancient Near Eastern Art Galleries

20th Century Art

19th Century European Paintings and Sculpture Galleries (See map)

Islamic Art Collection

EXPLORING

R Metropolitan Museum of Art
Second Floor

Source: Metropolitan Museum of Art

9. Drawings, Prints and Photographs
10. Nineteenth Century European Paintings and Sculpture Galleries
11. Islamic Art Collection
12. Ancient Near Eastern Art Galleries
13. Asian Art
14. 5000 Musical Instruments
15. European Paintings Galleries

LEGEND

Bathrooms   Water Fountain

Elevator   Stairs

Tour

decorative objects, costumes, armour, textiles, musical instruments, etc.) spread over 20 departments, the Metropolitan Museum of Art offers a whole array of services (lectures, guided tours, art courses, concerts, etc.) to the 4.5 million people who visit every year, and this in several languages. Moreover, the museum boasts a library comprising more than 350,000 books, three restaurants (see p 358), two bars, a large giftshop and even a rooftop garden!

To reach the main entrance of the **Metropolitan Museum of Art ★★★** *($8; free guided tours; ₰; access for the physically handicapped on 81st St., paid indoor parking; Tue to Thu 9:30am to 5:15pm, Fri and Sat 9:30am to 8:45pm, Sun 9:30am to 5pm; 1000 Fifth Ave., opposite 82nd St., ☎535-7710 or 570-3951, concerts and lectures ☎570-3949, ~472-2764)*, get off train 6 at the 86th Street subway station, at the corner of Lexington Avenue. Head west along 86th Street (toward Central Park) and turn left on Fifth Avenue. Or take one of the numerous buses going up Madison Avenue or down Fifth Avenue (lines M1, M2, M3 and M4).

After climbing up the main stairs, you will enter the Great Hall, designed in the style of an ancient Roman basilica. The hall is flanked by two cloakrooms (on either side of the entrance), the Gift and Book Shop (right of the Grand Staircase leading to the second floor), the Greek and Roman antiquities department (on the left), which leads to the museum's restaurant and cafeteria, and the Egyptian antiquities section (on the right), whence the tour begins.

First purchase your tickets at one of three wickets in the Great Hall, before heading to the **Egyptian Art ★★★** galleries. Several museums pride themselves on having the largest and finest collection of Egyptian antiquities apart from the Cairo Museum. Among these are the Louvre, the British Museum and, of course, the Metropolitan Museum of Art. The Met's collection was started in 1874, with over 35,000 artifacts discovered during archaeological excavations financed by wealthy Americans.

Walk through the long gallery on the right, where a rare painted wooden statue depicting Merti and his spouse (5th dynasty, circa 2350 BC) is notably displayed. At the other end of this gallery is the Meketra room (entrance on the right), where ancient Egypt's most beautiful funerary models can be admired. These come from the serdab of chancellor Mekutra (11th dynasty, 2009 BC). Both fascinating and instructive, these wooden models depict scenes of everyday life in Egypt, 4000 years ago. Among the settings are a brewery, a butcher shop, a garden as well as boats and their crews.

Cross the hall whose elevator leads to the Costume Institute, on Level G (see p 251), then turn right to enter the gallery where the impressive sarcophagus of Har-Khebi (26th dynasty, 664 BC) is on view. Opposite the gallery, a corridor lined with glass cases containing beautiful jewellery leads to a stunning collection of painted wood sarcophagi that fit into each other, much like Russian dolls.

Return to the previous gallery and turn right to reach the following room leading to the impressive Sackler Wing, where the Temple of Dendur has been reassembled.

The construction of the Aswan Dam, in Upper Egypt, caused the water level to rise considerably over several kilometres of the Nile Valley, flooding much of the land for evermore. The Temple of Dendur, one of ancient Egypt's architectural gems, was dismantled before the flood and given to the United States in 1965 as a gift for their help in saving the monument at Abu Simbel. Commissioned by the Roman emperor Augustus and erected in honour of the goddess Isis of Philae around 15 BC, the temple was rebuilt stone by stone in the Sackler Wing, whose huge windows look out on Central Park. The monument, marked by a great deal of 18th- and 19th-century graffiti, is recorded on a granite slab surrounded by a pool simulating the Nile.

Exit the Sackler Wing by the door behind the Temple of Dendur, which leads to the American art section.

The American art collection is spread over four floors, in a part of the museum appropriately named **The American Wing** ★★★. The first level, adjacent to the Egyptian galleries, is devoted to 19th- and 20th-century decorative arts. The collection, started from the museum's very foundation in 1870, notably comprises original woodwork and furnishings from bygone luxurious American homes.

EXPLORING

*Turn left, then right down the few steps by the washrooms.
Turn right again to reach the oval room on the left.*

In this room, the museum has reassembled John Vanderlyn's
panoramic painting of the palace and gardens at Versailles
(1818). It was formerly set up in a circular building erected in
City Hall Park. By exiting at the other end of the room, you will
reach the section devoted to exuberant Victorian furniture.
Among the more refined items is a beautiful chair designed by
architect Alexander J. Davis in 1857. At the back of the room
are three period living rooms from different 19th-century
American homes, with their original woodwork, decorative
appliqués and dark furnishings.

An opening on the left leads visitors to the finely wood-panelled
entrance hall of an old house from Buffalo (New York State),
designed in 1884 by architects McKim, Mead and White. The
following room is devoted to eccentric furniture created for
wealthy Americans by artists such as John La Farge and Louis
Comfort Tiffany. Particularly noteworthy is a stunning
solid-silver dressing table created in 1899. An L-shaped corridor
then leads to a magnificent living room designed in its entirety
(ceiling, chimney, stained-glass windows, furniture, vases, etc.)
by celebrated architect Frank Lloyd Wright in 1912. The room
was once part of the Little House in Wayzata, Minnesota.

Upon leaving the latter room, turn right to reach the interior
courtyard leading out into Central Park. The Charles Engelhard
Court is actually a winter garden where sculptures,
stained-glass windows and architectural elements from various
buildings by American architects are on view. The facade of the
Branch Bank of the United States, built on Wall Street in 1822,
is the pièce de résistance. Also to be seen here are Paul
Manship's interesting *Group of Bears* (1932), resembling Inuit
sculptures, the polychromatic main loggia of Louis Comfort
Tiffany's house and the Chicago Stock Exchange's
Art-Nouveau double staircase (Adler and Sullivan, architects,
1893).

A door across the hall from the Central Park entrance leads to
the **Arms and Armor Galleries ★★**, where you can take a quick
look at a few of the exceptional artifacts on display in glass
cases. This collection, the most comprehensive of its kind in
the world, comprises more than 14,000 weapons from Japan,

the Middle East and Europe (from the 5th century to the 19th century). Particularly exceptional are a beautiful helmet by Milanese armourer Filippo Negroli (1543), Charles Quint's personal pistol (circa 1540), the military helmets of Joan of Arc, Francis I and Cosimo de' Medici, the engraved armour of Anne de Montmorency and France's King Henry II (1555), as well as the hunting outfit of Napoleon I.

Return to the winter garden. Turn left and go through the doors of the Department of European Sculpture and Decorative Arts. Turn right and proceed to the far end.

It would take several days to fully explore all forty rooms devoted to **European Sculpture and Decorative Arts ★★★**. Several of them are, in fact, entire rooms recovered from European castles and mansions. The first room is adorned with the plaster decor that once graced the dining room of Lansdowne House's (London), designed by Robert Adam in 1768. On the way out, you will notice Giovanni Battista Borra's amusing *Monkey Door* (1755).

Go through the two following rooms to the south to reach the symposium gallery that accesses the Robert Lehman Wing, on the right (see p 250), and the Medieval Art Collection, on the left.

A brief look at the rooms devoted to medieval art is in order. Though the greater part of the collection is exhibited at The Cloisters, the museum's annex located in northern Manhattan (see p 268), the main room of the **Medieval Art Collection ★★** does boast the 17-metre high cast-iron gate from the Valladolid Cathedral (Spain, 17th century), as well as a small Romanesque chapel, set up beneath the Grand Staircase, where the *Vierges en Majesté* (France, 12th and 13th centuries) are on view.

Return to the Department of European Sculpture and Decorative Arts by crossing the length of the symposium gallery (turn left upon exiting the main room of the Medieval Art Collection).

On the left is the elegant shopfront of a boutique from 3 Quai Bourbon on Île Saint-Louis, Paris (circa 1775). Opposite are two minuscule Louis-XVI-style period rooms. The one on the left comes from the Hôtel de Crillon and served as a setting for

EXPLORING

Marie Antoinette's day-bed, created for the château at Saint-Cloud. The following room, devoted to Louis-XIV-style furnishings, notably comprises the Sun King's desk. By retracing your steps, you can see a beautiful salon on the right entirely decorated with Sèvres porcelain (including a set of dishes made for the prince of Rohan), another salon from the Hôtel de Lauzun (Paris) and yet another from the Hôtel de Varengeville (Paris); the latter contains the work desk of Louis XV, created for the palace at Versailles. Opposite the main drawing room of the Paar palace in Vienna (18th century) is a Louis-XVI salon once found in the Hôtel de Tessé (Paris) with Marie Antoinette's own furniture, created by Riesener.

Go through the latter living room, then turn right to reach the narrow interior courtyard where the exterior red-brick wall of the oldest part of the museum can be seen. This space, called the Carroll and Milton Petrie European Sculpture Court, is devoted to statuary art. A pleasant bar (Expresso, Wine and Beer Bar), which looks out onto Central Park, is located at the west end of the courtyard.

Of particular note around the courtyard and under the adjacent arcade are the marble busts of Diderot and Voltaire by Houdon, those of the Marquise de Pompadour by Pigalle and of Cosimo III de' Medici by Foggini, as well as the impressive *Flora and Priapus* by Bernini that once stood at the entrance of the Villa Borghese, in Rome. Closer to the park, several works by Maillol, Pajou and Rodin can also be admired.

Go through three of the rooms where beautiful 19th-century European furnishings are on display (in the opposite direction of the park), then turn right to access the collection of 20th-century art. The elevator that leads to the rooftop sculpture garden (open May to October, weather permitting) is on the right, just before the entrance to the Lila Acheson Wallace Wing for 20th Century Art. The bar-terrace set up here affords a spectacular view of Central Park and the New York skyline.

The **Lila Acheson Wallace Wing for 20th Century Art** ★★ features paintings, drawings, prints, sculptures, furniture, decorative objects and architects' blueprints created after 1900. The arrangement of the works in this department changes on a regular basis and is distributed over four floors.

For the purposes of the present tour, it is best to remain on the first floor. Among the masterpieces on display here are Picasso's portrait of Gertrude Stein, 90 paintings and drawings by Paul Klee as well as decorative items salvaged from the *Normandie* ship, which was destroyed by fire in the New York harbour during World War II.

Opposite the main entrance to the 20th-century art collections is that of the African, Oceanian and pre-Columbian art collections. After entering this department, turn right to see the large stained-glass window matching that of the Sackler Wing at the other end of the museum.

The **Arts of Africa, Oceania and the Americas ★★** department was entirely refurbished in 1982. It contains several unique objects, including art works from the court of Benin in Nigeria (16th to 18th centuries), *bisj* (totems of sorts) from the Asmat people of New Guinea, and gold objects from Central America, which belong to the Jan Mitchell Treasury for Precolumbian Works of Art in Gold (on loan to the museum since 1993).

Cross the rooms in the direction of Fifth Avenue. The cafeteria and restaurant share the same space on the left, at the south end of the Greek and Roman Art section (see p 358).

The rooms of **Greek and Roman Art ★★** are situated between the museum's food service area and the Great Hall, and can get annoyingly busy with people trying to get from place to place. This is unfortunate, for the works displayed here, spanning from the Neolithic age to the conversion of Emperor Constantine I's to Christianity in AD 337, deserve peace and contemplation. Half of the collection's some 30,000 objects are on display. Among these are mural paintings from two Roman villas built on the slopes of Mount Vesuvius, wooden furniture discovered in Pompeii (displayed in an alcove facing the Great Hall) as well as the largest collection of antique silver and glass artifacts outside Greece and Italy. Cycladic art is also well represented.

Return to the Great Hall. You have now completed the tour of the first floor. If you have the time and strength, go up the Great Hall's impressive Grand Staircase (facing the museum's main entrance) to the second floor. Turn left.

EXPLORING

You will first go through the **Drawings, Prints and Photographs ★★** section, a long corridor in which these works are displayed. From 1880 on, the museum acquired drawings by Michelangelo, Leonardo Da Vinci and Rembrandt (*The Three Crosses, Jews in the Synagogue*). Then in 1935, the institution acquired 50 drawings by Goya. Soon to follow were prints by Dürer, Van Dyck, Degas, Mary Cassatt, and others. Among the 12,000 photographs belonging to the museum are Fox Talbot's first photo album as well as precious works by Edouard Baldus, Nadar, Alfred Stieglitz, Berenice Abbott, Man Ray and Jean-Marc Bustamante. On the right, you can see a piece of the museum's original exterior wall, while on the left, a passage leads to a balcony above the superb Blumenthal Patio, from the Renaissance castle of Velez Blanco, in Andalusia (Spain, 1506-1515). The latter is part of the decorative arts collection exhibited on the first floor.

At the other end of the corridor are the 21 rooms of the Metropolitan Museum of Art's fabulous **Nineteenth Century European Paintings and Sculpture Galleries ★★★**. Most of the paintings on display here are world-famous — it might feel like you are walking through an art-history book. The great majority of these are masterpieces by French Impressionists such as Renoir and Monet.

After entering the Iris and B. Gerald Cantor Sculpture Gallery, turn left, then right (into the André Meyer Galleries) to explore this part of the museum in the chronological order in which 19th-century European painting evolved.

Particularly riveting among the neoclassical paintings in the André Meyer Galleries are Constable's *Salisbury Cathedral*, Delacroix's *The Abduction of Rebecca* and the portraits of Joseph-Antoine Moltedo and Madame Leblanc, by Ingres. At the very back, the Janice H. Levin Gallery, for its part, is dedicated to Corot and Rousseau. Turn right and walk through the Havemeyer Galleries (toward the Iris and B. Gerald Cantor Sculpture Gallery), where beautiful works by Daumier, Toulouse-Lautrec and particularly Degas (*Woman Ironing, After the Bath, Madame Valpinçon with Chrysanthemums, Dance Class, Horses*, etc) await you.

The column-framed paintings hanging on the walls in the main room are by Courbet, Fantin-Latour and Manet (*Young Woman*

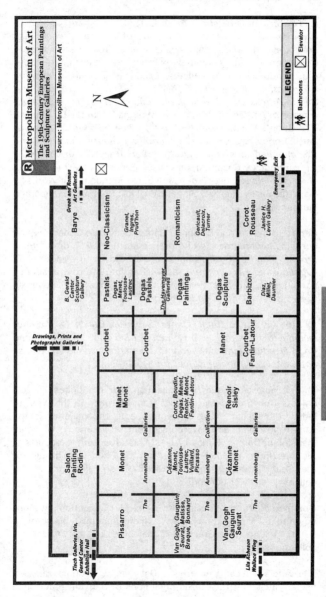

Metropolitan Museum of Art
The 19th-Century European Paintings and Sculpture Galleries
Source: Metropolitan Museum of Art

N

LEGEND

Bathrooms ⊠ Elevator

EXPLORING

in 1866; Woman with a Parrot). The Annenberg Collection Galleries, located on the other side of the main room, also boast several famous paintings (paintings from the Annenberg Collection are only exhibited six months a year; inquire about the timetable in advance), including Renoir's *Madame Charpentier and Her Children*, Monet's *Garden at Sainte-Adresse, La Grenouillère, Rouen Cathedral* and *London: Houses of Parliament* (the museum owns 37 works by Monet), Van Gogh's *Woman of Arles, Irises, Wheatfield with Cypresses* and *Sunflowers*, Cézanne's *Montagne Sainte-Victoire, Mme Cézanne dans la serre* and *Card Players* (the museum owns 21 oil paintings by Cézanne), as well as Gauguin's *La Orana Maria* and *Les seins aux fleurs rouges*. Not to mention major works by Pissarro, Sisley, Seurat, Signac, Vuillard, Bonnard, Braque and Picasso. Phew!

Return to the Iris and B. Gerald Cantor Sculpture Gallery, which contains several marble and bronze statues by Rodin (*Age of Bronze, Hand of God, Adam and Eve*, etc.) and by Carpeaux (*Ugolino and His Children*), as well as large-format academic paintings by Gérôme (*Pygmalion and Galatea*) and Puvis de Chavannes (*Allégorie de la Sorbonne*).

Exit the Iris and B. Gerald Cantor Sculpture Gallery by the door leading to the Greek and Roman Art section, on the second floor. Head straight to the rooms devoted to Islamic art, whose entrance is on the right, near the washrooms.

The museum's **Islamic Art Collection** ★★ comprises 12,000 objects from the Muslim world, from Morocco in the west to India in the east. Near the entrance to the galleries is the sumptuous Nur ad-Din Room, from a luxurious Ottoman mansion in Damas (Syria, 1707). Miniatures from the courts of Mughal (India) and Persia (including the Shah-nameh built for the Shah Tahmasp, Iran, 1514-1576) are also among the collection's major holdings.

Opposite the rooms housing the Islamic Art Collection are those devoted to Mesopotamian art, which you must go through before taking the Great Hall Balcony, to the Asian art collections.

The **Ancient Near Eastern Art Galleries** ★★ boast massive pieces, including the glazed-brick lions of Babylon (Iraq, circa

580 BC), made for king Nebuchadnezzar II, and the stone Human-Headed Winged Lions (Iraq, circa 860 BC), from the Assyrian palace of Ashurnasirpal II at Nimrud, as well as smaller objects, such as the headdress of gold and lapis lazuli worn by a young woman sacrificed to the gods at Ur (Iraq) around 2600 BC.

The rather broadly named **Asian Art** ★★ wing features Cambodian, Chinese, Korean, Indian, Japanese, Nepalese, Thai, Tibetan and Vietnamese works produced between the third millennium BC and the 20th century. Of particular note is the Astor Court, designed in 1981 on the pattern of interior courtyards of Ming-dynasty Chinese gardens (region of Suzhou), and its collection of period furniture.

Upon exiting Astor Court, turn right to enter the rooms consecrated to Japanese art. At the other end of these rooms is the second floor of the American Wing (see above). Turn right at the long gallery, where beautiful furnishings are on display, then left to admire a few 18th- and 19th-century American paintings and woodwork.

On the right is the former living room of the Rensselaer House in Albany (New York State, 1765) as well as the Marmion Room, from a Virginia plantation. These two rooms are decorated with wainscotting and wallpaper depicting rural landscapes. Stairs on the left lead next to the ballroom where George Washington celebrated his last birthday in 1798. Retrace your steps and turn left at the large corridor where, appropriately enough, you can gaze at a large painting entitled *Washington Crossing the Delaware*, by Emanuel Gottlieb Leutze in 1851.

Follow the corridor to the Charles Engelhard Court mezzanine, and walk around it to reach the entrance to the rooms displaying musical instruments.

The mezzanine is lined with silverware and glasswork. Particularly noteworthy are the pieces by Paul Revere, the hero of the American Revolution (18th century), the gem-covered gold vases by Tiffany senior as well as the beautiful Art-Nouveau-style glassware designed in the late 19th century by Tiffany junior.

EXPLORING

Enter the round gallery, which displays the Met's various musical instruments. Have a look before proceeding to the European Paintings Galleries.

The Metropolitan Museum of Art's **5,000 Musical Instruments** ★★ are veritable masterpieces of craftsmanship. Some 800 of them are on display, including the first fortepiano (Bartolomeo Cristofori, piano maker, Florence, Italy, 1720), three Stradivarius violins and Andrés Segovia's guitars. The highlights of this section, however, are the fantastic baroque harpsichords made for the 17th- and 18th-century European courts. Some of these instruments are used during the frequent concerts organized by the museum.

Paintings by great European masters are featured in the forty-four rooms of the **European Paintings Galleries** ★★★. These world-famous works constitute the core of the museum's collections. The visit begins in Room 16, adjacent to the musical instruments, notably featuring Velasquez's portrait of King Philip IV of Spain, and *The Supper at Emmaus*. Room 17 contains one of the museum's first acquisitions, *The Fortune Teller*, by Georges de La Tour. You must then go through Room 19 to reach Room 18, where Chardin's *The Silver Tureen,* Fragonard's *Madame Vigée-Lebrun* and Watteau's famous *Mezzetin* are on display. Room 20 is devoted to Tiepolo, while Room 21 features paintings by Goya (*Majas on a Balcony, Don Manuel Osorio Manrique de Zuñiga*, and more).

Next comes Room 22, which features depictions of beautiful views of Venice by Canaletto and Guardi, then Room 4A, topped by a magnificent ceiling from a 15th-century Italian palace, followed by Room 4B, where Boticelli's *Last Communion of Saint Jerome* is on view. Rooms 14A and 14 feature Bellini's *Madonna and Child*, Mantegna's *Adoration of the Shepherds*, Vermeer's *Young Woman with a Water Jug* and Rembrandt's *Aristotle with a Bust of Homer*. A detour through Room 15 allows you to admire English paintings by Gainsborough, Lawrence and Reynolds (*Portrait of Mrs. Elliott*).

The stunning whirl of masterpieces continues in Rooms 13, 12 and 10, where Rembrandt's *Man in Oriental Costume, Portrait of Saskia* and *Bathsheba at her Bath*, as well as Nicolas Poussin's *Midas se baignant dans la rivière Pactoles* are prominently displayed. From Room 10, go to Room 8, where

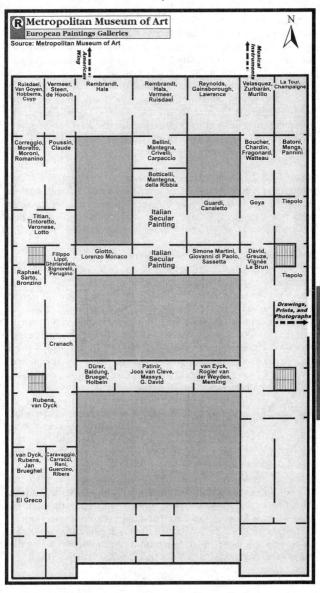

R Metropolitan Museum of Art
European Paintings Galleries
Source: Metropolitan Museum of Art

N

↑ American Wing

↑ Musical Instruments

| Ruisdael, Van Goyen, Hobbema, Cuyp | Vermeer, Steen, de Hooch | Rembrandt, Hals | Rembrandt, Hals, Vermeer, Ruisdael | Reynolds, Gainsborough, Lawrence | Velasquez, Zurbarán, Murillo | La Tour, Champaigne |

| Correggio, Moretto, Moroni, Romanino | Poussin, Claude | | Bellini, Mantegna, Crivelli, Carpaccio | | Boucher, Chardin, Fragonard, Watteau | Batoni, Mengs, Pannini |

Botticelli, Mantegna, della Ribbia

Guardi, Canaletto

Goya

Tiepolo

Titian, Tintoretto, Veronese, Lotto

Italian Secular Painting

Raphael, Sarto, Bronzino

Filippo Lippi, Ghirlandaio, Signorelli, Perugino

Giotto, Lorenzo Monaco

Italian Secular Painting

Simone Martini, Giovanni di Paolo, Sassetta

David, Greuze, Vignée Le Brun

Tiepolo

Drawings, Prints, and Photographs ▸▸▸

Cranach

Dürer, Baldung, Bruegel, Holbein

Patinir, Joos van Cleve, Massys, G. David

van Eyck, Rogier van der Weyden, Memling

Rubens, van Dyck

van Dyck, Rubens, Jan Brueghel

Caravaggio, Carracci, Reni, Guercino, Ribera

El Greco

EXPLORING

Titian's *Venus and the Organ-Player* is exhibited; then Room 6 via Room 5, which displays Giotto's *Epiphany*. From Room 6, head to Room 7, featuring paintings by Raphaël, then Room 27, devoted to Van Dyck (*James Stewart, Duke of Richmond and Lennox*) and Rubens (*Venus and Adonis, The Artist with his Wife and Son Peter Paul*). Brueghel the Elder is honoured in Room 28, where his famous *Harvesters* holds pride of place, while El Greco's *View of Toledo* stands out in Room 29. Finally, return to the museum's entrance via Rooms 30 (Carravaggio's *Concert*), 27, 26, 25 (works by Dürer and Holbein), 24, 23 (paintings by Mamling), 2 and 1.

Head back down the Grand Staircase to the Great Hall. Time permitting, you can explore either of the two sections described below. If not, why not reward yourselves for covering close to two-thirds of the largest museum in the Americas by treating yourself to a little gift at the museum's boutique?

The Robert Lehman Collection ★ ★ (first floor, at the very back, behind the Grand Staircase) is, as its name indicates, businessman Robert Lehman's former private collection of paintings, bequeathed to the museum in 1969. The collection was set up in its own wing in order to preserve its integrity. Several works are exhibited in rooms whose decor and antique furnishings come from Lehman's own New York residence. Paintings executed between 1880 and 1935 are visible from the entrance. Of particular note among these are *Girl at the Piano* by Renoir, *Vue du port de Marseilles* by Signac and *Maria* by Dutch painter Kees Van Dongen.

By wandering through the small rooms graced with dark wainscotting at the back, you can admire several Italian Renaissance masterpieces, including Botticelli's *The Annunciation*, Giovanni di Paolo's *Adam and Eve Driven from the Garden of Eden* and Ugolino da Siena's *Madonna and Child*. Also on display are Spanish (El Greco's *Christ Carrying the Cross*, Velasquez's *The Infanta Maria Teresa*), Flemish (Hans Memling's *The Annunciation*), French (an Ingres portrait, *La Princesse de Broglie*) and Dutch paintings (Rembrandt's *Portrait of Gérard de Lairesse*). Magnificent drawings by Degas, Dürer, Leonardo Da Vinci and Rembrandt are on display in the basement.

The Metropolitan Museum of Art's costume collection is under the direction of the **Costume Institute ★** (Level G, reached via the elevator in the Egyptian Art galleries). The institute boasts more than four centuries of some 60,000 costumes and fashion accessories from all over the world. The exhibitions change three times a year.

Several buses from lines M1, M2, M3 and M4 wait at the museum's exit to take visitors back to Midtown.

TOUR S: THE UPPER WEST SIDE ★★
(half a day)

Despite many attempts to attract upper-crust New Yorkers to the area, the Upper West Side finally realized that it could not compete with the unwaveringly popular Upper East Side, on the other side of Central Park. Efforts made by local developers to lure prospective residents are apparent in the ornamentation of the residential buildings scattered about the neighbourhood, which are without question the loveliest in New York. Ironically, the Upper West Side's efforts at self-improvement benefited its rival by enhancing the view enjoyed by residents of the posh apartments on the Upper East Side.

The Upper West Side dates back to about 1880. It developed around Bloomingdale Road, which used to run to Albany, the state capital. This winding rural road, which followed the route of an old Native American trail, was later widened and is now part of Broadway. The rocky terrain was levelled so that the area could be patterned after the grand boulevards of Paris. Home to stage and television actors, singers, dancers, comedians and musicians, the Upper West Side is one of the most appealing parts of Manhattan. There's a reason why the creators of *Mad About You* and *Seinfeld* decided to set their shows here.

Our tour of the Upper West Side starts at Columbus Circle, on the Central Park side. To get there by subway, take the A, C, D or 1 to the Columbus Circle/59th Street Station. The M5, M7 and M10 buses all stop at Columbus Circle as well.

Columbus Circle, located at the southwest corner of Central Park, where Broadway intersects with Eighth Avenue, is a big

EXPLORING

traffic circle with a statue of the "discoverer" of America in the middle, perched atop a column (Gaetano Russo, 1892). The Maine Monument, on the Central Park side, was erected in 1913 in memory of the sailors who died when the U.S.S. Maine was blown up in the port of Havana in 1898. This terrorist act was one of the causes of the Spanish-American War, which resulted in Cuba becoming an unofficial U.S. colony. To the right of the monument lies Central Park South, where the most expensive hotels with the best views are located. South of the circle stands a strange-looking building that could be a bank in an Arab country but was actually the New York Convention and Visitors Bureau until 1997. Finally, on the west side of the circle, you'll see the enormous New York Coliseum, whose days appear to be numbered. The building was a convention centre until the Jacob K. Javits Convention Center opened in 1986 (see p 280).

Head north on Central Park West. Walk next to the park for a better view of the buildings on the west side of the avenue.

Those of us who would like to have a pad in New York one day all dream of living in a place like the **Century Apartments ★ ★** *(25 Central Park W.).* These highly sought-after units, advertised for millions in the *Times*, are termed Prewar Apartments by rental agencies. This means that they predate World War II and have a more sophisticated decor, higher ceilings and a great deal more charm than those found in newer buildings. And no, they are not infested with cockroaches. A veritable masterpiece of the Streamlined Deco style, the Century Apartments were designed by French architect, Jacques Delamarre, in 1931. Their lofty twin towers are typical of buildings on the Upper West Side.

The section of **West 67th Street** between Central Park West and Columbus Avenue is lined with buildings designed to house artist's studios, hence their two-story picture windows. To the east, at West 67th Street, is the entrance to Tavern on the Green, the famous restaurant in Central Park (see p 355).

The Spanish and Portuguese Jewish community settled in New York in the mid-17th century, after being driven out of Europe and then the European colonies in South America. Since then, New York has welcomed thousands of Jewish immigrants, thus becoming the largest "Jewish" city in the world. The

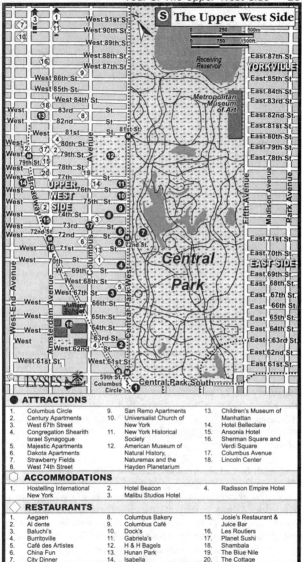

The Upper West Side

0   250   500m
0   750   1500ft.

Receiving Reservoir

YORKVILLE

Metropolitan Museum of Art

Central Park

EAST SIDE

UPPER WEST SIDE

Juilliard School

ULYSSES

Central Park South

● ATTRACTIONS

1.	Columbus Circle	9.	San Remo Apartments	13.	Children's Museum of Manhattan
2.	Century Apartments	10.	Universalist Church of New York	14.	Hotel Belleclaire
3.	West 67th Street	11.	New York Historical Society	15.	Ansonia Hotel
4.	Congregation Shearith Israel Synagogue	12.	American Museum of Natural History, Naturemax and the Hayden Planetarium	16.	Sherman Square and Verdi Square
5.	Majestic Apartments			17.	Columbus Avenue
6.	Dakota Apartments			18.	Lincoln Center
7.	Strawberry Fields				
8.	West 74th Street				

◯ ACCOMMODATIONS

1.	Hostelling International New York	2.	Hotel Beacon	4.	Radisson Empire Hotel
		3.	Malibu Studios Hotel		

◇ RESTAURANTS

1.	Aegaen	8.	Columbus Bakery	15.	Josie's Restaurant & Juice Bar
2.	Al dente	9.	Columbus Café	16.	Les Routiers
3.	Baluchi's	10.	Dock's	17.	Planet Sushi
4.	Burritoville	11.	Gabriela's	18.	Shambala
5.	Café des Artistes	12.	H & H Bagels	19.	The Blue Nile
6.	China Fun	13.	Hunan Park	20.	The Cottage
7.	City Dinner	14.	Isabella		

EXPLORING

Congregation Shearith Israel Synagogue ★★ *(99 Central Park W., at West 70th St.)*, the Spanish and Portuguese Jewish community's main synagogue, is the oldest temple in New York and thus enjoys a considerable level of prestige. It has been reconstructed several times on different sites. Designed in the Beaux-Arts style (1897), it contains furnishings from the community's first synagogue, erected in Lower Manhattan in 1730.

With their tall twin towers containing one or two apartments per floor, the **Majestic Apartments** ★★ *(115 Central Park W.)* are another classic example of the residential architecture of Central Park West. French architect Jacques Delamarre and sculptor René Chambellan collaborated on the design (1930).

Singer and songwriter John Lennon was shot in front of the main entrance to the **Dakota Apartments** ★★ *(1 West 72nd St.)* in 1980, turning the place into a shrine for rock 'n' roll fans. The former Beatle used to live in one of the immense, 20-room apartments in this building, which has the distinction of being the oldest of its kind north of 59th Street. When it was built in 1884 (Henry J. Hardenbergh), its detractors, who thought it was much too far from the centre of town, dubbed it "The Dakota" in reference to the remote Native American territories in the Midwest. A number of celebrities have lived here, including actress Lauren Bacall, dancer Rudolf Nureyev and John Lennon's widow, Yoko Ono.

Strawberry Fields ★ *(in Central Park, near the West 72nd St. entrance)*, a flower-filled garden named after the Beatles' lovely song, was given to the city by the inconsolable Yoko Ono, in memory of her soulmate. It was designed by landscape architect Bruce Kelly in 1983.

West 74th Street ★ *(between Central Park W. and Columbus Ave.)* boasts a lovely group of row houses with brick and stone façades. Architectural unity of this kind is extremely rare in New York. At the corner of the street stand the **San Remo Apartments** ★★ *(145 Central Park W.)*, designed by Emery Roth (1930). The small, circular temples pointing skyward atop the buildings disguise the water towers that used to supply the upper-floor apartments with drinking water.

Not far from the **Universalist Church of New York** *(4 West 76th St.)*, a neo-Gothic building dating from 1898, lies the **New York Historical Society** ★★ *($5; ৬; Wed to Sun noon to 5pm; 2 West 77th St., ☎873-3400*, an imposing neoclassical building designed by York and Sawyer (1908). An historical society, library and museum rolled into one, this venerable institution, founded by Mayor De Witt Clinton in 1804, hosts exhibitions of works from its own collections, which include a large number of precious documents, such as the contract for the Louisiana Purchase, signed by Napoleon I.

Kids who have always dreamed of going to the kind of museum that Indiana Jones might have put together will love the **American Museum of Natural History** ★★★ *($8; ৬; Sun to Thu 10am to 5:30pm, Fri and Sat 10am to 10:30pm; Central Park W., from West. 77th St. to West 81st St., entrance at West 79th St., ☎769-5100)*, which is packed with treasures from all over the world. A veritable Ali Baba's cave filled with some 35 million fascinating objects, this museum is the largest of its kind in the world. Founded in 1869 by a zoology professor named Albert Bickmore, it was moved to its current location on the Upper West Side in 1877.

An imposing brontosaurus skeleton and dinosaur eggs found in Mongolia are displayed in the Hall of Dinosaurs, while a blue whale over 30 metres long hangs in the Hall of Ocean Life. In the Hall of Minerals and Gems, visitors can admire the world's biggest sapphire, the Star of India, which weighs in at 563 carats. The collections devoted to the peoples of the earth include some superb totem poles from British Columbia (Canada), pieces of Mayan and Aztec temples and dioramas showing the customs of various cultures (an Amerindian village, a traditional Chinese wedding, etc.). The museum also has an Imax theatre, **Naturemax** ★★ *(admission fee; every day, hourly from 10:30am to 4:30pm, additional shows at 6pm and 7:30pm on Fri and Sat, ☎769-5034)*, which shows science and nature films on a giant, four-story screen. The **Hayden Planetarium** *(behind the museum, on Columbus Ave.)*, inaugurated in 1935, is currently closed for major renovations and is scheduled to reopen in the year 2000.

Turn left on West 81st Street, then walk across Columbus and Amsterdam avenues to Broadway.

EXPLORING

The **Children's Museum of Manhattan** *(admission fee; Mon, Wed and Thu 1:30pm to 55:30pm, Fri to Sun 10am to 5pm, closed Tue; 212 West 83rd St., between Amsterdam Ave. and Broadway, ☎721-1223)*, located a few streets north of the main tour, is designed specifically for children aged two to 10. Under the amused eye of their parents, kids can make lovely drawings, create their own TV show and take part in a marionette show, to name but a few of the activities offered by the museum.

Turn left on Broadway.

Broadway runs diagonal to the surrounding streets, which sparked the imagination of early 19th-century architects, who saw the perfect opportunity to create a wide avenue modeled on the grand boulevards of Paris. Among the buildings to have survived from this glorious era, characterized by mansard roofs, stone balustrades and small metal balconets taken straight from the École des Beaux-Arts in Paris, are the **Hotel Belleclaire** *(250 West 77th St.)*, built in 1901, and the **Ansonia Hotel ★★** *(2109 Broadway, south of West 74th St.)*, which is grander than anything dreamt up by Baron Haussmann, the man who beautified Paris under Napoleon III by widening the streets, creating boulevards and parks, etc. The French connection runs even deeper, though: during the Reign of Terror, Talleyrand took refuge in one of the farmhouses that were scattered about this area in the 18th century. Two years later, he was joined by the Duc d'Orléans, the future Louis-Philippe I, King of France (1830-1848), who taught languages and mathematics to young New Yorkers for a few months at a rural school in the vicinity. Famous former residents of the building itself include Arturo Toscanini, Lily Pons and Igor Stravinsky.

Sherman Square and **Verdi Square**, located on either side of West 72nd Street, attempt to lend some sort of structure to the shapeless space created by the multiple intersections in this area. The middle of the former is graced with one of the few original subway entrances still in existence (Heins and La Forge, 1904), while the latter is dominated by a statue of Italian composer Giuseppe Verdi, surrounded by characters from his most famous operas (Pasquale Civiletti, 1906).

Turn left on West 72nd Street then right on Columbus Avenue.

Between West 65th and West 82nd, **Columbus Avenue** ★ is lined with neighbourhood businesses (convenience stores, florists, dry cleaners, etc.) and good restaurants with sidewalk seating, lending it a relaxed, carefree air that contrasts with the frenetic, "high-society" atmosphere of New York's other affluent neighbourhoods. This refreshing change of pace is perhaps due to the presence of thousands of stage actors in the area.

Built at the same time as Montréal's Place des Arts, **Lincoln Center** ★★ *(admission fee; west of Columbus Ave. and Broadway, between West 62nd and West 65th, ☎546-2656; guided tours of the complex: ☎875-5350; guided tours of the opera house: ☎769-7020; to attend an orchestra rehearsal: ☎875-5656; Alice Tully Hall: ☎875-5050)* has a similar overall design, which is typical of cultural centres of the 1960s. Its four main buildings form a "U" around a concrete plaza with a fountain in the middle. The complex, whose architecture is modern but by no means daring, stands atop an underground parking lot that boosts it a few feet above street level. The **New York State Theater** (Philip Johnson, 1964), home of the New York City Ballet, stands on the left. Facing the street is the **Metropolitan Opera House** (Wallace K. Harrison, 1966), whose lobby is decorated with a series of murals by Marc Chagall; to its right are the **Vivian Beaumont Theater** (Eero Saarinen, 1965) and **Avery Fisher Hall** (Max Abramovitz, 1962), where the New York Philharmonic Orchestra performs. Damrosh Park, south of the opera house, adds a little greenery to this expanse of concrete. The orchestra gives outdoor concerts here at the **Guggenheim Band Shell**. Finally, the renowned **Julliard School**, attended by students of music and theatre, was moved north of West 65th Street in 1968. Chamber and classical music concerts are often presented in **Alice Tully Hall**.

To return to the starting point of the tour, head south on Broadway.

TOUR T: MORNINGSIDE HEIGHTS AND THE CLOISTERS ★★★ (one day)

North of Central Park, Manhattan Island narrows down to a point where the Harlem River, on the east side of the island,

Morningside Heights and The Cloisters

● ATTRACTIONS

12. Trinity Cemetery
13. Church of the Intercession
14. The Hispanic Society of America
15. American Numismatic Society
16. American Academy of Arts and Letters
17. MorrisJumel Mansion
18. George Washington Bridge Bus Station
19. Fort Tryon Park
20. George Washington Bridge
21. The Cloisters

◯ ACCOMMODATIONS

1. Fort Lee Hilton

◇ RESTAURANTS

1. Wilson's

INWOOD

WASHINGTON HEIGHTS

Dyckman

Broadway

190th St.

Henry Hudson PKWY.

Cabrini-Blvd.

Ft-Washington

W. 187th St.

NEW JERSEY
NEW YORK

Riverside Park

Fort Lee (N.J.)
George Washington
Bridge (toll)

1

W. 181st St.

W. 172nd St.

W. 162nd St.
W. 160th St.
W. 159th St.

W. 156th St.
W. 155th St.
W. 153rd St.

W. 154th St.

HIGH BRIDGE

MELROSE

Findley-Av.
College-Av.
Sherman-Av.
Morris-Av.

McClellan

River-Av.
Walton-Av.

E. 164th St.

E. 161st St.

Grand-Blvd.

Ogden-Av.

Jerome-Av.

Harlem-River-Dr.

Edgecombe-Av.

High-Bridge-Park

Harlem River

Major Deegan EXPWY.

E. 149th St.

Hudson River

Riverside Park

Riverside Dr.

St-Nicholas-Av.

Amsterdam

Broadway

W. 148th St.

W. 144th St.

W. 142nd St.
W. 140th St.

See map

W. 137th St.

W. 134th St.

W. 128th St.

W. 124th St.

W. 122nd St.

W. 119th St.

W. 115th St.

W. 113th St.

W. 111th St.

W. 108th St.

W. 105th St.

NEW JERSEY
NEW YORK

Riverside Park

Henry Hudson PKWY.

Broadway

Amsterdam Av.

Morningside Av.

Manhattan Av.

Convent

St-Nicholas-Av.

Frederick Douglass Blvd.

Adam-Clayton Powell Blvd.

Malcolm-X-Blvd.

Fifth-Av.

Madison-Av.

Park-Av.

Lexington-Av.

Third-Av.

Second-Av.

HARLEM

Marcus G. Pk.

E. 119th St.

E. 115th St.

E. 111th St.

E. 108th St.

E. 105th St.

Central-Park-North

Central Park

© ULYSSES

N

0   500   1000m.
0   0.25   0.5mi.

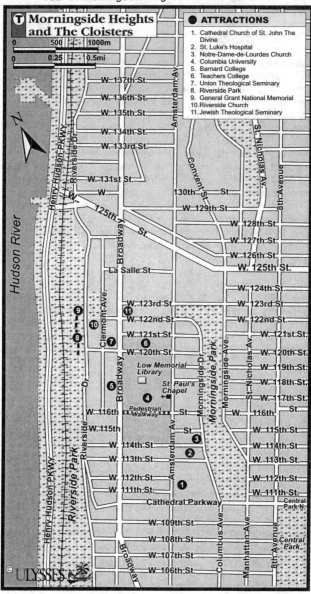

T **Morningside Heights and The Cloisters**

| 0 | 500 | 1000m |
| 0 | 0.25 | 0.5mi |

● ATTRACTIONS

1. Cathedral Church of St. John The Divine
2. St. Luke's Hospital
3. Notre-Dame-de-Lourdes Church
4. Columbia University
5. Barnard College
6. Teachers College
7. Union Theological Seminary
8. Riverside Park
9. General Grant National Memorial
10. Riverside Church
11. Jewish Theological Seminary

EXPLORING

© ULYSSES

meets the Hudson, on the west. The eastern part of this neck of land is occupied by the vast plain of Harlem while the western part of it forms a narrow, rocky, elevated strip that offers sweeping views over the Hudson River valley. A series of neighbourhoods, all of them called "Heights", developed on this high ground: Morningside Heights, between 110th Street and 125th Street; Hamilton Heights, which stretches to 145th Street; and Washington Heights, which borders Fort Tryon Park.

Because of their particular geographic situation, especially the range of visibility offered by their elevation, the Heights once constituted a strategic military location and several forts were erected here, including Fort Tryon, part of which has survived to this day. In 1776, when the area as a whole was still known as Harlem Heights, a critical battle took place here that was won by George Washington, thereby restoring the confidence of his troops, who had been routed a few days earlier on Long Island.

A number of important museums and religious and educational institutions are concentrated in the Heights. Columbia University stands out among these with a reputation that extends well beyond the borders of the United States, and the whole area is invaded by thousands of students at the beginning of the school year. A few ethnic groups also have deep roots in this area, including the Dominican community.

Part of this tour involves a bus ride, so it is important to have four tokens per person for the visit. For security reasons, it is best to avoid Morningside, St. Nicholas, Jackie Robinson and Colonial parks, which separate the Heights from Harlem to the east, as they are not very safe, even in the daytime.

The tour of Morningside Heights and The Cloisters begins at the corner of Cathedral Parkway (extension of Central Park North, which itself is the extension of east 110th Street) and Amsterdam Avenue (the extension of 10th Avenue). This corner is accessible by subway on the C train (Cathedral Parkway/West 110th Street Station) or by bus M4, which runs along the northern edge of Central Park and then branches off on Broadway.

As you walk north on Amsterdam Avenue, the first sight that comes into view is the Gothic-Romanesque mass of the **Cathedral Church of St. John the Divine** ★★★ *(admission charge; ⚥; Mon to Sat 7am to 5pm, Sun 7am to 7:30pm; guided tours Tue to Sat at 11am, Sun at 1pm; Vertical Tour, by reservation only, the 1st and 3rd Sat of every month at noon and 2pm; 1047 Amsterdam Ave., ☎316-7540 or 932-7314, Vertical Tour ☎932-7347).* Construction of New York's Episcopal cathedral began in 1892, according to traditional medieval craft methods, and it is still unfinished. Upon its completion, by the middle of the 21st century, it will be the largest Gothic cathedral in the world. The building's plans have been modified several times since the original design by architects Heins and Lafarge was selected in an 1891 contest. Unquestionably, however, the architect who has left the most lasting mark on the work is Ralph Adams Cram, who took over after 1911 and endowed it with its current allure, a combination of French and British Gothicism.

The steps up to the cathedral square are adorned with street lamps salvaged from Pennsylvania Station, which was torn down in 1963 (see p 171). The church's central portal has large, poured-bronze doors that were fashioned in the Paris shop of Barbedienne from a design by artist Henry Wilson. Across the threshold of this "cathedral-museum" is an immense nave 38-metres high and 182-metres long from the narthex to the end of the choir and contains myriad works of art, including many stained-glass windows (the themes of which are occasionally unusual for a church – sports and the arts, for example) and, even more impressive, beautiful 16th-century tapestries made for the Palazzo Barberini in Rome based on sketches by Raphael. The polychrome sanctuary is supported by eight granite columns that are each two metres in diameter and that stand in front of exceptional windows made by James Powell and Sons of London. A stroll on the ambulatory that runs along the back of the choir affords a view of seven distinctly decorated apsidioles. In St. Martin's Chapel, dedicated to the French people, there is an elegant **statue of Saint Joan of Arc** (Anna Huntingdon, sculptress), at the foot of which lies a stone from her cell in Rouen.

One of the most interesting ways to visit the cathedral is to take the Vertical Tour, which leads to the top of the bell towers (and is therefore not recommended to those who suffer from vertigo). From this vantage point it is possible to observe the evolution of the site as a whole and the meticulous, on-going work of artisans. Those interested in medieval construction techniques can attend a workshop where masonry and woodworking methods used to construct Europe's great cathedrals are explained. A group of buildings occupies the cathedral grounds, including a Greek-Revival orphanage from 1830 that now houses a religious art gallery (access from within the cathedral) and the bishop's palace, which resembles a medieval castle (private). East of the right transept is the Biblical Garden, made up of plants described in the Bible. In sum, the Cathedral Church of St. John the Divine, with its mandate to serve as a meeting place for all religions (eloquently attested by the menorahs in the sanctuary), is a colossal work in the image of the city that surrounds it.

Leave the cathedral and continue north on Amsterdam Avenue.

The block east of Amsterdam Avenue between West 113th Street and West 114th Street is entirely taken up by the imposing mass of **St. Luke's Hospital**, the oldest sections of which date from 1896 (Ernest Flagg, architect). The church of **Notre-Dame-de-Lourdes**, on West 114th Street, serves one of the largest French Roman-Catholic parishes in New York. Its sanctuary is a smaller-scale reproduction of the shrine at Lourdes (1910).

Turn left on West 116th Street, closed to car traffic from here, to reach the main campus of Columbia University, which stretches from 114th Street to 121st Street.

Founded as King's College in 1754, **Columbia University ★★** *(free admission; &; free guided tours every day 11am and 2pm; tours ☎854-4900)* has occupied its current Morningside Heights campus since 1897. This private university is one of the foremost post-secondary educational institutions in the United States. In order to set it apart from other American university campuses of the era, which were for the most part modelled after those of the medieval universities of Cambridge and Oxford in England, Columbia's administrators opted for a beaux-arts layout dominated by axes and perspectives and Italianate neoclassical architecture, which was considered modern at that time. Architects McKim, Mead and White were commissioned for and worked on the project until 1913.

The campus is centred around **Low Memorial Library**, named in honour of the former mayor of New York, Seth Low (1850-1916), who donated the building. The library building is preceded by a beautiful colonnade and is crowned by a dome, mimicking the Roman Pantheon. Guided tours of the campus leave the **Visitors Center** in the library. The library steps are graced by a beautiful **statue of the Alma Mater** created by sculptor Daniel Chester French in 1903, which symbolizes both knowledge and belonging. On the right, there is a view of the brick cupola of **St. Paul's Chapel** (1907), the interior of which is almost entirely covered in Gustavino tiles. The chapel's acoustics are much appreciated by music lovers and numerous concerts are presented in it every year from October to April. Among the more recent university buildings are the **Avery Library** *(north of St. Paul's Chapel)*, which assembles the largest collection of architecture books in the Americas, and the **Sherman Fairchild Center for the Life Sciences** *(near the intersection of Amsterdam Ave. and 119th St.)*, which houses the university's social sciences department. The modern look of this last building (Mitchell & Giurgola, architects, 1977) blends in harmoniously with the red and beige edifices from the early 20th century. Over the years, dozens of Columbia faculty and students have acquired celebrity status and many important breakthroughs have been made here. In all, the university's researchers have collected 16 Nobel prizes, including one awarded to Harold Urey in 1934 for his discovery of heavy water. A few years later, the power of the atom was detected in his laboratory, a finding that gave birth to the Manhattan Project, which in turn led to the fabrication of the first atomic bomb.

Return to 116th Street and head west. Then turn right on Broadway, which runs along the western edge of Barnard College.

Since its foundation, **Barnard College** *(on the west side of Broadway, between West 116th St. and West 120th St.)* has been a post-secondary educational institution exclusively for women. Named for its founder, Frederick A. Barnard, the college opened its doors in 1889 in an era when the neighbouring university still exclusively admitted male students. The institution, which lost its *raison d'être* the moment that Columbia opened its doors to female students in 1983 (!), is now part of the main university campus. Barnard College has also graduated its share of celebrities, including anthropologist Margaret Mead.

Teachers College *(525 West 120th St., east of Broadway)* is also affiliated with Columbia University. According to its promoters, it is the largest institution dedicated to teacher training in the Western World.

The very British neo-Gothic buildings of the **Union Theological Seminary** ★ *(on the north side of West 120th St., west of Broadway)*, which trains pastors of the United Church, stand across Broadway from Teachers College (Allens and Collens, architects, 1910).

Turn left on West 120th Street and then right on Riverside Drive.

To the left stretches the lush ribbon of greenery that is **Riverside Park** ★★ *(bordering the Hudson from West 72nd St. to West 125th St.)*, from which you can see the powerful Hudson River and the slopes of the New Jersey suburbs on the opposite shore. This linear park was established between 1888 and 1910 based on an idea dreamed up by Frederick Law Olmsted, who is also credited with the plans for Central Park. In 1937, the park was partially re-designed to accommodate Henry Hudson Parkway, which cuts off access to a good portion of the green space along the bank of the river below.

Enter the park and follow the paths to the level of West 122nd Street.

Riverside Park is punctuated with beautiful monuments. The most imposing of these is without question **General Grant National Memorial** ★ *(free; every day 9am to 5pm; Riverside Park, north of West 122nd St.)*, built in 1897 by John H. Duncan, which shelters the tombs of General Ulysses Grant and his wife. The great victor of the Civil War was laid to rest here following a petition signed in his honour by 90,000 people. His mausoleum, a replica of the tomb of Mausolus, one of the seven wonders of the ancient world, is entirely covered in white marble. Its interior holds stunning black porphyry statues of Grant and his wife reclining on their tombs. Admirers of the general have opened a small museum of Civil War memorabilia on the upper floor.

Exiting the mausoleum, visitors can enjoy an exceptional view of **Riverside Church** ★★ *(free, access to the bell tower $2; &.; Tue to Sat 9am to 4pm, Sun 12:30pm to 4pm, bell concert Sun 2:30pm; 490 Riverside Dr., ☎222-5900)*, which was erected thanks to a donation from billionaire John D. Rockefeller. Conceived in a late neo-Gothic style (1930) inspired by the medieval architecture of Flanders, the design of the church also reflects the architecture of modern skyscrapers: it has a steel structure hidden by stone decoration, and its bell tower reaches the respectable height of 21 stories. This tower shelters the Laura Spellman Rockefeller Memorial Carillon, the most powerful carillon in the world, which numbers 74 bells including one that weighs 20 tons and is considered to be the heaviest in the world. An elevator ride to the upper levels of the tower is an absolute must (although it is not recommended to those who suffer from fear of heights or vertigo), so you can see the carillon before moving on, via an open stairway, to the outdoor observatory, where there is a view over all of Morningside Heights. Riverside Church is interfaith, interracial and intercultural, and it frequently presents concerts and theatre pieces with religious tolerance and friendship among different peoples as principal themes.

Return to Broadway along West 122nd Street.

The remarkable concentration of institutions of higher learning in Morningside Heights is plainly apparent at the intersection of Broadway and West 122nd Street, which is entirely hemmed in by lay and religious schools. The **Jewish Theological Seminary**, one of the main centres of the Jewish religion outside of Israel, is at 3080 Broadway.

Hop on an M4 bus going north; the stop is on the east side of Broadway, near the Jewish Theological Seminary.

This tour really brings to light the colossal dimensions of Manhattan Island and the considerable distance between its southern and northern tips. Just as a reminder, the borough of Manhattan pretty much constitutes New York's "downtown core" and, despite its respectable size, it is by far the smallest of the five boroughs that make up the city.

Trinity Cemetery ★ *(between Riverside Dr. and Amsterdam Ave., from West 153rd St. to West 155th St.)* is visible on

EXPLORING

either side of Broadway, just before 155th Street. It was laid out on the farmland of French-born naturalist and ornithologist John James Audubon (1785-1851) in the second half of the 19th century when the little cemetery surrounding Trinity Church (see p 277), on Wall Street filled up. Audubon, who is famous for his paintings of North American birds and plants, was one of the first to be interred here. Among other celebrities buried here is furrier John Jacob Astor, patriarch of the famous dynasty that held sway over New York high society for over 50 years.

Get off the M4 bus at the corner of Broadway and West 155th Street (or continue to The Cloisters, at the very end of the bus route).

The **Church of the Intercession** ★ *(550 West 155th St.)* is right in front of the bustop at 155th Street. This Episcopal church (1914) and its cloister successfully interpret Gothic art of the Middle Ages and are masterpieces of Bertram Grosvenor Goodhue, who was later interred on the grounds. A recumbent statue of the architect can be seen in a recess of the north transept wall (Lee Lawrie, sculptor, 1929). Visitors lucky enough to enter the interior can also admire its rich marble floors, large organs to the left of the sanctuary and magnificent, exposed-framework, polychromatic wooden vault that shelters its nave.

Head to Audubon Terrace, an open courtyard on Broadway between 155th and 156th streets.

The **Hispanic Society of America** ★★ *(free; Tue to Sat 10am to 4:30pm, Sun 1pm to 4pm; 613 West 155th St., ☎926-2234)* is located at the end of Audubon Terrace. This Spanish and Portuguese art museum displays railroad magnate, Archer M. Huntingdon's collection of paintings, sculptures and furniture amassed at the beginning of the 20th century. His cousin, architect Charles Pratt Huntingdon, designed a lofty beaux-arts "palace" (1908) to house these treasures and an extensive research library. The name is a little misleading: this highly specialized institution has absolutely nothing to do with the large Hispanic community that emigrated from Central America and established itself in Washington Heights in the years after the museum was founded.

The **American Numismatic Society** ★ *(free; Tue to Sat 10am to 4:30pm, Sun 1pm to 4pm; 613 West 155th St., ☎234-3130)*, which possesses one of the largest collections of medals and coins from around the world, stands to the left of the Hispanic Society of America, and the **American Academy of Arts and Letters** *(632 West 156th St., ☎368-5900)*, which sometimes presents New York avant-garde exhibitions, can be seen on the right.

To visit the Morris-Jumel Mansion, walk east down West 155th Street, turn left on Amsterdam Avenue and then turn right on West 160th Street. It is recommended that visitors not dawdle along the way and that they keep their valuables concealed until they are on the grounds of this grand residence.

The **Morris-Jumel Mansion** ★ *($4; Wed to Sun 10am to 4pm; 65 Jumel Terrace, ☎923-8008)* is the oldest existing residence on Manhattan Island. It was built in 1765 for a Loyalist named Roger Morris and, ironically, it served as George Washington's New York headquarters after his victory at Harlem Heights, in the autumn of 1776. In 1810, the house was bought by French wine merchant Étienne Jumel, who updated his Georgian residence with a Federal portal. During a trip to France in 1815, Jumel met a then-dethroned Napoleon and offered him a haven at his home in the United States. Inside the house, you can tour a series of little rooms decorated with beautiful furniture pieces, some of which belonged to the emperor. The rose garden east of the house overlooks the Harlem River valley and offers a view of the huge borough of the Bronx across the water.

Backtrack to Broadway. Take bus M4 north to reach The Cloisters. Get off at the last stop, in front of Fort Tryon Park.

Along the way to Fort Tryon Park, the bus passes underneath the George Washington Bridge (see below), which is near the stunning **George Washington Bridge Bus Station**. This bus station serves the distant suburbs of New York, and it was designed in 1963 in the shape of a butterfly, by Italian engineer Pier Luigi Nervi, who is also responsible for the sports stadium in Rome, the exhibition centre in Turin and the tower of the Montreal Stock Exchange.

EXPLORING

Geroge Washington Bridge

The bus continues northward before finally stopping on the edge of **Fort Tryon Park ★★** *(west of Broadway, between 190th St. and Dyckman St.)*. This beautiful park was laid out on an escarpment overlooking the valley of the Hudson River. From the belvedere at the ruins of 18th-century Fort Tryon, visitors can look to the south and admire the **George Washington Bridge ★★**, described by Le Corbusier as the most beautiful bridge in the world (*Quand les Cathédrales Étaient Blanches*, 1937). Completed in 1931 by Swiss engineer O. H. Ammann, it was for a long time the longest suspension bridge on earth thanks to its incredible span of 1,066 metres. In 1962, a second level was added underneath the original deck to improve increasing traffic on the bridge.

Set at the highest point of Fort Tryon Park, **The Cloisters ★★★** *($8 including access to the Metropolitan Museum of Art; Mar to Oct, Tue to Sun 9:30am to 5:15pm; Nov to Feb, Tue to Sun 9:30am to 4:30pm; Fort Tryon Park, by subway take the A train toward Inwood to 190th Street Station, ☎923-3700)* is a fabulous museum made up of authentic cloisters and chapels imported from Europe stone by stone and reconstructed on this site beginning in 1934. These precious buildings lodge the exceptional collection of medieval art owned by the Metropolitan Museum of Art, whose main building is on Fifth Avenue (see p 235). The museum is particularly famous for its collection of tapestries, which is among the largest in the world.

The museum's first room, called Romanesque Hall, is affixed with the portal from the monastery of Moutiers-Saint-Jean (Burgundy, 13th century). A passage in the right wall leads to the 12th-century Fuentidueña Chapel, dedicated to Spanish Romanesque art and adorned with a fresco from the Catalan church of San Juan de Tredos. Adjacent to the chapel on the west, is the cloister of Saint-Guilhem-le-Désert Benedictine abbey (Hérault, France, 12th century). At the end of the Romanesque Hall, in the Langon Chapel, stands a medieval statue of the Virgin of Autun. Next to this is the chapter house of the Notre-Dame-de-Pontaut abbey (France), which borders the magnificent cloister of the Saint-Michel-de-Cuxa Benedictine monastery (Pyrénées, France, 12th century), pillaged during the French revolution. The south door of the chapter house gives way to the Early Gothic Hall, which exhibits, amongst other works, a 12th-century virgin that once decorated the cathedral of Strasbourg.

Take the stairs down to the lower level to visit Gothic Chapel, which is embellished by 14th-century Austrian stained-glass windows and a series of funerary statues. Gothic Chapel leads to the Glass Gallery, which displays stained-glass windows, and from there to the Treasury Room. The works exhibited in this last gallery include rich, 13th-century, Limoges enamel pieces; reliquaries; an ivory cross sculpted in a walrus tusk by the monks of an abbey in Suffolk, England (12th century); and, most impressive of all, the famous *Belles Heures de Jean de France, duc de Berry*, a precious work ornamented with golden miniatures crafted in Paris by the Limbourg brothers in 1406. At the entrance to the Treasury Room, two doors lead respectively to the cloisters of Trie and Bonnefont. A garden of medicinal plants used in the Middle Ages has been laid out at the latter, and the view of Fort Tryon Park and the George Washington Bridge is especially appealing from this cloister's terrace.

EXPLORING

Take the stairs back to the upper level and head to the Nine Heroes Tapestries Room, facing the stairway, on the way to the Unicorn Tapestries Room. The latter room displays seven exceptional and famous tapestries, each representing a hunt for the unicorn, the mythical animal with one twisted horn that symbolizes virginity and purity. These were woven as gifts for the marriage of Louis XII and Anne de Bretagne in 1499 and of François I and Claude de France in 1514. The visit wraps up with a peek at the Boppard Room, which features stained-glass windows from the German city of the same name; the Burgos Room, with its tapestry of Charles VIII, King of France; the Campin Room, with a superb triptych by Robert Campin from about 1425; and finally Late Gothic Hall, the Dominicans of Sens convent room from the 15th century, where German realist sculptures are exhibited.

To return to the tour's departure point, take bus M4 south (it runs all the way to Midtown), or take the A train at the 190th Street subway station toward Downtown, Lefferts Boulevard-Far Rockaway. This station is one of the deepest underground in the subway system and is equipped with an elevator so that transit users can bypass the long stairs that run from street level to the platforms.

TOUR U: HARLEM ★ (4 hours)

The most famous African-American district in the United States, Harlem evokes both the nostalgic blues of Billie Holiday and the grim shooting galleries set up in abandoned buildings. Yet Harlem is first and foremost a middle-class residential neighbourhood of small shops, brownstones and soaring neo-Gothic churches.

The general prosperity of the late 19th century led property developers to build thousands of apartment buildings north of Central Park, on the site of Harlem village, which was founded in the 17th century by Dutch colonists. This overdevelopment soon engendered a slump in rental rates and an unprecedented vacancy rate. The owners, who had always refused to rent to African Americans, had to resign themselves to do so in order to avoid bankruptcy. During the Roaring Twenties, Harlem established itself as the nucleus of African-American culture.

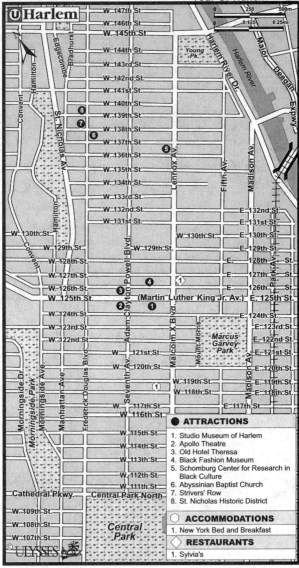

EXPLORING

Whites from Midtown also began crowding into its theatres and nightclubs to hear the first sounds of jazz. From 1960 on, however, Harlem became grey and dismal. Endemic unemployment and the omnipresence of drug dealers tarnished the district's reputation. Since 1980, though, Harlem has experienced a rebirth, as the staggering rent increases in Manhattan's other districts led a certain middle class to relocate here. Regrettably, this renaissance came to the detriment of less fortunate residents, mostly blacks who were gradually forced out toward other boroughs.

A few basic security measures should be taken while visiting Harlem: Explore the district in small groups of three or four people, avoid wearing showy jewellery, keep your camera concealed, avoid deserted areas and, above all, do not wander the streets come nightfall.

The tour of Harlem begins at the 125th Street subway station exit, located at Malcolm X Boulevard (formerly Lenox Avenue) and West 125th Street (now renamed Martin Luther King Jr. Boulevard). You can reach this station by taking trains 2 or 3. Head west on Martin Luther King Jr. Boulevard, considered Harlem's main street.

The **Studio Museum of Harlem ★** *(admission fee; Wed to Fri 10am to 5pm, Sat and Sun 1pm to 6pm; 144 Martin Luther King Jr. Blvd., ☎864-4500)* is a small museum devoted to art produced by black artists from the world over. The works on display include African masks, ancient statues and bold pieces by contemporary African-American artists.

Farther west is the famous **Apollo Theater ★** *(253 Martin Luther King Jr. Blvd.)*, where the biggest names in American jazz rose to fame, including Count Basie, Ella Fitzgerald and Duke Ellington. Back when Black performers were banned from other American venues, the Apollo played a pivotal cultural role for the African-American community. The gradual opening of Midtown halls to artists of colour, from 1960 on, led to the closing of the Apollo. Fortunately, the club reopened its doors in 1989, after complete renovations.

Despite their celebrity status, performers appearing at the Apollo had no choice but to be put up at the old **Hotel Theresa** *(at Martin Luther King Jr. Blvd. and Adam Clayton Powell Jr.*

Blvd.), because they were not welcome at other hotels in the city. Opened in 1913, the Theresa has since been converted into offices. Among its most notable guests was Cuban president Fidel Castro, who stayed here during his famous visit to New York in 1960.

Return to Adam Clayton Powell Jr. Boulevard. Head north along this main thoroughfare, then turn right on West 126th Street.

The **Black Fashion Museum** ★ *(admission fee; everyday noon to 5pm; 155 West 126th St., ☎666-1320)* features an interesting collection of garments worn by African Americans, from slavery to present day. Broadway stars' gowns, designed by great couturiers, are displayed alongside rags worn on Georgia plantations in the 18th century.

Turn left on Malcolm X Boulevard to explore the Harlem district more thoroughly. Follow this main thoroughfare for 10 blocks to West 136th Street.

The **Schomburg Center for Research in Black Culture** *(free admission; Mon to Wed noon to 8pm, Thu to Sat 10am to 6pm, Sun 1pm to 5pm; 515 Malcolm X Blvd., ☎491-2200)* is the world's largest research centre on the African diaspora. The centre boasts a few exhibition halls, but what makes it most noteworthy is its major library, which provides comprehensive information about the history and creative achievements of people of African descent worldwide. An annex of the New York Public Library, the centre opened in 1926 thanks to a donation from the Carnegie Foundation. Books can only be consulted on the premises.

Backtrack to West 135th Street. Head west along this street before turning right on Frederick Douglas Boulevard (formerly known by the more mundane name of "8th Avenue").

Located just east of Frederick Douglas Boulevard, the **Abyssinian Baptist Church** ★ *(132 West 138th St.)* played an important role in the African-American civil-rights movement during the forties and fifties. Its minister at the time was Adam Clayton Powell Jr. After fighting for the right of African Americans to obtain jobs within New York's public administration, Powell was the first black man to be appointed to the New York local council. He was later elected to the U.S.

EXPLORING

Congress in Washington D.C. The neo-Gothic church, built in 1923, is home to the oldest African-American denomination in the city, founded way back in 1808. If you're looking for something different that will get you off your feet, head to one of its two Sunday masses (9am and 11am) to hear the wonderfully uplifting gospel singers and the preachers' fiery sermons.

North of the church lie **Striver's Row** *(on West 138th St., between Adam Clayton Powell Jr. and Frederick Douglas boulevards)* and the **St. Nicholas Historic District ★** *(on West 139th St., between Adam Clayton Powell Jr. and Frederick Douglas boulevards)*. These two formerly well-to-do Victorian enclaves boast beautiful rowhouses built between 1889 and 1891 by renowned architects, including Stanford White. In the course of the twenties, a few well-off African Americans settled here, arousing the envy of some of their compatriots. A number of these houses have been restored over the last few years.

To get back to the subway, head east on 139th street, then turn right on Malcolm X Boulevard (formerly Lennox Avenue) to reach the 135th Street station, where trains 2 and 3 stop. You can also take the M2 bus (southbound), which runs along Adam Clayton Powell Jr. Boulevard.

TOUR V: BROOKLYN HEIGHTS ★★
(3 hours)

Here is a little riddle: What was the second largest city, after New York, in the United States at the end of the 19th century? Was it Boston, Philadelphia or Chicago? No, it was Brooklyn! In fact, before it was incorporated into the city of New York in 1898, which until then was limited to Manhattan Island, Brooklyn was a completely separate city engaged in a fierce rivalry with its neighbour across the East River. Brooklyn, whose name is a mutation of the Dutch *Breukelen*, was founded in 1646. At that time it was a vast agricultural estate that developed into distinct villages in different areas, which ended up all linked together.

Today, Brooklyn is the most populous of the five boroughs of New York, with 2.5 million residents. Its long ribbons of row

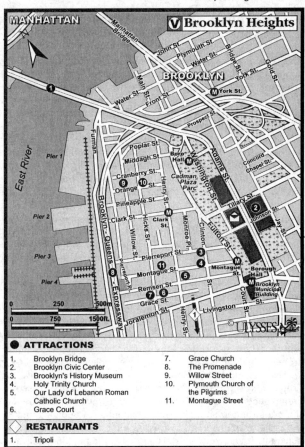

● **ATTRACTIONS**

1. Brooklyn Bridge	7. Grace Church
2. Brooklyn Civic Center	8. The Promenade
3. Brooklyn's History Museum	9. Willow Street
4. Holy Trinity Church	10. Plymouth Church of
5. Our Lady of Lebanon Roman	the Pilgrims
Catholic Church	11. Montague Street
6. Grace Court	

◇ **RESTAURANTS**

1. Tripoli

houses occupy 20,334 hectares of land – twice the area of inner-city Paris – at the western end of Long Island. Brooklyn is bordered to the north by the borough of Queens, to the south by the Atlantic Ocean, to the east by the endless suburbs of Long Island and to the west by the East River, which separates it from Manhattan Island. Brooklyn Heights represents just a tiny portion of Brooklyn. Situated on high ground overlooking the mouth of the East River, it faces the financial district of Lower Manhattan. Almost all of Brooklyn Heights is designated a historic neighbourhood because of the exceptional integrity of its architectural heritage, which for the most part dates from the second half of the 19th century.

This tour of Brooklyn Heights begins on Manhattan Island and suggests visitors take the walkway on the Brooklyn Bridge to cross the East River. This walk, which is very popular with New Yorkers, takes 45 minutes and offers both enjoyable, beautiful views of the surrounding area and a direct route to the heart of Brooklyn Heights on the opposite shore.

To reach the tour departure point, get off the subway at Brooklyn Bridge/City Hall Station, served by the 4 and 6 trains, or at City Hall Station, served by the N and R trains. Take the walkway that runs along the centre of Brooklyn Bridge, whose entrance is south of the Municipal Building (see p 277), at the intersection of Center Street and Park Row. To skip the walk and go directly to Brooklyn Heights, take the A train, which runs under the East River, to High Street/Brooklyn Bridge Station.

When it was completed in 1883, after 15 years of difficult work, the **Brooklyn Bridge** ★★★ *(at the mouth of the East River)* was considered the "eighth wonder of the world". Four times longer than the longest existing suspension bridge, it dominated the landscape like a medieval European cathedral with its two giant 90-metre-high pillars pierced by ogival arches. The bridge was designed by engineer John Roebling to link New York's Civic Center (City Hall, Courthouse, etc.) to Brooklyn's. Unfortunately, Roebling did not survive to see his dream become reality; he died in 1869 following an accident on the construction site. His son, Washington Roebling, took up the project, but he in his turn was bedridden by a work-related accident. It was younger Roebling's wife, Emily Roebling, who finally brought the project to completion. Before the Brooklyn Bridge was built, ferry service linked Brooklyn and New York. Praised by some and condemned by others, the bridge did succeed in bringing the citizens of the two cities closer together and launched, despite itself, the fusion process that would ultimately result in the creation of Greater New York in 1898.

Cross the Brooklyn Bridge on the pedestrian walkway at its centre. Turn right on Tillary Street to reach Cadman Plaza Park, around which hover the buildings of the Brooklyn Civic Center.

The **Brooklyn Civic Center** ★ *(east and south of Cadman Plaza Park)* unites a few beautiful public buildings, some of which recall the era when Brooklyn was still a separate city. Among these, a few that are worth mentioning are the neo-Romanesque Brooklyn General Post Office *(271 Cadman Plaza E.)*, erected between 1885 and 1892; the **Brooklyn Municipal Building** *(210 Joralemon St.)* from 1926, a conglomeration of various municipal departments; and Brooklyn Borough Hall *(209 Joralemon St.)*, an austere Greek-inspired creation from 1846 that once housed Brooklyn City Hall.

Turn left on Clinton Street.

Long Island stretches 150 kilometres into the Atlantic Ocean. Renowned for its beaches and its stylish resorts that serve as summer getaways for wealthy New Yorkers, Long Island has managed to preserve the rural allure that has made it so popular. On the other hand, the island possesses a quintessentially urban side, since the boroughs of Brooklyn and Queens are situated on its western end. The Long Island historical society once occupied the building that now houses **Brooklyn's History Museum** ★ *(admission charge; ⅃; Tue to Sat noon to 5pm; 128 Pierrepont St., at Clinton St., ☎1-718-624-0890)*. Erected in 1881 by architect George B. Post, this museum presents thematic exhibitions on the construction of the Brooklyn Bridge and on Brooklyn's short heyday in the second half of the 19th century.

Holy Trinity Church ★ *(157 Montague St.)* is tucked away behind the museum. This Episcopalian church, designed by architect Minard Lafever in 1844, has unfortunately lost its brownstone bell tower. Its terracotta and wood interior, is illuminated by beautiful stained-glass windows by William Jay Bolton.

Turn right on Remsen Street.

Immigrants from North Africa and the Middle East seem to congregate in the western section of Brooklyn, as witnessed by the numerous Lebanese and Moroccan restaurants on Atlantic Avenue. **Our Lady of Lebanon Roman Catholic Church** ★★ *(113 Remsen St.)* is a Maronite church that serves part of this community. Originally built for the Church of the Pilgrims, this temple is the oldest Romanesque-Revival building in the United

EXPLORING

States (Richard Upjohn, architect, 1846). The purity of its lines is in sharp contrast to the Victorian splendour of the era. Some of the church doors were salvaged from the *Normandie*, a ship that sank in the Port of New York in 1942.

Turn left on Hicks Street to see Grace Court and Grace Church.

Pretty **Grace Court ★** *(on either side of Hicks St.)* is actually a former service alley lined with stables and sheds that resembles similar lanes still seen today in London, England. Some of the buildings have preserved their original entrances.

The imposing neo-Gothic **Grace Church ★** *(2554 Hicks St.)* is another accomplishment by the prolific Richard Upjohn. Built in 1847, it contributes to the medieval allure of Grace Court.

Backtrack to the corner of Hicks and Remsen and turn left on Remsen. Follow this street to its end at The Promenade.

The Promenade ★★ *(between Remsen St. and Orange St.)* is a pleasant esplanade reserved to pedestrians overlooking the docks on the East River. From this elevated walkway dotted with benches and lampposts, strollers enjoy magnificent views of the Lower Manhattan financial district across the river. Along the way, there are beautiful brownstone row houses opening onto Pierrepont Place and Columbia Heights, the latter being where Washington Roebling lived when he was in charge of the construction of the Brooklyn Bridge. This is one of the most romantic spots in New York.

Turn right on Clark Street and left on Willow Street.

Some of the oldest houses in Brooklyn Heights are found along **Willow Street ★★** *(between Pierrepont St. and Middagh St.)*, a few of which were used as safe houses for runaway black slaves before and during the American Civil War (1861-1865). Number 57, which is adorned with a tall fire wall, is a beautiful example of Federal period architecture from 1824. Numbers 20 to 26, from 1845, have long galleries on their rear façades that directly overlook the river.

Turn right on Cranberry Street, right on Henry Street and right again on Orange Street (many of this neighbourhood's streets are named, amusingly, for fruit: in addition to Orange and Cranberry, there is a Pineapple Street).

Plymouth Church of the Pilgrims *(75 Hicks St., at Orange St.)* is a simple church that was a meeting place for American Abolitionists beginning in 1850. The church's pastor, Henry Ward Beecher, originated the underground railroad, a huge network of like-minded people who took in black slaves fleeing the southern states for Canada and other havens. Some neighbouring houses belonged to this network. A statue of Beecher stands in the garden of this Congregationalist temple.

Turn left on Hicks Street, then right on Montague Street.

Montague Street ★ *(between Pierrepont Pl. and Court St.)* is Brooklyn Heights' "Main Street", so to speak. It is lined with a few cafés and pretty shops, many of which are laid out on two floors to make the most of limited space.

To return to Manhattan, take the N or the R train at the Court Street subway station, at the eastern end of Montague Street (toward Uptown, Ditmars Boulevard, Astoria, 71-Continental Avenues, Forest-Hills).

 ## TOUR W: OTHER ATTRACTIONS

EXPLORING

Manhattan

The **Dyckman Farmhouse Museum** ★ *(free admission; Tue to Sun 11am to 4pm; 4881 Broadway, near 204th St., Train A to 207th Street station, ☎304-9422)* reminds us that New York City was once a Dutch colony and that the culture of the Netherlands is still felt here, long after the city was conquered by the British. The museum, located at the northern tip of Manhattan island, is set up in a beautiful farmhouse from 1783 surrounded by a lush garden. The structure is topped by a gambrel roof that slopes over the front and back porches, typical of Dutch colonial architecture in North America. The house contains an assortment of standard 17th- and 18th-century furnishings and objects that belonged to the Dyckman family, originally from the Netherlands.

The **Intrepid Sea-Air-Space Museum** ★★ *($10; Jun to Sep, everyday 10am to 5pm; Oct to May, Wed to Sun 10am to 5pm; Pier 86, at 12th Ave. and West 46th St.; trains A, C and E to 42nd Street subway station, ☎245-0072)* is set up on the imposing U.S.S. Intrepid aircraft carrier, moored at Pier 86 in New York Harbor. You can also go aboard four other ships – even a submarine docked at the Hudson River piers. Children will particularly appreciate this outdoor museum.

Situated in the westernmost reaches of Midtown, by the Hudson River, the **Jacob K. Javits Convention Center** ★ *(free admission; 11th Ave., between 34th and 39th streets; A, C and E trains to 34th Street-Pennsylvania Station subway station)* covers five whole blocks or 157,000 square metres of land. The glass- and steel-constructed New York Convention Centre, boasts a particularly impressive, 50-metre-high reception hall. The massive building is the work of architect Leoh Ming Pei, who is also accredited with the pyramid of the Louvre, in Paris.

Located in Riverside Park, the **Soldiers and Sailors Monument** ★ *(Riverside Park, at the west end of West 86th St., train 1 to West 86th St. subway station)* pays homage to those who perished in the American Civil War. The elegant cylindrical structure, built in 1902, was inspired by an Athenian monument from ancient Greece.

Brooklyn

The residential district of **Brighton Beach** *(at the southernmost tip of Brooklyn, D train to Brighton Beach subway station)* is spread out along the beach of the same name. A boardwalk stretches between the two, running parallel with the Atlantic Ocean. The many senior citizens who reside in the neighbouring high-rise buildings come to relax here every day. The district, made famous by Neil Simon's *Brighton Beach Memoirs*, is considered New York City's main Russian-Jewish district.

Founded in 1861, the **Brooklyn Academy of Music** ★ *(admission charge; ♿; 30 Lafayette Ave.; D, 2, 3 and 4 trains to Atlantic Avenue subway station, ☎1-718-636-4100)* has occupied the Lafayette Avenue Beaux-Arts building since 1907.

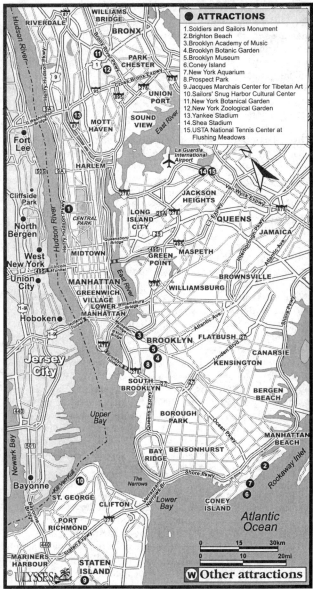

● ATTRACTIONS

1. Soldiers and Sailors Monument
2. Brighton Beach
3. Brooklyn Academy of Music
4. Brooklyn Botanic Garden
5. Brooklyn Museum
6. Coney Island
7. New York Aquarium
8. Prospect Park
9. Jacques Marchais Center for Tibetan Art
10. Sailors' Snug Harbor Cultural Center
11. New York Botanical Garden
12. New York Zoological Garden
13. Yankee Stadium
14. Shea Stadium
15. USTA National Tennis Center at Flushing Meadows

EXPLORING

Ⓦ **Other attractions**

This venerable institution, devoted to the performing arts, stages some of the most cutting-edge shows in New York City. Geared towards a more specific audience, it has thus created a name for itself alongside the big Manhattan halls, without robbing them of their clientele. The BAM notably presents baroque operas, avant-garde performances (Next Wave Festival) as well as dance-theatre productions by contemporary artists (Laurie Anderson, Philip Glass, Robert Lepage, etc.).

The 21-hectare **Brooklyn Botanic Garden** ★★ *(admission charge for the greenhouses; ㆑;Tue to Sun 10am to 4pm; 900 Washington Ave., near Eastern Pkwy.; ☎1-718-622-4433, lorigold@bbg.org)*, located south of the Brooklyn Museum (see below), boasts several beautiful thematic gardens, including three Japanese ones. The oldest of these was designed back in 1915 by architect-landscape gardener, Takeo Shiota.

Shadowed by the spotlight on Manhattan's Metropolitan Museum of Art, the **Brooklyn Museum of Art** ★★★ *(admission charge; ㆑, guided tours, lectures, concerts; Wed to Sun 10am to 5pm; 200 Eastern Pkwy., at Washington Ave., trains 2 and 3 to Eastern Parkway-Brooklyn Museum subway station, ☎1-718-638-5000, bma@echonyc.com)* is undeniably one of the finest art museums in the United States. Housed in a magnificent Beaux-Arts building designed by architects McKim, Mead and White (1897-1924), it is integrated into a grandiose setting of parks and gardens inspired by Baron Haussmann's grand Parisian boulevards. The museum contains galleries in over eight departments, including the Egyptian, Classical and Ancient Middle Eastern Art Department, which encompasses the museum's extensive collection of Egyptian art as well as 12 famous monumental bas reliefs from the ruins of an Assyrian palace. The Decorative Arts and Period Rooms Department displays exceptional collections of American decorative arts from 27 furnished rooms of various homes built throughout the United States. Among them is John D. Rockefeller's stunning Moorish smoking room (1885). Finally, the European Painting and Sculpture Department includes some of Cézanne, Courbet, Degas, Matisse, Monet and Pissarro's most beautiful works. Also of note are the 58 bronzes by Auguste Rodin in the Iris and B. Gerald Cantor Gallery. At the back of the museum, you can stroll through the intriguing Frieda Schiff Warburg Memorial Sculpture Garden, which is landscaped with architectural objects salvaged from various New York demolition yards.

The salad days of **Coney Island** *(by Surf Avenue; B, D, F and N trains to Stillwell Avenue-Coney Island subway station, Astroland, ☎718-372-0275)* are long gone, though the peninsula, which juts out into the Atlantic Ocean, has retained a few rusted *belle-époque* vestiges, giving it a certain charm. One of its large amusement parks, Luna Park, which was dominated by the metallic Parachute Jump ride, is now nothing more than a memory. Nevertheless, the boardwalk and adjacent beach continue to attract crowds of people on hot summer days.

The **New York Aquarium** ★★ *(admission charge; everyday 10am to 4:30pm; at West 8th St. and Surf Ave., D and F trains to West 8th Street-NY Aquarium subway station, ☎1-718-265-3474)* perfectly located right by the Atlantic Ocean, between Brighton Beach and Cony Island. The aquarium boasts a multitude of fish and sea mammals, such as whales, seals and penguins, that move about in its indoor tanks and outdoor ponds.

Created in 1860 by Calvert Vaux, **Prospect Park** ★★ *(west of Flatbush Ave., D and S trains to Prospect Park subway station, ☎1-718-788-0055)* is to Brooklyn what Central Park is to Manhattan, namely a large urban green space in the heart of the city. The park covers over 210 hectares and has a small wildlife centre (Brooklyn Zoo) as well as a winding lake and ponds perfect for rowboating. It is strongly recommended that you visit the park in groups of three or four and avoid it come nightfull.

EXPLORING

Staten Island

Built between 1668 and 1680 for Captain Christopher Billopp, **Conference House** ★ *(admission charge; Sat and Sun 1pm to 4pm; 7455 Hylan Blvd., bus S78 from the Staten Island Ferry Terminal on Staten Island, ☎1-718-984-6046)* is one of the oldest houses in New York City. In 1776, it was the site of a meeting between British and American forces to settle the American Revolution — hence its name. Needless to say, the conference came to naught. The solid stone manor occupies a choice site, at the southernmost tip of Staten Island.

Visitors will undoubtedly be surprised to find a Tibetan art museum bearing a French name in the very heart of Staten Island. The **Jacques Marchais Center for Tibetan Art ★★★** *(admission charge; Apr to Oct, Wed to Sun 1pm to 5pm; 338 Lighthouse Ave., bus S74 from the Staten Island Ferry Terminal on Staten Island, ☎1-718-987-3478)* was founded by an American woman with a passion for Tibet, who quite simply named it after her late husband. The museum features a Tibetan temple as well as numerous sculptures carefully arranged in a terraced garden. Since the Dalai Lama's visit in 1991, the museum has become a veritable Buddhist place of pilgrimage.

Historic Richmond Town Restoration Village ★★ *(admission charge; Apr to Dec, Wed to Sun 1pm to 5pm; 441 Clarke Ave., bus S74 from the Staten Island Ferry Terminal on Staten Island, ☎1-718-351-1611)* encompasses 28, 17th- and 18th-century buildings, through which the Historic House Trust of New York City re-creates past. Highlights include the Voorlezer's House (circa 1695), considered the oldest elementary school in the United States. Richmond Town is New York City's only historic village.

Located in an enchanting setting, the **Sailors' Snug Harbor Cultural Center ★** *(admission charge for museums and shows; park: everyday 9am to 5pm; museums: Wed to Sun noon to 5pm; 914 Richmond Terrace, bus S40 from the Staten Island Ferry Terminal on Staten Island, ☎1-718-448-2500)* is a huge performing arts centre that comprises a children's museum and theatre halls. The centre occupies several stately 19th-century Greek Revival buildings, dispersed throughout a park, which were once home to retired sailors. Of particularly note among these edifices and their portals is the Central Building, designed by architect Minard Lafever in 1833.

The Bronx

The **New York Botanical Garden ★★** *(admission charge for the greenhouses; &;Tue to Sun 10am to 6pm; at East 200th St. and Southern/Kazimiroff Blvd.; Metro North suburban train, which runs from Grand Central Station to Botanical Gardens station, ☎1-718-817-8700 or 817-8779, www.nybg.org)*

stands apart from its New York counterparts on account of its British character and remarkable surface area (close to 100 hectares).

Better known as the Bronx Zoo, the **New York Zoological Garden ★★★** *(admission charge; &; Tue to Sun 10am to 5pm; by the Bronx River Pkwy., train 2 to Pelham Parkway subway station, ☎1-718-367-1010)* is not only the largest of New York's five zoos, but also the biggest metropolitan wildlife conservation park in the United States. Its 120 ha shelter exotic animals from the equatorial jungle, the African savannah as well as the Himalayas and the mountains of Asia Minor, all in their respective natural habitats. Don't miss the nocturnal animal exhibit. The original buildings alone, designed by architects Heins and Lafarge between 1895 and 1908, are worth the visit.

Ardent fans of writer Edgar Allan Poe (1809-1849) won't want to miss visiting **Poe Cottage** *(admission charge; Sat 10am to 4pm, Sun 1pm to 5pm; in Poe Park, at East 192nd St. and Grand Concourse, D train to Kingsbridge Road subway station, ☎1-718-881-8900)*, where the author of *The Black Cat* spent the last years of his life.

Baseball is the United States' national sport. Every major city in the country has its own professional baseball team. Since New York does everything on a grand scale, it boasts two teams: the Mets and the Yankees. The latter play their home games at **Yankee Stadium** *(admission charge; &; at 161th St. and River Ave., train 4 to 161th Street-Yankee Stadium subway station, ☎1-718-293-6000, guided tours ☎1-718-293-4300)*, an open-air stadium deemed a veritable sports shrine by Americans.

Queens

Shea Stadium *(admission charge; at 126th St. and Roosevelt Ave., train 7 to the Willets Point-Shea Stadium subway station, ☎1-718-507-8499)*, a 55,000-seat, open-air stadium is home to New York's other baseball team, the Mets.

EXPLORING

The U.S. Open Tennis Championship is held every year at the **USTA National Tennis Center at Flushing Meadows** *(admission charge; in Flushing Meadows-Corona Park, train 7 to Willets Point-Shea Stadium subway station, ☎1-718-271-5100)*. The fully equipped centre, with both indoor and outdoor tennis courts, is laid out on the site of the 1964 World's Fair.

ACCOMMODATIONS

With some 60,000 hotel rooms to its name, New York City has plenty of establishments to choose from, making it easy to find something that will satisfy your needs. Be prepared to pay, however, because accommodations in New York do not come cheap. As in most major cities throughout the world, the hotel occupancy rate is exceptionally high, year-round. With rooms in such popular demand, prices are adjusted accordingly — an ideal situation for hotel-owners. Reserving a room at least two months in advance is essential if you don't want to end up stranded on the sidewalk, bags in tow. Most establishments require a credit card number to guarantee reservations.

Like several other American cities, New York now has hotel room wholesalers. These companies operate much the same as those who buy blocks of airplane seats, but can offer accommodation at the best hotels in the city. By reserving your room through these services, you can save up to 40% off the regular price advertised by the establishment.

If you visit New York City during the summer, make sure that your room is air conditioned, or risk getting a very bad night's sleep since the nights in July and August can be stifling. It is worth keeping in mind is that any hotel with less than 200 rooms is considered "small" in New York City (!), and that several have over 1,000 units. Hotels are arranged by tours and listed in order of price (starting with the least expensive) in this guide. Note that the 13,25% New York State tax, as well as a $2 per night municipal occupancy tax, must be added to the prices given, which apply to a standard double-occupancy room during the high season. Unless otherwise indicated, all rooms have fully equipped private bathrooms, air conditioners, telephones, television sets and in-room safes.

There are also a number of bed and breakfasts available in New York City. These are housed in private homes, some of which are very beautiful. This type of accommodation is relatively new to the American metropolis. Bed and breakfasts are generally less expensive, and allow you to meet people from New York and abroad over breakfast, which is usually included in the price. While the service does not compare with that of Fifth Avenue luxury hotels, the welcome and upkeep in these places varies, depending on the association in charge (see p 289). Note that in this kind of establishment, visitors usually, share a bathroom with the other guests.

Wholesalers

The **Central Reservation Service** *(11420 North Kendall Dr., Suite 108, Miami, Florida 33176, ☎1-800-950-0232 or 305-274-6832, ≈305-274-1357, www.reservation-services.com)* operates both as a call-centre for hotel room reservations throughout the United States, and as a wholesaler in major American cities, including New York. Paying a membership fee will enable you to obtain the best discounts.

The **Hotel Reservations Network** *(Mon to Fri 8am to 6pm; 8140 Walnut Hill Lane, Dallas, Texas 75231, ☎1-800-964-6835, www.180096hotel.com)* is a Dallas-based firm which offers a wide variety of hotel rooms at very good prices in major cities worldwide. There are no membership fees or service charges, though you must pay the firm directly for your room prior to your stay. In the event of last minute cancellations, HRN reserves the right to keep the full payment.

Old meets new in the Financial District.
- T. B

Legendary Central Park: nature surrounded
by skyscrapers. - *T. B.*

Quikbook *(Mon to Fri 9am to 7pm; 381 Park Ave. S., NY 10016, ☎1-800-789-9887 or 779-7666, ⇰779-6120, www.quikbook.com, info@quikbook.com)* is the biggest discount hotel reservation service in New York City. Its service is fast and efficient service for groups or individuals, and it lets you choose among about thirty different types of establishments scattered throughout Manhattan's various districts. Quickbook has no membership fees or service charges. Moreover, you are not required to pay for your room until you check out (at the reception desk), which is a definite advantage.

The **Room Exchange** *(Mon to Fri 9am to 5pm; 450 Seventh Ave., NY 10123, ☎1-800-846-7000 or 760-1000, ⇰760-1013)* offers discounts averaging 35% off the price of rooms in several New York hotels. This wholesaler, however, requires full payment for the room at least 48 hours prior to your stay. There are additional charges for last-minute cancellations.

Bed & Breakfasts

The **Abode Bed and Breakfast** association *(PO Box 20022, NY 10021, ☎472-2000)* consists of over 150 establishments throughout Manhattan. You can also rent an apartment for a week or two through this organization.

The **Bed and Breakfast Network of New York** *(☎645-8134 or 1-800-900-8134)* offers rooms in typical New York apartments. Some of these only provide the basic comforts, though.

As its name indicates, **Bed and Breakfast Ultra-Luxurious International** *(☎1-800-352-4497)* provides luxurious rooms in particularly charming apartments and houses (Victorian homes with 19th-century decor, modern penthouses overlooking Central Park, etc.). You can expect to pay significantly higher rates here than in other New York bed and breakfasts.

New York Bed and Breakfast *($40-$60 bkfst incl.; sb; 134 West 119th St., ☎666-0559)* has six rooms (shared bathroom only), spread out over several floors in an old brownstone located in the very heart of Harlem.

ACCOMMODATIONS

TOUR A: THE WALL STREET DISTRICT

Only a stone's throw from the World Trade Center and Battery Park City, the **Marriott Financial Center Hotel** *($375-$450; ⊘, ≈, ℛ, △; 85 West St., NY 10006, ☎385-4900 or 1-800-228-9290, ⇝227-8136)* occupies a red-brick high-rise built in the early nineties. Its 504 ultramodern rooms are equipped with all the amenities for business travellers (fax machine, modem hookups, etc.).

TOUR C: THE SOUTH STREET SEAPORT

Located in the heart of the South Street Seaport Historic District, the **Best Western Seaport Inn** *($144-$174 bkfst incl.; ⅃, ⊛, ℛ; 33 Peck Slip, near Pearl St., NY 10038, ☎766-6600, ⇝766-6615)* is housed in an early-19th-century red-brick building that used to be a warehouse, and is more reminiscent of colonial New England than the American metropolis. The small seven-story hotel only has 65 rooms, each of which has a mini refrigerator and VCR (you can rent movies from the reception desk). Breakfast is served every morning in the lounge adjacent to the lobby. Try to get one of the rooms with a balcony; though slightly more expensive, they are equipped with metal garden furniture and afford spectacular views of the Wall Street district and the Brooklyn Bridge. You will receive a warm reception and an excellent deal at this hotel, which is gay friendly.

The **Manhattan Seaport Suites** *($195-$235; K, ℛ; 129 Front St., NY 10005, ☎742-0003 or 1-800-427-0788, ⇝742-0124)* provides studios and suites that can accommodate up to four people each. The suites include a living room with sofa bed and a dining-area, a fully equipped kitchen (stove, microwave oven, fridge, mini bar) and a bedroom. The marbled bathrooms are equipped with hair dryers. The rooms are simply furnished. The place could be charming, were it not for the rather unfriendly welcome.

TOUR F: SOHO

 Inaugurated in 1996, the **SoHo Grand** *($229-$369; ♿, ✖,*
☺, ℋ; 310 West Broadway, near Canal St., NY 10013,
☎965-3000 or 1-800-965-3000, ≈965-3200) is the first hotel
to be built in Soho in the last 100 years. A symbol of the
district's gentrification, this luxury establishment is located on
West Broadway (not to be confused with Broadway, farther
east), a main thoroughfare lined with trendy cafés and
restaurants. The hotel lobby is unconventional in that it is
located on the top floor, rather than the main floor. A hallway
with comfortable armchairs links the hotel bar to the Canal
House Restaurant (see p 328). Blending the district's
old-fashioned industrial architecture with the exotic styles of
the twenties, the common rooms' and guestrooms' innovative
decor was designed by William Sofield and might make you feel
as if you are in a Batman movie. The beige-toned rooms have
beautiful views of the Downtown and Midtown skylines, and
are equipped with hair dryers, modem hookups and mini bars.
The newspaper is delivered to your room in the morning, and
local phone calls are free. CD players and VCRs are available at
the reception desk upon request. Another welcoming touch is
the tea and coffee machines set up on every floor. The SoHo
Grand welcomes cats and dogs with open arms, and even puts
litter boxes and rubber toys at the disposal of its four-legged
guests.

TOUR G: GREENWICH VILLAGE

A former apartment building, the **Larchmont Hotel** *($85-$99*
bkfst incl.; pb, sb; 27 West 11th St., NY 10011, ☎989-9333,
≈989-9496) is ideally located in the heart of Greenwich Village,
only a short distance from Chelsea, on a quiet street lined with
typical New York brownstones. There is a complex system of
access codes which you must use to get to your room and to
the private café, located in the basement, where breakfast is
served. The rattan furnishings give the modest-sized rooms a
tropical look. The less expensive rooms share bathrooms.

ACCOMMODATIONS

The **Washington Square Hotel** *($120-$160 bkfst incl.; ⊘, ℜ; 103 Waverly Pl., NY 10011-9194, ☎777-9515 ⇒979-8373, www.vyp.com/washington_square)* is a charming little place located near lovely Washington Square Park. Its 170 rooms are clean and attractively decorated. The hotel, whose common rooms can be described as intimate, boasts its own restaurant. The place has a large gay clientele.

TOUR H: CHELSEA

Don't be put off by the facade of the **Chelsea Savoy Hotel** *($90-$140; ♿; 204 West 23rd St., NY 10011, ☎929-9353, ⇒741-6309)*; its interior decor is on par with that of most other Midtown hotels, and its level of comfort is superior to that of other hotels in Chelsea. Each room has a hair dryer, an iron and ironing board, and windows that open (a rarity in New York City). There are special rooms for disabled and non-smoking guests.

The **Colonial House Inn** *($115 bkfst incl.; sb, pb; no credit cards accepted; 318 West 22nd St., ☎243-9669)* welcomes gay patrons, who benefit from the proximity of restaurants and bars in what is becoming the new "village". The hotel is a mere 10-minute walk from Greenwich Village. The rooms are small but well furnished and, like the rest of the hotel, are very clean and tastefully decorated. A rooftop terrace allows guests to sunbathe in the heart of the city. Very friendly welcome. Light breakfast buffet included.

The well-located **Chelsea Pine Hotel** *($120; pb, tv; 317 W. 14th St., ☎929-1023, ⇒645-9497)* caters mainly to a gay clientele. It has about 24 clean, safe rooms, each with a different decor inspired by the movies. The hotel also has a pretty garden with a rustic atmosphere, where free coffee is served all day.

TOUR I: THE EAST VILLAGE

St. Marks Hotel *($70-$110; 2 St. Mark's Pl., NY 10003, ☎674-2192, ⇒420-0854)* is a moderately-priced establishment which caters to the young, hip clientele that frequents the East

Village's bars and nightclubs. Its rooms contain simple and sturdy blond wooden furniture. There are several trendy cafés in the vicinity.

TOUR J: THE SQUARES

The **Gershwin Hotel** *($22 sb $150 pb; 3 E. 27th St. between Madison and Park, ☎545-8000, ⇒684-5546)* is both a youth hostel and a hotel with comfortable, well-equipped rooms. It is a favourite with well-informed, budget-conscious globe-trotters. At $22 per person, this is definitely one of the best bargains in New York, if you don't mind sharing a room and bathroom. The walls are decorated with pop art, and there is a rooftop terrace where you can relax and contemplate the glittering lights of the city after a long day of pounding the pavement. The hotel also has a small bar and shuttlebus service to the airports. The Gershwin's only shortcoming is its elevator, which has to be one of the slowest in town.

Officially opened in 1924, **Gramercy Park Hotel** *($145-$220; ℜ; 2 Lexington Ave., at 21st St., NY 10010, ☎475-4320 or 1-800-221-4083, ⇒505-0535, telex 668755, cable GRAMPARK)* is one of New York City's oldest luxury hotels. The clientele here consists of foreign tourists and the "regulars", who reside at the hotel for several months of the year or simply come to enjoy their daily sherry at the bar. Among its most famous residents is actor Matt Dillon, who lived here in the eighties. The hotel faces the only private park in New York City. Like those who reside around the park, the establishment's clients are given a key to the park gate. Because some of the Gramercy Park Hotel's 509 rooms have seen better days, request one of the recently renovated rooms, some of which have mini refrigerators or kitchenettes.

TOUR K: FROM THE EMPIRE STATE BUILDING TO THE UNITED NATIONS

True to its name, the **Murray Hill Inn** *($75; sb; 143 East 30th St., 10016, ☎683-6900 or 1-888-996-6376, ⇒545-0103, www.murrayhill.com)* is located within the residential enclave of Murray Hill. Housed in a former apartment building, this small, moderately-priced hotel is especially well-suited for students and young couples with modest budgets. Not all rooms are air conditioned and the six-story building has neither lobby nor elevator.

You will feel as if you have arrived at a *belle-époque* luxury hotel when you see the neo-baroque façade of the **Hotel Wolcott** *($85-$95; 4 West 31st St., NY 10001, near Fifth Ave., ☎268-2900, ≈563-0096, www.wolcott.com)*. The rooms themselves, however, are extremely stark. Every year, this budget hotel, located just three blocks from the Empire State Building, welcomes hundreds of groups of French and British tourists. In addition to its 260 rooms with private bathrooms, the hotel has several rooms with shared bathrooms available at a lower price.

There are a number of budget hotels between Broadway and Fifth Avenue, from West 30th Street to West 42nd Street. Most, however, are run down. One of the few exceptions is the **Herald Square Hotel** *($95-$125; sb or pb; 19 West 31st St., NY 10001, ☎279-4017 or 1-800-727-1888, ≈643-9208)*, a simple but clean establishment. The decor, however, is less than spectacular: the lobby looks like a hospital corridor and the rooms, which vary considerably in size from one floor to the next, are rather drab. In addition to units with private bathrooms, the establishment offers single-occupancy rooms with shared bathrooms for $50 a night. The hotel has no in-room safes.

With its distinctly French name, **Hotel Deauville** *($110; 103 East 29th St., NY 10016, ☎683-0990 or 1-800-333-8843, ≈683-5921)* attracts numerous visitors from France. This family-run establishment is situated in a quiet neighbourhood near Midtown Manhattan's fabulous attractions. Its 58 soberly furnished rooms are in stark contrast to its lavish neo-baroque façade, which was erected in 1912. Part of the hotel serves as a boarding house. Several celebrities, including Sid Vicious and Courtney Love, appear on the list of former tenants.

The **Quality East Side** hotel *($129; 161 Lexington Ave., NY 10016, ☎545-1800 or 1-800-567-7720, ≈481-7270 or 790-2760)* has 100 rooms in a building dating from 1905. The building was once a boarding house for single women, known as The Rutledge. Each room has an iron and ironing board as well as a coffee maker. Take care not to trip over the step in front of the bathroom, which is almost 50 cm high!

The **Hotel Metro** *($130 bkfst incl.; ⊘; 45 West 35th St., NY 10001, ☎947-2500, ⇒279-1310)* tries to look like a small European hotel, with a library that has a chimney, and conspicuous postmodern pediments in its 175 rooms. Hair dryers are provided in the marbled bathrooms. Check out the communal rooftop terrace.

The **Howard Johnson Hotel on 34th** *($130 bkfst incl.; ℜ; 215 West 34th St., NY 10001, ☎947-5050 or 1-800-446-4656, ⇒268-4829)* is part of the Pan-American chain of the same name and offers standard comfort. Its 125 rooms were renovated in 1995.

Situated opposite Penn Station (train station), **Hotel Pennsylvania** *($140; ⊘, ℜ; 401 7th Ave., at 33rd St., NY 10001, ☎736-5000 or 1-800-223-8585, ⇒502-8712)* is one of the giants of New York's hotel industry, with its 1,705 rooms, 42 suites and 600-seat ballroom. Built in 1919, the hotel reached the pinnacle of its glory during the big band era, when it featured musicians like Benny Goodman and Glen Miller. The latter even immortalized the hotel's phone number in his song *Pennsylvania 6-5000*. The Pennsylvania is now somewhat shabby and decorated with ultra-kitsch rococo furniture, reminiscent of a honeymoon in Las Vegas. Also, the place is located in a particularly busy and noisy district of Manhattan.

The **Best Western Manhattan** *($179; 17 West 32nd St., NY 10016, ☎736-1600 or 1-800-551-2303, ⇒563-4007)* is located on Korean Restaurant Row. The welcome here is rather indifferent and the service hasty. The hotel's baroque portal leads to 176 rooms, renovated in 1996 in the style of certain Manhattan neighbourhoods. Each room is equipped with a coffee maker, hair dryer, iron and ironing board, but there are no in-room safes.

🏨 The charming little **Hotel Bedford** *($180; ℜ; 118 East 40th St., NY 10016-1724, ☎697-4800 or 1-800-221-6881, ⇒697-1093)* is nestled among the brownstones of Murray Hill. Its soberly furnished studios and suites are fitted with kitchenettes.

ACCOMMODATIONS

In the heart of Murray Hill, the **Jolly Madison Towers Hotel** *($190; ☺, ℜ, ☎; 38th St. at Madison Ave., NY 10016, ☎802-0600 or 225-4340, ⇒447-0747)* is New York's branch of the Italian Jolly Hotels chain. Considering the good-sized rooms, the recent renovations and the pleasant neighbourhood where it is located, the establishment gives guests excellent value for their money. The welcome is warm and the service attentive. The hotel has retained the Whaler's Bar, a well-known neighbourhood watering hole, from its previous incarnation as the Lancaster Hotel. An Italian restaurant, the Cinque Terre, was added to the place a few years ago, as was the Madison Health Club, which offers shiatsu massages.

Several New York hotels offer business and leisure travellers studios and suites designed as furnished apartments, which can be rented by the day, the week or the month. **Murray Hill East Suites** *($240; ℜ, K; 149 East 39th St., NY 10016, ☎661-2100 or 1-800-248-9999, ⇒818-0724)* offer this kind of accommodation, which can be a good deal for large families and small groups. All 125 suites are furnished with a fully equipped kitchen, a living room with sofa bed and one or two bedrooms. The furnishings are comfortable, but the decor is rather mundane. The hotel is located on a quiet, tree-lined street, a few blocks from Manhattan's attractions.

 The sober and refined interior at **Morgans** *($245-$290 bkfst incl.; ℜ; 237 Madison Ave., NY 10016, ☎686-0300 or 1-800-334-3408, ⇒779-8352)* was designed by celebrated French designer Andrée Putman, who is also responsible for the Musée d'Orsay in Paris. The 154 rooms are decorated in various shades of grey, ranging from dark charcoal to off-white. Little attentions will be lavished on you, including fresh bedside flowers and an elegant afternoon tea, served in the dining room. Morgans Bar, on the main floor of the hotel, is one of the most select places in Manhattan. It is not uncommon to encounter international stars here. More retiring types can always enjoy the mini bar found in every room.

TOUR L: FIFTH AVENUE

The **Big Apple Hostel** *($55-$75; sb; 119 West 45th St., NY 10036, ☎302-2603, ⇒302-2605, BigApple@concentric.net)* is a very small, moderately-priced urban inn for young backpacking adventurers. Exceptionally well located for this kind of establishment (a short distance from Fifth Avenue and Times Square), the hostel offers both shared and private rooms with double beds (shared bathrooms only). The place boasts lockers, laundry facilities, and a communal kitchen, as well as a sombre but quintessentially New York back terrace. This is an ideal place to meet people from all over the world. Passports are required for identification purposes. Note that not all rooms are air conditioned and none have in-room safes.

The **Quality Hotel and Suites at Rockefeller Center** *($179; ⊘; 59 West 46th St., NY 10036, ☎719-2300 or 228-5151, ⇌768-3477)* occupies the former Wentworth hotel, now entirely renovated. Conveniently located between West 46th and 47th streets, the area comprising Little Brazil and Diamond Row, the establishment is a good deal in this highly prized Manhattan district. If possible, get a room facing 46th Street, since these face the building's lovely little private park at 1155 Avenue of the Americas. All units are equipped with a percolator, hair dryer, iron and ironing board.

Like other West 44th Street establishments, the **Hotel Iroquois** *($185-$225; 49 West 44th St., NY 10036, ☎840-3080 or 1-800-332-7220, ⇌398-1754)* occupies a choice location, midway between Fifth Avenue's shops and Broadway's theatres. Built in 1904, the 116-room hotel was fully restored in 1997. The welcome is warm, as it has always been, which is undoubtedly the reason James Dean chose to live here for two years (1949-1950)! The Iroquois has a babysitting service as well as a hairdressing salon. Because of its name, the hotel has welcomed many Native American chieftains attending aboriginal conferences over the last few years.

The **Mansfield** *($225-$275 bkfst incl.; 12 West 44th St., NY 10036, ☎944-6050, ⇌764-4477)* is a small hotel with 86 rooms, 24 suites and a great deal of character. Built in 1904, this former boarding house for wealthy singles was fully restored in 1996. The establishment has succeeded in preserving the ambiance of a turn-of-the-century private club, by paying meticulous attention to detail. Upon entering the lobby, adorned with Beaux-Arts mouldings, you will reach the lounge — graced with a fireplace and equipped with a giant-screen TV that shows taped concerts and operas — followed by the inviting library. The latter is topped by an amusing oval skylight and has a stage at the far end where harpists and pianists play in the evening. The hotel lends out books (available in several languages) as well as video tapes and CDs, which can be played on the VCRs and CD players supplied in each of the rooms. Breakfast and post-theatre buffets are also served here (both included in the price). The rooms at the Mansfield, decorated in shades of beige and black, are rather small, but cosy and elegant. A hair dryer is supplied in every bathroom. Only 3 of the 12 floors allow smoking.

The **New York Hilton and Towers** *($225-$335;* &, ⊘, ℛ, △; *1335 Ave. of the Americas, NY 10019,* ☎*261-5870 or 1-800-HILTONS,* ≈*315-1374, www.hilton.com)* resembles a gargantuan slab resting on a large podium, and contains 2041 rooms. The megahotel is typical of modern hotels built in the sixties. It is easy to get lost in its glittering lobby, which resembles a shopping centre and leads to huge conference rooms at the base of the tower and to the underground parking lot, free for guests. This veritable "city-within-a-city" offers every imaginable service, in over 30 languages. The New York Hilton has all the standard facilities. The rooms are comfortable, but unremarkable. Each room has a mini bar, modem hookup, hair dryer, iron and ironing board. Certain floors are reserved for non-smokers and several rooms have been specially fitted for physically handicapped travellers.

Closely associated with the Warwick-Champs-Élysées in Paris, **The Warwick Hotel** *($245-$295;* &, ℛ; *65 West 54th St., NY 10019,* ☎*247-2700 or 223-4099,* ≈*957-8915)* is a classic establishment located near Fifth Avenue, Central Park and Times Square. Built in 1927 for press tycoon Randolph Hearst, this luxury hotel of 434 rooms and suites recalls a time when travel was reserved for the elite. The Warwick was long the hotel of choice for stars at Paramount Pictures. James Dean, Elizabeth Taylor and Elvis Presley, to name but a few, have filed through its lobby. Cary Grant lived at suite 2706 for 12 years! The Beatles also stayed here during their first tour of the United States. The service is particularly attentive. The main floor boasts Randolph's bar, Ciao Europa restaurant and a small drugstore. The rooms are relatively large, and have mini bars and walk-in closets with irons and ironing boards.

A stone's throw from the Hotel Iroquois (see p297) is its main competitor and its namesake's historical rival, **The Algonquin Hotel** *($250-$275 bkfst incl.; &, ☺, ℜ; 59 West 44th St., NY 10036, ☎840-6800 or 1-800-555-8000, ⇒944-1419)*. The 142-room and 23-suite establishment dates from 1902. It made a name for itself during the twenties, when several eminent American writers, including Dorothy Parker and George Kaufman, regularly presided over the "Round Table" in its plush lobby. It has since become a landmark for authors passing through New York City, and a refuge for several well-known British actors, including Sir Anthony Hopkins and Jeremy Irons. The hotel is also renowned for its small concert hall, the Oak Room (not to be confused with the Oak Room at the Plaza hotel), where world-famous jazz musicians such as Henry Connick Jr. and John Pizarelli have appeared; for its Blue Bar, which has seen all the big names in American literature file; and its resident cat, Mathilda, who roams the lobby freely, welcoming guests in her own way. The Algonquin's guestrooms, nine of which are accessible to the physically handicapped, were partially renovated in 1995.

With 46 rooms and 38 suites, **The Shoreham** *($275-$295 bkfst incl.; ℜ; 33 West 55th St., NY 10019, ☎247-6700, ⇒765-9741)* is among the establishments New Yorkers describe as "upscale boutique-hotels". Its sobre and refined decor, in shades of grey taupe, blends American modernism of the forties and modern art of the nineties. Worth special mention are its chrome-plated armchairs, designed by Warren McArthur, and murals (1936) by Winold Reiss, which used to adorn Longchamps restaurant at the Empire State Building. In addition to a hearty breakfast, the hotel offers coffee throughout the day and well as an array of cakes and pastries come nightfall. Each room has a VCR and CD player (movies and CDs are on loan at the hotel reception desk at no extra charge). Several rooms have adjoining cedar closets, and the suites are fitted with sofa beds. Certain bathrooms only have shower stalls, but all are equipped with hair dryers.

Hollywood film-makers have made the **Plaza** *($305-$550; ≈, ℜ; 768 Fifth Ave., NY 10019, ☎759-3000 or 1-800-759-3000,*

☎759-3167) the most famous hotel in the world, thanks to the many big-budget films they shot here since the sixties, including *Breakfast at Tiffany's*, *Plaza Suite* to *Crocodile Dundee* and *Home Alone 2*. Classified as a historic monument, the Plaza is also the symbol of the New York hotel industry. Centrally located on Central Park, where Midtown meets the Upper East Side, the establishment built in 1907 and has kept its *belle-époque* charm intact. The hotel also boasts a famous bar and restaurant: The Palm Court and the Oak Bar (see p 383). The huge lobby of grey-veined white marble leads to the enormous rooms, some of which afford spectacular views over the park and the surrounding skyscrapers.

🏨 Stay at the **Royalton** *($315-$380; ⊘, ℛ; 44 West 44th St., NY 10036, ☎869-4400 or 1-800-635-9013, ⇝869-8965)* not only for the glamour, but also for the fabulous interior, which was designed in 1988 by Frenchman Phillippe Starck. Supermodels strut down the lobby's "runway", with its long blue carpet illuminated by a row of Starck's signature horned wall lights. A quarter of the rooms at the hotel, originally built in 1898, are graced with real fireplaces. Each room is equipped with a VCR (movies can be rented at the reception desk) and mini bar, though the odd, curved leather-padded bar on the main floor is not to be missed. The bathrooms are covered in green slate — a real treat for the feet.

The Peninsula New York *($395-$475; ⊛, ⊘, ≈, △, ℛ, ☎; 700 Fifth Ave., NY 10019, main entrance on 55th St., ☎247-2200 or 262-9467, ⇝903-3949, pny@peninsula.com)* is just the place if you enjoy being pampered in a *belle-époque* ambiance. This luxury hotel boasts a first-class health club and an excellent location, right on Fifth Avenue. Built in 1902, the 23-story Renaissance Revival hotel was long called The Gotham, then briefly known as Maxim's of Paris. In addition to the European-style spa where you can enjoy a mud bath, a massage or attend yoga classes, the establishment has three dining rooms, including the Adrienne restaurant, and a panoramic bar with a terrace overlooking Midtown Manhattan. The common rooms and guestrooms are graced with magnificent Art-Nouveau furnishings from Maxim's. The rooms all have mini bars, are spacious and flooded with ample natural light. Each of the marbled bathrooms has a hair dryer, bathrobes and a bidet — a rarity in North America.

The **New York Palace** *($400-525; ctv, pb; 455 Madison Ave., at 50th St., ☎1-888-7000, ⊷303-6000)* definitely lives up to its name. This splendid hotel was renovated in 1997 and is now considered one of the best in town. It boasts such amenities as a fitness centre equipped with the very latest in exercise machines, including a roller-blade simulator; a business centre where guests can send and receive E-mail and an excellent restaurant (see p 349). The ever-cheerful staff will do everything in their power to make your stay in New York as pleasant as possible. The bright, spacious, well-equipped rooms are impeccable. Those with even numbers are decorated in the Art Deco style, those with odd numbers in a more traditional manner. The suites all have fax machines and private minibars.

TOUR M: PARK AVENUE AND ITS SURROUNDING AREA

The **YMCA Vanderbilt Hotel** *($75-$95; ⚬, ⊘; 224 East 47th St., NY 10017, ☎756-9600, ⊷752-0210)* combines two seemingly contradictory names: YMCA (Young Men's Christian Association), synonymous with charity and physical fitness, and Vanderbilt, synonymous with ruthless capitalism and cream-filled pastries. And yet, this moderately-priced hotel has nothing to do with either. It is merely a noisy place where you can stay as a last resort.

The **Pickwick Arms Hotel**'s *($95-$120; ℜ; 230 East 51st St., NY 10022, ☎355-0300 or 1-800-PICKWIK, ⊷755-5029)* main attraction is its rooftop terrace, from where you can admire New York's skyline. The hotel's 400 rooms were partially renovated in 1996. It is the only non-luxury hotel in the Park Avenue area.

The **Hotel Beverly** *($169-$229; K, ℜ; 125 East 50th St., NY 10022, ☎753-2700 or 223-0945, ⊷759-7300)* has more suites and studios than rooms, at a ratio of 156 to 30. The suites are enormous and well-suited for large families; each comprises a living room with sofa bed, a bedroom, a large dining room and a kitchenette stocked with plates, cutlery, and pots and pans. Several studios also have kitchenettes. On the main floor of the hotel is the famous 24-hour Kaufman drugstore, which has been around since the thirties.

ACCOMMODATIONS

Several hotels in Midtown East have an equal number of standard rooms and suites equipped with kitchenettes. The latter type of accommodation is particularly popular with business people and UN delegations, who stay in New York for a few weeks or several months a year. The **Hotel San Carlos** *($179-$229; K; 150 East 50th St., NY 10022-7511, ☎755-1800 or 1-800-722-2012, ⊷688-9778)* is designed for this purpose. Each unit has a walk-in closet and a modem hookup.

The stretch of Lexington Avenue between East 42nd and East 52nd Streets has a high concentration of big luxury hotels. The **Doral Inn** *($189-$235; ℜ; 541 Lexington Ave., NY 10022, ☎755-1200 or 1-800-22-DORAL, ⊷421-3876)*, built in the twenties to serve nearby Grand Central Station, is trying to make a name for itself among these.

The **Hotel Lexington** *($219-$275; ℜ; Lexington Ave., at East 48th St., NY 10017, ☎755-4400 or 1-800-448-4471, ⊷751-4091, telex 426257 LEX UI, cable LEXTEL)* is one of the big classic hotels lining Lexington Avenue. Its 750 spacious rooms are tastefully furnished.

Like other Lexington Avenue hotels, the **Marriott East Side** *($265-$345; ℜ; 525 Lexington Ave., NY 10017, ☎755-4000 or 1-800-228-9290, ⊷751-3440, www.marriott-.com)* is centrally located, within easy reach of Midtown Manhattan's various attractions. Its plush lobby and lounges are panelled with dark wainscotting, resembling a 1940s film set on which Bette Davis would feel right at home. Each of the 643 rooms is equipped with a mini bar, an iron and ironing board. Some are reserved for the physically handicapped and non-smokers.

A true Art-Deco marvel, the **Waldorf-Astoria Hotel** *($325-$450; ⅋, ⊘, ℜ; 301 Park Ave., NY 10022-6897, ☎355-3000 or 1-800-WALDORF, ⊷872-7272 or 872-4784, www.hilton.com)* opened in 1931. Its 1,380 luxury rooms and some 200 ceremonial suites are distributed over the 59 stories of a stone-built high-rise dominating Park Avenue. This high-class establishment is considered one of the most famous places in the world not only for its extraordinary architecture, but also for the many celebrities who have stayed here (sometimes for several years at a time), including former president John F. Kennedy, Princess Grace of Monaco and composer Cole Porter.

Incidentally, the piano in the lobby is the one on which Porter composed some of his most beautiful songs. The hotel was fully restored by the Hilton hotel chain between 1994 and 1998. It has four gourmet restaurants, two bars and several richly decorated lounges.

TOUR N: TIMES SQUARE AND BROADWAY

Although the **Westpark Hotel** *($89-$99; 308 West 58th St., NY 10019, ☎246-6440 or 1-800-248-6440, ≈246-3131)* is on a quiet street, a little off the beaten path, but still close to the theatre district. The hotel has 99 simply furnished rooms, some of which afford views over Central Park. What more can you ask for at such reasonable rates?

The **Milford Plaza Ramada** *($99-$129; ⊘, ℜ; 270 West 45th St., NY 10036, ☎869-3600 or 1-800-221-2690, ≈944-8357)* is located in the heart of New York City's famed theatre district. The 1,300-room establishment is the lowliest of the colossal luxury hotels where musical-goers stay. This place might make you feel like a number, but this type of treatment seems to be the norm in "industrial" hotels. There is a unisex hairdressing salon on the main floor.

Very popular with Quebecers, the **Hotel Edison** *($102-$125; ⅄; 228 West 47th St., NY 10036, ☎840-5000 or 1-800-637-7070, ≈596-6850)* was totally revamped in 1996. The 1,000-room Art-Deco giant offers good value for your money, provided you do not expect overly personalized service. The hotel has its own theatre as well as a pleasant bar.

Located right near Carnegie Hall, the **Best Western Woodward** *($155-$185; 210 West 55th St., NY 10019, ☎247-2000 or 1-800-336-4110, ≈581-2248)* occupies a lovely Beaux-Arts building dating from 1903. The Carnegie Deli restaurant (see p 351), located next door, provides room service to hotel guests. The establishment's 140 rooms were renovated in 1997 and are now tastefully furnished.

If you appreciate grand hotel lobbies and do not object to rather confined living quarters, **The Paramount** *($175-$215; ⅄, ⊘, ℜ;*

ACCOMMODATIONS

235 West 46th St., NY 10036, ☎764-5500 or 1-800-225-7474, ⇝354-5237) is just the place for you. Its stunning lobby, designed by Phillippe Starck, features a grand staircase that everyone should descend dressed in their best attire at least once in their lives. The same Parisian designer renovated the 610 rooms which will surprise you with their innovative decor, but also with their size – which is rather small. The inverted, cylinder-shaped stainless steel sinks in the bathrooms — typical of the "Starck style" – are particularly worth mentioning. Movie-theatre architect Thomas Lamb constructed the original building in 1927. To top off its unconventional style, there is no outdoor sign indicating the hotel's name. The Paramount welcomes a large, stylish gay clientele, and liberal, well-to-do families who appreciate the game rooms and the daycare services provided by the hotel management.

With 474 pastel-coloured rooms, the **Novotel New York** *($185-$245; ⊘, ℛ; 226 West 52nd St., NY 10019-5804, ☎315-0100 or 1-800-221-3185, ⇝765-5369, www.novotel-northamerica.com)* is the largest North American hotel owned by this well-known French chain. Located in a commercial high-rise, the hotel isn't much to look at from the outside. This is not the case with the interior, however, which affords a spectacular bird's-eye view of Times Square and Broadway. The Café Nicole restaurant boasts an outdoor terrace, where you will truly feel above the fray. The hotel lobby is on the 7th floor. Do not be surprised to find yourself facing a simple elevator shaft once you've entered the hotel. Each tastefully and sparingly decorated room comes with a mini bar and a hair dryer.

After attending a big Broadway musical, why not pretend you are living in one by staying at the **Casablanca Hotel** *($225-$245 bkfst incl.; 147 West 43rd St., NY 10036, ☎869-1212 or 1-888-922-7225, ⇝391-7585, http://members.aol.com/casahotel)*, a small Moroccan-style luxury hotel straight out of *A Thousand and One Nights*, located in the heart of Times Square. This 48-room gem evokes colonial times with its rattan armchairs, "Play it again, Sam" piano and mosaic walls. Each room has a VCR and mini bar. Bathroom amenities include a hair dryer as well as a telephone.

Every weekday evening, the hotel offers complimentary pre-theatre wine and hors d'œuvres.

The 46-story-high **Crowne Plaza Manhattan** *($259-$319; ⅃, ⊘, ≈, ℛ, △; 1605 Broadway, at 49th St., NY 10019, ☎977-4000 or 1-800-243-6969 or 1-800-227-6963, ≈977-5517)* has 770 comfortable rooms and suites affording panoramic views of Times Square to the east and the Hudson River to the west. Every unit has a coffee maker, mini bar, hair dryer, iron and ironing board. The hotel entrance is right on Broadway, less than 100 metres from the theatres that feature some of the most famous American musicals. A fully-equipped fitness centre, comprising an indoor swimming pool, saunas, gym and aerobics rooms, is housed at the foot of the building. Boxing and yoga classes by professional instructors are also offered here. It must be added that this hotel, which opened in 1989, is one of the pillars of the newly refurbished Times Square.

An ultramodern hotel with 638 rooms and suites opened in 1990, the **Millennium Broadway** *($265-$315; ⅃, ⊘, ℛ, △, ☎; 145 West 44th St., NY 10036, ☎768-4400 or 1-800-622-5569, ≈768-0847)* is next to the Hudson Theatre, a relic from 1903 when the likes of Ethel Barrymore and Douglas Fairbanks performed there. Unlike several hotels in this district whose entrances face noisy Times Square, the Millennium is slightly set back from the road. Its impressive black-marbled lobby-hallway, decorated with Tamara Lempicka-style frescoes, connects 44th and 45th Street. The hotel has a fully equipped five-floor conference centre and rents out the 700-seat theatre next door for weddings and conferences. The guestrooms are large and very comfortable, and each has a mini bar, modem hookup, coffee maker, hair dryer and windows that open – even on the 52nd floor! Club rooms also have private fax machines. You can enjoy stunning views of the theatre district while seated in large leather armchairs beside the panoramic windows. Some rooms have been specially designed for physically handicapped travellers.

Synonymous with luxury and comfort, the **RIGHA Royal Hotel** *($325-$475; ⅃, , ⊘, ℛ; 151 West 54th St., NY 10019, ☎307-5000 or 1-800-937-5454, ≈765-6530)* is 54 stories above the fray, so if you are on one of the upper floors, you can enjoy a spectacular view of Central Park and the Hudson River. This modern establishment contains 500 deluxe suites that are not at all ostentatious. Amenities in each suite include a mini bar with ice-maker, a modem hookup, two television sets, a VCR, a hair dryer and scales. Unfortunately, the hotel's fitness centre leaves something to be desired for such an upscale establishment.

 TOUR P: THE UPPER EAST SIDE

On the border of Midtown and the Upper East Side, the **Bridge Apartments** *($140-$215; 351 East 60th St., NY 10022, ☎754-9388 or 1-888-754-9389, ⊷754-9593)* are more like typical New York apartments than hotel rooms. The buildings are on the approaches to the Queensborough Bridge roadway — hence the establishment's name. There are no elevators in this five-storey place. Each apartment contains simple and quaint rattan furnishings and a fully equipped kitchenette. The Bridge Apartments are a good choice for young families and those travelling in small groups, who are sure to enjoy chatting with other guests from all over the world while lounging in the back courtyard.

The Upper East Side boasts some of the most prestigious luxury hotels in New York City. Among these is **Hotel Pierre** *($345-$565; ℜ; at Fifth Ave. and East 61st St., ☎838-8000)* on Fifth Avenue. Housed in a magnificent Beaux-Arts building from 1929, whose roof is vaguely reminiscent of the Chapelle de Versailles, it offers rooms and apartments. It is probably the only hotel in New York that proudly hoists a Canadian flag outside, since it belongs to the Toronto-based Four Seasons chain.

 TOUR Q: CARNEGIE HILL AND YORKVILLE

With only 53 rooms, **The Franklin** *($169-$189 bkfst incl.; 164 East 87th St., NY 10128, ☎369-1000, ⊷369-8000)* offers a more personalized welcome than most other hotels. Behind its nondescript façade, architect-designer Henry Stolzman has created an original and modern decor, though this does not compensate for the extreme narrowness of the guestrooms. Artwork is displayed in the lounge where breakfast, four-o'clock tea and an assortment of evening desserts are served (all three included in the price). Other perks include free and safe parking (in the adjacent indoor tiered parking garage) and an excellent location that is ideal if you plan to visit the Fifth Avenue museums (all within a few blocks) rather than stay in your room.

Built in 1901, **Hotel Wales** *($185-$229 bkfst incl.; ℛ; 1295 Madison Ave., at East 92nd St., NY 10128, ☎876-6000, ⇝860-7000)* has preserved its original dark wainscotting, making it one of the only Victorian-style hotels still operating in New York City. An original staircase at the end of the lobby leads to the second floor, which boasts the large Pied Piper Room where you could easily spend days in the comfortable armchairs. Breakfast and an evening dessert buffet are served here (both included in the price). You can also enjoy afternoon tea free of charge while listening to a piano or harp recital. High-chairs for children are available upon request. The guestrooms at the Wales are small and contain a unique assortment of furniture. Most windows face an uninspiring, narrow interior courtyard. Request one of the few rooms facing the other side, or opt for one of the 40 suites overlooking the streets of the Upper East Side. Hair dryers and bottles of spring water are supplied in every room.

 TOUR S: THE UPPER WEST SIDE

New York's official youth hostel, **Hostelling International—New York** *(dormitory $30, room $75-$100; ℛ; 891 Amsterdam Ave., at West 103rd St., NY 10025-4403, ☎932-2300, ⇝932-2574)* has 480 beds in its dormitories and rooms for two, four or six people. Some rooms even have private bathrooms. A former 19th-century convent, the attractive red-brick hostel has a large, shaded back garden-patio that is a pleasant place to relax. The hostel also has a huge cafeteria and a small café in the lobby. You can also prepare your own meal in the communal kitchen. The hostel has coin-operated laundry machines and a game room. This place is clean, safe and inexpensive, and a great place to meet people from all over. Remember, however, that like all kinds of accommodations in New York City, it is essential to book a room way in advance.

ACCOMMODATIONS

The **Malibu Studios Hotel** *($79-$89 bkfst incl.; 2688 Broadway, at West 103rd St., NY 10025, ☎222-2954 or 1-800-647-2227, ₧678-6842, www.malibuhotelnyc.com)* is not far from the Hostelling International—New York, whose overflow of young travellers it welcomes during the hot summer months. The Malibu's 150 rooms, contain sparse, tubular furnishings and occupy the upper stories of a 19th-century building, whose main floor houses various neighbourhood shops. The establishment's narrow entrance is marked only by a slim black-and-white fabric awning emblazoned with a Californian palm tree. Once you have found it, you still have to climb a long staircase to reach the reception desk, then make your way through a maze of corridors before reaching your room, which will prove spartan but clean. The Malibu also rents out several rooms with shared bathrooms for as little as $49 a night.

All the rooms and suites at the **Hotel Beacon** *($135-$165; 2130 Broadway, at West 75th St., NY 10023, ☎787-1100 or 1-800-572-4969, ₧724-0839)* are equipped with kitchenettes stocked with plates and utensils, making this a sensible choice if you do not wish to spend too much money eating out. Housed in a brick high-rise from the twenties, the hotel is located in a very pleasant part of Manhattan, only a stone's throw from Lincoln Center and Columbus Avenue.

 Located opposite Lincoln Center, the **Radisson Empire Hotel** *($180-$240; ℛ; 44 West 63rd St., NY 10023, ☎265-7400 or 1-800-333-3333)* is a good deal. The hotel attracts a number of musicians. Each room is equipped with a CD player and VCR, as well as a hair dryer and mini bar.

🛏 NEW YORK CITY SUBURBS

Those who plan to reach New York City by car but loathe driving in the city itself can always check in at the **Fort Lee Hilton** *($145-$195; ⊘, ≈, ℛ; 2117 Route 4 East Fort Lee, New Jersey 07024, ☎201-461-9000, ₧201-585-9807)*. This suburban hotel, surrounded by a huge parking lot, is located in New Jersey, five minutes from the George Washington Bridge. Although it is not as grand as several luxury hotels in Midtown Manhattan, its rates are two-thirds the price. The hotel has an Italian restaurant, a sushi bar and a karaoke bar.

RESTAURANTS

New York's cosmopolitan character is reflected in its restaurants – some 17,000 in all, serving food from just about every country in the world. The city started attracting great chefs back in the early 19th century, and these culinary artists opened famous restaurants, a number of which have marked milestones in culinary history. For these reasons, New York is rightly considered one of the great gastronomic capitals of the western world. Because this city has everything, even some of the worst restaurants on the planet can also be found here. It is therefore wise to do a little research before choosing a place to eat.

The portions at American restaurants are generally very large – sometimes ridiculously so. Like their compatriots, New Yorkers eat a lot and are constantly snacking between meals. As a result, many are more portly than they'd like to be and try to shed their extra pounds jogging in Central Park. Others have opted to eat better or at least lighter food, which has led to the proliferation of deli and salad bars in Midtown Manhattan. In addition to fruit and vegetable salads, these places sell hot dishes by weight. Patrons serve themselves, then their food is weighed at the counter. Many of these places have seating on the second floor.

Deli and salad bars are an inexpensive alternative to New York's pricey restaurants. However, we recommend going right before noon to avoid the lunchtime crowds of workers, who fill these places for two hours, heaping food onto their plates with gusto. Another kind of budget restaurant that offers excellent value are noodle shops, which serve Chinese noodle dishes (soups, dumplings, etc.) for under $8. Lastly, if you're looking for a quick bite to eat, you can always grab a pretzel, hot dog, falafel or souvlaki from one of the vendors parked on the Midtown street corners with their little carts. These mobile businesses, strictly regulated by the city, are typical of New York. Fruit and vegetable vendors have followed suit, taking over unoccupied intersections.

Foreign visitors often forget that New York is a big seaport. It is also home to the largest fish market in the United States (the Fulton Fish Market, p 130), which supplies many restaurants. No matter what kind of restaurant, whether French, Italian or Chinese, seafood always figures on the menu.

For the past few years, spectacular food presentation has been in style in New York restaurants. In some places, the salads and desserts are easily 20 centimetres tall. These "skyscraper" dishes reflect the architecture of New York, as well as a desire to impress residents of and visitors to the Big Apple. In addition to their unusual appearance, they sometimes offer an interesting new experience for the palate, too. A gustatory tour of New York must also include a trip to a delicatessen, or deli (not to be confused with the deli and salad bars described above), for one of those famous pastramis on rye, which are served with pickles and bear no small likeness to the smoked meat sandwiches so popular in Montreal. The recipe was imported from Eastern Europe by Jewish immigrants back in the 1930s. The best-known delis in New York are clustered on 7th and 8th Avenues, just north of Times Square.

Brunch is generally served from 10am to 2pm on Saturdays and Sundays, often buffet-style. Many New York restaurants also have "after-theatre" menus (generally served between 10pm and midnight) for those who have worked up an appetite taking in a show.

Like most other Americans, New Yorkers make little distinction between the terms "bistro", "restaurant", "bar", "pub" and "café". These names have more to do with ambiance than what the place serves. You'll thus find Irish pubs labelled cafés, bistros with nothing French on their menu, bars that are actually restaurants, etc. Certain terms are more specific, though. Two examples are "grill", which generally refers to a place that serves grilled meat and fish, and "lounge", which is a place where customers can enjoy their apéritifs while ensconced in a comfortable armchair.

People still dress for dinner in New York. Many restaurants require proper attire, which in some cases means a jacket and tie for men and a dress for women. Of course, jeans and shorts are not permitted in these establishments, most of which are located in Midtown and on the Upper East Side. The atmosphere is much more relaxed in SoHo, Greenwich Village, Chelsea and the East Village, where you can wear pretty much whatever you want. However, in the best restaurants in every part of town, it is essential to make reservations several hours, days or even weeks in advance, depending on how popular the place is.

Be forewarned that smoking is now strictly forbidden in New York restaurants, except at the bar, if the place has one. This regulation, which has many New Yorkers grumbling, is enforced more rigorously in some neighbourhoods than in others. For example, don't expect places on the Upper East Side to be as lenient as those in the East Village. Finally, the tip is never included in the bill. Depending on the quality of the service, it is customary to leave the server around 15% of the total before tax. The same goes for the person who delivers your food if you order in.

This chapter contains listings for a number of New York restaurants, arranged by neighbourhood and by price, from the least to the most expensive.

Price categories for restaurants (in US dollars)

$	under $15
$$	$15 to $24
$$$	$15 to $34
$$$$	over $34

Unless otherwise indicated, this price scale refers to a meal for one person (appetizer, main course and dessert), before drinks, tax (8.25%) and tip (about 15%).

New York Restaurants by Type of Cuisine

RESTAURANTS

RESTAURANTS

TOUR A: WALL STREET

What could be more pedestrian than to start off a list of restaurants in an American city with a description of a **McDonald's** *($; &; every day 7am to 9pm; 160 Broadway, ☎227-3828)*. And yet, there's nothing bland about this particular bearer of the golden arches. Located in the heart of the business quarter, this restaurant has enlisted the services of a tuxedo-clad doorman and a Chopin-playing concert pianist perched on a mezzanine overlooking the entrance at lunchtime. Stock prices are displayed over the menu, and there is a souvenir shop on the second floor. To top it off, the place serves French pastries, espresso and cappuccino. Definitely not your typical Mickey D's.

Ellen's Café and Bake Shop *($; &; Mon to Sat 7am to 6pm; 270 Broadway, ☎962-1257)* is run by former Miss Subway beauty contest winner, Ellen Sturm, and the walls are hung with photographs of all past winners. Ellen's imaginative sandwiches are popular with the employees of City Hall, located right across the street.

The spectacular **Wall Street Kitchen and Bar** *($$; &; no jeans or shorts; Mon to Fri 11:30am to 9pm; 70 Broad St., ☎797-7070)* is in an old bank near the New York Stock Exchange. If you'd like to try eating in the company of dozens of brokers who keep shouting like they are still on the trading floor, this is the place for you. In the late afternoon, it turns into a bar, where suit-clad businesspeople come to calculate how many millions they've lost or made that day.

In neighbourhoods lacking in good, affordable places to eat, it is sometimes necessary to fall back on hotel restaurants. The **Greenhouse Café** *($$$; &; no jeans or shorts; every day 7am to 10pm; 3 World Trade Center, entrance on West St., at the corner of Liberty, ☎938-9100)*, in the Marriott World Trade Center Hotel, is one of the best places of its kind in the Wall Street area. Its skylights let in lots of natural light and offer views of the twin 110-story towers of the World Trade Center, at whose base it is located. Living up to its name, the café is bathed in natural light and doubles as an indoor garden strewn with plants. The menu includes dishes like ravioli with tomato and basil sauce, Caesar salad and traditional roast beef, which serves as the centerpiece of the buffet.

🦐 It takes whole string of superlatives to describe **Windows on the World** *($$$$; &: reservations required several days in advance, jacket required, no jeans or shorts; Sun brunch 11am to 2:30pm, lunch Mon to Fri noon to 2pm, dinner Sun to Thu 5pm to 10:30am, Fri and Sat 5pm to 11:30pm; 1 World Trade Center, use West St. entrance if arriving by car, ☎524-7000 or ☎524-7011, ≈524-7016)*, as you might have guessed by its understated name. It is located on the 107th floor of the World Trade Center, and its multi-level dining room can accommodate 240 guests, all of whom get to enjoy the breathtaking views of Midtown and New Jersey (in clear weather). Even so, we recommend asking for a table by the window on the Midtown side, unless you'd prefer to sit in one of the restaurant's romantic alcoves, reminiscent of gothic church vaults. The soft-coloured decor, which looks like some sort of futuristic cave, doesn't try to compete with the view but is nonetheless quite impressive (Hardy, Holzman, Pfeiffer, designers). We are pleased to report, furthermore, that the menu lives up to the setting, promising an outstanding gastronomic experience. You might start off with the *profiteroles aux escargots à l'ail* (garlic snails), move on to a grilled filet of buffalo, then top it all off with an iced hazelnut soufflé. You can wash down your meal with one of the 700 wines available from the cellar, whose stock of 20,000 bottles includes a number of famous vintages. The service is attentive but discreet. Two other restaurants, which double as bars, are also located on this floor (see below).

Like its next-door neighbour (see above), **The Greatest Bar on Earth** *($$$$, $10 cover charge after 9pm Wed to Sat; &; reservations required for brunch only, no jeans or shorts; brunch Sun noon to 3pm, lunch Mon to Fri noon to 2pm, dinner every day 4pm to 11pm; 1 World Trade Center 107th floor, ☎524-7000)* clearly does not have an inferiority complex. A young, well-heeled crowd comes here to chow down on oysters, sushi, pizza and burgers while enjoying the view of Midtown. The bar stocks 16 different kinds of vodka, and guests often knock back a few drinks to help their meal go down. Live music Wednesday through Saturday, starting at 9pm (lounge music on Wednesdays, R&B on Thursdays and Fridays and swing on Saturdays).

The **Cellar in the Sky** *($$$$; prix fixe; &; reserve a few days ahead of time, jacket required, no jeans or shorts; dinner Tue to Sat, at 7:30; 1 World Trade Center 107th floor, ☎524-7000)* is the most intimate of the three restaurants on the 107th floor of the World Trade Center. It has developed a very original concept in recent years: every night, the chef prepares a unique six-course menu, which is accompanied by five different wines from Windows on the World's 20,000-bottle cellar. The meal starts at 7:30 sharp and can easily last three hours. Between courses, and on a clear evening, you can entertain yourself by identifying the skyscrapers, bridges and avenues below.

 ## TOUR C: SOUTH STREET SEAPORT

Zigolini's Lavazza *($; Mon to Fri 7am to 7pm; 66 Pearl St., ☎425-7171)* sells delicious panini and focaccia, as well as pasta dishes, all at very reasonable prices. The coffee, prepared Italian-style (espresso, cappuccino, latte, etc.), is aromatic and full-flavoured. This quaint little restaurant is very popular with local office workers, so make sure to arrive before noon or after 1:30pm if you want to find a seat.

On the south side of Fulton Market, which was rebuilt in 1983, the **Fulton Street Café** *($$; &; every day 11:30am to 10pm; 11 Fulton St., ☎227-2288)* has a pleasant outdoor seating area that extends to the middle of the pedestrian walkway on Fulton Street. The menu features traditional fare like clambake (a stew made with clams, lobster and corn).

Contrary to what you might think, the **Paris Café** *($$-$$$; Mon to Sat 8am to midnight; 119 South St., ☎240-9797)* is not a French restaurant. It is first and foremost an Irish Pub (see p 383), a veritable neighbourhood institution; the dining room was only added in 1997. Located opposite the Fulton Fish Market, almost in the shadow of the FDR Drive elevated expressway, this place has a lot of character. A number of films have been shot in the area, including *The French Connection* and the latest, *Godzilla*. The menu features simple fare like sandwiches, salads, burgers and a whole slew of beer snacks, as well as more elaborate dishes, like Cajun chicken, salmon steaks and paupiettes of sole. Smokers can enjoy a cigarette with their meal if they eat at the bar.

A sign painted right onto the building and a dark, dingy interior set the tone at **Carmine's** *($$-$$$; Mon to Thu 11:30am to 10pm, Fri 11:30am to 11pm, Sat 1pm to 11pm; 140 Beekman St., ☎962-8606)*, which has barely changed since it opened in 1903. This restaurant is frequented mainly by locals, and it was here decades before tourists started coming to this area, which lends it a certain cachet. You'll forget how hard the wooden banquettes are when your food arrives from the open kitchen. Offerings include *zuppa di pesce* (seafood sauteed in a delicious marinara sauce), fried calamari and scallops sauteed in butter and lemon juice.

The **Bridge Café** *($$$; ♿: reservations recommended; Sun Brunch 11:45am to 4pm, lunch Mon to Fri 11:45am to 4pm, dinner Tue to Sat 5pm to midnight, Sun and Mon 5pm to 10pm; 279 Water St., at the corner of Dover, ☎227-3344)* is located on the outskirts of the South Street Seaport tourist zone, on a tiny street with views of the pillars of Brooklyn Bridge. The building is one of the oldest in Manhattan (1794), and has housed a restaurant since 1826. Don't expect to be transported back to the colonial era, though, as the building has been modified many times since it was built. Dishes like grilled duck and trout amandine figure on the menu, and the wine list consists exclusively of American products.

🏆 **Sequoia** *($$$; casual attire outside, dressier inside; summer every day 11:30am to 11pm, winter every day 11:30am to 7pm; Pier 17 South Street Seaport, ☎732-9090, ⌐732-2539)* occupies a large portion of the Pier 17 Pavilion of South Street Seaport, a shopping centre that straddles a long pier stretching out into the East River. The huge split-level dining room offers spectacular views of the water, the business district and the old boats docked at the neighbouring pier. Sequoia also has two bars (smoking permitted) and two outdoor seating areas alongside the boardwalk that runs around the pier. The clientele, mainly foreign tourists, tuck into dishes like boiled lobster, trout amandine and grilled swordfish. The lunch menu also includes salads, sandwiches and traditional soups like New England clam chowder.

Though **Sloppy Louie's** *($$$; every day 11:30am to 9pm; 92 South St., ☎509-9694)* has been absorbed into the South Street Seaport Museum complex; it is nonetheless an authentic neighbourhood restaurant that opened back when commercial fishermen still plied the waters off New York. Specialties of the house include bouillabaisse and breaded shrimp.

The main reasons to eat at the **Fraunces Tavern** *($$$; reservations required; Mon to Fri 8am to 9pm; 54 Pearl St., ☎269-0144)* are to soak up some history and admire the reconstructed colonial decor. Founded in 1762 by Samuel Fraunces, the tavern was the scene of George Washington's farewell to his officers 20 years later. During the cold weather, fires crackle in the hearths. The Fraunces Tavern Museum (see p 124) is located on the second floor.

Places like **The Yankee Clipper** *($$$$; seafood and grill; Mon to Sat 11:30am to 10pm, Sun noon to 9pm; 170 John Street, Burling Slip, ☎344-5959)* are common in the ports of New England. All-American families come here to eat steaks, fish and seafood in a muffled atmosphere. The building is an old, neoclassical warehouse faced with grey granite (1840). Its façade contrasts sharply with the three dining rooms, decorated with pseudo-French furniture and prefab woodwork. The menu includes boiled lobster, salmon steak and, on a more original note, grilled mahi mahi with avocado and mango sauce. A bar can also be found on the premises.

 ## TOUR D: BATTERY PARK CITY

There are a number of restaurants looking out onto the impressive indoor garden of the World Financial Center (not to be confused with the World Trade Center). One of these is **Sfuzzi** *($$; ⅄; every day 11:30am to 9pm; 2 World Financial Center, Winter Garden Atrium, ☎385-8080)*, which has an outdoor seating area at the foot of the garden's palm grove. The menu offers innovative pizzas and a variety of pasta dishes.

To get to the **Liberty Lounge** *($$; ⅄: no jeans or shorts; every day noon to 11pm; 85 West St., ☎385-4900)*, located in the New York Marriott Financial Center Hotel, you are better off taking the South Bridge of the World Financial Center rather than trying to walk across West Street. This bar/restaurant has a lovely *belle époque* decor adorned with old photographs of

Lower Manhattan. It's a good place to grab a snack after a long walk in Battery Park City.

Pipeline *($$$; &; reservations required; Sat and Sun brunch 11am to 2pm, lunch Mon to Fri noon to 2pm, dinner every day 6pm to 10pm; 2 World Financial Center, ☎945-2755)* looks out onto the North Cove sailing harbour alongside Battery Park City's beautiful promenade. The view is lovely in the spring, when splendid yachts owned by New York millionaires are tied up at the piers. The restaurant is an interesting sight in itself, with its decor inspired by the pipes and tanks of an oil refinery. The California-style cuisine includes dishes like creamed corn and Caesar salad with grilled chicken. On Saturday and Sunday evenings, the restaurant offers a special children's menu complete with games.

❌ TOUR E: CHINATOWN, LITTLE ITALY AND THE LOWER EAST SIDE

Chinatown

 Though it is not strictly speaking a restaurant or a café, we have to mention the **Chinatown Ice Cream Factory** *($; every day 11:30am to 11pm; 65 Bayard St., ☎608-4170)*, which serves cones of delicious Haägen Daazs ice cream in flavours like litchi and jasmine tea, which are only available in Chinatown. Despite its Scandinavian-sounding name, Häagen Dazs is a New Jersey company that first started selling its ice cream in New York, then went on to take the entire western world by storm.

The **Mandarin Court** *($$; every day 8am to 10:30pm; 61 Mott St., ☎608-3838)* serves the same kind of cuisine found in Hong Kong restaurants, which means an emphasis on fish and seafood. With its gleaming surfaces, typical of a certain kind of Asian modernism, the decor also reveals an attachment to the former British possession.

There are a few good Vietnamese restaurants in Chinatown as well, including **Vietnam** *($$; every day 11:30am to 10pm; 11 Doyers St., ☎693-0724)*, which really lives up to its name, offering a wide selection of dishes from all different parts of that Southeast Asian country.

The huge **Jing Fong Restaurant** *($$-$$$; &; every day 1am to 11pm; 20 Elizabeth St., ☎964-5256)* can serve nearly 1000 guests at once. Except for its outsized dimensions, this place is exactly what you'd expect from a Chinese restaurant in Chinatown. Colourful dragons illuminated by paper lanterns will keep you company during your meal, which will surely include several Cantonese seafood dishes.

Located east of old Chinatown, on a street that runs through what used to be the heart of the Lower East Side's Jewish neighbourhood, the **Triple Eight Palace** *($$-$$$; dim sum 8am to 3pm, dinner 6pm to 10pm; 88 East Broadway, ☎941-8886)* is the perfect place to go for dim sum. This traditional Cantonese meal, which starts before noon and often lasts several hours, offers a touch of the exotic. In a huge room filled with Chinese families, waiters push carts loaded with all different kinds of strange and delicious little morsels of food. They stop at each table, and each guest asks for the tidbits he or she wants to sample. Talk about instant gratification! You might not always know what you're getting, though, as the waiters don't speak English. Some of the more popular choices are the shrimp dumplings, the breaded chicken's feet and the boiled pork buns. To calculate the bill, the waiter adds up the number of little plates each person has accumulated.

Chinatown also has a few Thai restaurants, including the excellent **Mueng Thai** *($$$; Tue to Sun 11:30am to 11pm; 23 Pell St., ☎406-4259)*, where the dishes, seasoned with curry and coconut milk, are as spectacular as they are appetizing.

Little Italy

After a long walk in Little Italy, stop by the **Caffé Palermo** *($; Mon to Fri 11am to midnight, Sat and Sun 11am to 1am; 148 Mulberry St., ☎431-4205)* for some homemade tiramisú and a good cup of coffee. If it's hot, you might opt for a beer instead. For entertainment, you can watch the passersby weaving their way between the outdoor seating areas along

Mulberry Street, which are laid out right on the sidewalk and are often adorned with colourful umbrellas.

The Ferrara family has been making excellent desserts at their eponymous business, **Ferrara's** *($; every day 11am to midnight; 195 Grand St., ☎226-6150)*, since 1892. The place underwent major renovations in 1980 and has lost a lot of its charm, but the pastries are as delicious as ever. Italian sandwiches (panini and focaccia) are also available at lunchtime.

Unlike Ferrara's, the **Caffé Roma** *($; every day 11am to midnight; 385 Broome St., ☎226-8413)* has preserved its old-fashioned decor. Open since 1890, this place is a veritable New York institution. The tiramisú is not to be missed; nor are the sublime cannolis (crispy-fried pastry rolls filled with ricotta and coated with chocolate).

It's a well-known fact that the best Italian restaurants in New York are located outside Little Italy, in areas like Greenwich Village and Midtown. People come here more for the outdoor cafés and the friendly atmosphere than the cuisine. Even so, there are a few more highly rated places here, such as **Il Palazzo** *($$$; reservations recommended; lunch Mon to Fri noon to 2:30pm, dinner every day 6pm to 11pm; 151 Mulberry St., ☎343-7000)*, which serves dishes like veal marsala and lobster with vodka sauce on a bed of fettuccine. The dining room is small but luxuriously decorated with marble, and there is a tiny outdoor seating area at the back, which is surrounded by a high Roman-style brick wall with a waterfall.

If you like gangster stories, make sure to go to **Umberto's Clam House** *($$$; every day lunch 11:30am to 2pm, dinner 6pm to midnight, supper midnight to 4am; 129 Mulberry St., ☎431-7545)*, where mafioso Joey Gallo was assassinated in 1973, after eating his last meal. Fact meets fiction in this restaurant, where you might feel like you're in a scene from *The Godfather*. In addition to their famous clams, Umberto's serves homemade pasta and several veal and chicken dishes.

Those who like to end their meal with a good cigar will love **Florio's Grill & Cigar Bar** *($$$$; reservations required, jacket and tie required; every day 6pm to 11pm; 192 Grand St., ☎274-9414, http://www.florios.com)*. The owner, Lawrence Amoruso, has created a velvety atmosphere. Guests can dine by the fireside, then buy their favourite cigar and savour it in an adjoining room while sipping a fine old armagnac.

Lower East Side

If the Times Square delis seem too touristy to you, try one on the Lower East side. One option is famous **Katz's Deli** *($; ♿; Mon to Fri 8am to 8pm, Sat and Sun 10am to 7pm; 205 East Houston St., at the corner of Ludlow, ☎254-3346)*, a typical New York deli founded in 1888. If you're shy, this place is not for you, since you might have to shout to get served while waiting at the mile-long counter. The lighting is depressing, but the smoked meat sandwiches are good, and this is the real New York experience. No credit cards.

Ratner's *($$; Sun to Thu 6am to 11pm, Fri 6am to 3pm, Sat 9pm to 1am; 138 Delancey St., ☎677-5588)* follows the Jewish dietary laws to the letter. You can try traditional blintzes (pancakes stuffed with cottage cheese), *latkes* (a potato-based dish) or herring in a creamy sauce. A meal here can be an interesting change of pace for those unfamiliar with kosher cuisine.

 TOUR F: SOHO-TRIBECA

The Cupping Room Cafe *($; 359 West Broadway, ☎925-2898)* sets itself apart with its many entrances, each of which accesses a different area of this large, airy restaurant. If you want to relax over a cup of coffee, there is a small room with tables at the windows that is ideal for a quiet, soothing break. For a simple meal, enter the rustic bistro, which is reminiscent of an old-fashioned country home with its varnished floors. Finally, the restaurant-bar is the setting for a meal that is more formal, but equally inviting.

Shade *($; 241 Sullivan St., ☎982-6275)* is a charming little bistro ideal for sipping expresso at the counter or sinking into a comfortable leather booth to linger over a café au lait and a slice of cheesecake. To satisfy a larger appetite, the menu offers a variety of crisp pizzas, salads and sandwiches.

The allure of **Caffé Lure** *($-$$; 169 Sullivan St., ☎473-2646)* lies in its decor of woodwork and dried flowers. The quiet establishment with a pleasant terrace provides impeccable service. Gazpacho, Belgian waffles and pasta make up the menu along with fish that is always fresh.

Dean & DeLuca, an upscale grocery store chain, had the smart idea of opening a café in SoHo. The **Dean & DeLuca Café** *($-$$; Mon to Fri 7am to 7pm, Sat and Sun 8am to 6pm; 121 Prince St., ☎254-8776)* is particularly pleasant at breakfast time, when clients nonchalantly sit at their tables and read newspapers while dunking croissants in coffee.

Once upon a time, at the café **Once Upon a Tart** *($-$$; every day 8am to 7pm; 135 Sullivan St., ☎387-8869)*, there was an enormous slice of pecan pie that was trying to ingratiate itself with a patron who had just filled up on a delicious goat cheese, artichoke and black olive sandwich. Against all odds, it succeeded, with the help of a good, flavourful espresso.

Jerry's *($$; breakfast Mon to Fri 9am to 11am, lunch every day 11am to 5pm, dinner Mon to Sat 6pm to 11pm; 101 Prince St., ☎966-9464)* is the perfect place to have a salad in the middle of the afternoon, when the sun is the hottest in Manhattan. The decor is hip and the clientele, mainly artists meeting with their agents, tends toward the eccentric.

In a Moorish setting of walls covered in colourful mosaic, **Layla** *($$$-$$$; reservations recommended, suit jacket mandatory, no jeans or shorts; West Broadway, corner of Franklin St., ☎431-0700)* offers culinary creations with Mediterranean accents. You can savour Greek, Egyptian and Moroccan specialties around tables lit discreetly by little orange-toned lamps. The fragrances of the Middle East are revealed in the chicken stew, the grilled salmon wrapped in grape leaves and the Moroccan couscous. The wine list features amusing titles like "Cleopatra's Favourites" and "What to Drink When You're Lost in the Desert". For a delicious finale, try the dessert and a Turkish coffee. Belly dancing performances add a touch of Oriental exoticism to evenings here.

Nobu *($$-$$$; reservations recommended, suit jacket mandatory, no jeans or shorts; 105 Hudson St., corner of*

Franklin St., ☎219-0500 or 219-8095) is a Japanese restaurant renowned as much for its innovative cuisine as for its decor, which combines elegance and exoticism. The first element that catches the eye is the imposing row of birches with large branches attached to them, which run along the booths. Once seated, you'll notice the fantastic details of the decor, like the chopstick framework of the chairs lined up at the sushi bar and the false ceiling that opens to reveal colourful brickwork. Large blue velvet curtains section off a more intimate dining room that is ideal for romantic evenings. In addition to traditional sushi, sashimi and tempura dishes, the menu offers such delights as South American lobster *ceviche* and imported New Zealand mussels. For a slightly higher price, Chef Matsuhisa offers a menu of his favourite dishes.

The **Odeon** *($$-$$$; ♿; reservations recommended; every day 11:30am to 2am; 145 West Broadway, ☎233-0507)* is the night-owl hangout in TriBeCa, the former warehouse district just south of SoHo (Canal Street). A chic version of a 1950s-style diner with a heavy chrome decor, this place serves all the traditional American favourites, as well as a number of French dishes, like *steak-frites*.

The exotic decor at **Penang** *($$-$$$; reservations recommended; lunch every day noon to 2pm, dinner 6pm to midnight; 109 Spring St., ☎274-8883)*, with its waterfall, makes you forget for a moment that you are in the heart of SoHo. Waitresses garbed in the national dress bring patrons succulent dishes made with coconut and hot peppers, which you might have to wash down with a nice, cold glass of water.

🍰 **Balthazar** *($$$; reservations required; Sat and Sun brunch 11:30am to 4pm, lunch Mon to Fri noon to 6pm, dinner every day 6pm to 12:30am, supper Sun to Thu 12:30am to 2am, Fri and Sat 12:30am to 3am; 80 Spring St., ☎965-1414 or 965-1785, ≈343-1274)* looks like a big Parisian brasserie. All the ingredients are there: the little ceramic tiles on the floor, the big mirrors all around the dining room, the bustling waiters and the loud conversations. The place serves classic French cuisine (*cassoulet*, *bouillabaisse*, *confit de canard*, etc.), as well as simpler fare like *pan bagnat* (Provençale-style sandwich) and *steak-frites*. It also has an excellent oyster bar and a bakery that makes divine cakes.

RESTAURANTS

Il Barolo (*$$$*; &; *reservations recommended; Sun to Thu noon to 10pm, Fri and Sat noon to midnight; 398 West Broadway, ☎226-1102*) opens onto a pleasant garden with a few tables scattered about in it. The relaxed atmosphere makes it easy to sit back and savour the food, be it a plate of scallops or linguine with clam sauce. Make sure not to confuse West Broadway with Broadway.

L'École (*$$$, prix fixe; reserve several days in advance, no jeans or shorts; lunch Mon to Fri noon to 1:45pm, dinner Mon to Thu 6pm to 9:30pm, Fri and Sat 5:30pm to 10pm; 462 Broadway, at the corner of Grand St., ☎219-3300, ☎334-4866, http://www.frenchculinary.com*) is the restaurant of the French Culinary Institute, run by Mark F. Mainville. In the Institute's kitchens, apprentice chefs prepare complex dishes under the watchful eye of their professors. Guests get to taste the fruits of their lessons, which have usually been well-learned. To compensate guests for being guinea pigs, the restaurant charges less than the going rate. It has a series of five-course prix fixe menus that change with the days of the week. When we were there, on a Thursday, the menu consisted of consommé, *salade provençale*, filet of tuna with ginger, marinated pork loin and Grand Marnier soufflé. Guests are asked to rate the various dishes on a card at the end of the meal (optional).

Félix (*$$$-$$$$; reservations recommended; Mon 6pm to midnight, Tue to Thu noon to 2am, Fri and Sat noon to 3am, Sun 11:30am to 1am; 340 West Broadway, ☎431-0021*) looks like a typical little French bistro, making New Yorkers feel like they're in Paris. The French doors on the façade, left wide open in the warm weather, let lots of light and there is room near them for a few outdoor tables. Old French advertisements for products like Ricard have been framed and hung on the wall over a long banquette. Occupying the place of honour in the centre of the room is an old foosball (table soccer) game, making this fairly sophisticated place look a bit like a neighbourhood café. The menu, all in French, offers dishes like *cochon de lait à l'ancienne* (suckling pig), *aile de raie aux câpres* (skate with capers) and *salade de légumes marinés* (marinated vegetable salad). Don't confuse West Broadway with Broadway.

Over the years, **Zoë** *($$$-$$$$; &; reservations required; Sat and Sun brunch 11am to 2pm, lunch Mon to Fri noon to 2pm, dinner every day 6pm to 10pm; 90 Prince St., ☎966-6722)* has become one of the best restaurants in SoHo. In addition to original contemporary cuisine, the menu includes grilled chicken and red meat. Zoë also serves up one of the most imaginative brunches in New York and has a bar that offers a wide variety of wines by the glass.

The **Canal House** *($$$$; &; reservations required; every day 11:30am to 11pm; 310 West Broadway, ☎965-3588, contactus@sohogrand.com)* is located on the parlour floor of the Grand Hotel, which opened in 1996. This subtly designed space decorated in earthy tones, is particularly well-suited, like its menu, to a cold fall day, when the wind is sweeping the sidewalks of Manhattan. The regional specialties of the house include lamb pâté, pan-fried cod and grilled breast of Long Island duck.

 Just outside SoHo, in TriBeCa, **Capsouto Frères** *($$$$; reservations recommended; lunch Tue to Fri noon to 2pm, Sat and Sun brunch noon to 3:30pm, dinner every day 6pm to 10:30pm; 451 Washington St., south of Canal St., ☎966-4900)* occupies the ground floor of an old warehouse on the banks of the Hudson. If you'd like to have a gourmet meal off the beaten track, this spacious, airy restaurant, founded by three brothers of Egyptian origin, is the perfect place to go. The atmosphere is relatively relaxed, and you should feel free to bring along the kids. As in many New York restaurants, the menu is written entirely in the language of Molière. It features exquisite dishes like *noisettes de veau sauce au poivre vert* (veal with green pepper sauce), raspberry-grilled quail and *crevettes sautées nîmoise* (Nîmes-style sauteed shrimp). An unique cheese plate is also available. Smoking is permitted at the bar.

✕ TOUR G: GREENWICH VILLAGE

The **Factory Café** *($; 104 Christopher St., ☎807-6900)* has a superb ceiling of beautifully carved, brightly painted woodwork. Brick walls surround old furniture, chairs and sofas that are occupied by a largely gay clientele that likes to be seen, snack on sandwiches, and chat over coffee.

The lineup outside **John's Pizzeria** *($; 278 Bleeker St., at the corner of 7th Ave., ☎243-1680)* attests to the popularity of this modest restaurant where patrons munch on crisp, simple pizza. Rest assured; the fare is much better than the decor – graffiti-covered walls and tasteless paintings – might lead you to believe. The portions are generous, the service is quick, and the prices are not too much of a drain on the wallet. Beer and wine are also served.

Just a couple steps from John's Pizzeria, the charming **Mona Lisa** *($; 282 Bleeker St., corner of 7th Ave., ☎929-1262)* is a marvellous Victorian tea room, whose walls are adorned with huge mirrors and rococo-style paintings. This is an ideal spot to sip coffee or tea and gaze into a pair of friendly eyes.

Located just steps from the Gershwin Hotel (see p 293), **Naturally Tasty** *($; 234 5th St., corner of Madison Ave., ☎725-1804)* is the spot for a quick, healthy meal. This little restaurant's decor is nothing special, but simple, substantial home cooking may be savoured here. A few vegetarian dishes appear on the menu, including lasagna and tofu salad. The frozen yogurt is delicious and refreshing.

To satisfy mid-afternoon or post-clubbing hunger pangs, head to **Pommes Frites** *($; 123 2nd Ave., between 7th St. and 8th St., ☎674-1234)*. This tiny restaurant, nestled in a cramped location, prepares delicious Belgian-style fries accompanied by a variety of sauces such as mayonnaise, garlic, etc.

The **Village Delight Cafe** *($; 323 Bleeker St., ☎633-9275)* opens its doors at 6am to serve up tasty brownies, simple dishes like tabouli and falafels, home-made cakes, salads, croissants, and good coffee. The decor is rustic and enhanced by plants and dried flowers.

If you're looking for simple fare in a relatively low-key setting, head straight to the **Elephant & Castle** *($-$$; every day 11am to 11pm; 68 Greenwich Ave., ☎243-1400)*, which took its name an old pub in England. It is known for its Caesar salad and omelettes.

🦐 Decorated with antique world maps, globes and Chinese paper-covered lamps in the form of the earth, **Mappamondo** *($-$$; 8th Ave., between Bleecker St. and West 12th St., ☎675-3100)*, a little restaurant that prepares excellent Italian dishes at reasonable prices, is aptly named. The pasta is fresh and served with tasty sauces.

The **Cowgirl Hall of Fame** *($$; every day noon to 11pm; 519 Hudson Street, ☎633-1133)*, one of the ever more numerous theme restaurants in New York, is a fun place that serves Tex-Mex food in a Far West decor. It has a small museum devoted to cowgirls and women rodeo riders, as well as a shop that sells western gear (hats, boots, jackets, etc.). European visitors are sure to feel like they're far from home!

The **Figaro Café** *($$; ♿; every day 11:30am to 2am; 184 Bleecker St., ☎677-1100, ⌐388-0003)*, which used to be a beatnik and hippie hangout, is an important stop on the itinerary of anyone visiting the old haunts of Allen Ginsberg or Gregory Corso. With its outdoor seating area, awning and bistro-style dining room, it is reminiscent of a Parisian café, but the menu tends more toward the Italian, with an emphasis on pasta dishes. The noisy crowd would also fit right in at a Roman café. No credit cards.

Greenwich Cafe *($$; 75 Greenwich Ave., ☎255-5450)* is a pleasant locale with a streetside terrace and very convenient hours – it never closes! Its menu satisfies New Yorkers and tourists alike with its touch of sophistication, and the relaxed service reminds you that you are in the heart of the "Village".

Gay night owls of Greenwich Village flock to all-night **Manatus** *($$; every day, 24 hours a day; 340 Bleecker St., ☎989-7042)* when the bars close. The friendly, relaxed atmosphere makes it easier to readapt to a normal sound level after a night at the neighbouring clubs.

A restaurant-cum-microbrewery located at a busy intersection in Greenwich Village, the **Greenwich Pizza & Brewing Company** *($$; every day noon to 1am; 418 Avenue of the Americas - 6th Ave., at the corner of 9th St., ☎477-8744)* is a pleasant, affordable place with exposed brick walls and serves pizzas and burgers in a laid-back pub atmosphere. People come here in small groups to relax after a long day of sightseeing. In addition to its own beers, the place serves a wide variety of imported draft and bottled beers (Moosehead, Hoegaarden, St. Christoffel, La Trappe Enkel, etc.). Local pizza delivery available.

The **Rubyfruit Bar & Grill** *($$; Sun brunch 11am to 3pm, dinner every day 6pm to 11pm; 531 Hudson St., ☎929-3343)* is very popular with New York lesbians. The menu features dishes like lemon chicken and pasta with vodka sauce. Make sure to save room for one of the delicious homemade desserts, such as the famous key lime pie. The bar is on the second floor.

Open 24 hours a day, **Bouchon** *($$-$$$; 249 Park Ave., corner of 20th St., ☎254-5858)* is truly a beacon in the night and has the ambience of a friendly French bistro. The fare consists of such staples as eggs Florentine for breakfast and steak *tartare* or pepper steak for lunch or dinner. Simply put, this is a pleasant spot any time of day or night. Of course, the clientele varies depending on the hour. You can sit at the bar, around a wooden table, or squeeze into one of the leather booths set under a large mirror.

The **Café de Bruxelles** *($$-$$$; reservations recommended; Sun brunch 11am to 3pm, lunch Tue to Say 11:30am to 2:30pm, dinner Tue to Sat 6pm to 11pm; 118 Greenwich Ave., ☎206-1830)* is one of the all too few Belgian restaurants in New York. In a relaxed, occasionally noisy atmosphere, guests can enjoy typical Belgian fare like *carbonade flamande* (beef stew with beer) *waterzooi* (a sort of bouillabaisse) and, of course, mussels and fries served with mayonnaise-based sauces. The owners, Francis Chéru and Roger Delandre, have also put together a good selection of Belgian beers.

The back garden at **Grove** *($$$; reservations required; Sat and Sun brunch 11am to 3pm, dinner Sun to Thu 6pm to 11pm, Fri and Sat 6pm to midnight; 314 Bleecker St., ☎675-9463)* is so much more appealing than the dining room that it's best to wait for a nice warm day to go. The menu features dishes like grilled tuna and filet mignon with red wine sauce.

The homestyle cuisine at **Home** *($$$; reservations required; breakfast Mon to Fri 9am to 3pm, Sat and Sun brunch 11am to*

4pm, dinner Mon to Sat 6pm to 11pm, Sun 6pm to 10pm; 20 Cornelia St., ☎243-9579) offers a good idea of what East Coast American families eat for Sunday dinner. Dishes like grilled salmon steak and pork chops with applesauce or fruit ketchup are old standards. Weather permitting, you can eat in the restaurant's wonderful garden, surrounded by old buildings. Home also serves a delicious brunch, where you can stuff yourself with French bread, bacon, fried eggs, pork sausages and fruit pancakes.

Pó *($$$; reservations required; lunch Wed to Sun noon to 2pm, dinner Tue to Sun 6pm to 11pm; 31 Cornelia St., ☎645-2189)* is considered one of the best Italian restaurants in Greenwich Village. Guests who opt for the five- or six-course tasting menu will be treated to one delicious surprise after the next.

Sazerac House *($$$; reservations required, no shorts; Sat and Sun brunch 11am to 2pm, lunch Mon to Fri noon to 2pm, dinner every day 6pm to 11pm; 533 Hudson St., ☎989-0313)* occupies a picturesque old house (1826) that was once part of a manor owned by an English lord. The menu consists of typical Louisiana fare like jambalaya, gumbo and crabcakes.

Tapastry *($$$; reservations recommended; Sat and Sun brunch 10:30am to 3pm, dinner Sun to Thu 5pm to 11pm, Fri and Sat 5pm to 1am; 575 Hudson St., ☎242-0003)* has reinvented the traditional tapas of Spain and Portugal. To emphasize the play on words, the walls have been hung with tapestries. Smoking is permitted at the bar.

Thomas Scott's on Bedford *($$$; reservations recommended; dinner every day 6pm to 10pm; 72 Bedford St., ☎627-4011)*, located on a charming street lined with Georgian houses, serves grilled beef and fish in a tiny dining room with a big window through which guests can admire the surrounding architecture. The room is also decorated with a collection of miniature gilt-framed mirrors, lending it a warm, intimate atmosphere.

🦞 Successful thirty- and forty-somethings get together at the **Gotham Bar and Grill** *($$$$; reserve a few days in advance, no shorts; lunch Mon to Fri noon to 2pm, dinner mon to Thu 5:30pm to 10pm, Fri and Sat 5:30pm to 11pm, Sun 5:30pm to 9:30pm; 12 East 12th St., ☎620-4020, ≈627-7810)*, one of the best restaurants in New York, and also one of the only places in the Big Apple that dares to cross certain boundaries drawn in the sand – something that has largely contributed to its success. With great panache, chef and owner Alfred Portale has managed to bring together patrons from both the business and the art world; combine dishes typical of big Midtown restaurants with the relaxed atmosphere of Greenwich Village and marry mouth-watering cuisine with spectacular presentation. The restaurant, laid out beneath the high ceilings of a former warehouse, is spacious but gets very crowded. A bar stretches over 15 metres along the east side of the room, which is painted in light colours. The dishes, inspired by skyscraper architecture, are veritable masterpieces of culinary engineering; many are over 20 centimetres high. The salad served as an appetizer might remind you of one of Carmen Miranda's hats, while the desserts look like modern sculptures. Particularly noteworthy among the entrees are the saddle of rabbit with spinach, the Atlantic salmon with morels and the breast of duck with mango sauce and foie gras. Truly the best that American cuisine has to offer.

TOUR H: CHELSEA

People don't go to **Bachué** *($; Mon to Fri 8am to 10:30pm, Sat 10am to 10:30pm, Sun 11am to 7pm; 36 West 21st St., ☎229-0870)* for its ambiance, which is gloomy and faded, but for its healthy and affordable food. Try the whole-grain *crêpes* with maple syrup and tofu cream with fresh fruit for breakfast. For lunch, you can have the daily special or sample natural foods from around the world: Chinese seitan, Japanese brown rice rolls, Italian pasta or Latin-American burritos. The same menu is available in the evening, but the prices are higher after 6:30pm.

Since 1980, Chelsea has surpassed Greenwich Village in terms of numbers of businesses catering mainly to the city's gay community. One such place is the **Big Cup** *($; every day 8am to 1am; 228 8th Ave., ☎206 0059)*, where couples can sip coffee comfortably ensconced in soft, oversized sofas. It also has a counter where you can order coffee to go.

Whether in movies or in real life, we've all seen those gleaming chrome diners from the 1950s, often made out of metal pieces from buses and trolley cars. These ancestors of modern fast-food restaurants fell out of favour for a long time before enjoying a veritable renaissance in the mid-1980s. If you have a hankering for an authentic diner experience, head on over to the **Empire Diner** *($-$$; 24 hours a day; 210 10th Ave., ☎234-2736)*. Fortunately, the menu, somewhat of a hodgepodge, has not been caught in the same time warp as the rest of the place.

The **Food Bar** *($$; brunch Sat and Sun 11am to 2:30pm, lunch Mon to Fri noon to 2:30pm, dinner every day 6pm to 11pm; 149 8th Ave., ☎243-2020)*, with its parquet floor and pale wood walls, draws a motley crowd for brunch, while its dinner menu, made up of basic pasta dishes and salads, will suit those who prefer good company to gourmet dining.

Trois Canards *($$$; 184 8th Ave., ☎929-4320)* is located in the centre of Chelsea, the new, hip, laid-back gay district. This lively restaurant serves French food in its pleasant dining room or on the terrace, where you can watch the activity on the street.

TOUR I: EAST VILLAGE

 Noodles on 28 *($; 394 3rd Ave., northwest of 27th St., ☎679-2888)* is a little Chinese restaurant whose cuisine, though quite simple, is prepared and delivered astonishingly quickly and well, and at prices that are more than reasonable. While noodles are obviously the main feature, the menu also lists a variety of other dishes. In short, the place is inviting, good, quick, and a bargain.

The restaurant-café **Selka** *($; 144 2nd Ave., corner of 9th St., ☎228-9682)* is another 24-hour-a-day establishment. In the summer, buy one of the papers displayed at the entrance and grab a table on the pleasant terrace to sip a coffee and snack on a bagel with cream cheese. Relaxed ambience and somewhat casual clientele.

RESTAURANTS

The **Second Avenue Deli** *($-$$; 156 2nd Ave., corner of 10th St., ☎677-0606)* is a veritable institution in the East Village and a must for visitors in search of the New York deli experience. The prices are a touch high, but the portions are gargantuan. Smoked meat is the specialty of the house.

Transvestites are definitely in fashion in New York restaurants. At **Lucky Cheng's** *($$; Asian cuisine; every day 6pm to 2am; 24 First Ave., ☎473-0516)*, they attract a large, motley crowd made up of gays, stars from chic neighbourhoods and suburbanites, all curious to see the drag queens who serve the food. The building, a former Turkish bath, has only been slightly modified to accommodate the kitchens. Some of the old baths have been turned into fishponds. Lucky Cheng's does not take reservations, so guests can wait up to an hour for a table on some evenings. Cabaret shows are presented here nightly at 9pm and 11:30pm.

Passport *($$; Sat and Sun brunch 11am to 2pm, lunch Mon to Fri noon to 2pm, dinner 6pm to 11pm; 79 Saint Marks Pl., ☎979-2680)* will take you south of the border, where you can savour traditional seviche, burritos, enchiladas and tacos in a setting reminiscent of a *zocalo* in a colonial Mexican city. This two-floor restaurant has a bar near the entrance and a dining room below. The brownish terracotta floor, colourful ceramic tables and big vases all help create the illusion that you are a thousand miles from New York.

At **Stingy Lulu's** *($$; &; every day noon to 5am; 129 Saint Marks Pl., ☎995-5191)*, guests are served by heavily made-up transvestites in a setting that recalls a middle-class American kitchen from the 1950s. The chrome chairs covered with yellow and red vinyl are set up all the way out to the sidewalk, where you can take in a view of Tompkins Square Park and the motley East Village crowd. Stingy Lulu's hosts outrageous transvestite shows from Sunday to Wednesday, at 8pm and 10pm. The menu is as eclectic as the waiters' outfits, ranging from the basic burger to roast beef au jus. You are better off sticking to the simpler fare while soaking up the unique ambiance of this place, which has a large gay clientele.

Students and hip intellectuals get together at the **Yaffa Café** *($$; every day 24 hours a day; 97 Saint Marks Pl., ☎677-9001,* *delivery ☎674-9302)* at all hours of the day and night. The chrome furniture from the 1950s, covered with zebra-striped fabric, the back garden terrace, surrounded by typical New York buildings, and the colourful and somewhat comical fountain are sure to appear unique to European visitors. The young patrons carry on lively conversations between mouthfuls of Greek salad, Baba Ganoush sandwiches, Berber chicken or vegetable curry. The menu offers a good selection of vegetarian dishes with a Middle Eastern flavour and delivers locally between noon and 11pm.

Mitali *($$-$$$; reservations recommended; every day 11:30am to 10pm; 334 6th St., ☎533-2508)*, one of about 10 Indian restaurants near the intersection of First Avenue and 6th Street, serves good curry and Tandoori dishes in a somber setting steeped in the mysteries of the Orient.

🐚 There are so many Indian restaurants on the block of 7th Street between Second Avenue and First Avenue that it seems like little bit of India in the middle of New York. Among the many popular, respected Indian eateries in the neighbourhood, **Raga** *($$-$$$; 433 East 6th St., between 1st Ave. and Ave. A, ☎388-0957)* distinguishes itself with a sort of nouvelle Indian cuisine influenced by French and American cooking. The intimate setting, mouthwatering menu, and attentive service make the prices more than reasonable. An excellent selection of wines and several Quebec micro-brewery beers are served.

🐚 Every place in New York with a French name seems to be wildly successful. A good example is **Bistro Jules** *($$$; reservations recommended; Sat and Sun brunch 11am to 3pm, lunch Mon to Fri 11am to 5:30pm, dinner Sun to Thu 5:30pm to 11pm, Fri and Sat 5:30pm to 1am; 65 Saint Marks Pl., ☎477-5560)*, owned by Régis Courivaud. You can practice your French with the waiters, and the choice of dishes is very similar to what you'd find in a traditional Parisian bistro – *petatou*, *frisée aux lardons*, *cassoulet toulousin*, *boudin noir* and *moules frites*, to name a few. The atmosphere is relaxed, and smoking is permitted at the bar. Jazz musicians softly play at the back of the room from 9pm onward from Monday to Thursday and from 11pm onward on weekends.

RESTAURANTS

Indochine *($$$; reservations required; every day 5:30pm to 10pm; 430 Lafayette St., ☎505-5111)* serves cuisine that marries culinary traditions of the Orient with those of the Occident, reflecting both the sophistication of Europe and the subtlety of Asia. The restaurant is located on the ground floor of the famous Colonnade Row (see p 158), a handsome series of buildings fronted by a Corinthian colonnade dating from 1833.

The **Miracle Grill** *($$$; &; reservations recommended; Sat and Sun brunch 11:30am to 3pm, dinner 5:30pm to 11pm; 112 First Ave., ☎254-2353)* serves sophisticated, innovative Southwestern cuisine. The chef has taken pains to adapt dishes like grilled lamb kebabs with jalapeño peppers, quesadillas (served with chilis, corn, zucchini and cheese) and fajitas (stuffed with a delicious mixture of chicken, black beans, red onions, guacamole and sour cream) to New York tastes. There is a pretty garden out back.

Opaline *($$$; &; reservations recommended, no shorts; lunch Mon to Sat noon to 2pm, dinner every day 6pm to 11pm; 85 Avenue A, ☎475-5050)* is one of the pillars of French cuisine in the East Village. Its big dining room, which looks like a Parisian brasserie from the 1930s, is crowded with Midtown regulars, who come here to get a taste of the East Village without having to immerse themselves in the counterculture.

 # TOUR J: THE SQUARES

52 Irving Place *($; Mon to Fri 7am to 11pm, Sat 8am to midnight, Sun 8am to 11pm; 125 East 17th St., ☎995-5252)* is a pleasant neighbourhood café that can only seat about 15 people at a time. There is a bit more room during warm weather, when a few tables are set up outside. You can have a good, full-flavoured coffee, unless you'd rather try one of the 30 or so kinds of tea (regular and herbal) available. In summer, an assortment of fruit juices is offered as well. In addition to these beverages, the place sells soups, sandwiches and delicious cakes.

News Bar *($; 107 University Pl., corner of 13th St., ☎353-1246)* is not a bar but a little café that serves light meals including sandwiches, bagels, muffins and croissants. One wall is entirely covered by magazines that you can purchase and savour along with your snack.

The **open market at Union Square** *($; Union Sq.)* is a good place to pick up fruit, vegetables, organic bread, and home-made cheese: the basic provisions for a picnic on the benches in the park before an afternoon of sightseeing.

If you're craving a croissant for breakfast, head to the **Café Journal** *($-$$; Mon to Fri 8am to 5pm; 47 East 29th St., ☎689-6199)*, which makes delicious baked goods and also offers catering services. At lunchtime, the café serves sandwiches made with French bread (Brie, smoked turkey, ham, etc.), as well as meal-sized salads (Niçoise, Waldorf, etc.).

Noodles on 28 *($-$$; every day 11:30am to 11:30pm; 394 Lexington Ave., at 28th St., ☎679-2888)* is one of the best noodle shops outside Chinatown. The prices are low and the servings generous. The front part of the dining room gives onto an open kitchen, where you can see the chef making the noodles. The extensive menu includes shrimp dumplings, won ton soup and orange beef. The spicier dishes have a small green pepper next to them, and we can tell you right now that it's there for a good reason, as is your glass of water! On weekdays, the restaurant offers a lunchtime table d'hôte for under $6, including tea, soup, main dish and, of course, the indispensable fortune cookie.

For those who are into health food cuisine, the Japanese restaurant **Souen** *($-$$; 28 East 13th St., corner of University Pl., ☎627-7150)* offers a sugar-free, meat-free, dairy-free menu, printed on recycled paper. The selection includes numerous vegetarian specialties with a base of tofu, seitan and vegetables. Fish is the only non-vegetarian item served here and is prepared in a variety of ways: sushi, grilled, etc.

The **Turkish Kitchen** *($-$$; reservations recommended for dinner, no shorts or jeans; lunch Mon to Fri noon to 3pm, dinner every day 5:30pm to 11:30pm; 386 3rd Ave., ☎679-1810)* is considered one of the best Turkish restaurants in the United States. In a split-level dining room, guests can enjoy typical dishes like *ahtapot salatasi* (grilled octopus with onions) and *hunkar Begendi* (eggplant purée and pieces of lamb).

🍴 Vegetarians should keep **Zen Palate** *($-$$; 34 East Union Sq., corner of 16th St., ☎614-9291 or 614-9345)* in mind. Under the benevolent eye of the Buddha, you can savour your meal in several different settings: on the ground floor, on the terrace near the open kitchen, or upstairs where there are cushions and little wooden tables as well as a staircase leading to a slightly more stylish dining room with a view of Union Square. Among the many vegetarian creations listed on the menu, the tofu delight, which is made up of zucchini, tomatoes, and tofu and accompanied by black bean sauce, brown rice and vegetarian rolls, is especially noteworthy.

🍴 The **Parlour Café** *($$; ♿; breakfast Mon to Sat 10am to noon, lunch every day noon to 3pm, tea Mon to Fri 3:30pm to 5:30pm; 38 East 19th Street, ☎677-2233)* occupies the ground floor of an ABC Carpets and Home store. The mismatched tables and chairs that seat guests are actually part of the inventory, as you can tell by the price tags on their legs and backs. The fare consists of lovely salads and imaginative sandwiches. We particularly recommend the afternoon tea, featuring miniature sandwiches, traditional scones and fruit tartlets.

🍴 **Cafe Spice** *($$-$$$; 72 University Pl., corner of 11th St., ☎253-6999)* is a friendly Indian restaurant with a discreetly elegant decor. Little shelves on the walls hold glass bottles filled with spices. There are several booths for more intimate evenings. The menu is rather predictable, but the dishes are tasty.

🍴 Chef Normand Laprise has already made a name for himself in Montreal, and New Yorkers and visitors alike will be glad to discover his new restaurant **Cena** *($$-$$$; reservations recommended, suit jacket mandatory, no jeans or shorts; 12 East 22nd St., between Broadway Ave. and Park Ave., ☎505-1222)*, Spanish for "dinner". You will swoon with pleasure over the delicious, always market-fresh and beautifully presented cuisine in this modern, bright and airy setting. Efficient and attentive service.

Union Square is a lovely shady park in the heart of a dense, noisy part of town. **Luna Park** *($$-$$$; Apr to Oct, every day 11:30am to 6pm, depending on the weather; 17th St., ☎475-8464)*, in the north part of the park, is a pleasant, 250-seat outdoor café laid out around an elegant Beaux-Arts pavilion. The menu includes all sorts of salads and sandwiches, as well as more elaborate fish and pasta dishes.

The **Blue Water Grill** *($$$$; reservations recommended, no shorts or jeans; Mon to Sat 11:30am to 12:30am, Sun 11am to midnight; 31 Union Sq. W., ☎675-9500)* is set up inside an old bank, and some of its counters still grace the light-filled dining room. A long, narrow outdoor seating area with cane chairs runs alongside the street, and there is a big nightclub in the basement.

New Yorkers, who love anything and everything French, flock to the **Brasserie Les Halles** *($$$$; ᕀ; reservations recommended; every day noon to midnight; 411 Park Ave. S., at 29th St., ☎679-4111)* to savour the pleasures of Parisian life. The place might seem a little artificial to Europeans, but the locals seem to be having a blast. The restaurant also has a butcher's shop that sells French cuts of American beef.

The excellent reputation of the **Union Square Café** *($$$$; reserve several days in advance; lunch Mon to Sat noon to 2:30pm, dinner every day 6pm to 11pm; 21 East 16th St., ☎243-4020)* contrasts with its location, in the basement of an industrial building, and also with its simple decor, of hardwood floors and white walls. During warm weather, the chef bases his menu on the fresh produce from the neighbouring Union Square Market (see p 338).

🍴 Located on a charming street in the heart of peaceful Gramercy, **Verbena** *($$$$; reservations required; brunch Sun 11:30am to 3pm, lunch Mon to Sat noon to 2:30pm, dinner Sun to Thu 5:30pm to 10pm, Fri and Sat 5:30pm to 11pm; 54 Irving Pl., ☎260-5454 or 260-3595)* has an elegant 50-seat patio looking out onto a garden. The restaurant, with its sober, soothing decor, is run by owner and chef Diane Forley, an American born of a Guatemalan mother. She has managed to combine the cuisines of various countries in imaginative, mouth-watering dishes delicately seasoned with fresh herbs, peppers from Central America and spices from the Middle East. The menu, geared toward healthy eating, highlights dishes like squash ravioli with grilled oranges and sage, rabbit stew with vegetables and braised tuna steak in a crust of coriander and cumin.

TOUR K: FROM THE EMPIRE STATE BUILDING TO THE UNITED NATIONS

Chez Laurence *($-$$; reservations recommended for dinner; Mon to Sat 7am to 10pm; 245 Madison Ave., at 38th St., ☎683-0284)* is both a French pastry shop and an unpretentious bistro where you can take the kids without worrying that the waiters will look at you askance. The atmosphere is particularly pleasant and relaxed at breakfast time, when customers contentedly dunk their croissants in their coffee while watching the working folk pass by the windows facing onto Madison Avenue. At lunchtime, the menu includes hot, heartier fare like *poulet paillard* (chicken) and swordfish with mango chutney.

In many cities, museum restaurants are often unappealing cafeterias. In New York, however, most are charming. The **Morgan Court Café** *($$; Tue to Fri 11am to 4pm, Sat 11am to 5pm, Sun noon to 5pm; 29 East 36th St., ☎685-0610 or 685-0008)*, in the Morgan Library (see p 175) is a good example. Its tables are set up on a marble floor in the midst of a lovely winter garden with delicate Japanese trees.

Piccolino's *($$; ♿; every day noon to 10pm; 8 East 36th St. 10016, ☎683-6444 or 696-0191)*, located near the Empire State Building, serves a number of original pasta dishes, such as *farfalle La Gratzi* (farfalle with smoked salmon, capers and pickles), as well as imaginative pizzas, like *pizza Rabe* (broccoli, mild sausage, garlic and mozzarella), as well as hearty sandwiches and lovely salads. The decor is basic, but the atmosphere is nonetheless inviting, and the price is right. This is a good option for dinner in an area where it is often hard to find a happy medium between fast-food and gourmet cuisine (and the astronomical prices that go with it). The service is friendly and the clientele, mainly local. Piccolino's will even deliver within the neighbourhood.

RESTAURANTS

An incredible number of Korean restaurants are clustered on 32nd Street, between 5th and 6th Avenues – so many, in fact, that you'd almost think you were in Seoul. A number of places on what is now commonly termed "Korean Restaurant Row" have decent, inexpensive menus. On the down side, they don't have much ambiance, with their cafeteria-style counters and neon lighting. One of the few exceptions is **Spot** *($$$; &; reservations recommended; every day 10am to 5am; 34 West 32nd St., ☎629-8185)*, a futuristic bar/restaurant. As exotic as can be, this place transports you to 21st-century Asia, where traditional wooden trellises surrounding the tables, in enclosures around the edge of the room, contrast with severe black leather sofas facing a wall of TVs. The clientele, mainly hip young Asians who like the loud music and soft lighting, come here to munch on spicy, sauteed octopus casserole and dried, roasted calamari. Night-owls will be happy to note that Spot is open until 5am.

The secret is out: New Yorkers are crazy for the delicious dishes at the Morgan hotel (see p 296) restaurant, **Asia de Cuba** *($$$-$$$$; reservations recommended, suit jacket mandatory, no jeans or shorts; 237 Madison Ave., between 37th St. and 38th St., ☎726-7755)*. This infatuation is the result of the subtle blend of Asian cuisine and Caribbean flavours served in the classic elegance of a large dining room where logs crackle quietly on the hearths of two fireplaces. The service is professional and attentive without being pretentious.

Grand Central Station

At the entrance to the station, a large bar called **Michael Jordan's Steak House** *($$-$$$; suit jacket mandatory, no jeans or shorts; Grand Central Terminal, ☎655-2300)* invites you to sip a mug of beer or a glass of wine while waiting for your train. Time permitting, take a seat in one of the plush booths and admire the station's monumental architecture while somewhat removed from its chaotic hustle and bustle. The dining room, where you can sit at a table and get a splendid view of the interior of the station, is open only in the evening. Although the restaurant's name might lead you to believe that this is an informal sports bar, the decor is relatively stylish and there is a dress code.

As its name indicates, the **Oyster Bar & Restaurant** *($$-$$$; in the basement of Grand Central Terminal, ☎490-6650)* is both a bar and a restaurant, but we recommend that you head directly to the oyster buffet, since the restaurant is no place for anyone on a budget. The bar is much friendlier, and patrons can eat there for more reasonable prices while watching the head chef in the open kitchen. Good selection of wines.

Boby Van's *($$$-$$$; reservations required, suit jacket mandatory, no jeans or shorts; 230 Park Ave., corner of 46th St., ☎867-5490)* is a favourite haunt of New York businessmen, who come here to talk about everything under the sun and savour enormous, juicy steaks. The decor is sober and bright, and peach-painted walls form a pleasing contrast with the warm woodwork. There is a room reserved for cigar aficionados.

TOUR L: FIFTH AVENUE

La Bonne Soupe *($$; every day 11:30am to midnight; 48 West 55th St., ☎586-7650 or 765-6409)*, founded in 1973, serves much more than soup. In addition to fondues and quiches, you'll find traditional French favourites like pot-au-feu, bouillabaisse and rabbit with mustard sauce. The staff is French and the ambiance, authentic: leather banquettes, tables squeezed together, paper tablecloths and an unpretentious decor. Still, certain concessions have been made to appeal to American tastes, so insipid iceberg salads are systematically doled out as appetizers. The place has two floors; the first is warm and intimate, while the second is decorated with naif paintings and has a tiny, 12-seat patio. Owner Jean-Paul Picot and chef Romuald Fassenet, a "graduate" of the Tour d'Argent, are gradually revising the menu.

The **Garden Café** *($$; ♿; Thu to Tue 11am to 5pm; 11 West 53rd St., ☎708-9480)*, in the Museum of Modern Art (MoMA) figures on the list of charming New York museum restaurants – especially in warm weather, when you can eat your salad in the middle of the sculpture garden behind the galleries.

🦞 Open only in warm weather, the **Bryant Park Café** *($$; May to Oct every day 11:30am to midnight, brunch Sat and Sun 11:30am to 3:30pm, depending on the weather; West 42nd St., between 5th and 6th avenues, ☎840-6500)* in Bryant Park along the back wall of the New York Public Library (see p 179), has one of the loveliest outdoor seating areas in New York. With its cane chairs and European-style parasols, it draws flocks of Midtown working folk in the hot summer months. Among the many refreshing dishes on the menu, you might opt for gazpacho, a fresh salad or a club sandwich. The appetizing brunch menu includes tasty selections like banana pancakes with maple syrup (served with bacon and hazelnuts) and an asparagus *fritatta* served with Fontina cheese and hash browns.

Since 1995, Midtown Manhattan has been invaded by theme restaurants. The **Fashion Café** *($$; every day noon to 9pm, fashion shows Mon to Fri 12:30pm, 2pm and 7pm; 51 Rockefeller Plaza, ☎765-3131 or 765-3288)*, which follows on the heels of the Hard Rock Café, the Harley Davidson Café and the Jekyll and Hyde Restaurant, was founded by a group of supermodels, including Claudia Schiffer and Naomi Campbell. Its gimmick is to host daily fashion shows for its customers' entertainment. It also has a small museum that displays one of Madonna's bustiers and the Givenchy dress worn by Audrey Hepburn in *Breakfast at Tiffany's*, among other items of clothing.

Despite its name, **Lucky's Bar & Grill** *($$-$$$; jacket and tie required in the evening; breakfast every day 7:30am to 10am, lunch 11:30am to 2pm, dinner 6pm to midnight; 60 West 57th St., ☎582-4004)* is first and foremost a restaurant that cooks up typically hearty American fare like smoked pork loin with blackstrap molasses barbecue sauce and turkey meatloaf accompanied by a mountain of mashed potatoes. It also serves up a very affordable home-style breakfast in a neighbourhood where two eggs over easy can cost a fortune. In the late afternoon, Lucky's, which vaguely resembles a Parisian bistro, turns into a noisy bar crowded with businesspeople from the neighbouring offices. Stop in and sample a bourbon straight out of a 1950s detective novel or a glass of one of those fantastic American wines that could turn vintage Bordeaux green with envy. Go ahead and try one from Oregon, Long Island or Washington State. Come nightfall, you can relax to the sounds of a jazz trio (Mondays and Tuesdays only). The only sour note is the service, provided by a young and inexperienced staff who are in over their heads. Smoking permitted at the bar. Delivery service available within the area.

Located in a corner of the Trump Tower, on the top floor of the shopping centre, the **Trump Tower Café** *($$$; lunch Mon to Sat 10am to 6pm; 725 Fifth Ave., level 5, ☎754-4450 or 751-1930)* occupies an airy space bathed in natural light. It has two tiny outdoor seating areas, as well as a sandwich counter, which is located near the escalators and looks out onto a much larger terrace on the roof of the Nike Town store. Except for the Russian caviar at the top of the menu – the place *is* owned by Donald Trump, after all – the food is fairly conventional and affordable. Some of the better selections are the chicken Milanese, ravioli du jour and Caesar salad. The perfect place to go if you have an snack attack in the middle of an afternoon shopping excursion.

The section of 46th Street between 5th and 6th Avenues has been nicknamed Little Brazil, due to all the Brazilian businesses located here. Among these are a few good restaurants, including **Via Brazil** *($$$; reservations recommended; lunch every day noon to 3pm, dinner every day 6pm to 11pm, live music Wed to Sat 8pm to 10pm; 34 West 46th St., ☎997-1158)*, where patrons dine to the sounds of live Latin American music.

The **Bryant Park Grill** *($$$; reservations recommended, jacket and tie required for dinner, no shorts or jeans; lunch Mon to Fri 11:30am to 3:30pm, dinner every day 5pm to midnight; 25 West 40th St., ☎840-6500 or 840-8122)*, in the lovely park behind the New York Public Library (see p 179), has a splendid dining room. The hip, fashionable ambiance is reflected in the menu, which features tasty dishes like mahi mahi with hazelnuts, herbed filet mignon and shrimp penne.

The menu at **Oceana** *($$$-$$$$; 55 East 54th St., between Madison Ave. and Park Ave., ☎759-5941)* mainly features fresh fish and seafood dishes. The decor includes several models of antique ships and walls plastered with posters of boats. The wine list offers a vast selection of great vintages, and the service is impeccable.

The **Rainbow Room** *($$$$, $20 cover charge for the band; ♿; reserve several weeks in advance, jacket and tie required, no shorts or jeans; Tue to Sat 7pm to 1:30am, live music 7:30pm to 1am; 30 Rockefeller Plaza, entrance on 6th Ave., between West 49th and West 50th, ☎632-5000)*, located on the 65th floor of the old RCA Building (now the General Electric Building, see p 196) at Rockefeller Center, boasts a spectacular panoramic view of Manhattan and equally spectacular Art Deco architecture. It is considered the ultimate place for dinner and dancing in New York – a must for anyone wishing to immerse themselves in the atmosphere of the 1930s, the heyday of Glen Miller's and Benny Goodman's big bands.

Le Cirque 2000 *($$$$; reserve several weeks in advance, jacket and tie required, no jeans; lunch Mon to Sat 11:30am to 2pm, dinner every day 6pm to 11pm; 455 Madison Ave., ☎303-7788 or 303-7712)* is the perfect place to impress your guest. The setting is Henry Villard's sumptuous former residence, built in 1884 by McKim, Mead and White. This orgy of pink marble and gilt ornamentation from the Victorian era has been updated with futuristic, brightly coloured touches resembling the sets for the Cirque du Soleil. The prices are exorbitant, and the patrons enjoy flaunting their extravagance! If you can afford to, why not check it out? You can start off your meal with sautéed foie gras, continue with grilled lobster served with artichokes and wild mushrooms and top it all off with one of those spectacular desserts so typical of New York City.

Many people consider **La Côte Basque** *($$$$; reserve several days in advance, jacket and tie required, no shorts or jeans; lunch Mon to Sat noon to 2:30pm, dinner Mon to Thu 5:30pm to 10:30pm, Fri and Sat 5:30pm to 10:30pm, Sun 5pm to 10pm; 60 West 55th St., ☎688-6525)* to be one of the finest French restaurants in New York. Founded by Henri Soule in 1952, it was taken over by chef Jean-Jacques Rachou in 1987. Now located west of Fifth Avenue, it still has the famous mural painting, *Saint-Jean-de-Luz-à-la-Côte-Basque*, that helped make it famous. The decor, a blend of white stucco and dark wood beams, is exactly how Americans expected a French restaurant to look like back in the mid-1950s. The menu is written in the language of Molière, and the bilingual staff can help you choose between the *pomponette de foie de canard Jean-Jacques* and the *bavarois de homard et champignons avec son beurre de* *crevettes au safran* for your appetizer and the *suprême de volaille à l'étuvée d'endives périgourdine* and the *noisettes de veau au madère* for your main course. Despite their pretentious names, the dishes on the menu have been adapted to North American tastes. You can accompany your meal with a fine vintage wine from the restaurant's excellent cellar. As far as dessert is concerned, the choice is easier, since dessert soufflés are the specialty of the house. Since they take a long time to make, you have to order them at the beginning of your meal. La Côte Basque is a veritable Midtown institution, but certain flaws are inherent in its qualities, specifically its "Vieille France" atmosphere is a little stiff and the portions are as gargantuan as those served in the delis on 7th Avenue.

TOUR M: PARK AVENUE AND SURROUNDINGS

Burger Heaven *($; 20 East 49th St., between 5th Ave. and Madison Ave., ☎755-2166)* offers simple but substantial meals in a bright, modern, diner-style setting. The menu includes feta-cheese omelets, lobster salad and big juicy hamburgers. For this neighbourhood, this establishment is modest and relatively affordable.

To start the day off right, stop in at **Croissant & Gourmet** *($; 425 Madison Ave., corner of 49th St., ☎750-6970)* for pastries, bagels, sandwiches and salads.

Check out the wooden beams at **The Alamo** *($-$$; 304 East 49th St., corner of 2nd Ave., ☎759-0590)* to decide if they are real, and whether the dude ranch look is successful. This restaurant maintains that it has the largest selection of tequilas in New York, and a peek at the list seems to confirm that claim. Mexican knickknacks make up the decor, and the menu features classic dishes: guacamole, *camarones a la plancha* and, for those with fearless tastebuds, *jalapeños rellenos* (baked peppers stuffed with spicy cheese).

One of the most unusual restaurants in New York is the **Café St. Bart's** *($$; lunch Mon to Sat 11am to 4pm; Park Ave. and 50th St., ☎935-8434)*, which is set up inside the presbytery of St. Bartholomew's Church (see p 198). Its outdoor seating area opens onto the raised square next to the church, offering guests the dual pleasure of eating al fresco and admiring the Roman-Byzantine architecture surrounding them. A setting this interesting and a menu that is still relatively affordable are a rare combination in this part of town.

As soon as you step outside the Midtown tourist zone, restaurant prices drop by about a third. East of 3rd Avenue and west of 8th Avenue, you can usually find decent food at affordable prices. **Pescatore** *($$; Mon to Fri noon to midnight, Sat and Sun 5pm to midnight; 955 Second Ave., north of 50th St., ☎752-7151)*, a neighbourhood eatery divided into three sections (bar, café and restaurant), serves homemade pasta and delicious grilled fish.

For 50 years now, the **Caviarteria** *($$-$$$ 502 Park Ave., corner of 59th St., ☎759-7410 or 1-800-4-Caviar)* has offered a remarkable selection of imported caviar, including sevruga, osetra and beluga, from all over the world. The counter staff will be pleased to explain the variety of exclusive foods available, which includes salmon and different varieties of foie gras. The restaurant section, which opened several years ago, invites you to take a seat at a small bar with a view of the street, or, for more intimacy, at a little table, where you can leisurely savour caviar, smoked salmon and foie gras, all of it washed down with a goblet of champagne. The menu includes original dishes such as the Broken Grain Beluga Sandwich and the Caviarteria Club Sandwich, filled with Scottish salmon, Norwegian shrimp, watercress and cream cheese. A glass of champagne is available for a little under $10, while the price of caviar varies depending on the type. If there are no tables available in this stylish little restaurant, sample some of its delights by ordering take-out. There is also a mail-order catalogue of Caviarteria products.

At **Fresco** *($$-$$$; 34 East 52nd St., ☎935-3434)*, the term "fresh" takes on a whole new meaning. In a pastel-toned decor with tall blue glasses on every table, patrons savour delicious, attractively presented and marvellously well-seasoned Tuscan cuisine. The menu always features a pasta dish of the day, and other Italian specialties such as pepper salmon in wine sauce accompanied by potatoes and broccoli. The service is friendly and impeccable.

🦐 **Istana** *($$-$$$; no jeans or shorts; 455 Madison Ave., ☎303-6032)*, located in the New York Palace hotel (see p 301, offers outstanding Mediterranean cuisine and seems determined to completely alleviate patrons' tastebuds. Their breakfasts are simply exquisite, while a variety of elegantly presented and marvellously prepared dishes make up the lunch and dinner menus. The red snapper *ceviche* and the olive buffet, which offers about 50 varieties of olives from France, Greece, Italy, and other countries, are just two of the restaurant's many delights. The staff is pleasant and very attentive.

🦐 The main draw at the Indian restaurant **Nirvana** *($$-$$$; 30 Central Park South, ☎486-5700, www.nirvanarest.com)* is undoubtedly the spectacular view it offers of Central Park. Even though it is located just steps from the Plaza hotel, the restaurant is difficult to find because it is located in the penthouse of a commercial building. A slow elevator, which in no way reflects what awaits above, will carry you up to this hideaway. Once at the top, the first room on the left is a bar where you can enjoy a pre-dinner drink near an enormous aquarium that illuminates the room. Every piece of the restaurant's china is hand-painted and plated with 22-karat gold. If you are interested in buying any, you can do so as they are all sold separately. Indian fabrics cover the walls and create the intimate feeling of being in a tent. Fresh-cut flowers decorate every table, and mirrors on the walls make the place seem larger. The service is somewhat cool, but attentive. With advance notice, the chef will prepare special dishes not on the menu. There is a good selection of aromatic vegetarian dishes.

Though nothing like the famous Train Bleu in the Lyons train station, the **Train Bleu** *($$-$$$; reservations recommended; brunch Mon to Sat 10:30am to noon, lunch Mon to Sat noon to 3pm, tea Mon to Fri 3pm to 5pm; East 59th St. and Lexington Ave., level 6, ☎705-2100)*, in Bloomingdale's, still has a great deal of character. The long, narrow dining room looks like a dining car from the *belle époque*. Curiously enough, the carpet, chairs and wall coverings are all green. Brunch and afternoon tea are particularly pleasant here.

🦐 **Michael's** *($$$; suit jacket mandatory, no jeans or shorts; 24 West 55th St., between 5th Ave. and 6th Ave., ☎767-0555)* enjoys a solid reputation among artists and intellectuals. The kitchen's mainstays are seafood and grill dishes. The dining room is bright and airy, the service is flawless, and the staff glides discretely between tables. In brief, this spot is ideal for a quiet, savoury business meeting.

Next door to Burger Heaven (see p 347), but definitely in a superior category, **Seryna** *($$$; 11 East 53rd St., between 5th Ave. and Madison Ave., ☎980-9393)* is found just past a wall of graffiti and waterfalls. The decor is Japanese in inspiration, and waitresses dressed in geisha garb discretely serve fresh sushi and teriyaki dishes. There are several closed rooms reserved for traditional dining, which involves removing one's shoes at the door.

Vegetarians will do well to avoid the green façade of **Smith & Wollensky** *($$$; no jeans or shorts; 3rd Ave., corner of 49th St., ☎753-1530)*. Once through the door, a small glass case displaying precut pieces of meat ready to be grilled to taste will immediately catch your eye. Wooden tables, leather-covered benches and a sober, traditional decor make this an ideal spot for a business meal. The portions are generous and the service is attentive.

That **Vong** *($$$; 200 East 54th St., ☎486-9592)* has character is evident from the collages that cover its walls and ceilings, its dark wooden floor, red lacquered chests, asymmetrical Starck chairs, marble tables and above all its eclectic collection of pink molten glass lamps. The menu is among the best you will find in New York: everything is very fresh and exotic, meticulously prepared, though it seems spontaneously created (sesame tuna, crabs with herbs, strawberry puree and ginger ice cream). A meal here is truly an Asian feast for the senses. The pre-theatre menu served at 6pm from Monday to Thursday costs $35; on Fridays, there is a sampling menu for $65.

Maloney and Porcelli *($$$$; brunch Sat and Sun 11am to 2pm, lunch Mon to Fri 11:30am to 2pm, dinner 6pm to 10pm; 50th St., between Park and Madison, ☎750-2233)* is a place for people with hearty appetites and good digestion. Guests are served gigantic portions of food in an elegant setting popular with well-known politicians and affluent businesspeople. The waitress will no doubt recommend the crackling pork shank, which is served with a jarful of applesauce. Politely decline and opt for a more flavourful if less showy dish instead. Above the huge dining room, which is noisy and bustling with activity, is a more intimate mezzanine with a fireplace. Maloney and Porcelli has an outstanding wine cellar and hosts tastings at various times of the year.

TOUR N: TIMES SQUARE AND BROADWAY

Figaro *($-$$; every day 11:30am to 9:30pm; 26 West 44th St., ☎840-1010 or 840-2354)*, a bar/restaurant, offers excellent value for your money. The sandwiches, individual and family-size pizzas and appetizing pasta dishes are truly a bargain in this part of town, where a lettuce leaf can put a dent in your budget.

Zen Palate *($-$$; 663 9th Ave., corner of 46th St., ☎582-1669)* prepares mouthwatering vegetarian creations. Just a few bites will win over even the most dedicated carnivores. Tofu, seitan and vegetables prepared in different styles make up the varied and appetizing menu. Closed rooms have been furnished with low tables and comfortable cushions to make for a romantic candle-lit evening while enjoying delicious food.

The **Carnegie Deli** *($$; every day 8am to midnight; 854 7th Ave., near 54th St., ☎757-2245)*, which can be seen in Woody Allen's film *Broadway Danny Rose*, is one of the oldest delicatessens in the theatre district. Like other eateries of its kind, it serves enormous pastrami sandwiches, multi-storied burgers reminiscent of the surrounding skyscrapers and, of course, the obligatory cheesecake topped with fresh strawberries.

While it can be difficult to find a really charming restaurant in the Times Square area, keep this one in mind: the **Hour Glass Tavern** *($$; 373 West 46th St., corner of 9th Ave., ☎265-2060)*. For the last 30 years, the little kitchen of this country-house-style restaurant has been serving up delicious Italian dishes. Shelves full of knickknacks accentuate the intimacy and romantic ambience of this narrow two-story space, while the walls, decorated with framed hourglasses, evoke the passage of time. Savour seafood pasta, seasoned and grilled fettucini, or filet mignon, and top it off with a succulent home-made dessert. During the restaurant's busiest hours, a running hourglass ensures quick service and discretely reminds you that you have about an hour and a quarter to finish your meal.

The huge portions steal the scene at the **Stage Deli of New York** *($$; every day 6am to 2am; 834 7th Ave., ☎245-7850 or 245-7957, http//www.stagedeli.com)*, eliciting oohs and aahs from customers, who simply can't believe how big the sandwiches are and no doubt wonder how they're going to eat all that. Though the food can be disappointing, you have to try a real American deli at least once in your life, where smoked meat and cold cuts are served in big portions and sometimes in original combinations (not to be confused with deli and salad bars in the introduction to this chapter). The many celebrities who have frequented the Stage Deli since it opened in 1937 have created their own sandwiches and salads, which now appear on the menu; you can try a Julia Roberts sandwich (chicken salad, hard-boiled egg, lettuce and tomato) or a Fran "The Nanny" Drescher salad (a mixture of tuna, chicken, shrimp and gefilte fish salads). One portion is easily enough for two, especially if you want to save room for that deli classic, strawberry cheesecake. The restaurant also serves breakfast (eggs, bacon, sausages, etc.) all day.

Becco *($$-$$$; no jeans or shorts; 355 West 46th St., between 8th Ave. and 9th Ave., ☎397-7597, www.lidiasitaly.com)* is an inviting Italian restaurant with a pretty interior courtyard illuminated by skylights. The upstairs dining room provides a more intimate atmosphere. The traditional menu includes grilled salmon, rabbit, veal and, of course, pasta served with every kind of sauce. Dishes are carefully prepared and portions are very generous. A large selection of Italian wines is available at reasonable prices.

Thanks to splendid Brazilian windows hanging on its walls, the restaurant **Ipanema** *($$-$$$; no jeans or shorts; 13 West 46th St., between 5th Ave. and Avenue of the Americas, ☎730-5848)* is as warm, romantic and classic as the beautiful song by João Gilberto. The menu holds no surprises and the fare is quite satisfying.

Lounge C3 *($$-$$$; 103 Waverly Pl., ☎777-9515)* found in the Washington Square Hotel (see p 292) invites you to sample its eclectic menu in a relaxed atmosphere. You can enjoy mother's meat loaf or scampi with risotto in the intimacy of booths decorated with brightly coloured motifs. Paintings inspired by the work of Tamara de Lempicka and Gustave Klimt add an original accent to the decor. Come nightfall, live jazz livens up this stylish restaurant-lounge.

Jean-Lafitte *($$$; &; reservations recommended, no shorts or jeans; lunch Mon to Fri noon to 4pm, dinner every day 6pm to 11:30pm; 68 West 58th St., ☎751-2323)* has a warm, inviting, mahogany-panelled dining room. Seated on comfortable banquettes, guests enjoy delicious dishes like Creole tripes, Cajun catfish and New Orleans-style seafood jambalaya.

New Yorkers have a penchant for anything French – perfume, clothing, artists and, of course, restaurants. The city's many French restaurants have figured this out and do their best to recreate the atmosphere of little bistros and big Parisian brasseries. **Le Max** *($$$; &; reservations recommended; Mon to Fri 11:30am to 11pm, Sat 4pm to 11pm, Sun 11:30am to 10pm; 147 West 43rd Street, ☎764-3705 or 944-4805)* is no exception. In fact, it is a typical example, with its long bar and big mirror behind it, tile floors and painted columns supporting a high ceiling decorated with mouldings. The menu, composed of dishes like sole meunière and filet mignon with bordelaise sauce, matches the traditional decor.

The **Restaurant Charlotte** *($$$; reservations recommended for dinner, jacket and tie required; breakfast Mon to Fri 6:30am to 10:30am, Sat and Sun 7am to 9:30am, brunch Sat and Sun 10am to 2:30pm, lunch Mon to Fri noon to 2:30pm, dinner every day 5:30pm to 11pm; 145 West 44th St., ☎789-7508 or 789-7685)*, located on the ground floor of the Millenium Broadway Hotel, is the perfect place for a business lunch or dinner in the Times Square area. Over cold melon soup with prosciuto and mint, crabcakes with avocado or salade Niçoise, you can talk in peace, since the tables are far enough apart. What's more, the upholstered chairs are very comfortable. The decor, particularly the walls, with their lemonwood and African mahogany panels contrasting with grey marble slabs, recreates the "masculine" ambiance of the big ocean liners of the 1930s.

The **Russian Samovar** *($$$; reservations recommended; lunch Mon to Fri noon to 2:30pm, dinner Mon to Sat 5:30pm to*

11pm; 256 West 52nd St., ☎757-0168) is one of those authentic Russian restaurants filled with expatriates ordering pitchers of vodka, which they casually poor into water glasses. To the sounds of Slavic music, you can savour wild mushroom soup, duck with prunes and, of course, delicious caviar blinis.

🦀 Set at the foot of Manhattan's skyscrapers, the **Bernadin** *($$$-$$$$; reservations recommended, suit jacket and tie mandatory, no jeans or shorts; 155 West 51st St., between 6th Ave. and 7th Ave., ☎489-1515)* is one of New York's best-loved restaurants. The menu includes the requisite steak *tartare*, rib steak and filet mignon, but also offers delicious fish dishes. The elegant atmosphere, with cosy woodwork and discreet service, creates a uniquely enjoyable evening.

Le Marais *($$$$; ♿; reservations recommended, no shorts or jeans; Sun to Thu 11:30am to midnight, Fri 11am to 3pm, Sat 8pm to 1am; 150 West 46th St., ☎869-0900)* is both a Kosher butcher's shop that sells French cuts of American beef and a French restaurant, which serves traditional dishes like cassoulet, *poussin farci*, *onglet à l'échalote* and *steak-frites* under the watchful eye of three rabbis. The menu also includes a few appetizers rarely found in French restaurants in New York, such as *céleri rémoulade* and *rillettes d'oie*. The spacious dining room is decorated like a Parisian brasserie in the Marais district, with its dark wood floor and checkered tablecloths. Americans come here to soak up the French ambiance before heading off to see *Les Misérables* or *The Phantom of the Opera* in one of the neighbouring theatres. There is a private cigar lounge on the second floor.

The New York branch of the Parisian restaurant **Petrossian** *($$$$; reserve several days in advance, jacket and tie required, no shorts or jeans, brunch Sat and Sun 11am to 2pm, lunch Mon to Fri noon to 2pm, dinner every day 6pm to 10pm; 182 West 58th St., ☎245-2214)* is renowned for its vast selection of Russian caviar. This venerable institution, housed in one of the oddest buildings in Manhattan (see p 209) is patronized by exiled Russian aristocrats, among others. A glass of champagne with your meal?

TOUR O: CENTRAL PARK

Mickey Mantle, the Yankees' last great baseball player, opened his own restaurant before his death on Central Park Street South: **Mickey Mantle's Restaurant** *($$$$; 42 Central Park St. S., ☎688-7777)*. The presence of this "sports establishment" in such upscale surroundings might seem out of place, but its elegant, modern lighting, large windows and light wooden floors and furniture give it a more refined atmosphere than most restaurants of this type. That having been said, all the usual paraphernalia is also displayed: souvenirs of the legendary athlete adorn the walls along with photographs of baseball and other professional sports players; there are long bars at the front and a huge dining area in the back; waiters sport Mantle's famous number seven on their uniforms; large screens broadcast televised matches, etc. The menu features the typical hamburger and spare ribs, but also roasted chicken with herbs and filet mignon.

Up until 1934, the building that now houses **Tavern on the Green** *($$$$; ♿; reserve several days in advance, no shorts or jeans, Sat and Sun brunch 11am to 2pm, lunch Mon to Fri noon to 2pm, dinner every day 5:30pm to 10pm; Central Park, entrance near the corner of 67th St. and Central Park West, ☎873-3200)* was home to a flock of sheep that grazed in the neighbouring meadow. Their expensive upkeep (the Depression was in full swing) and the health threat they posed to local children spelled bad news for this "decorative" flock, which lent a pastoral air to the west part of Central Park. The restaurant, which has been renovated several times, now looks like a big greenhouse and is surrounded by trees decorated with lights (you can see it in Woody Allen's film *Crimes and Misdemeanors*). The Sunday brunch is particularly popular around Easter. During summer, make sure to ask for a table on big, breezy terrace.

TOUR P: THE UPPER EAST SIDE

With a name like **Blanche's Organic Take-Away and Juicebar** *($; Lexington Ave., corner of 71st St., ☎717-1923)*, this small restaurant, which prepares health-food cuisine, some of which is sold by weight, is almost self-explanatory. Inside, benches are set around a glass table facing the street. The brown rice and lentil salad is well-worth tasting. For an energy boost, try the "Beam Me Up" milkshake made of fresh fruit, spirulina, ginseng and protein supplements. Vegi-burgers, home-made soups, marinated tofu and other vegetarian specialties are also offered.

If you are in search of a place to refuel without emptying your wallet, head to **China Fun** (*$; 1239 2nd Ave., corner of 65th St., ☎752-0810*), where customers eat in a tightly packed area near the open kitchen. If you are put off by the sight of animal carcasses hanging in the kitchen, opt for one of the vegetarian dishes. The meals are simple, affordable and filling. There is also a good selection of meal-sized soups for under $10.

EJ's Luncheonette (*$; 1271 3rd Ave., corner of 73rd St., ☎472-0600*) is an unpretentious restaurant that is especially noisy and lively at dinnertime. Patrons eat elbow to elbow and engage in lively conversations. EJ's is also popular for its simple breakfasts of eggs, oatmeal or waffles.

House of Health (*$; 1014 Lexington Ave., between 72nd St. and 73rd St., ☎772-8422*) includes both a natural food store and "Salad Bar & Juice Bar". When you stop by for items like nuts in bulk or vitamins, you can also have a quick bite to take out or eat in, choosing from the selection of tofu and fresh vegetable dishes. There is also a small juice bar that serves excellent freshly squeezed fruit juices.

Just next door to House of Health, the small but friendly **Café Word of Mouth** (*$-$$; 1012 Lexington Ave., corner of 72nd St., ☎249-5351*) is set in a bright, minimalist space with an Art Deco design. This spot is ideal for conversation over a café au lait, a light meal of chili con carne, or a vegetable and goat cheese sandwich.

At **E.A.T.** (*$$-$$$; every day 9am to 9pm; 1046 Madison Ave., north of 80th St., ☎772-0022 or 628-1625*), you can eat in or order food to go at the takeout counter.

Sofia's Fabulous Grill (*$$-$$$; 29 East 61st St., between Madison Ave and Lexington Ave., ☎702-9898*) attracts a young, wealthy, good-looking clientele that comes here to see and be seen. The brick walls are covered with enticing drawings of various dishes and colourful culinary ingredients. Grill items and pasta are the mainstays of the menu.

Located on the second floor of a building containing several restaurants, **Contrapunto** *($$$; reservations recommended; Mon to Fri noon to 11pm, Sat and Sun 4pm to midnight; 200 East 60th St., at 3rd Ave., ☎751-8616)* serves original and sophisticated pasta dishes like papardelle with mushrooms and marsala sauce and tagliarini with calamari and jalapeño peppers in a basilic oil sauce. The desserts – chocolate timbale with tarragon accompanied by orange gelato and fruit minestrone served with kiwi sorbet, for example – are just as original. The wall-to-wall picture windows looking out onto Bloomingdale's are the only noteworthy part of the decor, so ask for a table next to one so you can watch the activity on the street.

Founded in 1962, **The Sign of the Dove** *($$$$; reserve several days in advance, jacket and tie required, no jeans or shorts; lunch Tue to Fri noon to 2:30pm, brunch Sat and Sun 11:30am to 2:30pm, dinner every day 6pm to 11pm; 1110 3rd Ave., at 65th St., ☎861-8080)* serves creative American cuisine. One of the great gastronomic institutions of New York, it is named after an 18th-century post house that was located nearby. It was here that Jackie Kennedy put an end to her first widowhood and President Richard Nixon showed off his talents as a pianist several years later. The restaurant's series of high-ceilings are surrounded by reddish brick arches, creating the impression that you're eating in the ruins of some Roman baths. Among the more noteworthy items on the extensive menu are the savory breast of duck with lentils, the shrimp lasagna and the marinated, grilled haunch of lamb. You are sure to find the perfect accompaniment to your meal on the excellent wine list. The service is very attentive but can be a bit clumsy at times. The restaurant has private party rooms upstairs and a pleasant piano bar to the left of the entrance (smoking permitted).

RESTAURANTS

TOUR Q: CARNEGIE HILL AND YORKVILLE

 Though its reputation originated with its preserves and fresh breads, hot commodities in the polite circles of the Upper East Side, **Sarabeth's Kitchen** *($$-$$$; reservations accepted for dinner only, no shorts; breakfast Mon to Fri 8am to 3:30pm, brunch Sat and Sun 9am to 4pm, lunch 11:30am to 3:30pm, afternoon tea 3:30pm to 6pm, dinner 6pm to 10:30pm; 1295 Madison Ave. 10128, ☎410-7335)* is also a trio of restaurants best known for their very popular breakfasts, where celebrities, politicians and eminent professors can often be spotted soaking up the serene, luminous morning ambiance. With its cream walls and pale Quaker furniture, the decor is reminiscent of a New England kitchen, and the service is correspondingly courteous and sober. The breakfast menu offers a vast selection of omelets, cereals, waffles and pancakes. If you want to try something original, opt for the delicious pumpkin waffles served with raisins, fresh cream and honey. At lunch- and dinnertime, Sarabeth's offers an eclectic menu inspired by California cuisine (chicken with peanuts served with cucumber and corn salad, grilled tuna with leaks and truffle oil, etc.). The wine list complements the menu, offering only California wines, with an emphasis on those from Napa Valley. Save room for some chocolate mousse cake with zabaglione, pecan pie with ginger ice cream or one of the other mouth-watering desserts.

TOUR R: THE METROPOLITAN MUSEUM OF ART

The Metropolitan Museum of Art is one of the largest and richest museums in the world. It has several bars and restaurants, including the **Museum Cafeteria** *($-$$; Tue to Thu and Sun 9:30am to 4:30pm, Fri and Sat 9:30am to 8:30pm; 1000 Fifth Ave.)*, which shares space with the Museum Bar and Café and the Museum Restaurant, both described below. The huge dining room, laid out like the atrium of a Roman villa, is ringed with a Doric colonnade that encircles a huge faux skylight. The cafeteria counters are across from the south entrance to the Greek and Roman art galleries. From the main lobby of the museum, you will first pay your respects to the white marble busts of a few emperors, then wind your way between dozens of tables before lining up in front of the display cases with your tray. You have a choice of hot pasta, meat and fish dishes, as well as salads, sandwiches, desserts and a whole slew of munchies. You can also help yourself to wine, beer, soft drinks, bottled water, tea and coffee before proceeding to the cash register. It can take a little time to find a free table, but remind yourself that few places in town offer better value for the money.

The **Museum Bar and Café** *($$; ♿; Tue to Thu and Sun 11:30am to 4:30pm, Fri and Sat 11:30am to 8:30pm; 1000 Fifth Ave.),* in a corner of the atrium described above, serves imaginative sandwiches as well as cakes and pastries. Tea time lasts all afternoon, so don't worry if you don't know the difference between low tea and high tea. If you're more in the mood for a glass of wine, there are two much more pleasant bars in the museum: the Expresso and Wine Bar at the west end of the European Sculpture Court *(level 1)* and the Roof Garden Expresso and Wine Bar *(on the roof; take the elevator to the right of the modern art galleries; May to Oct, open when weather permits).* The latter, laid out in the middle of a sculpture garden, offers extraordinary views of Central Park and the surrounding skyscrapers.

The **Museum Restaurant** *($$$; reservations required for dinner; Tue to Thu and Sun 11:30am to 3pm, Fri and Sat lunch 11:30am to 3pm, dinner 5pm to 10pm; 1000 Fifth Ave., ☎570-3964)* is in the center of the atrium where the cafeteria, bar and café are located. Though the restaurant has table service, a full menu, higher prices and is separated from the other eating areas, the atmosphere of the surrounding cafeteria is inescapable.

 TOUR S: THE UPPER WEST SIDE

For a quick, uncomplicated bite, opt for the tiny restaurant **Burritoville** *($; 451 Amsterdam Ave., between 82nd St. and 81st St., ☎787-8181).* There are just seven little tables inside, but the counter offers about 15 different types of *burritos* at hard-to-beat prices.

The **Columbus Bakery** *($; 474 Columbus Ave., corner of 83rd St., ☎724-6880)* serves excellent freshly squeezed orange juice, home-made cakes, pastries, and an assortment of sandwiches to satisfy sightseers' mid-day appetites. There is a little terrace with four shade-providing green parasols, if you want to enjoy a snack outdoors.

If decor and comfort are not top priorities, head to the **Columbus Café** *($; Columbus Ave., corner of 87th St., ☎721-9040)* for a quick bite. It is an ordinary sort of restaurant, and serves monstrous, freshly baked blueberry muffins. Take advantage of the opportunity to have a cup of coffee; a breakfast of a bagel and coffee costs only two dollars.

The **Daily Soup Meal** *($; 241 West 54th St., between 8th Ave. and Broadway, ☎765-soup)* is the place to go for an affordable meal on the run. For about five dollars, you can have a soup (the selection includes gazpacho, bouillabaisse and Indian shrimp with coconut milk), fruit, a slice of bread and a home-made cookie. The decor is modern, simple and clean.

Gabriela's *($; 685 Amsterdam Ave., corner of 93rd St., ☎961-0574)* is a lively Mexican restaurant that will please the whole family with its simple decor featuring colourful tablecloths, as well as its excellent food, amiable staff and modest prices. The menu is long and appetizing, and includes guacamole, *quesadillas*, enchiladas, *mariscos* and *empanadas*.

Decorated without a hint of pretence, **H & H Bagels** *($; 2239 Broadway, corner of 8th St., ☎595-8000)* is open 24 hours a day and boasts the best bagels in town. It is an ideal place to grab a quick and simple bite to eat.

Hunan Park *($; 235 Columbus Ave., between 71st St. and 70th St., ☎724-4411)* is another spot that will please travellers on limited budgets. You can enjoy a number of Chinese specialties in the unassuming interior at prices that are very affordable for this city. Soup and an order of beef in oyster sauce costs about $10. Several vegetarian dishes, most consisting of noodles, vegetables and sesame sauce, are also available.

The Tibetan restaurant **Shambala** *($; 488 Amsterdam Ave., between 83rd St. and 84th St., ☎721-1270)* offers fresh, honest, economical meals. Your appetite will be roused by the aroma of Oriental spices wafting from the kitchen. The long, narrow interior is decorated with Tibetan fabrics.

The little restaurant **Aegean** *($-$$; 221 Columbus Ave., between 71st St. and 70th St., ☎873-5057)* is a little more upscale than its next-door neighbour, Hunan Park (see above). Delicious Greek dishes of all sorts, including chicken or lamb kebabs accompanied by rice pilaf, grilled tomatoes and peppers, are served here. The Greek salad, the humus and the tzatziki are absolute musts.

For home-made pasta at reasonable prices, **Al Dente** *($-$$; 417 Amsterdam Ave., between 79th St. and 80th St., ☎362-1180)* is the place to go, despite its cramped quarters. The menu features a wide selection of pasta, including the particularly outstanding spinach-ricotta ravioli in tomato and thyme sauce.

The chef at the Indian restaurant **Baluchi's** *($-$$; Columbus Ave., between 73th St. and 74th St., ☎579-0456)* serves up delicious pieces of marinated chicken seasoned with garlic and ginger, accompanied by marvellously spicy vegetables covered in a delicious yogurt sauce, for only $6.95.

It's four o'clock in the morning, you're just leaving a bar on the Upper West Side, and suddenly you're struck by hunger pangs. Fear not, **City Diner** *($-$$; 2441 Broadway, corner of 90th St., ☎877-2406)* is open 24 hours a day. The menu offers a good variety of vegetarian dishes, as well as seafood, pasta and meat, including five-vegetable stir-fries, grilled fresh trout, rigatoni *bolognese* and Black Angus New York Sirloin steak. Delivery to hotels is also available.

The Cottage *($-$$; 360 Amsterdam Ave., corner of 77th St., ☎595-7450 or 595-7451)* is a real find in New York, especially since there isn't even a sign to identify it. Hidden amid the stylish, posh restaurants of the neighbourhood, this modest Asian establishment prepares mouthwatering dishes at affordable prices and offers patrons a complimentary carafe of wine in place of traditional Chinese tea as soon as they are seated. Szechwan-style dumplings covered in a lightly spiced peanut sauce and sesame chicken served with broccoli flowerets are among the delights to be tasted here. Don't be surprised when another carafe of wine is deposited on your table; it's still on the house. The restaurant's location near local bars makes it an ideal place to start off a night on the town.

All of the ingredients used at **Josie's Restaurant & Juice Bar** *($-$$; 300 Amsterdam Ave., between 78th St. and 79th St., ☎769-1212)* are organic, including chicken and fish, vegetables and flour; even the cooking water is filtered! The menu features such dishes as chicken stir-fry and vegi-burgers with tahini sauce. There is also a good selection of fresh juices and martinis, as well as several brands of imported beer to quench your thirst.

At **Planet Sushi** *($-$$;380 Amsterdam Ave., between 79th St. and 80th St., ☎712-2162)*, you can savour sushi à la carte (salmon, sea bass, shrimp, octopus, squid and clams). Main courses such as beef or salmon teriyaki and miso beef are also served. The kitchen opens onto the dining room, and the terrace is very pleasant during the hot summer months.

China Fun *($$; ♿; Sun to Thu 11am to midnight, Fri and Sat 11am to 1am; 246 Columbus Ave., near 71st St., ☎580-1516)* belongs to General Chiang Kai-shek's niece, who has put together a menu with over 200 different dishes, including 18 kinds of noodle soup. There is another China Fun on the Upper East Side (see p 356). Take-out counter and local delivery.

Les Routiers *($$; 568 Amsterdam Ave., between 88th St. and 87th St., ☎874-2742, www.les-routiers.com)* is unquestionably one of New York's best-kept secrets. The kitchen concocts marvellous French culinary delights, including duck cutlet, filet of tuna, and chicken suprême with wild mushrooms. The walls are decorated with regional maps of France, and woodwork that adds a warm touch to the setting. A second room in the back is transformed into a cigar bar after 10pm when it fills with after-dinner smoke. The service is pleasant and friendly.

A choice of meat and vegetables rolled in a crepe called *injera* makes the Ethiopian cuisine of **The Blue Nile** *($$-$$$; 103 West 77th St., between Columbus Ave. and Amsterdam*

Ave., ☎*580-3232)* absolutely mouthwatering. The decor is simple and pretty.

For fresh fish, you can rely on **Dock's** *($$-$$$; 2227 Broadway, corner of 89th St.,* ☎*724-5588)*. The dining room is large, modern and airy, and there is an oyster bar for aficionados. The menu is made up of a large selection of fish, all prepared to taste.

The sidewalk seating area is always packed at **Isabella's** *($$$; 359 Columbus Ave., near 77th St.,* ☎*724-2100)* during the hot summer months, when flocks of people stroll up and down Columbus Avenue in the evenings. The menu consists of pasta dishes and Italian-style grilled chicken and veal.

 On chilly evenings, it's a pleasure to warm up on the comfy banquettes of the legendary **Café des Artistes** *($$$$; &; reserve several days in advance, jacket and tie required, no shorts or jeans; brunch Sat and Sun 11am to 2pm, lunch Mon to Fri noon to 2:30pm, dinner every day 6pm to 11pm; 1 West 67th St.,* ☎*877-3500)*, which is popular with show-business celebrities. This outstanding Upper West Side restaurant was named after the building on whose ground floor it is located, which contains about 60 artist's studios. The dining room, with its dark woodwork, is adorned with a series of paintings of buxom nymphs by Howard Chandler Christy (1934), which the owner found rolled up in one of the studios upstairs. The cuisine, for its part, is classic French – pot-au-feu, *confit de canard*, salmon tartare and the like.

✗ TOUR T: MORNINGSIDE HEIGHTS AND THE CLOISTERS

A plain and honest welcome is guaranteed at **Wilson's** *($$; &; every day 8am to 10pm; 1980 Amsterdam Ave., at 158th St.,* ☎*923-9821)*, which also has a bakery. This restaurant is patronized mainly by neighbourhood residents, who come here to tuck into meatloaf, spare ribs and the like. For dessert, make sure to try the coconut cake or the sweet potato pie.

TOUR U: HARLEM

Located right in the heart of Harlem, **Sylvia's** *($$$; reservations recommended; Mon to Sat 8am to 10pm, Sun 11am to 10pm; 328 Lennox Ave., between 126th and 127th streets, ☎996-0660)* is sure to make you feel completely out of your element. Getting there is an adventure in itself, since you have to pass through the most famous African American neighbourhoods in New York. It is better not to dawdle on your way there and to take a taxi home in the evening; ideally, you should go with two or three other people. During Sunday brunch, guests eat to the sounds of live gospel music.

TOUR V: BROOKLYN HEIGHTS

There are a number of Middle Eastern and North African restaurants along the section of Atlantic Avenue immediately east of Brooklyn Heights. One of these, **Tripoli** *($$; reservations recommended; lunch every day noon to 2pm, dinner 6pm to 10pm; 156 Atlantic Ave., ☎596-5800)*, is on two floors. The bazaar decor on the ground floor contrasts with the stagelike setting upstairs, where pirate ships accompany you during your meal.

Williamsburg

The small interior of **Bean** *($; North 8th St., corner of Bedford Ave., ☎718-387-8222)* is completely stuffed with furniture and relics from the 1960s and 1970s. Guacamole, enchiladas and *quesadillas* constitute the classic dishes served in this little Mexican restaurant, while the grilled chicken accompanied by rice and beans daubed with sour cream is also worthy of mention. Feel free to bring your own wine or beer, and top off the meal with a piece of home-made cake.

 Across from Plane*at* Thailand (see below), **L Cafe** *($; Bedford Ave., ☎718-388-6792)* is an appealing place that serves pastries, bagels, and salads, and offers a selection of newspapers and magazines at the entrance. Weather permitting, you can sit on the back terrace shaded by trees and pretty fabric awnings. The service is friendly, and the clientele is made up of hip, young artists.

Plan*eat* Thailand *($; 184 Bedford Ave.,* ☎*718-599-5758)* offers a number of tables and curved benches facing an open kitchen. The chicken curry in coconut-milk sauce with basil and the ginger shrimp with onions and mushrooms are sure bets. The prices are remarkably low.

Oznots *($-$$; 79 Berry St., corner of North 9th St.,* ☎*718-599-6596)* is an amazing restaurant whose menu focusses on Mediterranean cuisine. The door's stained-glass casts a warm light over the interior, while a false metallic ceiling and colourful ceramics decorate the bar. The fish and seafood are marvellously well prepared, but the grilled steak with vegetables and *basmati* rice is also recommended. About 200 varieties of wine and some 50 beers are offered. Credit cards are not accepted.

Just steps away from L Cafe (see above), the Mexican restaurant **Veracruz** *($-$$; 195 Bedford Ave.,* ☎*718-599-7914)* is larger and more stylish than Bean. Its brick walls are graced with two wood-framed false fireplaces. There is also a pleasant terrace out back. The menu features all the classics of Mexican cuisine; the salads are especially well prepared. The margaritas are excellent and the service is attentive.

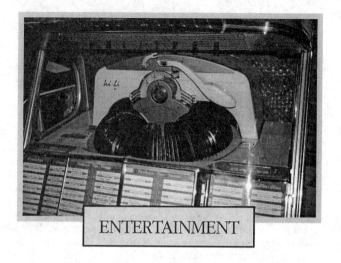

ENTERTAINMENT

New York City boasts a greater number of theatres per capita than any other big city in the Western world. Moreover, the theatre halls of the Big Apple attract huge audiences from all over North America. In fact, a number of Canadians and Americans go to New York City especially to see a famous Broadway musical or to attend an Off-Broadway play (in halls often located outside the Times Square district). Fans of the latter are usually experimental-theatre buffs, checking out plays presented in often small and sometimes hard-to-find halls. To obtain listings for the 40 or so musicals and some 200 plays, sometimes overlapping, consult the Friday and Sunday editions of *The New York Times*, which you can purchase prior to your trip at most shops carrying foreign newspapers.

The weeklies *The New York Press* and *The Village Voice (www.villagevoice.com)* provide exhaustive coverage of dance, music, restaurants, theatre and all of the other cultural and social activities going on in New York. These papers are free and available at many popular public places like bars, restaurants and some shops.

Time Out, which costs only $1.95, is another weekly that constitutes a veritable goldmine of information on live music to suit all tastes, keeps a current list of new restaurants, bars, cabarets and performance halls, and provides the schedules of the main movie theatres.

New York City On Stage *(☎768-1818)* is a telephone information line that provides schedules of dance, theatre and music performances in the five boroughs of New York.

THEATRE AND MUSICALS

Telecharge *(☎563-2929)* sells tickets to Broadway shows.

If you wish to see a Broadway musical, contact **Ticketmaster** *(☎307-7171 or 307-4100)* after making your selection. A $5 surcharge is added to the price of every ticket. This system has the advantage of ensuring that you get good seats and, if you order early enough, receive your tickets by mail prior to your departure (allow a minimum of 14 days for delivery).

If you prefer to see an Off- or Off-Off-Broadway play, contact **Ticket Central** *(☎279-4200)*, which offers a repertoire about a hundred plays and various shows.

Bargain-hunters will undoubtedly want to purchase their tickets while in New York City, but this may limit their options. To obtain rebates of up to 50% off regular ticket prices, head straight to the counter of **TKTS** *(no credit cards or cheques; expect a 2- to 3-hour wait; Mon, Tue, Thu and Fri 3pm to 8pm, Wed and Sat 10am to 2pm and 3pm to 8pm, Sun 11am to 7pm; at Broadway and 47th St., ☎768-1818)*, located on Times Square. Same-day performance tickets are sold here. There is another, generally less crowded TKTS counter at 2 World Trade Center in Lower Manhattan *(Mon to Fri 11am to 5pm, Sat 11am to 3pm)*. The latter is indoors, so you can camp out for tickets sheltered from the rain and cold.

COMEDY

New York is famous for its many comedy clubs where performers work hard to get a few laughs, sometimes challenging the bounds of good taste. The quality of the performances and the price of admission of course varies according to the stature of the comedians, but who knows, maybe you will have the chance to see the next Jerry Seinfeld during your stay in the city. Most shows start at about 6pm or 7pm, when new comedians take the stage to warm up the audience for their more experienced counterparts, who usually go on toward 9pm or 10pm. In addition to the cover charge, there is generally a two-drink minimum per person. In some nightclubs, it can be less expensive to order a bottle of wine for two people to cover the minimum, if that option is on the menu. Some nightclubs serve food. The range of services varies greatly form club to club so it might be best to call ahead for more information.

It is recommended to arrive about 20 minutes early to get a good table. The best table isn't always at the very front of the room, though, because sometimes comedians who lack other inspiration use nearby audience members as material, and this torture can last long enough to ruin an evening. If you think you are funny and quick enough to respond to the wit of a comedian, you might be interested in this challenge and may even come out ahead. But these professional jokers may be astonishingly quick on their feet and might put you in your place faster than you can say "knock, knock", making you the butt of the jokes.

Here is a list of the main comedy clubs in Manhattan

Boston Comedy Club *($5 wkdays, $10 wkends; 82 West 3rd St., between Thompson St. and Sullivan St., ☎477-1000)* is not much-frequented by visitors to New York, but this doesn't prevent the club from featuring excellent, highly professional comedians who will certainly win you over.

Caroline's Comedy Club *($8 to $15; 1626 Broadway, ☎757-4100, www.carolines.com),* near Times Square, often showcases experienced comedians who now star in their own sitcoms. The hall is spacious and includes a restaurant. We recommend a bottle of wine to cover the drink minimum.

Catch a Rising Star *($5 to $12.50; 253 West 28th St., between 7th Ave. and 8th Ave., ☎462-2824),* as its name indicates, is a launching pad for new comedians. The prices here are slightly lower than in the bigger clubs, and you might be pleasantly surprised by a talented, charming future star churning out a series of irresistible gags.

As its name indicates, **Dangerfield** *($8.45 to $12.50; 1st Ave., corner of 61st St., ☎593-1650)* is owned by American comedian Rodney "No Respect" Dangerfield. It ranks among the oldest stand-up comedy clubs in the city. Some very famous faces, like Jim Carrey and Andrew "Dice" Clay, have made appearances here. This spot is very popular with tourists and students.

New Yorkers regularly get together at the **Gotham Comedy Club** *($8 to $10; 34 West 22nd St., between 5th Ave. and 6th Ave., ☎367-9000)* for an evening of stand-up.

You will surely find something to perk up your ears at the **Original Improv** *(433 West 34th St., between 9th Ave. and 10th Ave., ☎279-3446)*.

On the Upper West Side, **Stand Up N.Y.** *($7 to $12; 236 West 78th St., corner of Broadway, ☎595-0850)* also features its share of celebrity comedians. For example, Jerry Seinfeld has entertained and won over audiences here.

TELEVISION TALK SHOWS

By far, the city of New York is the mecca of American talk shows, those programs where a host chats with guests, broaching various topics from the fantastic, to the comical, to the pitiful, all in front of a live audience. Those aged 16 years and over can attend a taping of one of these programs by reserving tickets at least six months in advance. Last-minute tickets are sometimes available at about 8am or 9am the day of the taping. The only problem here is the time involved: people have to wait hours at the studio doors to get these tickets.

Geraldo
(18 years of age and over) Geraldo Tickets, CBS Television, 524 West 57th St. , NY 10019, ☎265-1283.

Late Night
Conan O'Brien, NBC Tickets, 30 Rockefeller Center, NY 10112, ☎664-4000.

Late Show
David Letterman, Ed Sullivan Theatre, 1697 Broadway, NY 10019, ☎975-1003.

Regis and Kathie Lee Live
Live Tickets, Ansonia Station, NY 10023, ☎456-3054.

The Rosie O'Donnell Show
Rosie O'Donnell, 30 Rockefeller Center, NY 10112, ☎664-3056.

Saturday Night Live
30 Rockefeller Center, NY 10112, ☎664-3056.

 MOVIE THEATRES

New York is home to innumerable movie theatres that show the latest films. For schedules, consult the *New York Times* or the magazine *Time Out*.

The American Museum of Natural History houses an IMAX cinema.
79th St. Central Park West, between Columbus Ave. and Central Park West
☎769-5200
Wheelchair accessible
adults: $12
Children: $6.50
Students: $8.50
The museum tour (see p 235) includes admission to a screening.

 CLASSICAL MUSIC AND OPERA

Fans of classical music and dance, for their part, should head to the **Bryant Park Music and Dance Ticket Booths** *(Tue to Sun noon to 2pm and 3pm to 7pm; in Bryant Park, at 42nd St. and*

6th Ave., ☎382-2323), where slashed-price tickets for certain same-day shows are sold.

The **Brooklyn Academy of Music** *(30 Lafayette Ave., trains D, 2, 3 and 4 to the Atlantic Avenue subway station, ☎718-636-4100)* presents several classical and contemporary music concert. Baroque operas are sometimes staged here as well.

The famous **Carnegie Hall** *(154 West 57th St., ☎247-7800)* has presented the greatest names in song as well as popular and classical music over the course of its long history. The concert hall, which can accommodate close to 3,000 people, is renowned for its perfect acoustics.

The **Lincoln Center** *(at Columbus Ave. and 62nd St., orchestra ☎875-5656, opera ☎362-6000, ballet ☎870-5570 or 362-6000)* is a complex of several halls where the New York Philharmonic Orchestra, the Metropolitan Opera, the New York City Ballet and the American Ballet Theater perform.

The vast Art-Deco interior of **Radio Music Hall** *(1260 6th Ave., ☎247-4777, www.radiocity.com)* is worth the trip in itself. It can accommodate up to 6,000 people. The place shows Hollywood-produced film premieres and the famous Rockettes.

JAZZ CLUBS

Arthur's Tavern *(everyday 9pm to 3am; 57 Grove St., ☎675-6879)* presents New Orleans-style blues and jazz shows. There is no cover charge here, so the place is jam-packed on weekends.

The mere mention of the name Bird is enough to make real hard-core jazz fans goggle. **Birdland** *(Mon to Sat 5pm to 3am, Sun noon to 3am; 315 West 46th St., between 8th and 9th Ave., ☎581-3080)* has moved twice over the years. It first opened its doors in the forties to honour Charles "Yardbird" Parker, who could no longer play in clubs after his musician's licence had been confiscated! The original establishment was on 52nd Street. The club then moved to the Upper West Side, where it unfortunately only managed to attract a small handful of die-hard fans. The club's new digs, though cold in appearance, boast a first-rate sound system. The greatest modern-day jazz musi-cians flock here, including Jimmy Heath, Stanley Turrentine, Marc Johnson, Roy Haynes and Mark Whitfield. There are two sets a night, at 9pm and 11pm. Expect a cover charge of about $25 on the weekend and a $10 minimum for drinks, although two people can easily spend $20 at the bar. Most credit cards are accepted.

How Old Are You?

Before hitting the streets of New York and heading to a bar or nightclub, be sure to take identification cards that state your age, especially if you look young. It is not at all unusual to be asked to present ID before being admitted to a licensed establishment in this city.

The **Blue Note** *(Tue to Sat 10pm to 2am; 131 West 3rd St., ☎475-8592)* is the most famous jazz bar in the United States. Legendary musicians who were regular performers here include Duke Ellington and Charlie Parker. Rather steep cover charge.

At **Dharma** *(admission varies; 174 Orchard St., ☎780-0313)*, musicians take the stage and audiences to the fascinating world of jazz. The room is long and narrow, the ambience is intimate and warm, and the music is classic and lively.

The **Iridium Jazz Club** *(44 West 63rd St., between Columbus Ave. and Broadway, ☎582-2121)*, which opened its doors in 1993, has managed to avoid what most New York jazz bars suffered in the eighties and nineties: bankruptcy. The establishment prides itself on hiring the best up-and-coming musicians around, while avoiding overcharging its clients with exorbitant cover charges. Moreover, you can see celebrated guitarist Les Paul and his trio perform here every Monday night. Plan your evening at the Iridium either by consulting the *Village Voice* or listening to the radio station WBGO see who is playing, including several big names like McCoy Tyner, Charlie Haden and Michael Brecker.

The bar-restaurant **Peppers** *(349 Broadway, at Leonard St., ☎343-2824)* hosts Soul Wednesdays every week. The night features an eclectic mix of music, ranging from rhythm & blues and funk to reggae, Latin music and hip hop to spoken word. Doors open at 5pm and shows start at 7pm and 9pm. There is no cover charge before 6:30pm; after 6:30pm admission is $5. There is a one-drink minimum at the bar, and a two-drink minimum in the restaurant section. The place also boasts three televisions broadcasting sporting events.

The **Savoy Lounge** *(355 West 41st St., ☎947-5255)* proudly advertizes that it is the owner of a Hammond B-3, a legendary organ if there ever was one. There is also a jukebox inside, which plays blues and jazz tunes from noon to 4am. Take advantage of the happy-hour specials (until 9pm), which include $6 pitchers of beer, $2.50 beers and wine at $2 a glass. Blues devotees flock to the Savoy's Tuesday-night jam sessions, when the B-3 rocks for all its worth.

Small's *($10; 183 West 10th St., corner of 7th Ave., ☎929-7565)* lives up to New York's famous self-proclaimed reputation as the city that never sleeps. The first show here starts at 10pm and the last ends the next day at about eight in the morning. The atmosphere here is classic and inviting, the lighting is low key, and the music is excellent. Alcoholic beverages are not served here, but patrons are free to bring their own wine and beer – their own hard liquor: the bar sells an assortment of juices and soft drinks that can be used as mix, so those who prefer rum or vodka can make an evening of it without incurring too much damage to their wallets.

Few jazz bars have managed to stay in business for the last few decades. **Sweet Basil** *($17.50; 88 7th Ave. South, ☎242-1785)* is one of the sole survivors. This establishment has been welcoming great musicians such as Sam Rivers, David Murray, Steve Turre and Regina Carter since it opened in 1976. On the weekends, it is strongly advised to reserve a table in advance (call after noon). The first "dinner show" starts at 7:30pm (reservations are taken until 8pm) and the second begins at 8:30pm. From Sunday to Thursday, shows start at 9pm and 11pm; on Fridays and Saturdays, another show fires up the night crowd at 12:30am. Jazz brunches, hosted by Doc Cheatham, are offered on weekends (no cover charge), with shows starting at 2pm and 5pm. For the last two years, The Spirit of Life Ensemble has been livening up Monday evenings. There is a minimum table charge of $10 worth of food or drinks per person, whereas customers who sit at the bar are offered a drink on the house. Visa, MasterCard and American Express are all accepted.

One of the most illustrious jazz bars in New York City is unquestionably the **Village Vanguard** *(Thu and Sun 8:30pm to 1:30am, Fri and Sat 8:30pm to 2:30am; 178 7th Ave. South, between 11th St. and Perry St., ☎255-4037)*, which has been showcasing the day's hottest musicians since the sixties. Several momentous performances have been recorded here, including those of Bill Evans, John Coltrane, Miles Davis, Ornette Coleman and, more recently, Joshua Redman. The Vanguard also features the new blood of the Big Apple. Shivers will run down your spine as you descend the stairs and see all the legends who have played at this mecca of African-American music. Despite the photographs of some of the greatest jazz musicians of all time, the institution hardly boasts the best layout: the view isn't good from the bar and it isn't much better on the right of the stage. In other words, get here early, because the place quickly gets jam-packed.

BARS AND PUBS

The **Abbey Pub** *(237 West 105th St., corner of Broadway, ☎222-8713)* is a small, friendly neighbourhood bar. Whether for a glass of beer or a light meal, this quiet pub is perfect for making acquaintances and having long conversations with friends.

The **All-Star Café** *(1540 Broadway, ☎840-8326)* owned by restaurateur Robert Earle is the hangout of such star athletes as Wayne Gretzky, André Agassi, Monica Seles, Ken Griffey Jr., Joe Montana and Shaquille O'Neal. The restaurant is chock-full of paraphernalia, including a lock of tennis-"rebel" André Agassi's hair, a World Series ring that belonged to none other than Babe Ruth, and much more. This shrine has 20-metre-high ceilings, and 70 television sets (!) which broadcast sports matches, coming events and archival footage. You can sit at one of the tables shaped like a baseball, a baseball mitt or a race track (!) and, for about fifteen dollars, enjoy dishes traditionally associated with American sports: 17 kinds of burgers, five choices of hot dogs, chicken wings, T-bone steaks and more.

Located in Riverdale, in the Bronx, **An Beal Bocht** *(445 West 238th St., ☎718-884-7127)* can be described as a cross between an Irish pub and a typical college-student hangout. Patrons here sit at wooden tables with hand-painted Celtic effigies while listening to Irish music and poetry. Self-serve coffee and tea are free, but most people come here to drink "the best pint of Guinness in town".

Arleen Grocery *(95 Stanton St., between Ludlow St. and Orchard St., ☎358-1633)* is one block from Baby Jupiter and presents live music shows that are always free (to repeat, the shows are always free). Its façade is a reminder that this used to be a grocery store, although it is now a small bar with a stage area where up-and-coming musicians can exhibit their talent. As well, it is not unusual for already established bands, like the Jon Spencer Blues Explosion, to take the stage and get their kicks. The music ranges from rock to funk, by way of pop, and the acoustics here are excellent. Count on spending about $5 for a pint.

The **Astor Bar & Restaurant** *(316 Bowery St., corner of Bleecker St., ☎253-8644)* stands across the street from CBGB-OMFUG. At night, its scarlet neon sign gives it the look of a timeworn diner. You will be greeted at the door by a smiling hostess who will lead you to the elegant ground-floor restaurant or to the basement lounge to sip drinks. The latter has tortoise-shell-coloured walls and a low ceiling supported by pretty wainscotted columns. The lighting is low key and the music is subdued. Small candles identify the faces of people sitting either at tables or the comfortable booths against the walls. The staff is very welcoming and are happy to suggest a dish to share or to explain the selection of cocktails. Try the Long Island Ice Tea, a potent blend of vodka, rum, gin, and tequila topped off with a few drops of Coca-Cola – careful!

The bar **Baby Jupiter** *($3 to $8; 170 Orchard St., corner of Stanton St., ☎982-2229)* plays ambient electronic music and jazz. The establishment is divided into two rooms: on one side, there is a small restaurant-bar that serves Cajun cuisine, and on the other side of a velvet curtain, there is a room with a small dance floor and a stage where comedy shows are sometimes put on. The clientele ranges in age from 20 to 30.

The **Back Fence** *(approx. $5 on wkends; 155 Bleecker St., corner of Thompson St., ☎475-9221)* has been presenting rock and blues shows for 50 years. Simple, quiet and unpretentious.

The **Baggot Inn** *(approx. $5; 82 West 3rd St., between Thompson St. and Sullivan St., ☎477-0622)* is an unpretentious bar that presents rock and folk music shows. Good choice of beers.

Despite its great location, the **Barrow Street Ale House** *(15 Barrow St., between West 4th St. and Bleecker St., ☎206-7302)* is regularly invaded by New York University students, not leaving much room for tourists. You can refuel on burgers and fries or chicken to the sounds of rock music here. The establishment offers 21 kinds of beer on tap and happy hour allows you to knock back imported beers for $1.50 from Sunday to Wednesday.

Located near Amsterdam Avenue, the main draw of the **Bear Bar** *(Mon to Fri 5pm to 4am, Sat 4pm to 4am, Sun 1pm to 4am; 2156 Broadway, ☎362-2145)* is its cheap drinks. The early-bird special allows customers to pay as little as 50¢ for a beer before 5pm, after which prices go up one dollar an hour. Local brews can be sampled here as well: over 70 kinds of New York State beers are in stock.

Though the name is somewhat misleading, the **Big Bar** *(75 East 7th St., between 1st Ave. and 2nd Ave., ☎777-6969)*, is actually very small, darkish, and alluring. Happy hour here is a good way to start off the evening in a very comfortable atmosphere before heading off to make the rounds.

A certain Bob Dylan once went to the **Bitter End** *(admission varies; 147 Bleecker St., ☎673-7030)* to display his great talent as a story-teller. Today, many bands in search of fame liven up evenings here for visitors and a few regulars.

The **Bowery Bar** *(358 Bowery St., corner of 4th St., ☎475-2220)* is a meeting place for the beautiful-people crowd, whose deep pockets are stuffed full of green, whose smiles are radiant, and whose trendy wardrobe makes a statement.

Clients dressed in jeans and sneakers are categorically refused entry.

Fans of artist Giger (whose unbridled creations inspired the set design and the hideous creature in the film *Alien*) will appreciate **Caliban** *(360 3rd Ave., corner of 26th St., ☎889-0190)*, where some of his paintings and sculptures decorate this establishment's walls. People gather here to gab over a beer. A terrace out back is open in the summertime.

CBGB *($3 to $10; 315 Bowery St. corner of Bleecker St., ☎982-4052)* stands for "Country, Bluegrass & Blues", and resembles a dark, underground hallway plastered with posters and graffiti in blaring colours. There are shows (rock, reggae, punk, etc.) every night. Fans of thundering music and cheap beer will feel right at home.

For an evening of cigar lounging among models and flush visitors, try **Chaos** *(23 Watts St., between West Broadway and Broome St., ☎925-8966)*, a meeting place for professionals.

Models, starlets and artists get together at the stylish **Coffee Shop** *(29 Union Sq., corner of 16th St., ☎243-7969)* to chat, have a smoke, sip a drink and exchange business cards. The clientele is hand picked at the door.

The **Copacabana** *(admission varies; 617 West 57th St., between 11th Ave. and 12th Ave., ☎582-2672)* is undoubtedly one of the most popular Latin nightclubs in Manhattan. The services here include a restaurant, but salsa and merengue shows liven up the *muy calientes* evenings on Fridays and Saturdays. Appropriate dress is required: no jeans, T-shirts or sneakers.

If you care more about the quantity and quality of beer than the decor when choosing a bar, head straight to **d.b.a.** *(41 1st Ave, between 2nd and 3rd St., ☎475-5097)*, which has a great selection to choose from. This unpretentious bar carries approximately 60 kinds of beer, about forty brands of scotch, 20 kinds of tequila, etc.

Despite its name, **Decibel** *(240 East 9th St., between 2nd Ave. and 3rd Ave., ☎979-2733)* is a quiet, original spot where you can discover the virtues of *sake* and savour tasty little hors d'oeuvres. The bar offers a very wide selection of drinks to satisfy every kind of thirst.

Drinkland *(339 East 10th St., between Ave. A and Ave. B, ☎228-2435)* is somewhere to see and to be seen, as well as to drink. This recently opened establishment is decorated with furniture and trinkets straight from the 1960s and 1970s. The music ranges from retro to techno, and the beer is not too expensive. You can also play a game of pool.

The Dublin House *(225 West 79th St., between Broadway and Amsterdam Ave., ☎874-9528)* is a pub with subtle Irish nuances, where neighbourhood folk meet and chat a bit over a shared pitcher of beer. None other than Guinness is sold here. Tunes from the rock and roll songbook make up the background music.

The **Fashion Cafe** *(51 Rockefeller Center, between 5th St. and 6th St., ☎765-3131)* looks like stylish fashion magazine and is a meeting place for beautiful people, who come here to see, to be seen, to munch on health-food sandwiches and to sip cafés au lait.

Looking for a folky, laid-back atmosphere? Try the **Fast Folk Café** *(41 North Moore, between Varick and Hudson St., ☎274-1636)*, which presents acoustic music shows.

For a real Irish pub in New York City drop by **Fitzgerald's Pub** *(Mon to Sat 11am to 4am, Sun noon to 4am; 336 3rd Ave., ☎679-6931)*, where good beer is served in a dark-wood-panelled setting.

Upstairs from the **Flamingo East** *(219 2nd Ave., between 13th St. and 14th St., ☎533-2860)* restaurant, is a favourite spot of the city's nocturnal wildlife where the lively atmosphere of a party of friends meets the comfort of a grandiosely furnished living room. You can watch the constant traffic on Second Avenue from its large balcony. For a bite, try the grilled squid.

Situated in a building full of historical memorabilia, **Flute** *(205 West 54th St., between 7th Ave. and Broadway, ☎265-5169)* lives up to its name with an impressive selection of about 100 champagnes, about 10 of which are sold by the glass. Give in to the temptations of caviar, smoked salmon or foie gras as accompanying tidbits. If you are less enticed by the bubbly, the menu suggests a variety of scotches, cognacs, Porto, wines, grappa, calvados and imported beers.

The **Glocca Morra Pub** *(304 3rd Ave., at 23rd St.,* ☎*473-9638)* will make your eyes a 'smiling with its friendly Irish ambiance. Enjoy a game of darts or pool here while Jim Lillis, a.k.a. "the Sheriff", pours you a Rolling Rock, a Heineken or a Woodpecker Cider. We were treated to the sounds of Irish singers Dermit Henrey, Tom Birmingham and John Morrisson, who wehe featured here as part of the pub's Wednesday concerts.

If you're short on funds, you might have to pass off the posh **Greatest Bar on Earth** *(1 World Trade Center, 107th floor, at Liberty St.,* ☎*524-7000)* boasts three bars where you can munch on a few oysters *shabu-shabu*, or *sushi*. Live music and dancing every night to rhythm & blues and Roadhouse music. The magnificent view over Manhattan alone is worth the trip.

The **Greenwich Brewing Co.** *(everyday 11:30am to 1am; 418 6th Ave.,* ☎*477-8744)* is a microbrewery with a large adjacent bar and dining room (see p 330).

New York City, of course, has its own **Hard Rock Café** *(Mon to Thu 11am to 11:30pm, Fri and Sat 10:30am to 12:30pm, Sun 11am to 10:30pm ; 221 West 57th St.,* ☎*459-9320)*, a link of the famous British chain. This branch opened here in 1984 and like all others, is decorated with lots of memorabilia from various rock stars: electric guitars, clothing and posters. A veritable rock'n'roll museum, the place rocks to everything from the Rolling Stones to Cake and Portishead. You can also find your fill here *($$)* from a menu of burgers, club sandwiches and other typically American specialties. Reserving a table is a wise idea, since the place always fills up to capacity (especially on Saturday nights).

For those who prefer a lounge setting, you'll have to go to **Hell** *(59 Gansevoort St., near Washington St.,* ☎*727-1666)*. A mixed crowd, averaging 25-years-old, chats quietly over beers ($4 to $6 each) on one of the many sofas.

Located on the Upper East Side, **Hooligan's Tavern** *(Mon to Sat 8am to 4am, Sun 10am to 4am; 1804 2nd Ave., between 93rd and 94th Streets,* ☎*289-2273)* is a neighbourhood watering hole with a very friendly staff. You can watch a sports match here on one of 11 giant-screen televisions and, every Saturday, Sunday and Monday, take in a televised soccer match (in English and Scottish alike!). The pub's motto is: "Every Day is Christmas; Every Night is New Year's Eve; Every Sip is a Sonnet; and Every Bite is a Poem".

Right across from Hooligan's Tavern, the **Irish Times** *(1803 2nd Ave., at 93rd St., ☎426-8100)* will take you back to the 19th century. Modeled after quintessential early-19th-century English and Irish pubs, this establishment offers a whole slew of imported beers from all over the world, including Europe. The decor will take you back in time with its walls full of newspaper pages, photographs and other archival clippings from the Irish Times, some of which date as far back as the 16th century. Sean Quinn and his team will make sure you have a good time at their pub.

Jake's Dilemma *(430 Amsterdam Ave., between 80th St. and 81st St., ☎580-0556)* is choosing among the incredible selection of bottled beers offered at the bar (about 80). Dartboards, a pool table and a television broadcasting sports are part of the decor

Anything goes at the **Knitting Factory** *(74 Leonard St., between Church St. and Broadway, ☎219-3055)* in terms of music and bands. The music is sometimes rock and sometimes jazz, but it is always noisy. The crowd is lively and colourful.

A new creation from a designer duo, **Lot 61** *(550 West 21st St., between 10th Ave. and 11th Ave., ☎243-6555)* does what it takes to be a hot spot for Manhattan's beautiful people (always on the cutting edge of new trends) without the usual snobbishness. Stroll through the various rooms spread out in this large industrial space and admire the creations of local artists as well as the original decor made up of rubber sofas, booths with faunlike motifs and a stylized fireplace. A varied and interesting selection of snacks and hors d'oeuvres will satisfy picky eaters.

The Luna Lounge *(171 Ludlow St., between Houston St. and Stanton St., ☎260-2323)* stands out from other bars by letting any musician take the stage every night of the week. Monday nights feature comedians. These varied shows are always free.

ENTERTAINMENT

People pour in to hear well- and lesser-known artists. The retro decor features paintings by local artists that adorn the walls.

In the same neighbourhood, **Max Fish** *(178 Ludlow St., between Houston St. and Stanton St., ☎529-3959)* is a simple, unpretentious bar where you can sip drinks and check out temporary exhibitions of local artists' work, such as photographs, paintings and sculptures. A few bottled imported beers are available. To relax and change your frame of mind, there are a pool table, pinball machines and video games.

McSorley's *(15 East 7th St., between 2nd Ave. and 3rd Ave., ☎473-9148)* has been in business since 1854 but only opened its doors to women in 1970. This New York institution today is a popular meeting place for tourists to chat over a nice cool beer. Photographs and newspaper clippings relating the history of this old Irish pub are displayed on the walls.

Michael's Pub *($15 to $25; 109 East 56th St., between Park Ave. and Lexington Ave., ☎758-2272)* just moved at the end of 1998. This pub owes its notoriety to the fact that actor-director Woody Allen sometimes dropped in on Monday nights to play his clarinet. These days, Woody rarely announces his appearances and just pops in when he feels like it. Other excellent, lesser-known, but more talented musicians perform on different evenings. In addition to the cover fee, there is a two-drink minimum.

Motor City *(127 Ludlow St., between Rivington and Delancey, ☎358-1595)* will please old-time rock-and-roll fans with its rebellious atmosphere and music of years gone by. No tie is required to fit in with the unique decor strewn with car parts. Take a seat at the bar or in a booth and savour a very modestly price beer. No micro-brewery beers are available here.

Mulligan's Pub *(267 Madison Ave., between 39th St. and 40th St., ☎286-0207)* attracts a business clientele during the week, who stop in at the long bar after a full day of work to order from the large selection of cool, American and imported beers and even get a bite to eat. Tourists come in mainly on weekends. There is no live entertainment, but a stereo spouts out old hits that bring back faded memories. In addition, four televisions broadcast sports and national news programs. The service is friendly.

The inimitable **Naked Lunch Bar and Lounge** *(Tue to Sat 5pm to 4am, Sun and Mon 5pm to 2am; 17 Thompson St., ☎343-0828)*, based on William Burroughs' novel of the same name, is a bit nightmarish, but not to avid readers of the American author's horrific prose. Try one of the many special martinis offered here. The local beers are also worth a few greenbacks. A DJ gets the place moving from Wednesday to Saturday, and there is no cover charge.

Deconstruct the name **The Nuyorican Poets Cafe** *(236 East 3rd St., 2nd Ave. Subway station, ☎465-3167)* and you get: New Yorkers of Puerto Rican descent. This marginal café is a meeting place for poets, who come to read their works, which often deal with social themes in a contemporary style.

Not everyone can afford the Plaza Hotel, but its **Oak Bar** *(everyday noon to 1am; at Grand Army Plaza and Central Park South, ☎546-5330)* can be frequented by the most common of mortals. Enjoying a beer in the smoky and noisy ambiance of this dark-wood-panelled room is relatively reasonable and will leave you with long-lasting memories. While here, check out the hotel lobby.

OMFUG, "Other Music for Uplifting Gourmandizers", is CBGB's next-door neighbour and poetic counterpart. The ambience is relaxed, even romantic, thanks to warm candlelight. The cover charge is only about $6, so this is the perfect spot to begin an evening with a drink in good company, all the while listening to the recital of a local poet or live folk music.

The only beer on tap at **Paddy Reilly's Music Bar** *(519 2nd Ave., at 29th St., ☎686-1210)* is the ubiquitous Guinness, served with a five-centimetre head. Shows are presented here seven nights a week, and on Wednesdays musicians (amateurs and professionals alike) are invited to join host Tony DeMarco and his friends and guests for improvised jam sessions. Happy hour every day from 4pm to 7pm.

Despite its distinctly French name, the **Paris Café** *(Mon to Fri 8am to 4am, Sat and Sun 11am to 4am; 119 South St., in South Street Seaport, ☎240-9797)* is actually a marvellous Irish pub with a warm ambiance. The regulars here — including several truck drivers and the fishmongers from neighbouring Fulton Fish Market — are quick to welcome you to their gang.

The Paris Café is an excellent place from which to observe the night-time bustle around the New York fish market. Open since 1873, the pub has served some of the greatest names in American history among its regulars, including Thomas Edison, who divided his time between his inventions and his beer, and engineer W. A. Roebling, who supervised the construction of his brainchild, the Brooklyn Bridge, from his bar stool. Others include Buffalo Bill, Butch Cassidy and the Sundance Kid as well as Theodore Roosevelt, who used to come in toward the end of the day.

Imported-beer lovers gather at the **Peculier Pub** *(Mon to Thu 5pm to 2am, Fri 4pm to 4am, Sat 2pm to 4am, Sun 4pm to 1am; 145 Bleecker St., ☎353-1327)* for some 400 kinds of beer, imports from $5 to $6 and domestic brews from $3 to $4. It is best to come here during the week, for the place gets overrun with suburbanites come the weekend.

Fans of tranny (or transvestite) shows can watch some at **Pieces** *(everyday 2pm to 4am; 8 Christopher St., ☎929-9291)*, where the resident drag queens delight in making comments at the audience.

Pink Pony *(176 Ludlow St., between Houston St. and Stanton St., ☎253-1922)* is an unpretentious café-bar that occasionally presents comedy shows. It is frequented by a twenty-something clientele who chat about everything under the sun over brews.

If a noisy and excessively lively atmosphere is something you enjoy, pop round to **Planet Hollywood** *(Sun and Mon to Thu 11am to midnight, Fri 11am to 1am, Sat 10:30am to 1am; 140 West 57th St., ☎333-7827)*, where all of Hollywood seems to congregate. The decor here consists of pink-and-green zebra tablecloths and seats, a never-ending series of photographs and posters of American movie stars, costumes and accessories from film shoots scattered about. The owners of this restaurant chain, Arnold Schwartzeneger, Sylvester Stallone and Bruce Willis, have pulled out all the stops as far as flashiness is concerned — though these actors, of course, have never been known for their subtlety... True, this place can give you a headache, but the whole mass of celebrities parading through makes up for the establishment's garishness. Only in "America"!

Smack dab in bustling Greenwich Village, **Polly Esther's** *(Mon to Fri 11am to 2am, Sat and Sun 11am to 4am; 21 East 8th St., ☎979-1970; second location at 249 West 26th St.)* has cashed in big on the resurrected disco craze. The establishment, decorated with tacky but fun posters from the seventies, offers several good deals: happy hour, from 1pm to 9pm on weekdays and 1pm to 7pm on weekends, features beer at $3, etc.

A well-put-together clientele, waitresses that make men's heads turn, an excellent selection of vodkas and martinis, and a well-preserved, intimate decor await you at the lounge called **Pravda** *(281 Lafayette St., between Prince St. and Houston St., ☎226-4696)*.

Off the beaten track, far above the hustle-bustle of the city, the **Restaurant-Bar** *(49th St., corner of 1st Ave., ☎980-4796)* of the Beekman Tower Hotel is on the 26th story and offers sensational panoramic views of New York. A $10 minimum is in effect, but you can pay it in the form of seafood linguini, Atlantic salmon or filet mignon *($$$)*. From Tuesday to Sunday beginning at 9pm there is a live pianist. Davidoff cigars are sold. In the hot months of summer, you can enjoy a dreamy drink outside and admire the city shining with all its brilliant lights. Ideal for an intimate evening.

A clientele nostalgic for the 1960s and 1970s crowds into the **Rock & Roll Cafe** *(221 West 57th St., between 7th Ave. and Broadway, ☎459-9320)* to dance, drink and talk to the classic sounds of Lou Reed, AC/DC, Jimi Hendrix and David Bowie.

At the **Roxy** *(515 West 18th St., between 10th Ave. and 11th Ave., ☎645-5156)* you can don a pair of roller skates and get down to the funky, never outdated, disco beat. Bands of all musical genres occasionally perform. The clientele is a mix of gay and straight.

The **Russian Vodka Room** *(265 West 52nd St., between Broadway and 8th Ave., ☎307-5835)* attracts businessmen who come here after a long day at the office to lean on the bar and savour a few of the approximately 50 varieties of vodka available here. The atmosphere is sober, unlike some of the regulars, and a bit subdued.

ENTERTAINMENT

7B *(108 Ave. B, corner of 7th St., ☎473-8840)* is a bar that has appeared in numerous films including *Crocodile Dundee*, *Angel Heart* and *The Verdict*. It offers a good selection of cool beers and friendly service.

The **Sidewalk Café** *(94 Avenue A, corner of 6th St., ☎473-7373)* is a friendly café with a small performance room that hosts aspiring musicians and comedians. The quality of the shows widely varies, but they are always entertaining. During the dog days of summer, you can sit on a pleasant terrace while waiting for the performances to begin.

Don't be put off by the name of the **Slaughtered Lamb** *(182 West 4th St., between 6th Ave. and 7th Ave., ☎627-5262)*. This bar is a friendly spot that offers a hundred or so brands of beer. The basement looks like a haunted-house. On the weekend, this establishment is literally packed, so it's wise to come early.

To get a good idea of the kind of people populating the SoHo district, head to **Spy** *(101 Greene St., ☎343-9000)*, where an image-conscious, glamourous crowd struts right by you. The relatively affordable drinks ($4 to $5) will make you forget about the cost of the delicacies (Beluga caviar at $50, $12 cigars). The music, which is more "soft rock", is perfectly suited to this parade of celebrity wanna-bes.

The **Telephone Bar & Grill** *(149 2nd Ave., corner of 10th St., ☎525-5000)* is easily recognizable by its three scarlet-red phone booths imported from London standing next to the entrance. Obviously, this is a fun English pub. In addition to a good selection of imported beers, a few tasty American micro-brewery varieties figure on the menu. The service is smiling and friendly, adding to the jovial, relaxed atmosphere.

The Wha? *($5-$10; 115 MacDougal St., between Bleecker St. and 3rd St., ☎254-3706, ext. 190)* is a veritable Greenwich Village institution. Renowned for its monumental musical history, this club has witnessed the performances of many famous musicians and artists. For example, none other than Jimi Hendrix was discovered here, while other stars, like Bob Dylan, shook the crowd with their music, earning them a place in the rock and roll hall of fame. On Wednesdays and Sundays, there is no cover charge. Monday nights are usually reserved for Brazilian music, Tuesdays for funk bands, while Wednesday to Sunday all sorts of musical styles may be heard. Finally, guest comedians sometimes get things started on weekends.

The **Whitehorse Tavern** *(Sun to Thu 11am to 2am, Fri and Sat 11am to 4am; 567 Hudson St., ☎243-9260)* is the place where Welsh poet Dylan Thomas drank himself to death: 19 whiskeys can do that to you! A couple of beers, which cost $3 to $5, on the outdoor terrace might make a poet out of you instead.

The **Zinc Bar** *(approx. $5; 90 West Houston St., between Thompson St. and La Guardia St., ☎477-8337)* is a venue for different styles of music. On weekends, there are jazz shows, while during the week there might be Latin music or even poetry recitals.

 DANCE CLUBS

Life *(158 Bleecker St., ☎420-1999)* welcomes all kinds of people, from cross-dressers to the very conservative. Clearly, there is no dress code here. A twenty-something crowd comes here to dance to house and techno music, or relax in the lounge to the harmonic sounds of The Jackson 5, and other tracks. There is enough room to move on the dance floor without getting jostled by pimply teens. Drinks cost between $5 and $7.

The **Roseland** *(239 West 52nd St., ☎247-0200)* is a huge hall that can accommodate hundreds of people dancing the cha-cha, the samba and the rhumba. On Sunday afternoons, a 12-piece orchestra provides the music, just like in the good old days of big-band. On display at the entrance are several pairs of dance shoes that belonged to such dance legends as Fred Astaire and Ginger Rogers. Rock concerts are also held here.

The **Sound Factory** *(618 West 46th St., ☎643-0728)* attracts a clientele whose age varies between 21 and 35 years old, but all have one thing in common: to get in. And to gain entry, you must be dressed appropriately (no jeans, sneakers or shorts) and wear a big smile. Expect a cover charge of close to $20 and an electric ambiance. All levels of society seem to gather here and get along: everyone, from ravers and goths to the upper-class beautiful people crowd. The club boasts three floors: you can dance to rap on the first floor, while techno and jungle beats rattle the two floors above. Drinks range from $5 to $8.

Looking for an afterhours club? Then head to **Tunnel** *(220 West 27th St., at West Side Hwy.,* ☎*695-4682),*where a mixed and fairly young crowd comes here to worship DJ Dany Tenaglia, who spins old house, some trance and all the beats imaginable. It is best to get here before midnight if you want to get in and, although appearance is crucial at this trendy nightclub (especially if you want to avoid spending all night waiting in line), once inside, you will find virtually as many ravers and hipsters as thoroughly conventional people. You can dance here until the early hours of the morning (7am) and, if you can stand the heat, you'll have a great time. Drinks cost between $5 and $8.

The four floors of **Webster Hall** *(Thu to Sat 10pm to 4am; 11th St., between 3rd and 4th Ave.,* ☎*353-1600)* vibrate to the sound of techno music. All kinds of different people gather here, from leather-clad gay men to New Jersey secretaries. Rock concerts are sometimes held here as well.

Brooklyn

For an evening off the beaten track in a unique spot, try **Galapagos** *(70 North 6th St., Williamsburg,* ☎*718-782-5188 or 384-4586),* which is in an old mayonnaise factory. Take note of the open garage door, where merchandise used to be loaded onto trucks. There are no trucks parked here now – the parking lot has been filled with water to look like a small pond. Open the door on your left, walk along the edge of the water, and enter the intimate bar whose atmosphere is created by candlelight, electronic music and a regular clientele. Next door there is a repertory theatre called, **Ocularis** which shows classic films, like those of Fellini, sometimes preceded by the work of an unknown local director.

The **Brooklyn Brewerie** *(79 North 11th St., Williamsburg,* ☎*718-486-7422)* organizes guided tours of its facilities.

GAY BARS

A twenty-something female clientele fills up **Bar d'O** *(29 Bedford St., corner of Downing St., ☎627-1580)* to lounge on comfy sofas, sip beer and intimitely chat.

Barracuda *(275 West 22nd St., between 7th and 8th Ave., ☎645-8613)* a Chelsea institution, is always crowded with a diverse clientele patrons of all kinds.

Boiler Room *(86 East 4th St., ☎254-7536)*. A very popular bar in the East Village where drinks are not too expensive. Fairly interesting decor consisting of large wall hangings and high ceilings.

The two-storey, **The Crazy Nanny** *(21 7th Ave., corner of Leroy St., ☎366-6312)* is frequented by women who come to cruise, dance and let off steam.

Smack in the middle of the West Village, the little bar called **The Hangar** *(115 Christopher St., between Bleecker St. and Hudson St., ☎627-2044)* is very popular with tourists and regulars. The music is retro, and pool tables are available for your enjoyment.

The **Henrietta Hudson** *(438 Hudson St., between Morton St. and Barrow St., ☎924-3347)* is one of the most popular women's bars in the city. A mixed crowd meets here to play pool, dance like mad and trade phone numbers. On weekends there are live music shows.

In the category of more sophisticated joints, **Julies's** *(204 East 58th St., ☎688-1294)* is a quiet bar that is very popular with women looking for soul mates.

Julius *(Mon to Sat 8am to 2am, Sun noon to 2am; 159 West 10th St., ☎929-9672)* is a pleasant gay bar located in an old Greenwich Village building that was once home to a Prohibition-era speakeasy. It is one of the few gay bars where the music isn't blaring, so it's actually possible to have intelligible conversations.

The Monster *(80 Grove St., ☎924-3557)* has a typical piano-bar ambiance. The clientele here is a little older than that of other bars and more sophisticated, too. The bar also has a dance floor and features occasional shows.

A mixed crowd converges at **Splash** *(approx. $5; West 17th St., corner of 6th Ave., ☎691-0073)* to dance to techno beats, cruise, drink and play pool.

The **Stonewall Inn** *(everyday 11am to 4am; 53 Christopher St., ☎462-0950)* is considered the birthplace of the American gay revolution, because its patrons stood up to police harassment in 1969 by retaliating with stones and fists (see p 96, 150).

Wonder Bar *(505 East 6th St., between Ave. A and Ave. B, ☎777-9105)*. Probably the most pleasant gay bar in all of Manhattan, with its relaxed ambiance, elegant and soothing decor and hip clientele.

Hold onto your glass, because the dancers at **The Works** *(everyday 2pm to 4am; 428 Columbus Ave., at 81st St., ☎799-7365)* "shake their groove thing" right on the bar, blithely stepping over beers and spirits. This is one of the few gay bars on the Upper West Side.

 # PROFESSIONAL SPORTS

Yankees baseball games are played at **Yankee Stadium** *(at 161st St. and River Ave., train 4 to 161st Street-Yankee Stadium subway station, ☎718-293-6000)* in the Bronx.

To see the Mets in action, head to **Shea Stadium** *(at 126th St. and Roosevelt Ave., train 7 to Willets Point-Shea Stadium subway station, ☎718-507-8499)* in Queens.

Basketball fans can watch a Knicks game at **Madison Square Garden** *(on the west side of 7th Ave., between West 31st and West 33rd St., ☎465-MSG1)*. The amphitheatre also hosts New York Rangers National Hockey League games. The New York Islanders, also part of the NHL, play their games at the **Nassau Veterans' Memorial Coliseum** *(☎516-794-4100)*, in Uniondale.

To take part in the American football, head to **Giants Stadium**, in East Rutherford, New Jersey *(from NYC, take the Lincoln Tunnel and Route 3 West to the stadium; ☎201-935-8222)*, where you can catch a game played by one of New York's two teams, namely the Giants and the Jets.

SHOPPING

Question: What is the world's shopping capital? Answer: New York City, of course! The proof: millionaires from the world over come here for two to three days each month just to shop, knowing the selection is unbeatable. It is often said that if one cannot manage to find such-and-such an item in one of some 100,000 stores in the American metropolis, then that item simply does not exist – but there must be an American somewhere in the process of inventing it! The following list of shops represents but a trifling sample of what New York City has to offer. The best tool for finding that coveted item is The Yellow Pages, available in all hotels.

 DEPARTMENT STORES

Bergdorf-Goodman *(every day 10am to 6pm, Thu to 8pm; 754 5th Ave., ☎753-7300)*, the most exclusive department store in New York City, occupies two stately buildings on either side of Fifth Avenue, at 58th Street. The emporium carries the collections of several great French and Italian haute-couture designers, including Jean-Paul Gaultier, Christian Lacroix, Claude Montana and Emmanuel Ungaro, laid out in a plush, swanky decor.

Contrary to popular belief, **Bloomingdale's** *(Mon to Fri 10am to 8pm, Sat 10am to 7pm, Sun 11am to 7pm; 1000 3rd Ave., ☎705-2000 or 705-2098, ⊷705-2794)*, located on the edge of the fashionable Upper East Side district, mostly sells middle-of-the-range products at relatively affordable prices. The store carries most big-name American labels in women's fashions and menswear, such as Calvin Klein and Jones New York, who have their own boutiques inside the store itself. On the upper floors, you can pick up just about anything for the home, from night tables and flowered sheets to pancake griddles. The main floor is almost exclusively reserved for perfumes from all over the world, which are packaged in lovely bottles.

For a long time, the Wall Street district was entirely devoid of department stores. Seeing its thousands of workers roaming the streets at lunch hour, **Century 21** *(Mon to Fri 8am to 7pm, Sat 10am to 6pm; 22 Cortland St., ☎227-9092)* decided to open a store here where you could find electronics (cameras, VCRs, etc.), cut-price clothing and baggage in every possible colour, shape and size.

Macy's *(Mon to Sat 10am to 8pm, Sun 11am to 7pm; at 34th St. and 6th Ave., ☎695-4400)* prides itself on being the largest department store in the world. And it is. You can find anything and everything on its 10 floors or over 200,000 square metres of space. This venerable New York institution opened its doors in 1901. With the passing years, it most notably started the Macy's Thanksgiving Day Parade with Santa Claus, a tradition now emulated throughout North America.

Visitors who want to brag to their friends that they shopped on Fifth Avenue should head to **Saks Fifth Avenue** *(every day 10am to 6pm, Thu to 8pm; 611 5th Ave., at 49th St., ☎753-4000)*, where they can actually buy a shirt without having to mortgage the house. This quasi-mythical American fashion institution stocks big-name domestic lines on the main floor and international ones upstairs.

Japanese refinement rules on each of the seven floors of **Takashimaya** *(Mon to Fri 10am to 6pm, Sat 11am to 6pm; 693 5th Ave., ☎350-0100 or 800-753-2038)*, the New York branch of the well-known Nipponese department store. Wandering through the chic yet sober premises is a real visual treat.

Among the treasures to be found here are modern jewellery, silk sheets and, of course, traditional ceremonial teapots.

 CLOTHING

Alicia Mugetti *(999 Madison Ave., at 77th St., ☎794-6186; 186 Prince St., ☎226-5064).* Mugetti's collection of women's clothing is elegantly displayed at these two shops, the larger of which is on Madison Avenue. You'll find dresses, velvet jackets and hand-dyed pants, all bearing the designer's unique, personal touch.

Some **Benetton** *(597 5th Ave., ☎317-2501)* ads might be controversial, but the company's Fifth Avenue store is bright and airy, and the clothes are neatly displayed. There is a small café in the basement.

Betsey Johnson *(130 Thompson St., ☎420-0169)* embraces womanhood in all its forms, with her highly stylized, colourful clothing, some of which might appeal to the rebel or iconoclast in you.

World-renowned for its quality, impeccably styled suits and rainwear, **Burberrys** *(9 East 57th St., ☎371-5010)* also offers an impressive array of coats, tight-fitting garments and casualwear, for women and men.

At **Calvin Klein** *(654 Madison Ave., between 60th and 61st St., ☎292-9000)* you will fit right into the casual decor. Its three floors (one for menswear and two for women's fashions) — not to mention the mezzanine — contain everything from sweaters and pants to jeans, of course.

At **Canal Jean Co.** *(Mon to Thu and Sun 11am to 7pm, Fri and Sat 10am to 8pm; 504 Broadway, ☎226-3663)*, not only will you find all kinds of brand-name jeans, but Doc Marten shoes, accessories and even second-hand clothing, the whole on display in funky SoHo.

Get ready for the wave of European fashions that will be sweeping the runways for the next few seasons by stopping in at **Comme des Garçons**, whose avant-garde collection of

SHOPPING

menswear features high-end, loose-fitting, futuristic clothing made of modern fabrics. The shop itself is actually quite small and inviting, considering how famous the label is.

Geiger Park Avenue *(505 Park Ave., at 59th St., ☎644-34350)* will appeal to both women and men for its collection of designer clothes. This well-known European establishment, set up shop in New York City a few years ago and makes garments out of specially imported fabrics to clothe the very well-to-do.

The boutiques of the greatly missed Italian designer **Gianni Versace** *(816 Madison Ave., at 68th St., ☎744-5572; 817 Madison Ave., at 68th St., ☎744-6868; 647 5th Ave., between 51st and 52nd St., ☎317-0224)* continue to attract fans of his elegant clothing. The boutique located at 816 Madison Avenue is for men, and the women's one is across the street. The third, on Fifth Avenue, caters to both and even carries home-decor items.

The luxuriant gleaming colours of **Giorgio Armani** *(760 Madison Ave., at 65th St., ☎988-9191)* are proudly displayed in this Madison Avenue boutique, where the fabrics used are enough to make many a visitor linger. The **Emporio Armani** *(601 Madison Ave., between 57th and 58th St., ☎317-0800)*, carries less expensive streetwear and apparel. **Armani Exchange** *(568 Broadway, at Prince St., ☎431-6000)* carries the Italian designer's most casual pieces, at very affordable prices.

If you are looking to buy a scarf or a necktie for a friend, or perhaps a silk dress for your beloved, **Louis Féraud** *(3 West 56th St., ☎956-7010)* is just the place. This boutique is a work of art in itself, with its marble, bronze and polished-wood decor.

One of the stars of haute couture, **Miuccia Prada** *(45 East 57th St., between Madison and Park Ave., ☎308-2332)* to the extreme with her clothing designs. Her main collection bears her name and includes clothing, shoes and accessories which are highly coveted by the fashion world. Of course, you need deep pockets to shop here. Second location: **Prada** *(841 Madison Ave., at 70th St., ☎327-4200)*.

Nakazawa *(137 Thompson St., ☎505-7768, www.nakazawa)* sells hand-painted silk kimonos.

Those who prefer the comfort of denim can drop by **The Original Levi's Store** *(750 Lexington Ave., between 59th and 60th St., ☎826-5957; 1492-1496 3rd Ave., at 84th St., ☎249-5045; 3 East 57th St., at 5th Ave., ☎838-2188)*, which has everything of that material from jeans and shirts to jackets.

American designer Ralph Lauren sells his wares at **Polo Ralph Lauren** *(867 Madison Ave., at 72nd St., ☎606-1200)*. Here you can find four floors of clothing for men, women and children. The sells also antiques, men's and Women's shoes and a few accessories.

Lingerie

La Petite Coquette *(51 University Pl., between 9th and 10th St., ☎473-2478)* may be a small, but it has a good selection of quality lingerie.

It's very easy to find lingerie in New York City. **Victoria's Secret** *(34 East 57th St., ☎758-5592)* stands out for its outstanding quality and reasonable prices, not to mention its huge collection of sexy ladies' undergarments.

Hats

Women are sure to find something they like at **Amy Downs Hats** *(103 Stanton St., at Ludlow St., ☎598-4189)*.

Miu Miu *(100 Prince St., between Green and Mercer, ☎334-5156)*, also owned by Miuccia Prada, sells her less expensive line.

Worth & Worth *(331 Madison Ave., between 42nd and 43rd Sts., ☎867-6085)* specializes in quality hats for men. Good choice of panamas, berets and bowlers.

Shoes

Harry's Shoes *(Mon to Fri 10am to 6pm, Sat and Sun 11am to 5pm; at Broadway and 82nd St., ☎874-2035)* sells all the

SHOPPING

popular brands of footwear, including Clarks Wallabees, Rockport and Timberland, at very reasonable prices.

Women looking for something highly original should check out **I, Claudia** *(168 Ludlow St., between Stanton and Houston, ☎533-4722)*. We should add that the shoes are as expensive as they are bizarre.

Men looking for a pair of new shoes are sure to find what they want at **McCreedy & Schreiber** *(37 W. 46th St., between 5th and 6th Ave., ☎719-1552)*.

If you're looking for footwear for your kids, stop by **Richie's Children's Shoes** *(183 Ave. B, between 11th and 12th St., ☎228-5442)*, which has a varied selection and friendly staff.

Sporting Goods

Located on Herald Square, the biggest **Athlete's Foot** *(Mon to Sat 9am to 9pm, Sun 11am to 8pm; 46 West 34th St., ☎629-8200)* in the world is spread over several floors and stocks the best-known brand-name sneakers (Nike, Reebok, Adidas) as well as sportswear and accessories. An extra section with the Timberland, Rockport and Lugz footwear lines, is scheduled to open here as well. Caps and tracksuits with the logos of local professional sports teams — namely the Yankees, the Knicks, the Mets, etc. — can be purchased here as well.

Blades Chelsea Piers *(22nd St., Pier 62, ☎336-6199)* is the perfect place to buy a pair of skates or a hockey stick. Skate rentals and sharpening also available.

Blades West *(120 W. 72nd St., between Columbus Ave. and Broadway, ☎439-1234)* carries a good selection of in-line skates.

You've just moved to New York City and plan on staying for a while? Want to fit in with the city's hectic way of life? All you have to do is participate in a few of New Yorkers' favourite sports, such as jogging or squash, and you're there! But hold on! You have to be dressed accordingly. To avoid getting disapproving stares, be it at the gym or along the paths of

Central Park, you should go to a store such as **City Sports** *(Mon to Fri 10am to 8pm, Sat 11am to 7pm, Sun 11am to 6pm; 153 East 53rd St., ☎317-0541, ↝317-2756)*, which caters to inner-city sports enthusiasts with well-padded wallets. The staff here, equipped with individual microphone headsets, can advise career-oriented sports buffs and even sell them a high-tech baby carriage.

East End Tennis *(326 E. 61st St., ☎317-0144)* and **Mason's Tennis Mart** *(911 7th Ave., between 57th and 58th St., ☎757-5374)* both have a wide selection of tennis racquets and balls.

Though golf courses are a rare sight on the island of Manhattan, several stores here cater to adherents of this sport, which is becoming increasingly popular among the middle classes. **The New York Golf Center** *(Mon to Fri 10am to 7pm, Sat 10am to 6pm, Sun 11am to 5pm; 131 West 35th St., ☎564-2255 or 888-465-7890, ↝244-6941)* is one of these specialized shops.

Nike Town *(Mon to Fri 10am to 6pm, Sat 10am to 7pm, Sun 11am to 6pm; 6 East 57th St., ☎891-6453)* if frequented more for its high-tech decor than for the Nike-brand sporting goods it sells (running shoes, shirts, jogging pants, etc.). Anyways, this sportswear line is sold the world over. The five floor establishment used to be the Bonwit Teller department store, and then the short-lived New York Galeries Lafayette. Sports clips are shown on a giant-screen in the main atrium, while the trophies and medals on display impart something of a jeweller's appearance to this Mecca for budding sports buffs. Elevators of 26 tubes of compressed air, soar to the 200 models of shoes in stock, from the basement warehouse to the store's various floors.

The **Princeton Ski Shop** *(21 East 22nd St., between Park Ave. and Broadway, ☎228-4400)* has a good assortment of snowboards and skis, both downhill and cross-country, as well as in-line skates.

Believe it or not, several thousand New Yorkers get around the city by bicycle! A number of them have bought their bikes at **Toga Bike** *(Mon to Sat 10am to 6pm, Sun 11am to 5pm;*

SHOPPING

110 West End Ave., ☎*799-9625,* ⌨*799-2834),* which offers an unbeatable selection of such vehicles.

The World of Golf *(Mon to Fri 10am to 7pm, Sat 10am to 5pm; 147 East 47th St.,* ☎*755-9398 or 800-818-5840,* ⌨*207-8370)* is another golf equipment speciality store.

BOOKSHOPS

The shelves at **A Different Light** *(151 W. 19th St.,* ☎*989-4850)* are stocked with an excellent selection of gay literature.

The various branches of the giant bookstore chain **Barnes & Noble** *(1972 Broadway, at 66th St.,* ☎*595-6859; 2289 Broadway,* ☎*362-8835 and 1280 Lexington Ave.,* ☎*423-9900)* are great places to pick up someone and something from the countless paperbacks, reference books, bestsellers and magazines sold here at unbeatable prices.

Books of Wonder *(16 W. 18th St., between 5th and 6th Ave.,* ☎*989-3270)* sells marvelous children's books filled with colourful illustrations.

With over 200 outlets in the United States and abroad, **Borders** *(Mon to Fri 9am to 10pm, Sat 10am to 8pm, Sun 11am to 8pm; 461 Park Ave.,* ☎*980-6785,* ⌨*980-0529)* sell books, CDs and video tapes. Authors and musicians are often invited to speak about their work or perform in the bookshop.

Whatever magazine you're looking for, you'll find it at **Dina's Magazines** *(270 Park Ave., between 21st and 22nd St.,* ☎*674-6595),* which carries over 4,000 of them, as well as various local and foreign newspapers.

Film and theatre buffs will find their favourite plays and screenplays at the **Drama Book Shop** *(723 7th Ave., between 48th and 49th St.,* ☎*944-0595).*

Forbidden Planet *(840 Broadway, at 13th St.,* ☎*473-1576),* named after a science-fiction movie that came out about 50 years ago, has an incredible selection of sci-fi books and comics, as well as an assortment of works related to the supernatural.

The **Gotham Book Mart** *(41 W. 47th St., between 5th and 6th Ave., ☎719-4448)* has been in business for over a century now. You'll see its slogan on your way in: "Wise men fish here". With its creaky floors and dusty shelves, this place is full of that charm particular to old bookstores. The books themselves are top-quality and the service is excellent. This is just the sort of place where you might unearth an old classic sitting forgotten on a shelf.

The boutique of the **Guggenheim Museum** *(Mon to Fri 9:30am to 5:30pm; 1071 5th Ave., at 89th St., ☎423-3615 or 800-329-6109, ≈941-8784, sales@guggenheim.org)* has a good selection of books on modern and contemporary art as well as a unique assortment of "gifts", objets d'art and modern jewellery. The shop also carries educational children's books, posters, and items sporting the Guggenheim symbol. Take note that "friends of the museum" (i.e. contributing members) get a 10% discount on all purchases.

The shop at the **Guggenheim Museum (SoHo)** *(575 Broadway, at Prince St., ☎423-3500)* has a vast array of books on art.

Located on the main floor of the **Modern Museum of Art** *(every day 10am to 6:30pm, except Fri 9pm; 11 West 53rd St., ☎708-9700)*, the in-house boutique carries more than 6,000 books mainly dealing with 20th-century art. These works deal with most forms of art: architecture, design, painting, drawing, film and sculpture. The shop also stocks postcards, posters, greetings cards, slides and children's books. Like at the Guggenheim, members here get a 10% discount.

Black and red set the tone for **Murder Ink** *(2486 Broadway, between 92nd and 93rd St., ☎362-8905)*, which will plunge you into the dark, mysterious world of whodunits and thrillers full of black humour.

The Mysterious Book Shop *(129 W. 56th St., ☎765-0900)* boasts an impressive collection of new and used crime novels.

SHOPPING

A Photographer's Place *(133 Mercer St., between Prince and Spring St., ☎431-9358)* has an excellent selection of books related to photography.

Rand McNally *(150 E. 52nd St., between Lexington and 3rd Ave., ☎758-7488)* has a good selection of maps, atlases and globes, as well as a few travel guides.

The shelves at **Shakespeare & Co.** *(716 Broadway, ☎529-1330, 939 Lexington Ave., between 68th and 69th sts., ☎570-0201)* are stacked with an excellent selection of books on literature, painting and poetry.

St. Marks Comics *(11 St. Marks Pl., ☎598-9439)* carries an impressive array of classic and contemporary comics, both new and used.

Travel Bookshops

Here are a few bookshops where you are sure to find everything you're looking for on the subject of travel:

Complete Traveler Bookstore: 199 Madison Avenue, New York, NY 10016, ☎685-9007.

Hagstrom Map and Travel Center *(57 West 43rd Street, New York, NY 10036, ☎398-1222)*. This bookshop, which has been in operation for 80 years, makes and sells maps that can help you find your way anywhere in the State of New York. Both pocket-size and very large-format maps are available.

Traveler's Bookstore, *(75 Rockefeller Plaza, 22 West 52nd Street, New York, NY 10019, ☎664-0995)* Founded in 1982, Traveler's Bookstore aims to provide you with the best possible travelling tools (guide books, accessories, etc.).

Travel's Choice Bookstore: bookshop and travel agency; 111 Greene Street, New York, NY 10012, ☎941-1535.

French and European Publications

Librairie de France: Rockefeller Center Promenade, 610 5th Avenue, New York, NY 10020-2497, ☎581-8810, livresny@aol.com.

MUSIC

A-1 Record Shop *(439 E. 6th St., between 1st Ave. and Ave. A, ☎473-2870)*, next to the restaurant Raga (see p 336), sells old soul, disco, reggae and rap LPs. If you've got some of your own to sell, bring them here.

If you're in the market for a compact disk, cassette or video tape, you're sure to find what you're looking for at **HMV** *(1280 Lexington Ave., at 86th St., ☎348-0800; 57 W. 34th St., ☎629-0900; 2081 Broadway, ☎721-5900)*.

J&R Music World *(23 Park Row, between Beekman and Ann St., ☎238-9000)* is a huge store with a good music and video section. It also sells computers and VCRs.

NYCD *(426 Amsterdam Ave., between 80th and 81st St., ☎724-4466)* specializes in used CDs.

Stern's *(71 Warren St., ☎964-5455)*, right near the World Trade Center, is not a branch of the famous jewellery store of the same name but rather a record shop specializing in international music especially African artists.

As its name indicates, **Tower Records, Video and Books** *(Mon to Fri 10am to 10pm, Sat 10am to 8pm, Sun 11am to 6pm; 692 Broadway, ☎800-474-7890)* carries records, videos and books, in large quantities and at prices Europeans will find very reasonable.

The **Virgin Megastore** *(Fri and Sat 9am to 2am, Sun to Thu 9am to 1am; 1540 Broadway, between 45th and 46th Ave., ☎921-1020)* certainly lives up to its name, full of music for all tastes, from pop and classical music to jazz. The store also stocks a multitude of reasonably priced books. The main floor

SHOPPING

also has a travel agency, a videos and CD section, a café and a video-game and computer section.

MUSICAL INSTRUMENTS

Sam Ash Music *(160 W. 48th St., between 6th and 7th Ave., ☎719-2299)* is a huge store with a vast selection of electric and acoustic guitars, percussion instruments, synthesizers, amplifiers and microphones.

The **Main Drag** *(207 Bedford Ave., Brooklyn, ☎718-388-6365)* is the place to go for high-quality used guitars and amplifiers.

The Music Store *(44 W. 62nd St., ☎541-6236)* rents out a small number of musical instruments (flutes, guitars and violins) and sells sheet music of works by different artists like Bob Dylan, U2, Chopin, Beethoven, Tori Amos and Schubert.

If you've got money to burn and are in the market for a custom-made guitar or mandolin, head to **Carlo Greco Custom Guitar Maker** *(165 W. 48th St., ☎704-2042)*.

You probably won't buy anything at **48th St. Custom Guitars** *(170 W. 48th St., between 7th and 8th Ave., ☎764-1364)*, but the place is worth checking out if you're interested in antique musical instruments.

ART

The **Christie's** *(Mon to Sat 10am to 5pm, Sun 1pm to 5pm; 502 Park Ave., at 59th St., ☎546-1600)* and **Christie's East** *(Mon to Sat 10am to 5pm, Sun 1pm to 5pm; 219 East 67th St., ☎606-0400)* auction houses are open for business every day of the week.

Founded in 1744, **Sotheby's** *(Mon to Sat 10am to 5pm, Sun 1pm to 5pm; 1334 York Ave., at 72nd St., ☎606-7000)* is New York City's biggest auction house. Paintings by the great masters, refined artifacts, jewellery and modern art are exchanged for sometimes astronomical sums of money.

PHOTOGRAPHY, POSTERS AND FRAMES

Cinema Paradiso *(162 Bleecker St., ☎677-8215)*: original movie posters and frames.

If you're looking for a picture frame or a unique gift, try **Liquid Image** *(390 Broadway, ☎334-4443)*, which will make a montage of your pictures against a movie backdrop, a famous photo or a classic painting.

New York Film Works *(928 Broadway, between 21st and 22nd St., ☎475-5700, nyfw@worldnet.att.nett)*: film developing, photo touch-ups, camera and lens repairs, laser and colour photocopies, video transfers.

PhotoTech *(110 East 13th St., ☎673-8400, www.phototech.com)* will not only process your film but also repairs all brands of lenses.

TOYS

Located in the very heart of Times Square, the **Disney Store** is a retail branch of the Disney chain. You will find everyone here from Mickey Mouse and Donald Duck to Disney's most recent animated-movie stars, including the *Hunchback of Notre Dame* and *Mulan*, in the form of figurines and stuffed dolls, and adorning caps, T-shirts, beach towels, glasses and plates.

Santa Claus' does not live in the North Pole, but nowhere else than New York City, at **F.A.O. Schwarz** *(Mon to Sat 10am to 6pm, Sun 10am to 5pm; 767 5th Ave., ☎644-9400)*, unquestionably the biggest toy store on earth. They are all here, from stuffed teddy bears to Barbie dolls, of all possible and imaginable models.

Looking for a Sony Playstation or the latest version of Tekken? Head to the **Game Park** *(82 West Broadway, between Warren and Chambers St., ☎571-3466)*.

MARKETS

The **Antiques Fair and Flea Market** *(admission fee; Sat and Sun, from sunrise to sundown; 6th Ave., between 24th and 27th St., ☎243-5343)* brings together some 600 New York antique and secondhand-goods dealers. These merchants set up shop in various buildings and empty lots in Chelsea, where they sell every imaginable item to complete one's collection of plastic toys, baseball cards or china toadstools from Italy.

The most urbane of New York public markets is unquestionably **Union Square's Greenmarket** *(Mon, Wed, Fri and Sat 8am to 4pm; on the west side of Union Square, ☎477-3220)*, where farmers come to sell their fresh products (fruits, vegetables, herbs, flowers) right on the street. Residents of Chelsea and Greenwich Village do their shopping here, as do the chefs of the great neighbourhood restaurants.

 FOOD

Sausages and pasta are piled higgledy-piggledy right up to the ceiling at **Balducci's** *(every day 7am to 8pm; 424 6th Ave., ☎673-2600)*, a pleasant family-run grocery store synonymous with good and tasty Italian food since 1916.

Caviarteria (see p 348) carries a vast selection of caviar, smoked salmon and foie gras.

In New York City, the kingdom of ready-to-eat take-out food is ruled by **Dean and Deluca** *(Mon to Sat 8am to 8pm; 560 Broadway, ☎431-1691)*. The place boasts pasta and home-made sauces, desserts, meat and fish, among other treats.

At **Zabar's** *(Mon to Fri 8am to 7pm, Sat 8am to 10pm, Sun 9am to 6pm; 2245 Broadway, ☎787-2002)*, you'll find everything from ready-made take-out dishes and Jewish specialties to imported cheeses and stainless-steel kitchenware. Is it any wonder why residents of the Upper West Side flock here on weekends?

Sweets

If you've got a sweet tooth, you'll have a hard time resisting the delicious chocolates at **Godiva** *(701 5th Ave., ☎593-2845)* and **La Maison du Chocolat** *(25 East 73rd St., between 5th and Madison Ave., ☎744-7117)*.

WINE, BEER AND SPIRITS

Garnet Wines and Liquors *(929 Lexington Ave., between 68th and 69th St., ☎772-3211)* keeps its shelves stocked with new arrivals from Europe and the Americas.

New Beers Distributors *(167 Christie St., between Delancey and Rivington, ☎473-8757)*, on the Lower East Side, sells over 250 kinds of beer at prices reasonable enough to please veteran bargain hunters.

Wine-lovers won't be disappointed by the selection at **Union Square Wines** *(33 Union Square W., between 16th and 17th St., ☎675-8100)*, which carries all the famous vintages, a good choice of organic wines and a variety of bottle-openers ranging in price from $3 to $220.

CIGARS

The Smoke Scene *(841 7th Ave., ☎265-1425)* has a good selection of domestic and imported cigars, though the store itself looks a bit rinky-dink.

The **Three Little Indians Cigar and Trading Company** *(Mon to Fri 11am to 8pm, Sat 11am to 9pm, Sun 1pm to 8pm; 140 Mulberry St., ☎334-5839, ≈274-9414)*, located right in the heart of Little Italy, sells fine cigars and other hand-picked "smokables". Shopkeeper Lawrence Amoruso will be only too pleased to introduce you to the art of cigar smoking.

LEATHER

If you are considering splurging on luggage, attaché cases, handbags, shoes or other leather accessories, look no further than **Gucci** *(685 5th Ave., ☎826-2600)*; the Italian boutique world-famous for the quality of its wares for the last 70 years.

Louis Vuitton *(49 East 57th St., ☎371-6111)* also sells leather goods. This boutique, the most famous of the celebrated chain outlets, will satisfy those who appreciate quality made worked leather goods, such as handbags, attaché cases, travel accessories, etc.

 COSTUMES

Abracadabra *(10 Christopher St., ☎627-5745)* not only sells all sorts of magic tricks but also rents out unusual costumes.

Halloween Adventure *(104 4th Ave., between 11th and 12th St., ☎673-4546)* sells costumes, accessories and makeup for both children and adults.

 ACCESSORIES

If you're looking for the ultimate in fashion accessories to go with your best clothing, make sure to check out the impressive array of retro handbags at **Deco Jewel** *(131 Thompson St., between Houston and Prince, ☎253-1222)*. The owner has a passion for beautiful, rigid-form purses that are more decorative than practical, and has been seeking them out, buying them up and selling them for years. Apparently, she has dozens of her favourite styles at home. The bags vary in texture, from metallic to transparent plastic to the kind of precious materials used only for luxury goods. Some are decorated with stones, while others look more like little jewellery boxes. Worth a stop, if only to admire the unique storefront decorations.

If you're looking for a brand-name watch, take the time to stop by **Montre Tourneau Timemachine** *(Madison Ave., at 52nd St.,*

☎758-7300 or 800-772-7836), which sells a whole range of Piaget, Cartier, Rolex, Gucci, Wittnauer and ESQ products.

If you're looking for a pair of shades to protect your eyes from the bright summer sun, **Sunglass Hut** *(477 Madison Ave.,* ☎317-9898) is the place to go.

The **Uncle Sam Umbrella Shop** *(161 West 57th St., between 6th and 7th Ave.,* ☎582-1977) makes, sells and repairs all different kinds of umbrellas.

 JEWELLERS

Incomparably elegant, **Cartier** *(653 5th Ave., at 52nd St.,* ☎753-0111; Trump Tower, 725 5th Ave., at 57th St., ☎308-0840) boasts an exquisite collection of jewellery, objets d'art, diamonds and antiques.

Fortunoff *(681 5th Ave.,* ☎758-6660) has a lovely selection of jewellery for all special occasions.

Piaget *(730 5th Ave.,* ☎246-5555) has no reason to be envious of Cartier, because it carries jewellery-artist Piaget's creations, namely 18-carat-gold or (merely!) platinum watches, some of which are studded with gems. The rest of the jewellery here will also please the most capricious of shoppers.

Sally Hawkins *(448 W. Broadway,* ☎477-5699) is a sunny gallery that displays American jeweller Bill Schiffer's magnificent creations, which are set with Swarovski crystals. Each superb and unique necklaces, pair of earrings and bracelet, are enhanced by the colour and elegant cut of the crystals. The original design of these works of art is truly remarkable – for example, we saw a necklace with chlorophyll-green cloverleaves and a delicate pair of "ultraviolet"-coloured earrings. The prices range from $80 to $2000. The gallery also has a lovely assortment of Schiffer's silver jewellery.

The consistent popularity of Swatch watches necessitates a detour to the **Swatch Store** *(5 East 57th St.,* ☎317-1100; 500 5th Ave., between 42nd and 43rd St., ☎730-7530; Pier 17 at South St. Seaport, second floor, ☎571-6400), which still

SHOPPING

offers the latest models of their sometimes outrageous, sometimes very conventional, but always striking watches. Hard-core Swatch fans can also pick up older models.

Known throughout the world, **Tiffany & Co.** *(727 5th Ave., at 57th St., ☎755-8000)* offers an amazing and always growing selection of diamonds, pearls as well as gold and silver jewellery. In short, all kinds of luxury goodies. Whatever you're looking for, Tiffany's probably has it in stock!

 ## CHINA, CRYSTAL AND SILVERWARE

Baccarat *(625 Madison Ave., between 58th and 59th St., ☎826-4100)* has been selling crystal wear for over 200 years. The store also carries silverware, Reynauld-Ceralene china and Gien earthenware.

Honoring the memory of crystal-engraver René Lalique, the **Lalique** *(680 Madison Ave., between 61st and 62nd St., ☎355-6550)* boutique offers breathtaking decorative and functional pieces, not to mention crystal jewellery, perfume, and accessories such as handbags and beautiful scarves.

After eating at **Nirvana** *(30 Central Park South., ☎486-5700, www.nirvanarest.com)* (see p 349), why not leave with the dishes and the silverware? Each piece is sold separately – plates, coffeepots, ashtrays, etc. The dishes are hand-painted and plated with 22-karat gold.

 ## HAIRDRESSERS

The **Jean-Louis David** *(1180 6th Ave., at 46th St., ☎944-7389)* hair salons have eight locations throughout Manhattan catering to both sexes Some of these are Quick Service salons, providing decent haircuts in under 15 minutes for men, and in less than 30 minutes for women.

FLORISTS

If fresh flowers make your heart go pitter-patter, make sure to stop by **Denis Flowers** *(526 Lexington Ave., between 48th and 49th St., ☎355-1820)* or **Eva's Garden Flowers** *(1506 1st Ave, at 79th St., ☎744-8710)*.

If you're looking for a bouquet of roses, try the specialist: **Roses Only** *(45 Christopher St., ☎243-4052)*.

 PET SHOPS

Cat lovers take note: it is time to offer your best feline friend a well-deserved treat. **Just Cats** *(244 East 60th St., between 2nd and 3rd Ave., ☎888-CATS)* sells everything humanly imaginable with regard to cats: beds, leashes, collars, clothing, jewellery, etc.

The **Not Just Dogs** *(244 East 60th St, between 2nd and 3rd Ave., ☎752-8669)* shop carries designer-made clothes. Hard to believe, but even Chanel takes an interest in our four-legged friends! Among the items to be found in this decadent shop are unusual beds, coats and collars; and if your dog is disabled, you'll be happy to know that this shop sells specially made ramps for your physically challenged pet.

 FURNITURE

Scores of New Yorkers who like to fill their homes with traditional furniture on thick Persian rugs head to **ABC Carpet and Home** *(Mon to Fri 10am to 8pm, Sat 10am to 7pm, Sun 11am to 6pm; 888 Broadway, at 19th St., ☎473-3000)*. Original antiques and copies of American and European furniture are to be found here along with curtains, cushions, towels, wallpaper and other accessories.

SHOPPING

MISCELLANEOUS

CompUSA'S Super Store *(1775 Broadway, at 57th St., ☎262-9711, ⊶445-1698; 420 5th Ave., at 37th St., ☎764-6224, ⊶782-7798)* has a huge selection of computers, printers and software.

Before going club-hopping, some of you might want to check out the widest array of condoms at **Condomania** *(351 Bleecker St., ☎691-9442)*.

Perfume Palace *(233 5th Ave., ☎481-1942)* offers a good selection of reasonably priced fragrances.

WRITE TO US

INDEX

INDEX

INDEX

ORDER FORM

ULYSSES TRAVEL GUIDES

☐ Affordable B&Bs	$12.95 CAN	☐ Lisbon	$18.95 CAN
in Québec	$9.95 US		$13.95 US
☐ Atlantic Canada	$24.95 CAN	☐ Louisiana	$29.95 CAN
	$17.95 US		$21.95 US
☐ Beaches of Maine	$12.95 CAN	☐ Martinique ...	$24.95 CAN
	$9.95 US		$17.95 US
☐ Bahamas	$24.95 CAN	☐ Montréal	$19.95 CAN
	$17.95 US		$14.95 US
☐ Belize	$16.95 CAN	☐ New Orleans .	$17.95 CAN
	$12.95 US		$12.95 US
☐ Calgary	$17.95 CAN	☐ New York City	$19.95 CAN
	$12.95 US		$14.95 US
☐ Canada	$29.95 CAN	☐ Nicaragua ...	$24.95 CAN
	$21.95 US		$16.95 US
☐ Chicago	$19.95 CAN	☐ Ontario	$24.95 CAN
	$14.95 US		$14.95US
☐ Chile	$27.95 CAN	☐ Ottawa	$17.95 CAN
	$17.95 US		$12.95 US
☐ Costa Rica ...	$27.95 CAN	☐ Panamá	$24.95 CAN
	$19.95 US		$16.95 US
☐ Cuba	$24.95 CAN	☐ Portugal	$24.95 CAN
	$17.95 US		$16.95 US
☐ Dominican ...	$24.95 CAN	☐ Provence - ...	$29.95 CAN
Republic	$17.95 US	Côte d'Azur	$21.95US
☐ Ecuador	$24.95 CAN	☐ Québec	$29.95 CAN
Galapagos Islands	$17.95 US		$21.95 US
☐ El Salvador ...	$22.95 CAN	☐ Québec and Ontario	$9.95 US
	$14.95 US	with Via	$7.95 US
☐ Guadeloupe ..	$24.95 CAN	☐ Toronto	$18.95 CAN
	$17.95 US		$13.95 US
☐ Guatemala ...	$24.95 CAN	☐ Vancouver ...	$17.95 CAN
	$17.95 US		$12.95 US
☐ Honduras	$24.95 CAN	☐ Washington D.C.	$18.95 CAN
	$17.95 US		$13.95 US
☐ Jamaica	$24.95 CAN	☐ Western Canada	$29.95 CAN
	$17.95 US		$21.95 US

ULYSSES DUE SOUTH

☐ Acapulco	$14.95 CAN	☐ Cartagena ...	$12.95 CAN
	$9.95 US	(Colombia)	$9.95 US
☐ Belize	$16.95 CAN	☐ Cancun Cozumel	$17.95 CAN
	$12.95 US		$12.95 US

☐ Puerto Vallarta $14.95 CAN   ☐ St. Martin and $16.95 CAN
                    $9.95 US   St. Barts $12.95 US

ULYSSES TRAVEL JOURNAL

☐ Ulysses Travel Journal . . . . $9.95 CAN
(Blue, Red, Green, Yellow, Sextant) $7.95 US

ULYSSES GREEN ESCAPES

☐ Cycling in France $22.95 CAN   ☐ Hiking in Québec $19.95 CAN
                    $16.95 US $13.95 US
☐ Hiking in the . . $19.95 CAN
  Northeastern U.S. $13.95 US

TITLE	QUANTITY	PRICE	TOTAL

Name _____	Sub-total	
Address _____	Postage & Handling	$8.00*
_____	Sub-total	
_____		
Payment : ☐ Money Order ☐ Visa ☐ MasterCard	G.S.T. in Canada 7%	
Card Number _____		
Signature _____	TOTAL	

ULYSSES TRAVEL PUBLICATIONS
4176 St-Denis,
Montréal, Québec, H2W 2M5
(514) 843-9447 fax (514) 843-9448
www.ulysses.ca
* $15 for overseas orders

U.S. ORDERS: **GLOBE PEQUOT PRESS**
P.O. Box 833, 6 Business Park Road,
Old Saybrook, CT 06475-0833
1-800-243-0495 fax 1-800-820-2329
www.globe-pequot.com